T0383174

DEVELOPMENT OF INTERNATIONAL ENTREPRENEURSHIP BASED ON CORPORATE ACCOUNTING AND REPORTING ACCORDING TO IFRS

ADVANCED SERIES IN MANAGEMENT

Series Editors: Miguel R. Olivas-Luján and Tanya Bondarouk

ADVANCED SERIES IN MANAGEMENT   VOLUME 33B

DEVELOPMENT OF INTERNATIONAL ENTREPRENEURSHIP BASED ON CORPORATE ACCOUNTING AND REPORTING ACCORDING TO IFRS: PART B

EDITED BY

MANSUR P. ESHOV
Tashkent State University of Economics, Uzbekistan

GULNORA K. ABDURAKHMANOVA
Tashkent State University of Economics, Uzbekistan

AKTAM U. BURKHANOV
Tashkent State University of Economics, Uzbekistan

NODIRA B. ABDUSALOMOVA
Tashkent State University of Economics, Uzbekistan

AND

SHAKHLO T. ERGASHEVA
Tashkent State University of Economics, Uzbekistan

United Kingdom – North America – Japan – India – Malaysia – China

Emerald Publishing Limited
Emerald Publishing, Floor 5, Northspring, 21-23 Wellington Street, Leeds LS1 4DL

First edition 2024

Editorial matter and selection © 2024 Mansur P. Eshov, Gulnora K. Abdurakhmanova, Aktam U. Burkhanov, Nodira B. Abdusalomova and Shakhlo T. Ergasheva.
Individual chapters © 2024 The authors.
Published under exclusive licence by Emerald Publishing Limited.

British Library Cataloguing in Publication Data
A catalogue record for this book is available from the British Library

ISBN: 978-1-83797-670-6 (Print)
ISBN: 978-1-83797-669-0 (Online)
ISBN: 978-1-83797-671-3 (Epub)

ISSN: 1877-6361 (Series)

Printed and bound by CPI Group (UK) Ltd, Croydon, CR0 4YY

INVESTOR IN PEOPLE

CONTENTS

PART 1: SPECIFICS OF INTERNATIONAL
ENTREPRENEURSHIP DEVELOPMENT ACROSS
SECTORS OF THE MODERN ECONOMY

PART 2: INTERNATIONAL EXPERIENCE IN THE DEVELOPMENT OF TRADE COOPERATION AND INTERNATIONAL ENTREPRENEURSHIP

ABOUT THE EDITORS

Mansur P. Eshov – Doctor of Science, Vice Rector of Academic Affairs of Tashkent State University of Economics (Tashkent, Uzbekistan). Mansur P. Eshov has more than 30 scientific research are reflected in the results of scientific works published, in particular, 1 textbook, 8 scientific articles, as well as the most prestigious international journals in 5 scientific articles published. He is the winner of the republican stage of the Best Pedagogical Contest of Higher Education; winner of the Qualifying Selection for Candidates nominated on the basis of the Istedod Foundation; winner of the city stage of the intellectual contest "Stars of Science" is organized by the Association of Women of Uzbekistan "Olima ayollar". The author's research interests are methodology for determining the tax burden on the mechanism of taxation of small enterprises; the theoretical and practical aspects of the mechanism of the successful implementation of government grants guided; management and marketing; business or sector business; finance, money circulation, and credit.

Gulnora K. Abdurakhmanova – Vice Rector of Research and Innovations at Tashkent State University of Economics (Tashkent, Uzbekistan). She actively participates in conferences and has numerous research materials in international scientific books and journals in English, Uzbek, and Russian languages. Gulnora K. Abdurakhmanova is a member and an Editor-in-Chief in "Economics and innovation technologies" scientific-electronic journal of Tashkent State University of Economics. The author's research interests are teaching the disciplines of Labor, Demography, Migration; conducting doctoral scientific research on labor economics; development and implementation of educational programs and strategies.

Aktam U. Burkhanov – Doctor of Economic Sciences, Professor, Dean of the Finance and Accounting Faculty, Tashkent State University of Economics (Tashkent, Uzbekistan). Aktam U. Burkhanov is the author (coauthor) of more than 200 scientific and educational works. During his scientific and pedagogical activity, he authored 8 textbooks, 4 monographs, 5 training manuals, and 14 teaching-methodical manuals, including the textbooks "Financial Market and Investments" (2021), "Investments and Innovations" (2021), "Financial Management" (2020), "Financial Market" (2020), "Financial Security" (2019), and "Crisis Management of Enterprises" (2013). The monographs "Investment of Small Business Entities: Theory and Practice" (2014) and "Financial Stability of Enterprises: Theory and Practice" (2019) aim to improve the quality of education in educational institutions. The author is a member of the editorial board and Chief Editor of scientific journals "Uluslararası İşletme, Ekonomi ve Yönetim Perspektifleri Dergisi" and "Journal of Turkish Studies."

Nodira B. Abdusalomova – Head of the "Accounting" Department of Tashkent State University of Economics (Tashkent, Uzbekistan), Doctor of Economic Sciences, Professor. She got her Bachelor's degree at the Tashkent State University of Economics in the field of

"Accounting and Auditing." She completed her Master's degree at the Tashkent State University of Economics, specializing in "Public Finance Management." In 2017, she defended her Candidate Dissertation on "Improving cost management and accounting in ferrous metallurgy enterprises." In 2019, she received the degree of Doctor of Economic Sciences with a dissertation on the topic "Improvement of the budgeting and internal control system in the management accounting system." Currently, four of her students have successfully defended their Dissertation of Candidate of Science. The author conducts scientific research in the direction of management accounting, strategic management accounting, and international standards of financial reporting. She is the author of more than 100 scientific works, including 20 foreign articles, 3 textbooks, 3 monographs, and 2 educational manuals.

Shakhlo T. Ergasheva – Candidate of Economic Sciences, Professor of Accounting Department, Director of the Innovation Resource Center for IFRS of Tashkent State University of Economics (Tashkent, Uzbekistan); International School of Finance Technology and Science (Tashkent, Uzbekistan). Shakhlo T. Ergasheva organizes republican and international scientific and practical conferences and scientific activities. She is the author and editor of collective monographs. Her research interests include accounting and auditing according to international financial reporting and auditing standards, as well as accounting in the public sector of the economy. Shakhlo T. Ergasheva is the author of more than 200 works published in Uzbek and foreign publications, including 10 works in Scopus and 3 in Web of Science. She is a performer of research works supported by grants of the Republic of Uzbekistan.

ABOUT THE CONTRIBUTORS

Tolonbek Sh. Abdyrov – Doctor of Economic Sciences, Professor, International University of the Kyrgyz Republic (Bishkek, Kyrgyzstan). His scientific interests include the formation and development of clusters in the economy of the Kyrgyz Republic, regional economic development, economic specialization of regions, issues of innovative development of the national and regional economy, issues of sustainable economic development, and formation of a digital economy. He is the author of more than 130 scientific and methodological works published in scientific publications of the Kyrgyz Republic, Kazakhstan, Russia, the United States, and South Korea, including 2 monographs, a textbook with the stamp of the Ministry of Education and Science of the Kyrgyz Republic for undergraduates, and 5 textbooks. The author is a developer (Head of the working group) of the state educational standard in the direction "State and municipal administration" for bachelors and undergraduates. He is the head of the working group on the development of proposals for the agro-industrial complex to the road map for the entry of the Kyrgyz Republic into the EAEU. Tolonbek Sh. Abdyrov is a member of the working group on the development of methods for the formation of cluster initiatives in the Kyrgyz Republic.

Nelli I. Akylbekova – Doctor of Economics, Professor, Head of Management Program of the Kyrgyz National University named after Jusup Balasagyn (Bishkek, Kyrgyzstan). She has over 140 scientific publications. Nelli I. Akylbekova conducted scientific research in the following areas: development of the social sector, demographic processes, development of tourism, small and medium enterprises, and development of the banking system.

Ahmad S. Al Humssi – (PhD in Economics), Associate Professor of Economic Statistics at the RUDN University (Moscow, Russia), Associate Professor of National Economics at the Financial University (Moscow, Russia). His research interests include international economics, economic analysis, international statistics, national economics, and other studies in Middle Eastern and North African economies. The author has more than 50 publications written on economics and statistics published in Russian and international peer-reviewed scientific journals.

Mireya Jay Alcántara – Candidate of Economic Sciences, Intern Researcher at the Institute of World Economy and Business of the Faculty of Economics at RUDN University (Moscow, Russia). Her scientific interests include the theory of economic growth, sustainable development, globalization, humanization of economic growth, and economic, sociopolitical, international, and cultural problems. Mireya Jay Alcántara participates in Russian and international scientific and practical conferences.

Alina S. Alymkulova – Candidate of Economic Sciences, Associate Professor, International University of the Kyrgyz Republic (Bishkek, Kyrgyzstan). Her scientific interests are quite diverse and include problems of the world, national, and regional economy. Particularly, the author is interested in the issues of integration processes, financial crises, interregional crisis, etc. Alina S. Alymkulova has published about 50 research papers in Kyrgyzstan and abroad. She is also the author of collective monographs, textbooks, and scientific manuals.

Inna V. Andronova – Professor, Doctor of Economics, Academic Secretary of the Dissertation Council, Head of the Department of International Economic Relations, Dean of the Faculty of Economics, RUDN University (Moscow, Russia). Her scientific interests include foreign economic security, economic interests of Russia in the regions of the world, and international economic relations. Inna V. Andronova is the author of more than 100 scientific papers, including monographs and chapters in monographs, articles in peer-reviewed journals of Higher Attestation Commission (VAK) of the Russian Federation and foreign citation databases. Under her supervision, Peoples' Friendship University annually hosts international conferences to discuss topical issues of the world economy.

Raykhona A. Artikova – Senior Lecturer, Tashkent State Transport University, Tashkent, Uzbekistan. Raykhona A. Artikova has scientific works published and indexed in Scopus and Web of Science databases.

Tolendi A. Ashimbayev – PhD, Senior Lecturer of the Department of Economics, Services, and Law, Almaty University of Humanities and Economics (Almaty, Kazakhstan). He was awarded with the badge "Excellence in Education – 2023" of the first degree of the Republic of Kazakhstan. The list of scientific papers includes 36.8 printed sheets in articles and abstracts of conferences, including 25 articles published in leading scientific journals. The author published 3 articles in Scopus.

Almagul T. Attokurova – Candidate of Economic Sciences, Associate Professor, International University of the Kyrgyz Republic (Bishkek, Kyrgyzstan). The author conducts scientific research on demographics, population, migration processes, problems of feminism and gender studies, current problems of development and implementation of green economy, and aspects of national social policy, including a special study of vulnerable segments of the population. She is the author of more than 30 articles and 2 textbooks.

Irina N. Belova – Candidate of Economic Sciences, Professor, Department of International Economic Relations and Foreign Economic Activity, Faculty of Economics, Peoples' Friendship University of Russia named after Patrice Lumumba (RUDN University, Moscow, Russia). She is the author of more than 10 manuals and more than 40 key papers on world economy. Her scientific interests include world economic relations, international trade, world commodity markets, and China's economy.

Aktam U. Burkhanov – Doctor of Economic Sciences, Professor, Dean of the Finance and Accounting Faculty, Tashkent State University of Economics (Tashkent, Uzbekistan). Aktam U. Burkhanov is the author (coauthor) of more than 200 scientific and educational works. During his scientific and pedagogical activity, he authored 8 textbooks, 4 monographs, 5 training manuals, and 14 teaching-methodical manuals, including the textbooks "Financial Market and Investments" (2021), "Investments and Innovations" (2021), "Financial Management" (2020), "Financial Market" (2020), "Financial Security" (2019), and "Crisis management of enterprises" (2013). The monographs "Investment of Small Business Entities: Theory and Practice" (2014) and "Financial Stability of Enterprises: Theory and Practice" (2019) aim to improve the quality of education in educational institutions. The author is a member of the editorial board and Chief Editor of scientific journals "Uluslararası İşletme, Ekonomi ve Yönetim Perspektifleri Dergisi" and "Journal of Turkish Studies."

Natalya I. Bykanova – Candidate of Economic Sciences, Associate Professor, Department of Innovation Economics and Finance, Institute of Economics and Management, Belgorod State National Research University (Russia). Her scientific interests include bank marketing, financial market, internet banking, digital banking, digitalization, digital transformation, digital marketing, remote banking, financial technology, and banking ecosystems. She has been a reviewer of articles for scientific journals multiple times. The author has participated in international scientific and practical conferences. She has published more than 150 works in Russian and foreign peer-reviewed journals and books.

Vladimir Z. Chaplyuk – Doctor of Economics, Professor of the Department of Accounting, Auditing, and Statistics, Faculty of Economics, RUDN University (Moscow, Russia). His scientific interests include the theory of economic growth, public and corporate finance, international economic relations, and is the author of collective monographs. He has published more than 100 works in Russian and foreign peer-reviewed scientific journals and books.

Alexandra A. Chudaeva – Candidate of Economic Sciences, Associate Professor, Department of Economics, Organization, and Strategy of Enterprise Development, Samara State University of Economics (Samara, Russia). Alexandra A. Chudaeva is a Business Coach, a Lecturer at the Higher School of Management of the Samara State University of Economics, a member of the Public Council at the Ministry of Economic Development and Investment of the Samara Region, and a member of the expert council to determine the winners and finalists of the contest "Best Mentoring Practices in the Samara Region" organized by the Ministry of Industry and Trade of the Samara Region. In 2022, Alexandra A. Chudaeva became the winner of the All-Russian contest "Golden Names of Higher School" in the nomination "For the development of practice-oriented higher education." Her scientific interests include investments, assessment of economic efficiency of investment projects, uncertainty, risks, investment risks, financing of investment projects, digitalization, peculiarities of assessment of efficiency of projects of digitalization of production enterprises, and economics and finance of industrial enterprises.

Olga B. Digilina – Doctor of Economics, Professor, Department of Political Economy, Faculty of Economics, RUDN University (Moscow, Russia). Her research interests include the theory of economic growth, sustainable development, managerial economics, digitization, innovation management, human resource management, strategic planning, competition development, creation of information systems, management, and finance. Olga B. Digilina is the author of more than 100 scientific papers, including 12 monographs. Olga's Hirsch Index is 13.

Li Dingbang – PhD student at the Department of International Economic Relations, Faculty of Economics, RUDN University (Moscow, Russia). His research interests include multinational corporations, foreign direct investment, China's "Belt and Road" economic policy, and Chinese investment in Kazakhstan.

Zarina T. Duishenalieva – Senior Lecturer, Department of Management, Higher School of Economics and Business, Kyrgyz State Technical University named after I. Razzakov (Bishkek, Kyrgyzstan), PhD student of the Kyrgyz National University named after Jusup

Balasagyn (Bishkek, Kyrgyzstan) with a degree in Economics and Management. She has more than 20 scientific papers, including 3 methodological manuals for undergraduate students. Main research areas include the development of the banking sector and the development of the financial market.

Elena A. Egorycheva – Candidate of Economic Sciences, Senior Lecturer, Department of National Economy, Faculty of Economics, Peoples' Friendship University of Russia named after Patrice Lumumba (RUDN University, Moscow, Russia). She is the Head of the Master program "International Business" at Faculty of Economics in RUDN University. The author's scientific interests include international business, world economy, and China's economy.

Elza R. Gasimova – PhD student. In 2021, she received a Master's degree in "International Trade" from the Peoples' Friendship University of Russia named after Patrice Lumumba. Since 2022, she continues her education at the Department of International Economic Relations in the profile "World Economy" of the RUDN University (Moscow, Russia).

Alexey V. Groshev – postgraduate student, Department of International Economic Relations and Foreign Economic Activity, Faculty of Economics, Peoples' Friendship University of Russia named after Patrice Lumumba (RUDN University, Moscow, Russia). He is the Managing Partner of the outsourcing contact center "Interstellar." The author's scientific interests include world economic relations, world commodity and services markets, international marketing, and outsourcing.

Abdoulaye M. Hassane – postgraduate student of RUDN University (Moscow, Russia). A. M. Hassane is the winner of the contest Volunteer of the Year RUDN University 2021. He was awarded with a certificate and gratitude for social activity on behalf of the Rector of the Peoples' Friendship University of Russia three times. From 2017 to the present, he has been actively involved in international and regional volunteer activities, including (1) World Festival of Youth and Students (WFYS), Sochi 2017; FIFA World Cup – Russia 2018; (2) First Russia-Africa Economic Summit and Forum – Sochi 2019; (3) St. Petersburg International Economic Forum – St. Petersburg 2021; (4) Economic Forum Russia-Islamic World – Kazan 2023; (5) Second Summit: Economic and Humanitarian Forum Russia-Africa – St. Petersburg 2023. A. M. Hassane, he is one of the founding members of the Future Team Chad Association (FTT), an active member of the RUDN University Volunteer Center and a permanent member of the AIS Russia.

Ekaterina A. Isaeva – Candidate of Economic Sciences, Associate Professor, Department of Banking and Monetary Regulation, Financial University under the Government of the Russian Federation (Moscow, Russia). She is the author of the textbook "Strategic management in financial and credit organizations." The author's research interests include change management, including in the credit activities of banks, banking marketing, and management. Ekaterina A. Isaeva is the current chief expert on conducting a Demonstration exam in the specialty "Banking." She has practical experience working in companies dealing with problem debts as well as in the department of budget revenues and expenditures in the State Fisheries Committee of Russia.

Nasiba N. Ismatullaeva – Assistant, Department of Accounting and Business, Tashkent State Transport University, Tashkent, Uzbekistan. Nasiba N. Ismatullaeva conducts research in the field of accounting and auditing.

Abdumalik M. Kadirov – Doctor of Economic Sciences, Head of the Department of Management at Fergana Polytechnic Institute, Researcher at the Tashkent State University of Economics (Tashkent, Uzbekistan). He is the honored worker of science and economics of Uzbekistan and the honored worker of higher professional education. He is the author of more than 90 publications and a number of monographs on issues of economic and financial sustainability, public administration, industrial economics and research on scientific methodology in economic specialties. He is the author (coauthor) of more than 90 scientific and educational works, including 3 textbooks and 3 monographs.

Nikolay D. Keosya – postgraduate student at RUDN University (Moscow, Russia). The author is a specialist in the field of investments and the Deputy Director of a large company in the field of construction equipment.

Nargiza A. Khaydarova – born on May 4, 1973, in the Buka district of the Tashkent Region in a family of public servants. In 1991, she entered Tashkent State Agrarian University and graduated in 1996. Since her graduation, the author has been working in the field of education. She has 22 years of teaching experience, with several scientific articles published. Until now, she has been working as an Acting Associate Professor of the Accounting Department at the Tashkent State University of Economics (Tashkent, Uzbekistan).

Mutabar Kh. Khodjayeva – defended her candidate's dissertation at the Banking and Finance Academy on the topic "Accounting and audit of insurance activities in the Republic of Uzbekistan" in July 2001. Since 2001, she has been an Associate Professor at the Department of Financial Analysis and Audit at Tashkent State University of Economics (Tashkent, Uzbekistan).

Marina V. Krasnova – Candidate of Sciences (Pedagogy), Associate Professor, Associate Professor of Commerce and Hospitality Department, Vladimir State University named after Alexander and Nikolay Stoletovs (Vladimir, Russia). Her research interests include the innovative technologies of service activities in the tourism and hospitality industry, spheres of economic (entrepreneurial) activity, subjects and forms of their interaction, and contemporary management tools (business communication) in the process of regional economic development. Marina Krasnova has published more than 30 papers in Russian and foreign peer-reviewed scientific journals and 3 textbooks and teaching aids.

Elmira D. Kuramaeva – Candidate of Economic Sciences, Associate Professor, Deputy Director for Academic Affairs of the Higher School of Economics of the Kyrgyz National University named after Jusup Balasagyn (Bishkek, Kyrgyzstan). She has more than 45 scientific articles and 4 methodical works. She received her PhD in Economics in 2016. Courses taught include "Money, Credit, and Banking," "Banking management," "Monetary and credit regulation in the economy," "Payment system," and "Banking – risk management."

Mohichekhra T. Kurbonbekova – Doctor of Economic Sciences, Associate Professor, Project Manager of the Department of Commercialization of Scientific and Innovative Developments, Tashkent State University of Economics (Tashkent, Uzbekistan). She is an Associate Professor at the Department of Banking and Investments of Tashkent State University of Economics. She is the author of more than 50 publications and monographs on economics, finance, monetary policy, and banking. The author is a member of four innovative projects at the university and the Head of a targeted project "Ensuring sustainable growth in the field of tourism through the development of national crafts of the Republic of Karakalpakstan, creating the 'SMART QNatCraft' platform." She is a member of the leading women's club organized at Tashkent State University of Economics. She is the coauthor of Scopus-indexed articles "Ensuring the stability of banks during the COVID-19 pandemic," "Financial technologies and innovations (Fin Tech-I)," and "The interdependence of education and development, organizational learning capabilities and on organizational effectiveness in the field of service delivery." Mohichekhra T. Kurbonbekova is the author of the study guide "Banking."

Ainura K. Kydykbayeva – MBA, Associate Professor, International University of the Kyrgyz Republic (Bishkek, Kyrgyzstan). She is a participant of international projects, including an Expert Consultant on Marketing, Green Financing, and Digital Economy. Her scientific interests include banking innovations, sustainable development, and poverty eradication. Ainura Kydykbayeva had an experience of organizing scientific and practical conferences at the national and international level on regional sustainable development and poverty eradication. She is a member of the working group of the project "Ensuring quality assurance and accreditation of online programs in Kyrgyzstan," implemented with the financial support of INQAAHE Agency for Quality Assurance in Education "EdNet." She is the author of more than 20 scientific and educational publications.

Diana M. Madiyarova – Doctor of Economics, Professor of the Department of International Economic Relations of RUDN University (Moscow, Russia). She completed her PhD at the Maastricht Business School, Holland. From 2005 to 2010, she was the Head of the Department of "Economics" of the Eurasian National University named after L. N. Gumilyov. The author's research interests include economics of integrated structures and socioeconomic and political–economic problems of ensuring economic security. She has prepared 20 Candidates of Economic Sciences. D. M. Madiyarova is the author of more than 30 textbooks in Kazakh and Russian. In 2015, the author was awarded with the medal "For merits in the development of science of the Republic of Kazakhstan."

Ousman N. Mahamat Nour – postgraduate student of RUDN University (Moscow, Russia). O. N. Mahamat Nour is a member of the Association of African Students in the Russian Federation (2019). He had 1 month of internship at the Hilton Hotel in Moscow and 2 weeks of internship at the Institute of Hotel and Tourism (2017–2018); 1 month of internship at the Radisson Blu Hotel in Moscow (Russia) and 1 month of internship at the Modern Hotel in Bonghor City (Chad 2017–2018).

Shokhina U. Mamayusupova – Student of Tashkent State University of Economics (Tashkent, Uzbekistan). She is the honored student of Faculty of Finance and Accounting. Her major is budget control and treasury. She is the author of more than 50 publications, including papers about budget management, treasury, finance, and globalization. She is a member of "Developing a national model of a dualistic system through the formation of an alternative financial ecosystem" project.

Roman V. Manshin – Candidate of Economic Sciences, Associate Professor, Department of International Economic Relations, Faculty of Economics, RUDN University (Moscow, Russia); Leading Researcher, Institute of Demographic Research, Federal Research Sociological Center, Russian Academy of Sciences. The author's research area is "International Labor Market and Migration."

Daria O. Maslakova – Senior lecturer of the Department of Commerce and Hospitality of Vladimir State University named after Alexander and Nikolay Stoletovs (Vladimir, Russia). Author and coauthor of about 59 published works. Professional interests: institutional analysis of investment processes; financial literacy and digital financial literacy.

Ainura J. Murzataeva – Candidate of Economic Sciences, Associate Professor, International University of the Kyrgyz Republic (Bishkek, Kyrgyzstan). She carries out scientific research on developing securities markets, corporate governance, insurance, investments and investment attractiveness of the state, digital finance, and topical aspects of the nonbanking financial market, and problems of social insurance of the population. She is the author of more than 25 articles and the coauthor of 2 textbooks.

Zhyldyz B. Myrzakhmatova – Candidate of Economic Sciences, Associate Professor of the Department of Banking and Taxation of the Higher School of Economics of the Kyrgyz National University named after Jusup Balasagyn (Bishkek, Kyrgyzstan). On June 2, 2015, she received the degree of Candidate of Economics. She teaches disciplines such as "Modern payment systems," "Monetary regulation of the economy," "Banking risk management," and "Banking analytics." The number of publications in elibrary.ru is 19.

Jahonmirzo Z. Nizomiddinov – first-year Master's student at Tashkent State University of Economics (Tashkent, Uzbekistan). He is the recipient of numerous prestigious honors and awards, including the Alisher Navoiy State Scholarship, the Muqimiy Badge and Scholarship, and the Student of the Year award. He achieved second place in the International Olympiad in Accounting at L. N. Gumilev Eurasian National University in the Republic of Kazakhstan. Additionally, he has authored over 50 publications and 1 monograph "Improving the financial impact of small business and promoting private entrepreneurship in innovative areas." His work has been published in prestigious journals, including the "Academic Journal of Digital Economics and Stability," the "American Journal of Social and Humanitarian Research," "World Bulletin of Management and Law," "American Journal of Social and Humanitarian Research," and "Global Transformations: Economics, Finance, and Pedagogy."

Sanjar Omanov – PhD Researcher, Senior Teacher, Department of Financial Analysis and Audit, Tashkent State University of Economics (Tashkent, Uzbekistan). He is the honored worker of science and technology of the Uzbekistan and the honored worker of higher professional education. He is the author of more than 20 publications. In 2018–2020, he worked as a specialist in the Department of Financial and Economic Development Planning of the Ministry of Preschool Education of the Republic of Uzbekistan. In 2020, he worked as an Assistant in the "Financial Analysis and Audit" department of the Tashkent State University of Economics and as a Senior Teacher since February 2023. Sanjar Omanov is the author (coauthor) of more than 20 scientific and educational works, including 1 textbook.

Ilya E. Pokamestov – Candidate of Economic Sciences, Associate Professor. Since 2014, he has been teaching at the Financial University under the Government of the Russian Federation (Moscow, Russia) (Associate Professor of the Department of Financial and Investment Management). He was trained in leading factoring companies in the United Kingdom and France. In 2007, he created FACTORing PRO, which develops and maintains the first information portal about factoring and trade finance in Russia and the CIS. He has 20 years of experience in senior positions in the factoring business at FC

UralSib, Societe Generale Group, and VTB Group. He is the Editor-in-Chief of the journal "Factoring and Trade Finance." Ilya E. Pokamestov is the author of the books "Factoring," "Factoring: sales, technology, risk management," and more than 30 publications on the topic of factoring and trade finance. He has more than 20 years of teaching experience and a solid list of publications at the Russian Science Citation Index and Scopus. He cooperates with the HSE and Moscow State University.

Gulsher A. Qalandarshoev – postgraduate student of the Department of International Economic Relations at RUDN University (Moscow, Russia). His research interests include world economy, international economic relations, and international investment cooperation. He has previously published scientific works on the selected topic in peer-reviewed journals of Higher Attestation Commission (VAK) of the Russian Federation and other journals.

Ismail U. Rakhimberdiev – Candidate of Economic Sciences, Associate Professor, Department of Accounting and Business, Tashkent State Transport University, Tashkent, Uzbekistan. He is a Scientist in the field of taxes, taxation, and economic analysis in road transportation.

Munisa E. Saidova – Doctor of Biological Sciences, Professor, Department of Agronomy and Soil Science, Tashkent State Agrarian University (Salar, Uzbekistan). She has published more than 120 scientific works, including works on the ways to solve the problems of soil degradation under climate change, reclamation soil science and soil protection, soil assessment and mapping, soil biology and biodiagnostics of degraded soils, scientific research methods in agro-soil science, sustainable soil science, scientific-pedagogical activity in directions such as the basis of development, the use of advanced geo-information systems in soil science, and reclamation of saline soils. The author is a member of the editorial board of the journal "Uzbekistan zamini" and the Editor-in-Chief of the international journal "European Journal of Agricultural and Rural Education (EJARE)." Munisa E. Saidova is the author (coauthor) of more than 120 scientific and educational works, including 4 textbooks, 4 training manuals, 3 monographs, and 2 scientific treatises.

Dono A. Sativaldiyeva – born July 2, 1961. In 1982, after graduating from the National Economic Institute, she began her activities as a Deputy Chief Accountant. Dono A. Sativaldiyeva switched to teaching in 2001, starting to work at the Department of Accounting in Foreign Economic Activity at the Tashkent State University of Economics. She teaches students subjects such as "Accounting," "Financial Accounting," "Budget Accounting," "Financial and Management Accounting," "Management Accounting," and "Introduction to Accounting." She is the author of more than 50 theses and articles, published monographs, published textbooks, including "Accounting," "Collection of problems on financial and management accounting," "Collection of problems on accounting," "Financial and management accounting," "Accounting in other industries," and many other publications. Nowadays, Dono A. Sativaldiyeva is an Associate Professor at the Department of Accounting at the Tashkent State University of Economics (Tashkent, Uzbekistan). She conducts scientific work with students of the Faculty of Finance and Accounting. She is hardworking, sociable, and responsive. Students love and respect her. The author has her rightful place among the university teaching staff.

Saltanat T. Seytbekova – Head of the Department "Accounting, Audit, and Finance" of the Kazakh National Agrarian University "Higher School of Business and Law" (Almaty, Kazakhstan). The author's scientific interests include accounting, auditing, and statistics.

Khonzoda M. Shamsitdinova – student of Tashkent State University of Economics (Uzbekistan). She is the honored student of Faculty of Finance and Accounting. She is the author of more than 45 articles on attracting investments to the financial market, profitability of securities, budget control and treasury, and Islamic finance (including articles with coauthors from Tashkent State University of Economics).

Alexey V. Shleenko – Candidate of Economic Sciences, Associate Professor, Head of the Department of Industrial and Civil Engineering, Southwest State University (Kursk, Russia). He is a doctoral student of the Orel State University named after I. S. Turgenev. Alexey V. Shleenko is the author of more than 234 scientific and methodological publications, including international ones. His research interests include regional and sectorial economics, spatial economy, evolution and development of spatial economy, and the research of factors of economic growth of regional clusters and spaces.

Irina N. Shvetsova – Candidate of Economic Sciences, Associate Professor, Director of the Institute of Economics and Management, Pitirim Sorokin Syktyvkar State University (Syktyvkar, Russia). Her scientific interests include strategic management of regional ecosystems, digital transformation, finance, and investment. The candidate's dissertation "Improving investment policy based on capital assessment" was devoted to topical issues of the development of investment activity and investment potential of the Komi Republic. She is the author of the more than 120 scientific works, including monographs and more than 30 articles in scientific journals. Irina N. Shvetsova was awarded a certificate from the Free Economic Society of Russia for a significant contribution to the activities of the Free Economic Society of Russia, aimed at promoting the socioeconomic development of the country, active expert and educational work, participation in the implementation of socially significant projects, and a certificate from the Ministry of Science and Higher Education of the Russian Federation for significant contribution to the development of the education sector and many years of conscientious work.

Daria S. Sokolan – Candidate of Economic Sciences, Assistant, Department of International Economic Relations, RUDN University (Moscow, Russia); Deputy Dean, Faculty of Economics for International Affairs; curator of the Master's degree in the areas of "International trade" and "International logistics." The author is a specialist in the field of international direct investment and investment activity of China. Darya S. Sokolan teaches more than 10 disciplines. She is a regular commentator in leading Russian magazines and TV channels.

Larisa N. Sorokina – Candidate of Economic Sciences, Associate Professor, Head of the Department of Accounting, Auditing, and Statistics, RUDN University (Moscow, Russia). Her research interests include problems of economic security of the country under conditions of external and internal restrictions. Larisa N. Sorokina is the author of collective monographs and a reviewer of textbooks. She has published more than 120 works in Russian and foreign peer-reviewed scientific journals and books.

Bobir Tashbaev – PhD (Economics), Associate Professor, Department of Financial Analysis and Audit, Tashkent State University of Economics (Tashkent, Uzbekistan). He is the author of a series of monographs on improving the budget deficit and its debt financing mechanism, including two textbooks and one monograph. The author is the editor of the scientific journal "Editorial Board Member of Economical Science."

Irina B. Teslenko – Doctor of Economics, Professor, Head of the Department of Business Informatics and Economics of Vladimir State University named after Alexander and Nikolay Stoletovs (Vladimir, Russia). Author and coauthor of about 400 published works. Corresponding member of the International Academy of Sciences of Pedagogical Education (since 2005). Corresponding member of the Academy of Natural Sciences (since 2012). Professional interests: institutional analysis of transformation processes in the Russian economy (intellectual capital, intersectoral partnership, and national and regional innovation system); spheres of economic (entrepreneurial) activity and subjects and forms of their interaction; modern management tools (information technologies) in the process of formation of national and regional innovation systems, and digital transformation of socio-economic systems.

Malika S. Tugizova – Student of Tashkent State University of Economics (Tashkent, Uzbekistan). She is the author of more than 40 articles. Her articles have been published in international journals and conference collections, including an international journal "World Economics & Finance Bulletin," "Journal of Science, Research, and Teaching," "Innovative Society: Problems, Analysis, and Development prospects," and "International Journal of Social Science & Interdisciplinary Research."

Minovar M. Tulakhodjaeva – defended her doctoral dissertation at Moscow State University on the topic "Company and methods of financial control in the Republic of Uzbekistan" in October 1998. Since 2001, she has been a Chairman of the Board of the National Association of Accountants and Auditors of Uzbekistan (Tashkent, Uzbekistan).

Ibrokhimjon U. Tursunaliev – born on September 22, 1998, in the Tashkent Region, Uzbekistan. In 2021, he graduated from Westminster International University in Tashkent with a degree in Finance at the Faculty of Economics. In the following 2 years, he studied at the Master's program of Tashkent State University of Economics, specializing in accounting. He is currently working as an Assistant Teacher of the Department of Accounting in the Tashkent State University of Economics (Tashkent, Uzbekistan). He is contributing to the learning environment with a positive and professional manner to help other peers to reach their full potential.

Bobir O. Tursunov – Doctor of Economic Sciences, Professor, Head of the "Economic security" department, Tashkent State University of Economics (Tashkent, Uzbekistan). Bobir O. Tursunov is the author (coauthor) of more than 100 scientific and educational works. During his scientific and pedagogical activity, he authored 2 textbooks, 3 monographs, and 6 teaching-methodical manuals, including the books "Economic Security" (2023), "Business Evaluation" (2021), "Food Security" (2022), "Methods for Analyzing Economic Security" (2023), "National and Regional Economic Security" (2020), and "Security and Technology" (2022). The monographs "Financial Security Management at Textile Enterprises" (2022) and "Methodology for Financial Security Management at Textile Enterprises" (2021) serve to improve the quality of education in educational institutions. The author has published 16 papers in Scopus/WoS journals. The author's h-index in Scopus is 8. Bobir O. Tursunov is a member of the editorial board of the scientific journals "International Journal of Arts and Social Science," "International Journal of Progressive Sciences and Technologies," "International European Extended Enablement in Science, Engineering, and Management," "Uluslararası İşletme, Ekonomi ve Yönetim Perspektifleri Dergisi," "Global Journal of Business and Management," and "Journal of Turkish Studies."

Rustam F. Urakov – Acting Associate Professor, Department of Accounting and Business, Tashkent State Transport University, Tashkent, Uzbekistan. The author's research interests include accounting, economic analysis, and auditing.

Bunyod Usmonov – PhD (Economics), Associate Professor, Department of Financial Analysis and Audit, Tashkent State University of Economics (Tashkent, Uzbekistan). He is the honored worker of science and higher professional education. He is the author of more than 30 publications and monographs on state of financial management and economics of entities. The author is the editor of the scientific journal "International Advance Journal of Engineering Research." Usmonov Bunyod Aktam ugli is the author (coauthor) of more than 40 scientific and educational works, including 2 textbooks and 2 monographs.

Natalia A. Volgina – Doctor of Economics, Professor, Department of International Economic relations, Faculty of Economics, RUDN University (Moscow, Russia). Her academic interests are connected with TNCs, foreign direct investment, international production, and global value chains. She has more than 100 publications, including papers presented at the conferences, articles in academic journals, chapters in the books, and 3 monographs, including "Global Value Chains in the Automotive Industry in Central and Eastern Europe" (2018) and "China in Global Value Chains" (2023). She is the author of the textbooks "International Economics" (2005 and 2010), "International Trade" (2019), and "International Finance" (2020).

Zhang Xiao – Candidate of Economic Sciences, Department of International Economic Relations, Faculty of Economics, RUDN University (Moscow, Russia); The author is engaged in studying "World Economy."

Akram A. Yadgarov – Doctor of Economic Sciences, Professor, "Green" Department of Economics and Sustainable Business, Tashkent State University of Economics (Tashkent, Uzbekistan). He has published more than 150 scientific works, particularly on ways to solve climate change problems, agricultural insurance relations, ecology, environmental improvement issues, agricultural development, education development, and leasing relations. Akram A. Yadgarov is the author of research monographs on international standards in quality management, implementation of environmental management, issues of food safety, and development of real sector networks. He is a member of the editorial board of "Uzbekistan insurance market" and "International Journal of Trend in Scientific Research and Development." He is the author (coauthor) of more than 200 scientific and educational works, including 4 textbooks, 8 training manuals, 5 monographs, and 4 scientific treatises.

Olga B. Yares – Candidate of Science (Economics), Associate Professor, Head of Commerce and Hospitality Department, Vladimir State University named after Alexander and Nikolay Stoletovs (Vladimir, Russia). Her research interests include the theory of regional economics, problems of formation and development of the consumer regional market, anti-crisis regulation tools, areas of economic (entrepreneurial) activity, subjects, and forms of their interaction. Olga Yares is the author and coauthor of more than 80 published works, including 2 monographs, 4 textbooks, and 62 articles published in Russian and foreign peer-reviewed scientific journals.

Nurselen T. Yildirim – postgraduate student in the field of "World Economy" at the RUDN University (Moscow, Russia). In 2018, she received her Bachelor's degree from the Faculty of Political Sciences (Mulkiye), Department of Political Science and Public Administration, Ankara University. In 2021, she received her Master's degree from the Faculty of Economics, the People's Friendship University of Russia (Moscow). Her scientific interests are world economy and international economic relations.

Irina F. Zhuckovskaya – Candidate of Science (Economics), Associate Professor, Associate Professor of Commerce and Hospitality Department, Vladimir State University named after Alexander and Nikolay Stoletovs (Vladimir, Russia). Her research interests include the theory of human capital, intellectual capital, digital economy, and Industry 4.0 and their impact on the development of certain sectors of the national economy (trade and services). Irina Zhuckovskaya organizes Russian scientific and practical conferences. She is an author of collective monographs and a reviewer in Russian scientific journals. She has published more than 200 papers in Russian and foreign peer-reviewed scientific journals and 30 textbooks and teaching aids.

APPLIED PERSPECTIVE ON MANAGING INTERNATIONAL ENTREPRENEURSHIP BASED ON CORPORATE ACCOUNTING AND IFRS REPORTING: INTRODUCTION

Mansur P. Eshov, Gulnora K. Abdurakhmanova, Aktam U. Burkhanov, Nodira B. Abdusalomova and Shakhlo T. Ergasheva

Tashkent State University of Economics, Uzbekistan

Managing international entrepreneurship is complicated by the need for comprehensive coverage. First, in the geographical aspect, an international enterprise must cater to the interests of its home country since the management apparatus is situated there. Contributions to the state budget, generated through corporate income tax, flow into this country. The most knowledge-intensive jobs are created here for managerial personnel and employees engaged in corporate research and development (R&D).

On the other hand, international business must also consider the interests of countries where its production units are located and where its products are sold. For this reason, each branch and representation of an international enterprise must adapt to the specifics of the local business culture and the requirements of local stakeholders. This should be reflected in International Financial Reporting Standards (IFRS). Second, in the transactional aspect, in the contemporary era of globalization characterized by the creation and dynamic development of international trade partnerships, international enterprises may often be participants in several integration chains of countries and companies simultaneously. Each transboundary supply and sales chain, as well as each integration union of countries, pursues its own interests and has its own traditions of business communication and enterprise management – all of which must be considered by IFRS. Third, in the market aspect, an international enterprise is a participant in a specific global market (industry). Thus, it must adhere to its requirements dictated by its "invisible hand" and supranational regulators. On the other hand, an international enterprise is also a subject of the economy as a whole, where business traditions may differ from the practices of a specific market. Therefore, as it expands its geographical presence to new countries and diversifies its product range, an international enterprise must constantly adapt its

Development of International Entrepreneurship Based on Corporate Accounting and Reporting According to IFRS
Advanced Series in Management, Volume 33B, 1–4
ISSN: 1877-6361/doi:10.1108/S1877-63612024000033B001

management practices to the market environment of its presence. Actively used in international business, IFRS can assist in this.

Fourth, in the technological aspect, an international enterprise must fully engage advanced technologies in its management practices. On the other hand, it is necessary to prevent and reduce technological barriers to stakeholders' access to corporate reporting. In this regard, IFRS should encourage the digital modernization of corporate accounting and reporting, ensuring mass accessibility of corporate reporting for all stakeholders, regardless of their digital competence and access to telecommunication infrastructure.

Fifth, in the stakeholders' aspect, shareholders, creditors, investors, and the management of an international enterprise are interested in increasing its profitability and commercial success. On the other hand, the employees of an international enterprise are interested in its socially responsible human resources (HR) management. In turn, consumers and representatives of local communities are interested in the environmentally friendly treatment of international business, the ecological aspects, and the high quality of its products, as well as their affordable price and convenience of acquisition and consumption.

Finally, the regulatory authorities of all countries where international business is present are interested in maximizing the volume and completeness (de-shadowing) of its tax contributions to state budgets, compliance with labor legislation, protection of consumer rights, compliance with national quality and safety standards for products, as well as maintaining healthy market competition without price dumping by international enterprises to preserve local business. To remain competitive, an international enterprise must consider the interests of all stakeholders. IFRS can and should assist in this. The following two management issues for contemporary international business arise at the intersection of all mentioned aspects.

The first issue involves adapting IFRS to the specifics of the development of international business in different sectors of the economy. The areas of corporate accounting are specific in each economic sector, which should be reflected in the content of corporate reporting. For example, to strengthen the international brands of export-oriented agricultural enterprises, it is important to emphasize the naturalness of their products and the climatic sustainability of their production. IFRS should provide such an opportunity. In turn, the ecological aspects of production and distribution processes are of great importance in the industry, which should also be reflected in corporate reporting according to IFRS.

The second issue concerns the transition of IFRS from traditions to innovations through a more comprehensive consideration of international experience in the development of trade cooperation and international entrepreneurship. In the dynamically changing global economic system in the new era of globalization, IFRS must consider and fully meet the growing needs of international enterprises from around the world in the field of foreign trade partnerships when building international value chains.

For example, IFRS should consider new categories of countries – not relying on the template experience of developed countries but adapting to the unique experience of each category of developing countries. For instance, new customs unions involving developing countries – the Eurasian Economic Union (EAEU) and the expanding Brazil, Russia, India, China, and South Africa (BRICS) bloc – require their own IFRS that correspond to the specifics of their markets. Consequently, it is necessary from the unification of IFRS to their diversification. In the era of flexible foreign trade partnerships, numerous new IFRS should emerge, easy to implement in the practice of international entrepreneurship and ensuring the improvement of corporate management efficiency.

Existing literature separately addresses the identified aspects of managing international enterprises in accordance with IFRS, along with the related issues. This fragmentation of existing scholarly knowledge is the cause of unresolved questions. These questions have been extensively studied at the theoretical level; the concept of IFRS as instruments for managing international enterprises has been formed to a considerable extent. However, at the empirical level, the integration of IFRS into the corporate accounting and reporting of international entrepreneurship is insufficiently explored and remains largely uncertain.

This book aims to fill the identified gaps in the existing literature and create a comprehensive scientific understanding of managing international entrepreneurship in the implementation and adherence to IFRS. This book aims to comprehensively study applied issues related to the use of IFRS in managing international entrepreneurship. Consequently, the book provides an applied perspective on managing international entrepreneurship based on corporate accounting and reporting according to IFRS, forming the basis for the scientific novelty and originality of this volume.

The scientific novelty and theoretical significance of this book lie in its comprehensive coverage of the practice of applying IFRS at all levels of economic management. At the microlevel, the book explains the essence and justifies the advantages of implementing IFRS into the practice of corporate management, accounting, and reporting. At the meso-level, the book reflects the benefits of transitioning local enterprises to IFRS for economic growth and sustainable regional development. The influx of foreign investments stimulates business activity in the region, and the entry of international enterprises into local markets contributes to increased competition. This creates additional jobs, raises income levels in society, enhances purchasing power, and boosts economic activity in the region.

At the macro-level, the transnationalization of activities by national enterprises, facilitated by the transition to IFRS, contributes to diversifying the markets for their products, increasing profits (a tax base), and consequently, tax contributions to the national budget. The expansion of the presence of national enterprises in global markets strengthens the international status of the country. On a global scale, IFRS support the establishment and development of international trade partnerships and customs unions. This promotes the development of international trade and the sustainable growth of the global economic system.

The uniqueness of this book and its practical significance lie in its pioneering and comprehensive examination of the rich contemporary experience of developing countries, among themselves and in collaboration with developed nations, in the development of mutual trade based on the integration of IFRS into international entrepreneurship. Specifically, the book unveils the progressive experiences of foreign trade partnerships involving China, Japan, Tajikistan, Kazakhstan, Turkey, Russia, African countries, Kyrgyzstan, and Uzbekistan. Practical recommendations aimed at enhancing IFRS are proposed for the development of foreign trade cooperation with these countries, underscoring the practical significance of this book.

The book is logically structured and systemically presents the outcomes of cutting-edge scientific research on the topic of managing international entrepreneurship through the integration of IFRS into corporate accounting and reporting practices. The first part reflects and explains the specifics of the development of international entrepreneurship across various sectors of the contemporary economy, including the financial sector, Industry 4.0, agriculture, manufacturing and extractive industries, and the service sector. The second part presents and analyzes international experience in the development of trade cooperation and international entrepreneurship.

The primary target audience for this book includes members of the academic community who study IFRS in the theory and practice of international entrepreneurship. Within the book, they will find a detailed overview and analysis of contemporary practical experiences in applying IFRS in corporate accounting and formation and publication of corporate reports in international entrepreneurship. Consequently, the book supports an ongoing scholarly discussion on the development of international trade through the modernization and implementation of IFRS.

An additional audience for this book comprises representatives of the management bodies of international enterprises. Within the book, they will find examples from international practice and scientific and practical recommendations for risk management and leveraging the benefits of transitioning to IFRS. The additional audience also includes government and supranational economic regulators. Their representatives will find scientific developments and practical recommendations for intensifying the development of international trade through flexible and highly effective integration of IFRS into corporate management practices (accounting and reporting).

PART 1

SPECIFICS OF INTERNATIONAL ENTREPRENEURSHIP DEVELOPMENT ACROSS SECTORS OF THE MODERN ECONOMY

DIGITAL FINANCIAL LITERACY AS A CONDITION FOR THE POPULATION TO ADAPT TO DIGITAL TRANSFORMATION

Irina B. Teslenko and Daria O. Maslakova

Vladimir State University, Russia

ABSTRACT

The research aims to analyze the priority areas for developing the digital financial literacy (DFL) of the population. During the research, the authors applied comparative analysis, synthesis, a systemic approach to data evaluation, and the dialectical method. The research found that the main components of DFL include the level of digital financial knowledge, the level of digital financial attitudes, and the level of digital financial behavior. There are also scientifically based theses about the importance of digital transformation of society due to the new global requirements for the level of basic knowledge and skills to use digital financial technologies effectively. Based on the analysis, the authors defined DFL as a basic digital process of forming financial concepts based on the ability of people to make informed decisions in dealing with financial services and their awareness of the risks arising in the digital environment, as well as the possibility of their neutralization. The research identifies and analyzes the most promising areas that make it possible to develop trends in the field of DFL.

Keywords: Financial literacy; digital financial literacy; risks; financial services; financial behavior; digital environment

JEL Codes: G5; G53

Digitalization creates new opportunities and risks for consumers of digital financial instruments. The research describes the key trends in the consumption of financial services, the risks faced by citizens, and open questions in connection with their management. This research presents materials on the topic that may be of interest to the professional community.

The introduction of advanced digital technologies creates new realities for professional and individual investors and significantly modernizes the existing ones. Big data and

Development of International Entrepreneurship Based on Corporate Accounting and Reporting According to IFRS
Advanced Series in Management, Volume 33B, 7–14
Copyright © 2024 Irina B. Teslenko and Daria O. Maslakova
Published under exclusive licence by Emerald Publishing Limited
ISSN: 1877-6361/doi:10.1108/S1877-63612024000033B002

artificial intelligence (AI) open up huge opportunities for developing a new economic structure. However, the digitalization processes of citizens and their distancing, which intensified during the COVID-19 pandemic, contributed to a sharp acceleration of digital processes worldwide.

New opportunities for the country and the economy are accompanied by new, serious threats and risks to the rights and interests of people. Knowledge and practical application of skills in the field of personal finance management are relevant to every citizen. The demand for information in this area generates a supply from a considerable number of specialists with different levels of training.

Financial market participants use elements of social engineering to convince the audience and draw attention to their financial instruments. People have difficulty verifying large amounts of data, its validity, timeliness, and (very importantly) the availability of digital financial information. Financial and technological services continue to increase in quantity, becoming more complex. Such technological advances stimulate changes in financial markets, which leads to the emergence and growth of the need to form a population with digital skills to expand participation in economic activities and promote economic development and competition in the national and global economy.

The digital transformation of society dictates new requirements for the level of basic knowledge and skills to use digital financial technologies effectively.

According to the Organization for Economic Cooperation and Development (OECD), globalization and an increase in the spread of new financial technologies have several positive aspects. First, there has been an intensification of financial inclusion. For example, people who cannot visit bank branches in person have received online access to financial services. Second, the speed and quality of the provision of financial services that meet the consumer's needs have increased. Third, the productivity of interaction between financial service providers and consumers has increased due to the possibilities of the digital environment.

MATERIALS AND METHOD

Considering the pace of change in fintech and the possibilities of digital work with financial instruments, digital skills mean an expanding range of skills that change over time. Financial and digital skills include a variety of behaviors, experiences, knowledge, work habits, character traits, and predispositions.

Thus, they include financial, technical, and cognitive skills, as well as cognitive-social skills (e.g., interpersonal communication skills).

Citizens use digital skills to work with various digital technologies, including computers, laptops, mobile phones, and other Internet-connected or smart devices. Some skills may be device-specific, while others may be more versatile.

Before considering methods for evaluating digital financial skills, it is necessary to understand what digital financial skills are and how they are classified. These skills are sometimes also referred to as digital competence or digital competencies. They may include the knowledge and skills a person needs to use digital financial instruments.

The acceleration of digitalization in the financial sector of the economy has led to an awareness of the importance of financial knowledge and the emergence of the phrase "Digital financial literacy" (DFL). This phrase appeared in the late 1990s in Russian and foreign academic sources. However, the relevance of defining the essence of this concept and interest in it arose relatively recently, 7–6 years ago (Dmitrova, 2020). Therefore, the unity of approach to understanding the term in scientific circles has not yet developed.

In 1997, the concept of "digital literacy" was considered by P. Glister. According to the scientist, the concept includes media literacy, Internet literacy, computer literacy, and the ability of people to critically perceive information in the digital environment (Glister, 1997).

S. G. Davydov and O. S. Logunova believe that DFL is a person's involvement in the digital environment, supported by certain competencies in using, searching, processing, and protecting digital information (Davydov & Logunova, 2015).

E. A. Sorokina argues that there is a direct relationship between knowledge, skills, and attitudes in the field of DFL and the effectiveness of using digital tools and predicting the financial future of people (Sorokina, 2021).

Representatives of the MARA Technology University (UiTM) take the position that people with financial knowledge, self-confidence, and various practical experience in financial transactions are limited in the area of digital financial risks in the field of digital financial services. This predetermines the importance of studying the DFL of the population at all levels (Baistaman et al., 2022; Rahim et al., 2022).

A group of scientists from the University of Jyväskylä defines three main areas in the formation of the concept of DFL: financial technology, financial behavior in the digital environment, and behavioral intervention (adaptive inclusive programs for people with special needs) (Koskelainen et al., 2023).

RESULTS

Russia is one of the world leaders in digitalizing the financial sector. It occupies leading positions in various international rankings.

For 2022, the Russian Federation ranked fifth in terms of the number of Internet users; at the end of the year, their number was 129.8 million, which is 5.8 million more than in the same period in 2021 (Kemp, 2022). In terms of the level of penetration of mobile devices into the daily life of consumers, Russia has a stable sixth position in world leadership. The development of financial and technological services allowed Russia to enter the top five leading countries in digital banking in 2022, along with such countries as Switzerland, Spain, Turkey, and Poland.

The financial technology index has grown since 2017 by 42% and amounted to 86% in 2022, which is 23% higher than the value for the countries of North America and 27% higher than the value of the Eurozone countries.

According to a survey by the rating agency Expert RA for 2022, 87% of bank customers in Russia used digital channels, 30% of Russians reduced the number of visits to bank branches, and 92% of respondents opted for cashless payments. The presented analytical data allow us to conclude that there is a positive trend in the development of the provision of digital services to the population of the Russian Federation.

The large-scale development of financial and technological services predetermines the direction for developing digital financial competencies. They will enable citizens to properly and effectively use fintech products and avoid the negative impact of fraudsters in the digital environment.

In our opinion, DFL is based on basic knowledge of digital financial concepts and reflects the ability of a citizen to make informed decisions in handling financial instruments and consider possible risks arising in the digital environment.

For the first time in Russia, a comprehensive assessment of DFL was carried out in February 2023 by the National Agency for Financial Research (NAFI) analytical center.

Until now, only some of its aspects have been studied. The study involved 1,600 respondents aged 18–70 years. DFL was measured using the Digital Financial Literacy Index, which includes three partial indices (the level of digital financial knowledge, the level of digital financial attitudes, and the level of digital financial behavior).

The DFL index is measured in points. In 2022, it was 5.63 points out of 10 possible for Russia. The private indices that make up the assessment were as follows:

- Digital financial knowledge – 1.61 points out of 3 possible.
- Digital financial behavior – 2.34 points out of 4 possible.
- Digital financial attitudes – 1.79 out of 3 possible points (NAFI Analytical Center, 2023).

More than 70% of Russians demonstrated an average level of DFL, 73% among versus 63% among men, 73% among urban residents versus 61% among rural residents, 81% among married couples versus 45% among single people.

A fairly high level of digital financial knowledge about financial products was revealed. According to it, 66% of respondents are well aware of the principle of using personal data on the Internet, and 49% are aware of the need to sign a digital financial contract in order for it to be considered valid for receiving a service.

Simultaneously, misconceptions about cryptocurrency are common among residents of the Russian Federation. Thus, 38% of respondents believe cryptocurrency can be used as legal tender. Also, 60% of respondents expressed the opinion that there are many simple and easy ways to increase capital. Such incorrect beliefs are often shared by young people between 18 and 30. In general, this category of respondents is the most vulnerable in terms of digital financial security.

The level of digital financial attitudes is assessed satisfactorily. For example, Russian citizens have proper attitudes regarding the possible risks of using websites when purchasing online. More than 81% of respondents check the site for a security condition before purchasing payment for services or goods; 56% of citizens participating in the survey read the terms and user agreements before making an online purchase. Simultaneously, 31% of respondents use public Wi-Fi when paying for purchases on the Internet and are not aware of the risks of personal data leakage.

The majority of Russians demonstrate the right behavior regarding the protection of their personal data in the digital financial environment. Thus, 75% of respondents say that they do not even disclose their passwords and personal identification number (PIN) codes to close friends; 79% of respondents do not share personal information about their finances on the Internet. Simultaneously, survey participants quite often neglect to change passwords on online shopping websites regularly, only 34% of survey participants do this, and 38% almost never change them.

The relationship between DFL and the digitalization of services is apparent. There are positive and negative sides to the spread of digital financial services. We consider it positive that such an increase in the financial accessibility of financial services is received by citizens who previously could not use banking services in bank branches due to the lack of proper infrastructure or limited mobility. The positive sides include the timeliness of the necessary transactions. The expansion of the relationship between financial service providers and end users can also be called a positive side, considering the opportunities provided by the digital environment.

It should also be noted that the spread of digital financial services has negative sides, which lead to the following:

• Financial losses.
• A decrease in confidence in the financial system due to the lack of positive experience.
• An increase in the creditworthiness of the population (due to the ease of obtaining services).
• Exclusion of certain socially vulnerable groups from the financial system due to the impossibility of using digital channels due to the lack of Internet access, sufficient knowledge, and experience.
• Greater vulnerability of the consumer to the actions of third parties (cyber criminals) (Pearson & Korankye, 2022).

The development and widespread use of digital technologies creates new risks for the consumer of financial services. The following is a grouping of financial risks regarding the level of DFL.

Group of risks by their sources of occurrence.

(1) Risk group arises due to the consumer's behavior of digital financial services.
Risk sources:
1.1. Lack of digital knowledge (low DFL). When comparing digital financial services, there is a false illusion of understanding a financial instrument.
1.2. "Virtuality" in the perception of money. The ease of use of a digital resource can lead to an increase in errors.
1.3. Behavioral distortions. Overestimation of true benefits or overconsumption of digital financial services.
(2) Risk group arises due to the imperfection of the digital financial services market and the uneven distribution of market power between the service provider and the consumer (Shvaher et al., 2021).
Risk sources:
2.1. Consumer digital footprint. Knowledge of user activity allows companies to push citizens to various financial transactions.
2.2. Intensive influence of companies on consumers. Due to the variety and diversity of digital services or the imposition of additional digital services that the consumer, in the absence of the necessary knowledge, cannot recognize.
2.3. Exposure of services to digital fraudsters who can fraudulently obtain passwords and other personal data from the users of financial services.
(3) Risk group arises due to irrelevant regulation of the digital environment.
Risk sources:
3.1. Weak protection by the holder (companies) of the personal data of citizens. Insufficient control over compliance with the requirements for the security of personal data storage.
3.2. Disclosure mechanisms, which arise due to unscrupulous financial service providers.
(4) Risk group arises due to the peculiarities of the functioning of digital financial services.
Risk sources:
4.1. Decision-making based on rigid algorithms leads to a refusal to provide the service because the influence of factors under unforeseen circumstances is not considered.
4.2. Software failure makes it impossible to get a financial service.

To minimize the presented risks, it is necessary to take the following measures:

(1) To tighten regulation of the digital sphere.

With expanded opportunities for digitalization, attracting funds from the public (P2B lending) by companies has become much more accessible. Crowd technologies, particularly crowdlending, began to be actively used abroad. Consumers receive a working financial instrument with very high risks compared to traditional ways of capital investment. The user of an advanced financial instrument must be competent enough in the matter of finance to make an independent and well-considered decision on managing this instrument.

(2) To develop the financial and DFL of the population.

To improve the DFL of the population, it is necessary to develop an initiative to teach the elements of DFL within the framework of existing educational programs (including for people with limited access to digital financial services). It is recommended to use digital technologies to improve training effectiveness, including launching distance courses and developing training simulators and learning gamification. It is recommended to develop a framework for digital financial competencies in the following areas:

- The first direction is based on the knowledge of means of payment (e.g., electronic money, digital ruble, etc.), asset management (e.g., mobile bank and electronic wallet, etc.), and alternative financing forms (e.g., crowdfunding).
- The second direction accumulates knowledge on digital financial risks associated with fraud in the digital environment by phishing, pharming, installing spyware, hacker attacks, involving citizens in digital financial pyramids, etc.
- The third direction is the ability to manage digital financial risks and master the skills of digital hygiene (e.g., safe use of financial instruments in a digital environment, rules for storing personal data, rules for using public Wi-Fi, etc.).
- The fourth direction extends to form a certain level of knowledge of one's civil rights and obligations as a consumer of digital financial services (algorithm for the procedure for indemnification, etc.).
- The fifth direction is the assessment of existing programs to improve the level of financial and DFL of the population, which makes it possible to select only effective programs that have been tested at different levels.

(3) To form digital nudging (devices that push the consumer to the responsible use of finances, navigator in the financial sector).

The term nudging was introduced in 2017 by American economist Richard Thaler to refer to a system that allows people to make the right choice. Using this system in the digital environment, it is possible to create or improve mobile applications that allow citizens to keep track of their expenses and plan their budgets. An example of the current digital nudging is the automation of payment for housing and utility services, credit debt, etc.

The complex of the above activities will make it possible to organize high-quality and efficient receipt of digital financial services by the population.

DISCUSSION

The development of DFL is of macroeconomic importance. It can significantly contribute to the country's economic growth.

To develop a new digital financial culture, it is necessary to know the behavioral models that actually work for the country and its regions. It is necessary to understand that it is not enough to read a textbook on behavioral economics. It is necessary to conduct regional monitoring on sociocultural characteristics.

To achieve the necessary level of development of DFL, it is necessary to develop a development strategy that can adapt to contemporary economic and technical conditions of national and global fluctuations.

Another important aspect of discussing the topic of DFL is fraud on the Internet. A person faces various types of monetary settlements and payments daily. Earlier, many transactions were carried out using cash; now, a lot of simple and convenient payment instruments for conducting financial transactions are provided for the choice of a citizen. In addition to simplicity and comfort, there are new risks.

Cyberbullying is represented by two main types (phishing and skimming). Phishing is a way in which attackers extract information on a bank card remotely. By establishing a connection with a citizen by phone, a "fake" bank employee (an attacker) asks to provide personal SMS data with PIN and Card Verification Value (CVV) codes. There is another option for obtaining data via the Internet – a phishing website, which is a fake site that records a username and password when a user logs in, after which fraudsters can use them for various illegal purposes.

In 2022, the volume of monetary losses of Russian citizens from telephone fraud amounted to 14,200 million rubles, which is 42.25% more than in 2021. According to the Central Bank of the Russian Federation, 83% of Russian citizens have encountered cyberbullying (OECD, 2018). Negative statistics suggest that it is necessary to increase the level of financial literacy and consider the possibility of opening hotlines or services to solve problems and complaints of consumers of financial services.

It is necessary to be as attentive as possible when participating in various surveys. Scammers often conduct surveys under the guise of popular financial organizations (e.g., a bank), offering to play a cash prize at the end. To confirm the receipt of the winnings, the scammers ask to send a certain amount to their account to confirm that the citizen is allegedly a client of their financial organization.

Another way to extract information from gullible citizens is the creation of fake personal pages for the purpose of familiarization and obtaining personal information that can serve as access to the real finances of citizens.

As the number and complexity of financial and digital products (tools) grows, society begins to feel the need for properly structured approaches to determine the existing levels of digital skills and organize future needs in the financial sphere.

CONCLUSION

The growing digitalization of financial services requires a change in the approaches of the population to managing their money in the online environment. According to the data presented in the research, the index of DFL of Russian citizens so far has average values. This indicates that the population knows how to use financial instruments on the Internet but often ignores important basic security rules.

The dissemination of knowledge and skills about the proper use of digital resources can change the behavioral attitudes of people in managing personal and public finances and thereby increase their level of financial literacy.

REFERENCES

Baistaman, J., Nawi, F. A. M., Mustapha, W. M. W., & Mamat, M. (2022). Exploratory factor analysis of financial literacy in the Malaysian context. *Proceedings*, *82*(1), 24. https://doi.org/10.3390/proceedings2022082024

Davydov, S. G., & Logunova, O. S. (2015). Project "Digital literacy index": Methodological experiments. *Sociology: Methodology, Methods, Mathematical Modeling*, *41*, 120–141.

Dmitrova, A. V. (2020). Theoretical aspects of digital literacy formation: Features of representation in pedagogical research. *Azimuth of Scientific Research: Pedagogy and Psychology*, *1*(30), 111–114.

Glister, P. (1997). *Digital literacy*. Wiley.

Kemp, S. (2022, February 15). *Digital 2022: The Russian Federation*. DataReportal. https://datareportal.com/reports/digital-2022-russian-federation. Accessed on 12 May 2023.

Koskelainen, T., Kalmi, P., Scornavacca, E., & Vartiainen, T. (2023). Financial literacy in the digital age – A research agenda. *Journal of Consumer Affairs*, *57*(1), 507–528. https://doi.org/10.1111/joca.12510

NAFI Analytical Center. (2023, February 1). NAFI conducted the first measurement of the Digital Financial Literacy Index of Russian residents. https://nafi.ru/analytics/nafi-provel-pervyy-zamer-indeksa-tsifrovoy-finansovoy-gramotnosti-zhiteley-rossii/. Accessed on 15 April 2023.

OECD. (2018). *G20/OECD INFE policy guidance on digitalization and financial literacy*. OECD Publishing. https://www.oecd.org/g20/summits/buenos-aires/G20-OECD-INFE-Policy-Guidance-Digitalisation-Financial-Literacy-2018.pdf. Accessed on 12 May 2023.

Pearson, B., & Korankye, T. (2022). The association between financial literacy confidence and financial satisfaction. *Review of Behavioral Finance*, *9*, 1–19. https://doi.org/10.1108/RBF-03-2022-0090

Rahim, N. M., Ali, N., & Adnan, M. F. (2022). Students' financial literacy: Digital financial literacy perspective. *GATR Journal of Finance and Banking Review*, *6*(4), 18–25. https://doi.org/10.35609/jfbr.2022.6.4(2)

Shvaher, O. A., Degtyarev, S. I., & Polyakova, L. G. (2021). The effect of social media on financial literacy. *International Journal of Media and Information Literacy*, *6*(1), 211–218.

Sorokina, E. A. (2021). Historiographical analysis of the problem of formation of digital financial literacy of university students. *The World of Science, Culture and Education*, *6*(91), 100–103.

ACCELERATION OF DIGITALIZATION OF TRADE DURING THE PANDEMIC: MOVING TOWARD TRADE 4.0

Irina F. Zhuckovskaya, Olga B. Yares and Marina V. Krasnova

Vladimir State University named after Alexander and Nikolai Stoletovs, Russia

ABSTRACT

The research aims to investigate trade transformation in the context of technological transition and acceleration of its digitalization during the SARS-CoV-2 (COVID-19) pandemic. The methodological basis of this research includes analysis, synthesis, induction, deduction, causality, comparison, description, and logical thinking. The research found that during the COVID-19 pandemic, the digitalization of trade accelerated for several years to come. Industry enterprises (wholesalers and retailers) began to actively implement Industry 4.0 technologies (artificial intelligence, Internet of Things, cloud computing, big data analysis, and augmented and virtual reality) and adapt them to their needs. The main characteristics of today's trade are the creation of smart trade and technological space, platforming, digital automation, omnichannel, personalized sales, etc. Therefore, we can say that trade is undergoing revolutionary transformations, as a result of which Trade 4.0 is being born. A definition of Commerce 4.0 as a customer-oriented business with industry characteristics and digital models that meet the scientific and technical requirements and regulations of Industry 4.0 is given based on the analysis. Key features of Trade 4.0 are digitization of buyers, business processes, products, and services; transforming supply chains into customer-centric organizations; building a digital ecosystem around the company; variety of formats used by trade enterprises; omnichannel interaction with customers and sales; and flexibility of order execution options.

Development of International Entrepreneurship Based on Corporate Accounting and Reporting According to IFRS
Advanced Series in Management, Volume 33B, 15–22
ISSN: 1877-6361/doi:10.1108/S1877-63612024000033B003

Keywords: Trade; Trade 4.0.; digitalization of trade; e-commerce; Internet of Things; artificial intelligence; big data; COVID-19 pandemic

JEL Codes: F14; O14

The present era is the era of large-scale use of digital technologies in the economy, which form Industry 4.0. Information and communication technologies developed for the industry have gradually been adopted and adapted in trade, leading to its transformation toward the digitalization of trade and technology processes.

Responding to the pandemic caused by the SARS-CoV-2 (COVID-19) coronavirus, the governments of more than 150 countries worldwide have taken stringent anti-pandemic measures that have negatively impacted the development of the global economy, including trade. Global gross domestic product (GDP) fell by 3.3% in real terms in 2020 compared to 2019. The decline in global industrial production and trade in the first half of 2020 was as deep as during the 2009 Global Financial Crisis (GFC). However, as quarantines and self-isolations became the norm, businesses and consumers began to increasingly go digital, providing and buying more goods and services online, which contributed to the growth of the share of e-commerce in global retail to 17% in 2020 (its share was 14% in 2019). As a result, by the end of 2020, production and trade adjusted to the new conditions, contributing to their V-shaped recovery.

Digital transformation has accelerated during the COVID-19 pandemic. According to new McKinsey research from a survey of company executives, the digitization of customer, supplier, and internal operations has accelerated by 3–4 years during the COVID-19 pandemic. Simultaneously, the share of digital products and their portfolios accelerated by 6–7 years (McKinsey & Company, 2020). Trade (especially retail) has begun to actively apply Industry 4.0 technologies – artificial intelligence (AI), Internet of Things (IoT), cloud computing, big data analysis (BDA), augmented reality (AR), and virtual reality (VR) – to satisfy customer needs.

The research aims to analyze the trends in the digitalization of trade and the transition to Trade 4.0. During the research, the authors tested the hypothesis that the change in the technological structure and the introduction of Industry 4.0 technologies led to the transformation of the conditions for trade development. During the COVID-19 pandemic and after it, the digitalization of trade is accelerating, and a new era (Trade 4.0) is emerging.

METHOD

The scale of the use of digital technologies over the past decades in almost all sectors of the economy, including trade, is reflected in the works of many authors. Part of the research of the prepandemic period was devoted to the analysis of innovative processes and the use of digital technologies in trade (Strelets & Chebanov, 2020; Zhuckovskaya et al., 2023), trends in the development of e-commerce (Krupenskiy, 2020; Santos et al., 2023), its impact on business performance (Azeem et al., 2015; Falk & Hagsten, 2015), traditional trade (Liu et al., 2013), and prices (Hillen & Fedoseeva, 2021).

The cardinal changes that have occurred in the economy and society under the influence of the pandemic and anti-pandemic restrictions have contributed to the growth of research into the state of society, the economy, and its industries, as well as trade in a pandemic

(Bellora et al., 2020; Panshin et al., 2022; Zagashvili, 2021). Studies were also carried out by individual organizations, such as the World Bank, Organization for Economic Cooperation and Development (OECD), and World Trade Organization (WTO) (OECD, 2020; Research and Markets, 2020; Smeets, 2021; UNCTAD, 2021a, 2021b). Studies have shown that during the lockdown periods, the activities of most commercial enterprises were suspended (offline trade and nonfood retail); the forced self-isolation of the population provoked an increase in demand for online services for groceries and medicines home delivery (Chub, 2020; Perera et al., 2021, etc.). The support of the population and businesses from the state was also required during this period (Saif et al., 2021).

The acceleration of the digitalization of trade during the COVID-19 pandemic and the adaptation of Industry 4.0 technologies in retail led to revolutionary changes and the emergence of the terms "Trade 4.0" and "Retail 4.0." However, they are quite new to the academic environment and among practitioners. Therefore, there is still little research in this area. These include the works of Gliss and Lakert (2017), Loh et al. (2022), Sakrabani et al. (2019); and others. However, there is no clear definition of the terms "Trade 4.0" and "Retail 4.0" yet.

RESULTS

Over the past decade, the global economic system and international trade have been characterized by an increase in instability, uncertainty, the development of multidirectional trends, frequent cataclysms, and crisis phenomena.

Prior to the global financial and economic crisis, there was a significant increase in global trade. Thus, the average annual growth rate of global merchandise exports in 2002–2008 amounted to 14.76% and world imports – 14.54%. In 2009, accompanied by the global crisis, there was a sharp drop in the volume of world trade. In value terms, the volume of international merchandise exports decreased by 22.24% and imports – by 22.91%.

The recovery period that began at the end of 2009 led to increased trade turnover worldwide in 2010–2011. However, a significant slowdown in growth rates was observed in the subsequent period (2012–2014).

However, the sanctions imposed in March 2014 against the Russian Federation by the United States and Western European countries, as well as the fall in prices on the global fuel and raw materials market, had a negative impact on the global economy and led to a decline in global exports and imports in 2014–2016. As a result, according to the United Nations Conference on Trade and Development (UNCTAD), the value of world exports fell to $16.04 billion and imports to $16.21 billion.

After this disastrous period, global trade (with an annual growth rate of about 10%) started to pick up in 2017–2018. In 2018, the volume of world merchandise exports in value terms reached its maximum of $19.56 billion. Then there was a new decline due to the crisis caused by COVID-19.

Anti-pandemic measures introduced by countries worldwide have had a negative impact on the efficiency of the global economy and world trade. The value of world trade fell by 7.4%. In 2020, world merchandise exports in value terms reached $17.6 trillion (UNCTAD, 2021a).

There has been a transformation of demand in individual markets for goods and services. For example, demand for aircraft, automobiles, and their parts, fuel, and mechanical equipment fell sharply, while the demand for pharmaceuticals, protective and disinfection products, food, and certain household goods sharply increased. In terms of supply chains, there were occasional disruptions in the first months of the COVID-19 pandemic (especially in the transport of medicines and personal protective equipment). However, large supply chains proved to be more resilient in a crisis, which allowed them to play a significant role in economic recovery. This applies, for example, to trade in parts for the production of passenger cars, where the reduction in volumes was much smaller compared to trade in passenger cars themselves.

Due to the removal of the most restrictive anti-pandemic measures in 2021, the growth of world trade in goods amounted to 26.5% and in services – 17.2%.

The COVID-19 pandemic has accelerated the digital transformation of the global economy and has led to profound changes in business and lifestyle. Steel consumers rapidly shift to online channels in B2B and B2C markets. This required all sellers to urgently expand the adoption of digital technologies in their enterprises, which led to a qualitative transformation at the organizational and industry levels. For example, resale platforms have become the rebirth of traditional thrift stores in a new digital reality. Compared to them, online resale platforms offer additional advantages, including a huge range and services for authenticating branded goods. This led to a significant increase in e-commerce sales (Fig. 1), especially in retail, which amounted to $4.9 billion in 2021. According to forecasts, they will grow by more than 50% over the next four years (Statista, 2022).

However, sales digitization has not progressed at the same pace in all countries. According to UNCTAD, despite the widespread use of e-commerce in all regions of the world, the largest shift to online shopping has been in emerging market economies. For example, the Latin American online marketplace Mercado Libre sold twice as many items per day in the second quarter of 2020 compared to the same period the previous year. African e-commerce platform Jumia reported a 50% increase in transactions in the first six months of 2020. In China, the share of online sales in total retail volume rose from 19.4% in August 2019 to 24.6% in August 2020 (UNCTAD, 2021b).

According to the McKinsey Business Survey, the pace of digitalization of customer interactions during the COVID-19 pandemic and digital adoption is "years ahead of previous surveys, and even faster in developed Asia than in other regions (Fig. 2). Now respondents are three times more likely than before the crisis to say that at least 80% of their customer interactions are digital" (McKinsey & Company, 2020).

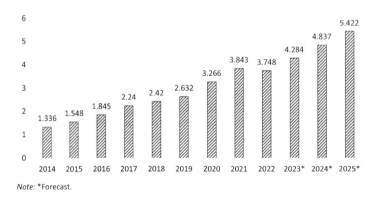

Fig. 1. Global eCommerce Revenue From 2014 to 2025 (in $ Billion). *Source:* Compiled by the authors based on Statista (2022).

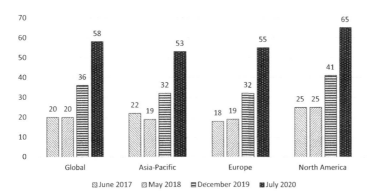

Fig. 2.   The Average Share of Digital Customer Interactions (in %). *Source:* Compiled
by the authors based on McKinsey & Company (2020).

Indeed, during the COVID-19 pandemic, retailers were forced to create and apply new forms of activity for their stores (create online platforms or use the services of market-places) and look for new ways to deliver goods to the buyer to limit personal communi-cation and protect customers from COVID-19. Many marketplaces have introduced additional services for the delivery of goods to consumers. For example, delivery was carried out in the country where the marketplace was located and other world sites.

At this time, the role of traditional retail stores and shopping centers has also changed. Some of them have turned into delivery points for online orders, showrooms, outlets for placing stock goods, etc.

Even after the restrictions were lifted, when life gradually began to return to normal, many consumers continued to shop online (58.4% of Internet users buy something online every week). In 2020–2021, "there were more IoT connections (such as connected cars, smart home gadgets, and connected industrial equipment) than non-IoT connections (laptops and computers). It is expected that by 2025 there will be more than 30 billion IoT connections, almost 4 IoT devices per person on average" (Lueth, 2020).

In 2021–2022, merchants continued to focus on personalized customer relationships. To do this, they focused on the further use of AI technologies, AR, subscription models, payment for purchases through mobile applications, digitalization of workflow through integration with Customer Relationship Management (CRM), Enterprise Resource Planning (ERP) systems, and internal databases, and expanded partnerships with various delivery services. As a result, retail sales revenue in physical stores for many companies almost equal to their digital sales (Shopify Plus, 2023). Brands are investing in omni-channel tools that allow them to sell anywhere. This aspect has intensified with the development of resale platforms that host a wide range of products. Turning to their services, the user is immersed in viewing, searching, and selecting an object, getting the emotions of a person who has found a rare exhibit because Internet websites may have exclusive copies from limited series or cult items.

Thus, merchants have gained a competitive advantage when using digital technologies. There has been a paradigm shift from Retail 3.0 to Retail 4.0. This signals a shift from broad industrial digitalization to technological digital systems that integrate with smart objects and IoT in other industries. Websites now provide customers with a wide range of services to meet their needs (e.g., delivery, examination of the authentication of the goods sold, payment, communication, etc.). This is how they attract consumers. Given their requirements and motives and providing the desired value to the buyer, this category of retailers creates a competitive advantage for themselves and increases customer loyalty.

Based on the preceding, we will define trade: "Trade 4.0 is a customer-oriented business with industry characteristics and digital models that meet the scientific and technological requirements and provisions of Industry 4.0."

Features of Trade 4.0 include the following:

- Digitalization of all – buyers, business processes, products, and services.
- Transforming supply chains into customer-centric organizations that ensure the rapid flow of goods and information between channels while providing customers with personalized services.
- Building a digital ecosystem around the company, which is a client-centric business model that combines several groups of goods, services, and information focused on customers' needs.
- A variety of formats of trade enterprises (offline and online).
- Omnichannel interaction with customers and sales. Omnichannel combines different technology platforms to provide consumers with a seamless and convenient shopping experience. As a result, the consumer gets a seamless experience of interacting with the seller.
- Flexibility of order fulfillment options.

DISCUSSION

A new paradigm for the development of the world economy, a change in the technological structure, the transition to the Fourth Industrial Revolution, and the introduction of Industry 4.0 technologies transform the development factors of the economic system and the sphere of circulation.

Many authors note that retail, traditionally classified as a low-tech industry, is currently being transformed into an industry with advanced intensive implementation of Industry 4.0 technologies – AI, IoT, cloud computing, BDA, AR, and VR. The systemic and integrated use of digital technologies also led to the transformation of business models in this industry in accordance with the requirements of Industry 4.0, which allowed scientists and practitioners to assert the transition to Retail 4.0.

However, it should be noted that IoT technologies are being increasingly used not only in retail trade but also in intermodal transportation, which has contributed to the expansion of the use of digital services for customers among logistics providers, whose services are also used by wholesale trade. This corresponds to the current interests of trade, including international trade.

Therefore, the statement that only Retail 4.0 is currently being transitioned is narrow because Industry 4.0 technologies are being increasingly applied throughout the trade and technology space, forming the model of Trade 4.0 (wholesale and retail).

CONCLUSION

Thus, the working hypothesis is proven. Based on the analysis, it is shown that the change in the technological structure and the introduction of Industry 4.0 technologies led to the transformation of the conditions for trade development. It evolves and adapts to current requirements. The acceleration of digitalization in the context of the COVID-19 pandemic contributed to the birth of a new era – Trade 4.0. It is based on changing customer needs and the growing importance of the customer experience. The desire of sellers to make this customer experience unforgettable and customers loyal leads to the development of new approaches, business models, technologies, and tools.

The most prominent role in today's trade is played by the following areas: collection and analysis of big data, cloud computing, omnichannel sales, ecosystem building, AI, IoT, smart loyalty programs, speech technologies, etc. Currently, they are only being introduced into trade and will become its basis and development driver in the future.

REFERENCES

Azeem, M. M., Marsap, A., & Jilani, A. H. (2015). Impact of e-commerce on organization performance: Evidence from banking sector of Pakistan. *International Journal of Economics and Finance, 7*(2), 303–309. https://doi.org/10.5539/ijef.v7n2p303

Bellora, C., Clemence, C., & Jean, S. (2020). European trade in the health crisis: Problems of dependency more than vulnerability. In *CEPII. La Lettre du CEPII* (pp. 412–413). http://www.cepii.fr/PDF_PUB/lettre/2020/let412.pdf. Accessed on 10 December 2022.

Chub, A. A. (2020). COVID-19 and the role of digital technologies in the consumer behavior on the food market. *Problems of Theory and Practice of Management, 8*, 40–58.

Falk, M., & Hagsten, E. (2015). E-commerce trends and impacts across Europe. *International Journal of Production Economics, 170*(Part A), 357–369. https://doi.org/10.1016/j.ijpe.2015.10.003

Gliss, R., & Lakert, B. (2017). *Trade 4.0. Digital revolution in trade: Strategies, technologies, transformation.* Alpina Publisher. (Original work published 2017).

Hillen, J., & Fedoseeva, S. (2021). E-commerce and the end of price rigidity? *Journal of Business Research, 125,* 63–73. https://doi.org/10.1016/j.jbusres.2020.11.052

Krupenskiy, N. A. (2020). Digital trade: Current status and development prospects in Russia and EAEU countries. *Trade Policy, 1*(21), 15–24. https://doi.org/10.17323/2499-9415-2020-15-24

Liu, T. K., Chen, J. R., Huang, C. C. J., & Yang, C. H. (2013). E-commerce, R&D, and productivity: Firm-level evidence from Taiwan. *Information Economics and Policy, 25*(4), 272–283. https://doi.org/10.1016/j.infoecopol.2013.07.001

Loh, L. H., Umi, K. R., Lee, T. C., Seah, Ch. S., & Loh, Y. X. (2022). Revolution of retail industry: From perspective of retail 1.0 to 4.0. *Procedia Computer Science, 200*, 1615–1625. https://doi.org/10.1016/j.procs.2022.01.362

Lueth, L. K. (2020, November 19). State of the IoT 2020: 12 billion IoT connections, surpassing non-IoT for the first time. *IoT Analytics.* https://iot-analytics.com/state-of-the-iot-2020-12-billion-iot-connections-surpassing-non-iot-for-the-first-time/. Accessed on 5 January 2023.

McKinsey & Company. (2020, October 5). How COVID-19 has pushed companies over the technology tipping point—And transformed business forever. https://www.mckinsey.com/capabilities/strategy-and-corporate-finance/our-insights/how-covid-19-has-pushed-companies-over-the-technology-tipping-point-and-transformed-business-forever. Accessed on 20 February 2023.

OECD. (2020, October 7). *E-commerce in the time of COVID-19.* http://www.oecd.org/coronavirus/policy-responses/e-commerce-in-the-time-of-covid-19-3a2b78e8/. Accessed on 10 December 2022.

Panshin, I. V., Digilina, O. B., & Teslenko, I. B. (2022). Labor productivity in a pandemic. In A. V. Bogoviz, A. E. Suglobov, A. N. Maloletko, & O. V. Kaurova (Eds.), *Cooperation and sustainable development* (pp. 843–851). Springer. https://doi.org/10.1007/978-3-030-77000-6_100

Perera, K. J. T., Fernando, P. I. N., Ratnayake, R. M. C. S., & Udawaththa, U. D. I. C. (2021). Consumer behavior within the COVID-19 pandemic a systematic review. *International Journal of Research and Innovation in Social Science (IJRISS), 5*(12), 806–812.

Research and Markets. (2020, October 21). *2020 Global e-commerce and online payments analysis: The health crisis affects retail and service sectors unequally.* https://www.globenewswire.com/news-release/2020/10/21/2111703/0/en/2020-Global-e-Commerce-and-Online-Payments-Analysis-The-Health-Crisis-Affects-Retail-and-Service-Sectors-Unequally.html. Accessed on 8 December 2022.

Saif, N. M. A., Ruan, J., & Obrenovic, B. (2021). Sustaining trade during COVID-19 pandemic: Establishing a conceptual model including COVID-19 impact. *Sustainability, 13*(10), 5418. https://doi.org/10.3390/su13105418

Sakrabani, P., Teoh, A. P., & Amran, A. (2019). Strategic impact of retail 4.0 on retailers' performance in Malaysia. *Strategic Direction*, *35*(11), 1–3. https://doi.org/10.1108/SD-05-2019-0099

Santos, V., Augusto, T., Vieira, J., Bacalhau, L., Sousa, B. M., & Pontes, D. (2023). E-Commerce: Issues, opportunities, challenges, and trends. In J. Santos & B. Sousa (Eds.), *Promoting organizational performance through 5G and agile marketing* (pp. 224–244). IGI Global. https://doi.org/10.4018/978-1-6684-5523-4.ch012

Shopify Plus. (2023). *Ecommerce trends 2023: Industry report "Social ecommerce gets more interactive"*. https://www.shopify.com/plus/commerce-trends/ecommerce. Accessed on 5 February 2023.

Smeets, M. (Ed.) (2021). *Adapting to the digital trade era: Challenges and opportunities*. WTO. https://www.wto.org/english/res_e/publications_e/adtera_e.htm. Accessed on 25 December 2022.

Statista. (2022). *From frenzy to fall: E-commerce back to normal?* https://spaces.statista.com/1bea0ce6-d0124704887a35377c6a4749.pdf?utm_source=Statista+Webinar+Contacts&utm_campaign=4f39c7ce83-DoS_Webinar_eCommerce_-Show_EN_KW38_2022_LHA&utm_medium=email&utm_term=0_f5ac47a287-4f39c7ce83-344273366/. Accessed on 25 December 2022.

Strelets, I. A., & Chebanov, S. V. (2020). Digitalization of world trade: Scope, forms, implications. *World Economy and International Relations*, *64*(1), 15–25. https://doi.org/10.20542/0131-2227-2020-64-1-15-25

UNCTAD. (2021a, December 9). Global merchandise trade exceeds pre-COVID-19 level, but services recovery falls short. https://unctad.org/news/global-merchandise-trade-exceeds-pre-covid-19-level-services-recovery-falls-short. Accessed on 8 December 2022.

UNCTAD. (2021b). *COVID-19 and E-commerce a global review*. United Nations. https://unctad.org/system/files/official-document/dtlstict2020d13_en_0.pdf. Accessed on 8 December 2022.

Zagashvili, V. (2021). International trade in the aftermath of the COVID-19 pandemic. *World Economy and International Relations*, *65*(10), 15–23. https://doi.org/10.20542/0131-2227-2021-65-10-15-23

Zhuckovskaya, I. F., Kosorukova, I. V., Tazikhina, T. V., & Sergeyeva, N. V. (2023). Retail trade in digitalized economy: Development tendencies for agro-industrial enterprises in Russia. In V. I. Trukhachev (Ed.), *Unlocking digital transformation of agricultural enterprises* (pp. 105–114). Springer. https://doi.org/10.1007/978-3-031-13913-0_12

GREEN BANKING AS AN INNOVATIVE BENCHMARK FOR THE DEVELOPMENT OF THE BANKING SYSTEM UNDER THE CONDITIONS OF GLOBAL TRANSFORMATIONS

Nelli I. Akylbekova[a], Zarina T. Duishenalieva[b], Elmira D. Kuramaeva[a], Zhyldyz B. Myrzakhmatova[a] and Tolendi A. Ashimbayev[c]

[a]*Kyrgyz National University named after Jusup Balasagyn, Kyrgyzstan*
[b]*Kyrgyz State Technical University named after I. Razzakov, Kyrgyzstan*
[c]*Almaty University of Humanities and Economics, Kazakhstan*

ABSTRACT

The research aims to identify changes in the banking system of the Kyrgyz Republic, as well as the application of green banking and its promotion as an innovative benchmark. To conceptually understand the problem, the authors applied abstract-logical methods of comparison and generalizations to study and comprehend the current results of scientific research by scientists from around the world. The authors analyzed the time series of development indicators of the banking sector for 2017–2022. The information base was statistical information provided by the National Bank of the Kyrgyz Republic. The banking system of the Kyrgyz Republic is developing progressively positively, in which green principles are beginning to be used to support green initiatives. For green banking to fully function, it is necessary to create an efficient and secure payment system that would help stimulate environmentally responsible financial transactions. For this purpose, the use of advanced technologies (e.g., blockchain technologies) will contribute to the modernization of the payment system. The high degree of dollarization of the banking sector helps attract foreign investment and makes it possible to develop foreign capital, which reduces the independence of the banking sector and hinders the free choice and implementation of priority green projects. Currently, there is a trend of

Development of International Entrepreneurship Based on Corporate Accounting and Reporting According to IFRS
Advanced Series in Management, Volume 33B, 23–30
ISSN: 1877-6361/doi:10.1108/S1877-63612024000033B004

de-dollarization, which poses new challenges for the banking sector to find compromises with foreign partners.

Keywords: Banking system; green economy; green banking; payment system; dollarization of the banking sector; de-dollarization of the banking sector

JEL Codes: E44; G21; N25; O16; Q57

The research topic is relevant in that global natural changes create new risks for the national economy, requiring immediate response from the state and additional funding for urgent projects. In such conditions of global changes, banks can be useful by providing financial resources for priority socially significant projects on favorable terms. On the other hand, banks should also benefit from such transactions because they perform the social functions assigned to them, form a positive image, and interact with partners in the long term. However, Kyrgyzstan lacks long-term credit instruments, which hinders the development of green projects that need long-term financing at a low-interest rate.

Despite this, the principles and mechanisms of green banking are being promoted in the Kyrgyz Republic through the State Program for the Development of the Green Economy in the Kyrgyz Republic for 2019–2023, aimed at implementing green banking mechanisms, maintaining favorable living conditions, preserving nature and biological diversity, and developing measures to ensure sustainable economic development (Government of the Kyrgyz Republic, 2019). Such a state policy aims to form a healthy person to create the potential of human capital as one of the main production factors.

We can note the successful steps in the implementation of green projects thanks to the financing of international donor organizations through commercial banks.

However, this is not enough. External and internal financing of priority projects and areas is required to form a highly effective multilevel complex for developing a green economy and mitigating environmental change.

This topic is becoming relevant and attracts the attention of economists to study its theoretical and practical aspects. The authors studied the views of scientists on green banking. For example, some authors offer a scientometric analysis of the literature on green banking (Sarma & Roy, 2020).

MATERIALS AND METHODS

The authors used abstract-logical and special methods to study economic phenomena. Relevant studies of green banking in the publications of scientific publications were studied to identify the possibility of application in the Kyrgyz Republic. Methods of logical generalization and comparison contributed to defining general patterns, principles of green banking, and its positive features.

To analyze the development of the banking system of the Kyrgyz Republic, statistical information provided by the National Bank of the Kyrgyz Republic was taken. The authors analyzed the main performance indicators of commercial banks, such as capital, liabilities, total assets, and indicators of the capital adequacy of commercial banks for 2017–2022.

The development of the payment system, including noncash payments and the use of electronic money, was assessed by such indicators as the number of plastic cards in circulation, Point of sale (POS) terminals, ATMs, and dollarization of the banking system. The authors traced the share of deposits and loans in foreign currency.

RESULTS

The transformation of the banking sector on the terms of green principles is a trend in developed countries. The banking system is a complex and integral structure, which consists of many elements. As intermediaries in the redistribution of financial resources, commercial banks should be the first to spread green principles in the economy and encourage enterprises to comply with green business rules, join the implementation of environmental projects, and contribute to the transformation of society's consciousness to preserve their living environment for future generations (Akylbekova & Bayguttiev, 2019).

At the beginning of 2023, there were 23 commercial banks and 318 branches of such banks operating in the Kyrgyz Republic. To identify trends in the development of the banking system of the Kyrgyz Republic, the authors analyzed key indicators of the banking system, such as total liabilities and capital assets, which increased for 2017–2022 (Fig. 1).

The ratio of net total capital to risk-weighted assets increased by 1.4%, amounting to 25.6% in 2022 against 24.2% in 2017. The ratio of Tier 1 net capital and risk-weighted assets also decreased over the studied period by 1%, amounting to 19.2% in 2021 against 20.2% in 2008. The ratio of net total capital and total assets decreased by 0.1%, amounting to 17% in 2022 (Fig. 2).

Some indicators of the capital adequacy of commercial banks have decreased, which indicates a weakening of their stability. This is due to the influence of negative global processes, including the COVID-19 pandemic and global economic and political crises.

Thus, before the COVID-19 pandemic, the banking sector developed steadily and had a positive trend. However, in March 2020, during the global COVID-19 pandemic, the exchange rate of the Kyrgyz som significantly decreased. The negative impact of the COVID-19 pandemic was subsequently overcome by commercial banks, which continued their progressive development and showed a positive trend in key indicators.

The conducted research allows us to state that the payment system of the Kyrgyz Republic is developing positively, aimed at increasing the volume of noncash payments and settlements (Akylbekova et al., 2019).

The general trend in these data indicates the increased popularity and prevalence of electronic payments. Growth in the number of plastic cards in circulation, POS terminals,

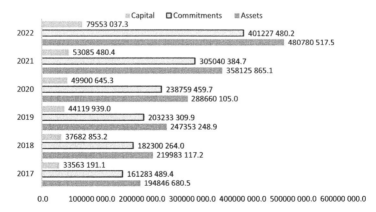

Fig. 1.   Key Indicators of the Banking System Kyrgyz Republic, Thousand Soms.
Source: Compiled by the authors based on National Bank of the Kyrgyz Republic (n.d.).

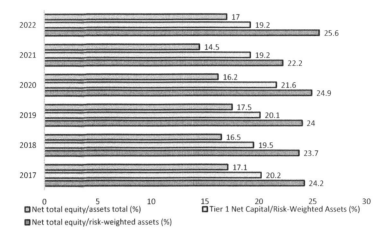

Fig. 2. Dynamics of Capital Adequacy Indicators of Commercial Banks of the Kyrgyz Republic for 2017–2022, %. *Source:* Compiled by the authors based on National Bank of the Kyrgyz Republic (n.d.).

and ATMs indicates the development of banking infrastructure and the satisfaction of customer needs in electronic financial services (Sayakbaeva et al., 2020). Additionally, more than 4.7 million electronic wallets are open in the Kyrgyz Republic.

Thus, the payment system is developing. However, the spread of noncash payments among the rural population lags behind the urban population.

The study of green banking is hampered by the lack of statistical information because there is no separation of information on environmental and social projects. However, in 2022, loans for agriculture amounted to 15.58%, social services – 1.6% and procurement and processing – 0.46%. This is an extremely low share of the total volume of loans provided by commercial banks.

The analysis of the structure of loans from commercial banks by loan terms in 2022 allows us to conclude that the loans provided are mostly issued for a short period. Loans over three years account for only 28%. Long-term financing is required to solve environmental and social problems, which is extremely insufficient.

Some work has been done to introduce green principles and transform the banking system into green banking. Fourteen commercial banks and one microfinance company signed a declaration on establishing a Green Economy Charter to unite common banking efforts toward forming sustainable financing. Roadmaps were developed for using green financing in the banking system and the sector of microfinance organizations according to green economy principles.

Such initiatives need funding and the development of the payment system in accordance with contemporary requirements for security and reliability of functioning. Interaction with international partners and accelerating the process of transferring funds within the Kyrgyz Republic and from abroad requires using the latest digital financial platforms and high-tech communication tools to strengthen control over the smooth processing of payments.

Another global factor influencing the development of the banking sector and green banking in the Kyrgyz Republic is the influence of the US dollar.

The share of foreign currency deposits in the deposit base decreased from 44.5% in 2018 to 39.1% in 2019, after which it slightly increased to 43.4% in 2020. It then declined to 42.2% in 2021 and increased again to 48.3% in 2022. The general trend shows some variation in the share of foreign currency deposits. In general, it has remained at a relatively stable level. The share of loans in foreign currency in the loan portfolio also decreased over the reviewed period. It was 38% in 2018, 35.2% in 2019, 33% in 2020, 28% in 2021, and 23.6% in 2022. This indicates that the bank made fewer foreign currency loans over time (National Bank of the Kyrgyz Republic, n.d.).

These indicators show that the bank was reducing its dependence on foreign exchange transactions. A decrease in the share of foreign currency deposits may indicate a decrease in customer interest in foreign currency deposits or a change in the bank's strategy. A decrease in the share of foreign currency loans may mean that the bank is reducing its activity in this area or increasing its focus on the local currency.

The impact of the global financial system on the banking sector has led to a high degree of dollarization. In the conditions of the transformational economy, this had positive aspects, such as attracting foreign investment and grants from international organizations to the social sector. This reduces the independence of decision-making when choosing priority green projects that benefit the Kyrgyz Republic. Simultaneously, the process of de-dollarization has recently been outlined in the global economy, which also significantly affects the transformation of banks into green banks. However, compromises should be sought and negotiated with foreign partners to find opportunities for external borrowing to implement green initiatives, overcome poverty, and create favorable living conditions for the population.

DISCUSSION

Green banking provides new tools for financing environmentally and socially significant tasks. An analysis of the research of contemporary authors on this issue confirms its relevance and significance for achieving the goals of sustainable economic development and minimizing environmental risks.

Ajaz Akbar et al. discuss the practice of green banking in the leading public sector of the Bank of India and the leading commercial bank in Malaysia (Mir & Bhat, 2022). Green banking principles enhance the image and profitability of traditional banks (Sharmeen et al., 2019; Sharmeen & Yeaman, 2020; Zheng et al., 2021). Using the example of a study of green banking in Pakistan, it was found that the image of Islamic banks can be improved through the adoption of green banking initiatives that will lead to improved climate outcomes in Muslim societies (Qureshi & Hussain, 2020; Rehman et al., 2021). Climate change challenges require a rapid response from financial institutions, governments, and all stakeholders (Park & Kim, 2020; Shaumya & Arulrajah, 2017; Zafar et al., 2019). Green financing in these conditions is necessary to finance environmental programs (Chen et al., 2022; Khan et al., 2023; Tara et al., 2015). Some researchers consider the view of bankers on green banking (Masukujjaman et al., 2015; Raihan, 2019). Some researchers study the view of stakeholders on the effectiveness of green banking products and services (Linh & Anh, 2017; Podsakoff et al., 2003).

Green financial products serve banks to perform several important tasks. Banks can strengthen their image and provide green loans to develop a green economy (Kondyukova et al., 2018; Nath et al., 2014; Ratnasari et al., 2021). Green finance can help banks manage risk more effectively and help achieve sustainable development goals by creating sustainable financial systems. Ensuring a sustainable banking sector is a condition for the sustainability of the economy (Nizam et al., 2019; Nwagwu, 2020).

In Kyrgyzstan, the use of the principles and tools of green banking is at an early stage, which requires the study of effective foreign practices in the development of green banking.

CONCLUSION

The transformation of financial flows toward environmentally responsible projects requires market participants to have clear and accessible information about each transaction. Modernization of the payment system requires introducing new information and tele-communication technologies that ensure safe and efficient payments between various business entities.

The payment system for green banking should be closely integrated with the offer of green investment products. Opening accounts and making payments should be easy and convenient for customers to encourage them to engage in sustainable financial trans-actions. Banks can offer customers various options for green investments and provide information about the positive impact of such investments on the environment. The development of a payment system for green banking should be based on innovative technologies. Mobile applications and digital wallets can greatly simplify and speed up green payments. Electronic payments also help reduce the consumption of paper money and save resources. The main direction at the present stage is to expand the range of mobile banking services to attract savings from the population and mobilize them for environmental and social projects. Introducing a system of rewards and bonuses for environmentally responsible purchases can help implement environmental habits among consumers. Banks can also actively promote the benefits of green finance solutions by raising customer awareness and education.

The development of a payment system for green banking is a part of society's desire for sustainable development and a more responsible attitude toward the environment. Its implementation can raise awareness of environmental issues and enhance the participation of all financial market participants in solving these problems.

However, the banking sector lacks financial resources for long-term lending; long-term loans are needed to finance green projects.

Dollarization of the banking sector contributes to the development of foreign capital, which reduces the independence of the banking sector and hinders the free choice and implementation of priority green projects. The process of de-dollarization is taking place globally, which also affects the transformation of banks into green banks. It is necessary to look for compromises and negotiate with foreign partners to maintain the pace of banking development, increase the implementation of green projects, and introduce innovative green banking tools to overcome poverty and create favorable living conditions for the population.

Further research should be aimed at conducting a detailed study of green banking in the Kyrgyz Republic, studying the dynamics of green finance, and finding effective green banking tools. The advanced experience of foreign countries is interesting, which will also be traced and discussed. Globalization processes strongly impact the development of the banking system, climate change, the environment, and the economy, which also requires additional study to develop measures to mitigate negative impacts.

REFERENCES

Akylbekova, N. I., & Bayguttiev, S. S. (2019). The role of the banking sector in the economy of Kyrgyzstan. *Proceedings of the Issyk-Kul Forum of Accountants and Auditors of Central Asian Countries, 4*(27), 21–27.

Akylbekova, N. I., Bayguttiev, S. S., & Ashimbayev, T. A. (2019). Banking sector as a key factor for economic development. *Eurasian Scientific Association, 12*(58), 183–187.

Chen, Z., Mirza, N., Huang, L., & Umar, M. (2022). Green banking—Can financial institutions support green recovery? *Economic Analysis and Policy, 75*, 389–395. https://doi.org/10.1016/j.eap.2022.05.017

Government of the Kyrgyz Republic. (2019). *Program for the Development of a Green Economy in the Kyrgyz Republic for 2019–2023* (accepted by Resolution No. 605 on November 14, 2019). https://climate-laws.org/document/program-for-the-development-of-a-green-economy-in-the-kyrgyz-republic-for-2019-2023_934c. Accessed on 12 July 2023.

Khan, I. U., Hameed, Z., Khan, S. U., & Khan, M. A. (2023). Green banking practices, bank reputation, and environmental awareness: Evidence from Islamic banks in a developing economy. *Environment, Development and Sustainability*. https://doi.org/10.1007/s10668-023-03288-9

Kondyukova, E. S., Shershneva, E. G., & Savchenko, N. L. (2018). Green banking as a progressive model of socially responsible business. Upravlenets *[The Manager]*, *9*(6), 30–39.

Linh, D. H., & Anh, T. V. (2017). Impact of stakeholders on the performance of green banking products and services: The case of Vietnamese banks. *Economic Annals-XXI, 165*(5–6), 143–151. https://doi.org/10.21003/ea.V165-29

Masukujjaman, M., Siwar, C., Mahmud, M., & Alam, S. S. (2015). Bankers' perception on green banking: An empirical study on Islamic Banks in Bangladesh. *Management and Marketing Journal, 13*(2), 295–310.

Mir, A. A., & Bhat, A. A. (2022). Green banking and sustainability – A review. *Arab Gulf Journal of Scientific Research, 40*(3), 247–263. https://doi.org/10.1108/AGJSR-04-2022-0017

Nath, V., Nayak, N., & Goel, A. (2014). Green banking practices – A review. *IMPACT: International Journal of Research in Business Management, 2*(4), 45–62.

National Bank of the Kyrgyz Republic. (n.d.). *Official website.* http://www.nbkr.kg. Accessed on 19 July 2023.

Nizam, E., Ng, A., Dewandaru, G., Nagayev, R., & Nkoba, M. A. (2019). The impact of social and environmental sustainability on financial performance: A global analysis of the banking sector. *Journal of Multinational Financial Management, 49*, 35–53. https://doi.org/10.1016/j.mulfin.2019.01.002

Nwagwu, I. (2020). Driving sustainable banking in Nigeria through responsible management education: The case of Lagos Business School. *The International Journal of Management Education, 18*(1), 100332. https://doi.org/10.1016/j.ijme.2019.100332

Park, H., & Kim, J. D. (2020). Transition towards green banking: role of financial regulators and financial institutions. *Asian Journal of Sustainability and Social Responsibility, 5*, 5. https://doi.org/10.1186/s41180-020-00034-3

Podsakoff, P. M., MacKenzie, S. B., Lee, J.-Y., & Podsakoff, N. P. (2003). Common method biases in behavioral research: A critical review of the literature and recommended remedies. *Journal of Applied Psychology, 88*(5), 879–903. https://doi.org/10.1037/0021-9010.88.5.879

Qureshi, M. H., & Hussain, T. (2020). Green banking products: Challenges and issues in Islamic and traditional banks of Pakistan. *Journal of Accounting and Finance in Emerging Economies, 6*(3), 703–712. https://doi.org/10.26710/jafee.v6i3.1177

Raihan, M. Z. (2019). Sustainable finance for growth and development of banking industry in Bangladesh: An equity perspective. *MIST International Journal of Science and Technology, 7*(1). https://doi.org/10.47981/j.mijst.07(01)2019.135(%25p)

Ratnasari, T., Surwanti, A., & Pribadi, F. (2021). Implementation of Green Banking and financial performance on commercial banks in Indonesia. In W. A. Barnett & B. S. Sergi (Eds.), *Recent developments in Asian economics international symposia in economic theory and econometrics* (pp. 323–336). Emerald Publishing Limited. https://doi.org/10.1108/S1571-038620210000028018

Rehman, A., Ullah, I., Afridi, F. A., Ullah, Z., Zeeshan, M., Hussain, A., & Rahman, H. U. (2021). Adoption of green banking practices and environmental performance in Pakistan: A demonstration of structural equation modelling. *Environment, Development and Sustainability, 23*, 13200–13220. https://doi.org/10.1007/s10668-020-01206-x

Sarma, P., & Roy, A. (2020). A scientometric analysis of literature on Green Banking (1995-March 2019). *Journal of Sustainable Finance and Investment, 11*(2), 143–162. https://doi.org/10.1080/20430795.2020.1711500

Sayakbaeva, A. A., Akylbekova, N. I., & Taalaibek, T. (2020). Digitalization as a platform for online business development in the banking sector of the Kyrgyz Republic. *Actual Issues of the Modern Economy, 9*, 394–404. https://doi.org/10.34755/IROK.2020.43.49.054

Sharmeen, K., Hasan, R., & Miah, M. D. (2019). Underpinning the benefits of green banking: A comparative study between Islamic and conventional banks in Bangladesh. *Thunderbird International Business Review*, *61*(5), 735–744. https://doi.org/10.1002/tie.22031

Sharmeen, K., & Yeaman, A. M. (2020). Benefits that Islamic and conventional banks can attain by implementing green banking. *Journal of Islamic Monetary Economics and Finance*, *6*(4), 833–860. https://doi.org/10.21098/jimf.v6i4.1134

Shaumya, K., & Arulrajah, A. (2017). The impact of green banking practices on bank's environmental performance: Evidence from Sri Lanka. *Journal of Finance and Bank Management*, *5*(1), 77–90. https://doi.org/10.15640/jfbm.v5n1a7

Tara, K., Singh, S., & Kumar, R. (2015). Green banking for environmental management: A paradigm shift. *Current World Environment*, *10*(3), 1029–1038. https://doi.org/10.12944/CWE.10.3.36

Zafar, M. W., Zaidi, S. A. H., Sinha, A., Gedikli, A., & Hou, F. (2019). The role of stock market and banking sector development, and renewable energy consumption in carbon emissions: Insights from G-7 and N-11 countries. *Resources Policy*, *62*, 427–436. https://doi.org/10.1016/j.resourpol.2019.05.003

Zheng, G.-W., Siddik, A. B., Masukujjaman, M., Fatema, N., & Alam, S. S. (2021). Green finance development in Bangladesh: The role of private commercial banks (PCBs). *Sustainability*, *13*(2), 795. https://doi.org/10.3390/su13020795

MODELING THE IMPACT OF AGRICULTURE, FISHING, AND LIVESTOCK SECTOR ON THE UAE'S GDP

Ahmad S. Al Humssi[a,b], Larisa N. Sorokina[a] and Vladimir Z. Chaplyuk[a]

[a]RUDN University, Russia
[b]Financial University under the Government of the Russian Federation, Russia

ABSTRACT

This research aims to determine the impact of the agriculture, fishing, and livestock sector (AFL sector) on the gross domestic product (GDP) of the United Arab Emirates (UAE) from 1975 to 2022. The authors use the Augmented Dickey–Fuller test (ADF), Granger causality, Vector autoregression (VAR), Ordinary least squares (OLS), and Autoregressive conditional heteroskedasticity (ARCH) techniques. The causal relationship between the UAE AFL sector and the GDP and its main sectors was studied in the short and long terms. The research concludes that the total GDP, oil GDP, and nonoil GDP respond to changes in the AFL sector and vice versa, which explains the positive role played by such a sector in the UAE's economy in the short and long terms. The study recommends that the government direct attention to the AFL sector as an additional source of income for the state, which will reduce dependence on the country's oil sector. The study also emphasizes the necessity of economic development in the AFL sector and at the level of all economic sectors to achieve the country's comprehensive long-term Sustainable Development Goals (SDGs).

Keywords: Agriculture; economic growth; oil GDP; nonoil GDP; alternative source; sustainable development; national economy; UAE

JEL Codes: C51; N55; O13; Q14; Q15; Q17; Q18

Although agriculture accounts for a comparatively small share of the global economy (Alston & Pardey, 2014), the sector is considered one of the mainstays of the national economy (Beckman & Countryman, 2021; Loizou et al., 2019; Sertoglu et al., 2017). The

Development of International Entrepreneurship Based on Corporate Accounting and Reporting According to IFRS
Advanced Series in Management, Volume 33B, 31–40
Copyright © 2024 Ahmad S. Al Humssi, Larisa N. Sorokina and Vladimir Z. Chaplyuk
Published under exclusive licence by Emerald Publishing Limited
ISSN: 1877-6361/doi:10.1108/S1877-63612024000033B005

local production of food is a major contribution to the country's food security (Harkness et al., 2021). The agricultural sector also provides an alternative source of income for the country (Besley & Persson, 2023; Komarek et al., 2020; Oya et al., 2018), especially for those countries that are largely dependent on oil exports (Al Humssi et al., 2023), which applies to many countries in the Middle East region, including Saudi Arabia, the United Arab Emirates (UAE), and Kuwait. It thus plays a role in improving the external trade balance by reducing agriculture imports and helping the country in achieving self-sufficiency, poverty reduction, and structural transformation (Bezemer & Headey, 2008).

Most Middle Eastern countries suffer from a number of factors that negatively affect the agricultural economy. The most important factor is climate change due to the proximity of these countries to the equator and their relatively high temperatures compared to other regions. Most Middle Eastern countries also suffer from the problem of increasing desertification, which negatively affects the agricultural economy (Haque et al., 2023).

Many Middle Eastern countries depend mainly on the oil sector for their economic development, which makes them vulnerable to Dutch disease and such crises as the global financial crisis of 2008–2009 and the COVID-19 pandemic (Chaplyuk et al., 2021, 2022; Petrovskaya et al., 2022).

One of the main strategic objectives of agriculture is to achieve abundance in agricultural production, both crop and livestock. By achieving a surplus in agricultural production, a country can improve its trade balance and balance of payments, helping it to achieve self-sufficiency. This involves working to ensure the optimal use of the main resources affecting production (land, water, etc.).

Given the importance of the agricultural economy in sustainable economic development, many studies have examined its impact on macroeconomic indicators.

Besley and Persson (2023) propose a dynamic model that differs from the approach most commonly used in economics in two ways. First, they focus on transformations of values and technologies that create a dynamic integration, which can either help or hinder the green transition. Second, they note that in countries with a democratic political system, policymakers cannot commit to future policies and elections. Their research results show that market failures and government failures can negatively affect the green transition and the country's well-being.

Jacobs (2012) studied the relationship between the green economy and economic growth. The researchers compared different views on the role of the green economy, concluding that the relationship of the green economy to growth depends on the type of green economy targeted.

Hussain et al. (2022) used the long- and short-run cross-sectional distributed autoregressive estimator approach to measure the effects of green technology, environmental factors, and gross domestic product (GDP) on green growth in high-income countries. Their study concludes that green technology and GDP have a linear positive effect on the green economy, while environmental factors (e.g., emissions) have a nonlinear negative impact on green growth. The authors of the study conclude that high-income countries need to manage their economic and environmental activities properly.

Mo et al. (2023) investigate the impact of institutional investment and financing on green growth in several Asian countries using an The Autoregressive Distributed Lag (ARDL) bounds testing approach. This approach allowed the authors to conclude that green investment positively affects the agricultural economy in countries such as China, India, and Russia, while institutional financing has positive effects on green growth in China, India, and Japan.

In previous research, many methods have been used to select mathematical models that represent the causal relationship between indicators, whether in the short or long term. In this research, the authors present a new econometric approach that represents the relationship between the UAE's green economy on the one hand and the country's GDP (oil and nonoil) on the other.

METHODOLOGY AND DATA

The research aims to model the impact of the agriculture sector on the GDP in 1975–2022 using the least squares technique, Granger causality, an augmented Dickey-Fuller test, and Autoregressive conditional heteroskedasticity (ARCH) test. This research mainly uses the data issued by the UAE statistics office because it consists of 48 observations covering the period 1975–2022 (UAE Federal Competitiveness and Statistics Authority, 2023a, 2023b).

One of the main problems in studying linear relationships between variables is the problem of false correlation, in which there is no causal relationship between the variables, but the linear correlation coefficient has a high value. Therefore, the last coefficient cannot be adopted as a criterion to determine whether there is a linear relationship between the economic coefficients. One of the main tools used to reveal the existence of a causal relationship between variables is the Granger Causality methodology.

In this research, the authors used the Augmented Dickey–Fuller test (ADF), Vector autoregression (VAR), cointegration test, and ARCH techniques for long-term modeling purposes. The authors rely mainly on modern mathematical modeling techniques to achieve the ultimate goal of these models, namely, economic planning and forecasting in the short and long terms.

MODEL CONSTRUCTION AND RESULTS

In this research, the authors will consider the following variables: agriculture, fishing, and livestock (AFL) sector, mining and quarrying (MQ) sector, manufacturing industries (MI) sector, electricity, water, and gas (EGW) sector, construction (C) sector, wholesale retail trade, hotels, and restaurants (WRTHR) sector, transports, storage, and communication (TSC) sector, real estate and business services (RSBS) sector, social and personal services (SPS) sector, financial corporations sector (FCS), government services (GS) sector, domestic services of households (DSH) sector, total GDP (TGDP) sector, and total of nonoil (TNO) sectors.

Using Granger's methodology (PGS) to reveal causality between variables related to the UAE economy in 1975–2022, the authors obtain the following results (Table 1):

Table 1. PGS Tests, for UAE Economic Sectors.

Null Hypothesis: Zn Does Not Granger Cause $\left(\overset{NPGC}{\Rightarrow}\right)$ Zm	F-Stat.	Prob.	Test Result Bidirectional Causality $\left(\overset{PGC}{\Leftrightarrow}\right)$ Unidirectional Causality $\left(\overset{PGC}{\Leftarrow};\overset{PGC}{\Rightarrow}\right)$ Independence Causality $\left(\overset{NPGC}{\Leftrightarrow}\right)$
MQ-SECTOR $\overset{NPGC}{\Rightarrow}$ AFL-SECTOR	3.41291	0.0426	MQ-SECTOR $\overset{PGC}{\Leftrightarrow}$ AFL-SECTOR
AFL-SECTOR $\overset{NPGC}{\Rightarrow}$ MQ-SECTOR	5.94534	0.0054	
MI-SECTOR $\overset{NPGC}{\Rightarrow}$ AFL-SECTOR	0.93086	0.4024	MI-SECTOR $\overset{PGC}{\Leftarrow}$ AFL-SECTOR
AFL-SECTOR $\overset{NPGC}{\Rightarrow}$ MI-SECTOR	6.45398	0.0037	
EGW-SECTOR $\overset{NPGC}{\Rightarrow}$ AFL-SECTOR	5.70807	0.0065	EGW-SECTOR $\overset{PGC}{\Rightarrow}$ AFL-SECTOR
AFL-SECTOR $\overset{NPGC}{\Rightarrow}$ EGW-SECTOR	1.70158	0.1950	
C-SECTOR $\overset{NPGC}{\Rightarrow}$ AFL-SECTOR	2.28648	0.1144	C-SECTOR $\overset{PGC}{\Leftarrow}$ AFL-SECTOR
AFL-SECTOR $\overset{NPGC}{\Rightarrow}$ C-SECTOR	5.99691	0.0052	
WRTHR-SECTOR $\overset{NPGC}{\Rightarrow}$ AFL-SECTOR	2.69354	0.0796	WRTHR-SECTOR $\overset{PGC}{\Leftarrow}$ AFL-SECTOR
AFL-SECTOR $\overset{NPGC}{\Rightarrow}$ WRTHR-SECTOR	4.39428	0.0187	

(Continued)

Table 1. *(Continued)*

Null Hypothesis: Zn Does Not Granger Cause $\left(\overset{NPGC}{\Rightarrow}\right)$ Zm	F-Stat.	Prob.	Test Result Bidirectional Causality $\left(\overset{PGC}{\Leftrightarrow}\right)$ Unidirectional Causality $\left(\overset{PGC}{\Leftarrow}; \overset{PGC}{\Rightarrow}\right)$ Independence Causality $\left(\overset{NPGC}{\Leftrightarrow}\right)$
TSC-SECTOR $\overset{NPGC}{\Rightarrow}$ AFL-SECTOR	7.57638	0.0016	TSC-SECTOR $\overset{PGC}{\Leftrightarrow}$ AFL-SECTOR
AFL-SECTOR $\overset{NPGC}{\Rightarrow}$ TSC-SECTOR	6.51584	0.0035	
RSBS-SECTOR $\overset{NPGC}{\Rightarrow}$ AFL-SECTOR	10.0910	0.0003	RSBS-SECTOR $\overset{PGC}{\Leftrightarrow}$ AFL-SECTOR
AFL-SECTOR $\overset{NPGC}{\Rightarrow}$ RSBS-SECTOR	9.13326	0.0005	
SPS-SECTOR $\overset{NPGC}{\Rightarrow}$ AFL-SECTOR	6.20086	0.0044	SPS-SECTOR $\overset{PGC}{\Leftrightarrow}$ AFL-SECTOR
AFL-SECTOR $\overset{NPGC}{\Rightarrow}$ SPS-SECTOR	3.37564	0.0439	
FCS-SECTOR $\overset{NPGC}{\Rightarrow}$ AFL-SECTOR	4.97406	0.0116	FCS-SECTOR $\overset{PGC}{\Rightarrow}$ AFL-SECTOR
AFL-SECTOR $\overset{NPGC}{\Rightarrow}$ FCS-SECTOR	2.35337	0.1078	
GS-SECTOR $\overset{NPGC}{\Rightarrow}$ AFL-SECTOR	1.75798	0.1851	GS-SECTOR $\overset{NPGC}{\Leftrightarrow}$ AFL-SECTOR
AFL-SECTOR $\overset{NPGC}{\Rightarrow}$ GS-SECTOR	1.08223	0.3483	
DSH-SECTOR $\overset{NPGC}{\Rightarrow}$ AFL-SECTOR	3.38582	0.0436	DSH-SECTOR $\overset{PGC}{\Rightarrow}$ AFL-SECTOR
AFL-SECTOR $\overset{NPGC}{\Rightarrow}$ DSH-SECTOR	1.06588	0.3538	
TGDP $\overset{NPGC}{\Rightarrow}$ AFL-SECTOR	4.73906	0.0141	TGDP $\overset{PGC}{\Leftrightarrow}$ AFL-SECTOR
AFL-SECTOR $\overset{NPGC}{\Rightarrow}$ TGDP	4.00491	0.0258	
TNO-SECTOR $\overset{NPGC}{\Rightarrow}$ AFL-SECTOR	4.95063	0.0119	TNO-SECTOR $\overset{PGC}{\Leftrightarrow}$ AFL-SECTOR
AFL-SECTOR $\overset{NPGC}{\Rightarrow}$ TNO-SECTOR	3.61609	0.0358	

Source: Compiled by the authors based on UAE Federal Competitiveness and Statistics Authority (2023a, 2023b).

Using the Granger causality approach, our results can be summarized as follows. In the short term, there is a two-way causality between agriculture and other sectors such as MQ-sector, TSC-sector, RSBS-sector, SPS-sector, GS-sector, TGDP, and TNO-sector.

The EGW-sector, C-sector, and WRTHR-sector have an impact on the AFL-sector. In this case, there is a one-way causal relationship.

Agriculture affects other sectors, such as the FCS-sector and DSG-sector. However, these sectors have no impact on the AFL-sector.

Moreover, there is independence or a two-way causality between the GS-sector and the AFL-sector.

To consider the models in the long term, the authors converted them to error correction models, in which the time series of the residuals of the mathematical models must be stable at the first level. To detect the unit's root, the authors used the ADF test as in Appendix 1 (Step 1).

In the ADF test, the null hypothesis is that U has a unit root under Lag Length $= 0$. Thus, the time series of the residuals U4, U9, and U410 contain the root of the unit; it is unstable. Therefore, we cannot use mathematical models to represent the long-term impact of agriculture on other sectors (e.g., C-sector, FCS-sector, and GS-sector). Therefore, the authors exclude these from the following treatment.

For the purposes of cointegration, when the authors tested the time series of the variables, they found that they were all stable at the first difference.

One of the most important methods used to improve linearity in error correction models is to transform them into log-linear regression models as follows:

$$Y = B_0 + B_1 X + u \to \log(Y) = B_0 + \log(B_1 X) + u \tag{1}$$

The analysis of the data in Appendix 1 (Step 2) shows that there is a long-term linear relationship between the UAE's agriculture sector on the one hand and its GDP and other sectors of the economy on the other hand. Therefore, the authors formulated log-transformed models according to the following formulas (Eqs. 2–11):

$$\text{Log}\left(\frac{\text{MQ} - \text{sector}_n}{\text{MQ} - \text{sector}_{n-1}}\right) = -0.0328666332111$$
$$+ 1.13854149134 * \text{Log}\left(\frac{\text{AFL} - \text{sector}_n}{\text{AFL} - \text{sector}_{n-1}}\right) \tag{2}$$
$$+ 0.19582236612 * \text{U1}(-1)$$

$$\text{Log}\left(\frac{\text{MI} - \text{sector}_n}{\text{MI} - \text{sector}_{n-1}}\right) = 0.0509691932278$$
$$+ 0.876259323706 * \text{Log}\left(\frac{\text{AFL} - \text{sector}_n}{\text{AFL} - \text{sector}_{n-1}}\right) \tag{3}$$
$$-0.214065866255 * \text{U2}(-1)$$

$$\text{Log}\left(\frac{\text{EGW} - \text{sector}_n}{\text{EGW} - \text{sector}_{n-1}}\right) = 0.0624503613595$$
$$+ 0.6919961505 * \text{Log}\left(\frac{\text{AFL} - \text{sector}_n}{\text{AFL} - \text{sector}_{n-1}}\right) \tag{4}$$
$$-0.023302215 * \text{U3}(-1)$$

$$\text{Log}\left(\frac{\text{WRTHR} - \text{sector}_n}{\text{WRTHR} - \text{sector}_{n-1}}\right) = 0.04741377199$$
$$+ 0.23969878882 * \text{Log}\left(\frac{\text{AFL} - \text{sector}_n}{\text{AFL} - \text{sector}_{n-1}}\right) \tag{5}$$
$$-0.112965312676 * \text{U5}(-1)$$

$$\text{Log}\left(\frac{\text{TSC} - \text{sector}_n}{\text{TSC} - \text{sector}_{n-1}}\right) = 0.039139092489$$
$$+ 0.551699975665 * \text{Log}\left(\frac{\text{AFL} - \text{sector}_n}{\text{AFL} - \text{sector}_{n-1}}\right) \tag{6}$$
$$-0.149663454511 * \text{U6}(-1)$$

$$\text{Log}\left(\frac{\text{RSBS} - \text{sector}_n}{\text{RSBS} - \text{sector}_{n-1}}\right) = 0.00815715185419$$
$$+ 0.8985148361 * \text{Log}\left(\frac{\text{AFL} - \text{sector}_n}{\text{AFL} - \text{sector}_{n-1}}\right) \tag{7}$$
$$-0.162887831066 * \text{U7}(-1)$$

$$
\text{Log}\left(\frac{\text{SPS} - \text{sector}_n}{\text{SPS} - \text{sector}_{n-1}}\right) = 0.0540683992106
$$
$$
+ 0.482857306515 * \text{Log}\left(\frac{\text{AFL} - \text{sector}_n}{\text{AFL} - \text{sector}_{n-1}}\right) \quad (8)
$$
$$
-0.0864602591426 * \text{U8}(-1)
$$

$$
\text{Log}\left(\frac{\text{DSH} - \text{sector}_n}{\text{DSH} - \text{sector}_{n-1}}\right) = 0.0609569549558 + 0.723022098082
$$
$$
* \text{Log}\left(\frac{\text{AFL} - \text{sector}_n}{\text{AFL} - \text{sector}_{n-1}}\right) \quad (9)
$$
$$
-0.0372303251396 * \text{U11}(-1)
$$

$$
\text{Log}\left(\frac{\text{TGDP}_n}{\text{TGDP}_{n-1}}\right) = 0.02843029697640 + 0.54133522131400
$$
$$
* \text{Log}\left(\frac{\text{AFL} - \text{sector}_n}{\text{AFL} - \text{sector}_{n-1}}\right) \quad (10)
$$
$$
-0.0672008688952 * \text{U12}(-1)
$$

$$
\text{Log}\left(\frac{\text{TNO} - \text{sector}_n}{\text{TNO} - \text{sector}_{n-1}}\right) = 0.0411846626103
$$
$$
+ 0.519990243193 * \text{Log}\left(\frac{\text{AFL} - \text{sector}_n}{\text{AFL} - \text{sector}_{n-1}}\right) \quad (11)
$$
$$
-0.0359265394403 * \text{U13}(-1)
$$

To determine the economic importance of the previous models for planning and forecasting purposes, they performed a homogeneity test. One of the methods used to test for the presence of standard errors in economic models is the ARCH test because Prob. Chi-Square >0.05. The results of applying this test are shown in Appendix 1 (Step 3).

The results of the homogeneity test show that the linear regression models represent the relationship between the direct long-term impact of the green sector on the GDP and other sectors of the economy.

Decision-makers can thus use these models for the purposes of long-term planning and forecasting, as shown in Appendix 1 (Step 4), which shows the annual growth of the UAE economic sectors in 2024–2033 under the influence of a 1% annual growth in the UAE's agriculture sector.

DISCUSSION AND RECOMMENDATIONS

The results given in the previous section show that the UAE's agricultural sector plays an important role in its overall economy because it has a direct impact on most other sectors of the economy in the UAE, in addition to contributing directly to the growth of the UAE's total GDP and oil and nonoil GDP.

Using the models referred to in the previous section, if the agricultural sector grows at 1% per annum in 2024–2033, it will result in an intermediate level of annual growth of 0.56% in the UAE's GDP and 0.46% in its nonoil GDP. Other economic sectors will be as follows: MQ (1.74%); MI (0.54%); EWG (0.43%); WRTHR (0.26%); TSC (0.49%); RSBS (0.88%); SPS (0.38%); and DSH (0.45%).

In this research, the authors used the ADF, Granger causality, Ordinary least squares (OLS), and ARCH techniques to select the appropriate mathematical model to explain the relationship between measurement variables, which, in our example, is the effect of changes in agriculture on the UAE economy. In addition to their significance in the regression model, the importance of these techniques is that they simplify the structural model by removing factors that do not have a significant impact on the outcome.

Following an analysis of the impact of the agriculture sector on the UAE economy, the authors identified the following main priorities:

- The preparation of state plans to determine priority areas in the production, transportation, logistics, tourism, fishing, and mining sectors. By doing business, the UAE occupies an important position in the economy of the Arab world and in that of the wider global community (The World Bank Group, 2023). This factor positively affects the attraction of foreign investment, which can be directed to economic sectors other than the oil sector to strengthen and further diversify the national production-based economy (Al Humssi, 2018).
- Investment in and development of the agricultural sector, including foreign investment and state support. The UAE's agricultural sector has considerable potential, despite the fact that most of its territory is desert. The country's government has implemented several successful agricultural projects in desert areas (e.g., Project Suihan, the Al-Jourif project, and others) (Al Humssi, 2018).

CONCLUSION

This research investigates the impact of the agricultural sector on the GDP and other sectors of the economy in the UAE over 1975–2022 using the ADF, Granger causality, OLS, and ARCH techniques. In the research, the authors studied the causal relationship in the short and long term between the UAE's agricultural sector, the GDP, and the major contributing sectors of the economy.

Using the models referred to in the previous section, the authors conclude that if economic growth occurs at the rate of 5% in 2024–2033, it will result in an intermediate level of annual growth of 3.07% in the UAE's GDP and 2.56% in its nonoil GDP. The other economic sectors will grow at the following intermediate rates: MQ (7.70%); MI (2.92%); EWG (2.41%); WRTHR (1.50%); TSC (2.71%); RSBS (4.51%); SPS (2.15%); and DSH (2.50%). The total GDP and total of the nonoil sectors will grow at an intermediate rate.

ACKNOWLEDGMENTS

This paper has been supported by the RUDN University Strategic Academic Leadership Program.

REFERENCES

Al Humssi, A. (2018). The impact of falling oil prices on the United Arab Emirates economic development. In V. M. Matyushok & I. V. Lazanyuk (Eds.), *New trends, strategies and structural changes in emerging markets: Proceedings of the VII International Scientific Conference* (pp. 11–13). RUDN University. https://www.e-library.ru/download/elibrary_35651632_96089913.pdf. Accessed on 2 June 2023.

Al Humssi, A., Petrovskaya, M., & Abueva, M. (2023). Modeling the impact of world oil prices and the mining and quarrying sector on the United Arab Emirates' GDP. *Mathematics, 11*(1), 94. https://doi.org/10.3390/math11010094

Alston, J. M., & Pardey, P. G. (2014). Agriculture in the global economy. *The Journal of Economic Perspectives, 28*(1), 121–146. https://doi.org/10.1257/jep.28.1.121

Beckman, J., & Countryman, A. M. (2021). The importance of agriculture in the economy: Impacts from COVID-19. *American Journal of Agricultural Economics, 103*(5), 1595–1611. https://doi.org/10.1111/ajae.12212

Besley, T., & Persson, T. (2023). The political economics of green transitions. *Quarterly Journal of Economics, 138*(3), 1863–1906. https://doi.org/10.1093/qje/qjad006

Bezemer, D., & Headey, D. (2008). Agriculture, development, and urban bias. *World Development, 36*(8), 1342–1364. https://doi.org/10.1016/j.worlddev.2007.07.001

Chaplyuk, V. Z., Akhmedov, F. N., Zeitoun, M. S., Abueva, M. M.-S., & Al Humssi, A. S. (2022). The impact of FDI on Algeria's economic growth. In E. G. Popkova & B. S. Sergi (Eds.), *Geo-economy of the future* (pp. 285–295). Springer. https://doi.org/10.1007/978-3-030-92303-7_32

Chaplyuk, V. Z., Alam, R. M. K., Abueva, M. M. S., Hossain, M. N., & Al Humssi, A. S. (2021). COVID-19 and its impacts on global economic spheres. In E. G. Popkova & B. S. Sergi (Eds.), *Modern global economic system: Evolutional development vs. revolutionary leap* (pp. 824–833). Springer. https://doi.org/10.1007/978-3-030-69415-9_94

Haque, F., Fan, C., & Lee, Y.-Y. (2023). From waste to value: Addressing the relevance of waste recovery to agricultural sector in line with circular economy. *Journal of Cleaner Production, 415*, 137873. https://doi.org/10.1016/j.jclepro.2023.137873

Harkness, C., Areal, F. J., Semenov, M. A., Senapati, N., Shield, I. F., & Bishop, J. (2021). Stability of farm income: The role of agricultural diversity and agri-environment scheme payments. *Agricultural Systems, 187*, 103009. https://doi.org/10.1016/j.agsy.2020.103009

Hussain, Z., Mehmood, B., Khan, M. K., & Tsimisaraka, R. S. M. (2022). Green growth, green technology, and environmental health: Evidence from high-GDP countries. *Frontiers in Public Health, 9*, 816697. https://doi.org/10.3389/fpubh.2021.816697

Jacobs, M. (2012). *Green growth: Economic theory and political discourse*. GRI Working Papers No. 92. Grantham Research Institute on Climate Change and the Environment. https://www.lse.ac.uk/granthaminstitute/wp-content/uploads/2012/10/WP92-green-growth-economic-theory-political-discourse.pdf. Accessed on 10 September 2023.

Komarek, A. M., De Pinto, A., & Smith, V. H. (2020). A review of types of risks in agriculture: What we know and what we need to know. *Agricultural Systems, 178*, 102738. https://doi.org/10.1016/j.agsy.2019.102738

Loizou, E., Karelakis, C., Galanopoulos, K., & Mattas, K. (2019). The role of agriculture as a development tool for a regional economy. *Agricultural Systems, 173*, 482–490. https://doi.org/10.1016/J.AGSY.2019.04.002

Mo, Y., Ullah, S., & Ozturk, I. (2023). Green investment and its influence on green growth in high polluted Asian economies: Do financial markets and institutions matter? *Economic Research-Ekonomska Istraživanja, 36*(2), 1–11. https://doi.org/10.1080/1331677x.2022.2140302

Oya, C., Schaefer, F., & Skalidou, D. (2018). The effectiveness of agricultural certification in developing countries: A systematic review. *World Development, 112*, 282–312. https://doi.org/10.1016/j.worlddev.2018.08.001

Petrovskaya, M. V., Chaplyuk, V. Z., Alam, R. M. K., Hossain, M. N., & Al Humssi, A. S. (2022). COVID-19 and global economic outlook. In E. G. Popkova & I. V. Andronova (Eds.), *Current problems of the world economy and international trade* (pp. 127–139). Emerald Publishing Limited. https://doi.org/10.1108/S0190-12812022000042013

Sertoglu, K., Ugural, S., & Bekun, F. V. (2017). The contribution of agricultural sector on economic growth of Nigeria. *International Journal of Economics and Financial Issues, 7*(1), 547–552. https://www.econjournals.com/index.php/ijefi/article/view/3941. Accessed on 10 September 2023.

The World Bank Group. (2023). *Doing business*. https://www.doingbusiness.org/content/dam/doingBusiness/country/u/united-arab-emirates/ARE.pdf. Accessed on 2 June 2023.

UAE Federal Competitiveness and Statistics Authority. (2023a). *National account estimates 1975–2009*. UAE Ministry of Cabinet Affairs. https://fcsc.gov.ae/en-us/Pages/Statistics/Statistics-by-Subject.aspx. Accessed on 7 August 2023.

UAE Federal Competitiveness and Statistics Authority. (2023b). *National account estimates 2012–2022*. UAE Ministry of Cabinet Affairs. https://fcsc.gov.ae/en-us/Pages/Statistics/Statistics-by-Subject.aspx#/%3Ffolder=Economy/National%20Account/National%20Account. Accessed on 13 August 2023.

Appendix 1. Causality and Forecasting Tests for UAE Economic Sectors.

Step 1: ADF Test

Resd.	T stat.	1%	5%	10%	Prob.	Acceptable H_1, H_0
U_1	-5.919511	-3.581152	-2.926622	-2.601424	0.0000	H_1
U_2	-2.872608	-3.577723	-2.925169	-2.600658	0.0562	H_1
U_3	-3.452473	-3.581152	-2.926622	-2.601424	0.0140	H_1
U_4	-1.729914	-3.584743	-2.928142	-2.602225	0.4097	H_0
U_5	-7.175577	-3.581152	-2.926622	-2.601424	0.0000	H_1
U_6	-7.175577	-3.581152	-2.926622	-2.601424	0.0000	H_1
U_7	-2.679041	-3.581152	-2.926622	-2.601424	0.0854	H_1
U_8	-6.506060	-3.581152	-2.926622	-2.601424	0.0000	H_1
U_9	-1.028160	-3.577723	-2.925169	-2.600658	0.7357	H_0
U_{10}	-1.171689	-3.581152	-2.926622	-2.601424	0.6788	H_0
U_{11}	-5.261348	-3.581152	-2.926622	-2.601424	0.0001	H_1
U_{12}	-5.720458	-3.581152	-2.926622	-2.601424	0.0000	H_1
U_{13}	-7.842198	-3.588509	-2.929734	-2.603064	0.0000	H_1

Step 2: Model Outputs

Model	R^2	F	p value	AIC	D – W	H_1/H_0
D(log(MQ-sector))	0.185	4.987	0.011	0.285	1.632	H_1
D(log(MI-sector))	0.352	11.960	0.000	-0.548	1.691	H_1
D(log(EGW-sector))	0.258	7.633	0.001	-1.367	1.209	H_1
D(log(WRTHR-sector))	0.219	4.958	0.042	-1.309	1.623	H_1
D(log(TSC-sector))	0.227	6.450	0.003	-1.040	1.674	H_1
D(log(RSBS-sector))	0.333	10.973	0.000	-0.763	1.505	H_1
D(log(SPS-sector))	0.193	5.272	0.009	-1.171	2.218	H_1
D(log(DSH-sector))	0.368	12.826	0.000	-1.706	1.490	H_1
D(log(TGDP))	0.170	4.520	0.016	-1.013	1.676	H_1
D(log(TNO-sector))	0.204	5.651	0.007	-1.744	1.578	H_1

(Continued)

Appendix 1. (Continued)

Step 3: Heteroskedasticity Test: ARCH for UAE Economic Sectors

VAR Model	F-statistic	Obs*R-squared	Prob. F(1,44)	Prob. Chi-Square(1)	Acceptable H_1, H_0
D(log(MQ-sector))	0.267497	0.277966	0.6076	0.5980	H_1
D(log(MI-sector))	0.068865	0.071883	0.7942	0.7886	H_1
D(log(EGW-sector))	1.119458	1.141305	0.2958	0.2854	H_1
D(log(WRTHR-sector))	0.001859	0.001943	0.9658	0.9648	H_1
D(log(TSC-sector))	0.362711	0.376097	0.5501	0.5397	H_1
D(log(RSBS-sector))	0.214866	0.223541	0.6453	0.6364	H_1
D(log(SPS-sector))	3.213280	3.130705	0.0799	0.0768	H_1
D(log(DSH-sector))	3.581364	3.462338	0.0650	0.0628	H_1
D(log(TGDP))	0.788154	0.809479	0.3795	0.3683	H_1
D(log(TNO-sector))	0.944081	0.966261	0.3365	0.3256	H_1

Step 4: Forecasting Results

Year	MQ-sector	MI-sector	EGW-sector	WRTHR-sector	TSC-sector	RSBS-sector	SPS-sector	DSH-sector	TGDP	TNO-sector
2024	1.8	0.53	0.42	0.25	0.48	0.88	0.37	0.44	0.55	0.45
2025	1.79	0.53	0.42	0.25	0.48	0.88	0.37	0.44	0.56	0.45
2026	1.77	0.53	0.42	0.25	0.48	0.88	0.37	0.44	0.56	0.46
2027	1.76	0.53	0.43	0.25	0.49	0.88	0.37	0.44	0.56	0.46
2028	1.75	0.54	0.43	0.25	0.49	0.88	0.38	0.44	0.56	0.46
2029	1.73	0.54	0.43	0.26	0.49	0.88	0.38	0.45	0.57	0.46
2030	1.72	0.54	0.43	0.26	0.49	0.88	0.38	0.45	0.57	0.47
2031	1.71	0.54	0.44	0.26	0.5	0.88	0.38	0.45	0.57	0.47
2032	1.7	0.55	0.44	0.26	0.5	0.89	0.39	0.45	0.57	0.47
2033	1.69	0.55	0.44	0.26	0.5	0.89	0.39	0.46	0.57	0.47

Source: Compiled by the authors based on UAE Federal Competitiveness and Statistics Authority (2023a, 2023b).

THE IMPORTANCE OF STRATEGIC COST MANAGEMENT AND ITS IMPLEMENTATION IN MANUFACTURING INDUSTRIES: A CASE STUDY OF METAL PRODUCING INDUSTRIES IN UZBEKISTAN

Dono A. Sativaldiyeva, Nargiza A. Khaydarova and Ibrokhimjon U. Tursunaliev

Tashkent State University of Economics, Uzbekistan

ABSTRACT

This research focuses on determining the necessity of strategic cost management in manufacturing industries. Additionally, the research negates the need for its implementation in practice with the intention of strategic accounting for managing industrial enterprises. During the research, the authors used observation, data collection, generalization, grouping, comparison, and monographic observation. The focus is placed specifically on analyzing the cost management systems of steel industries in Uzbekistan. The problems of reducing the cost of manufactured products and improving cost accounting are one of the most urgent issues. In the conditions of limited resources, the prices of basic raw materials and energy sources are increasing daily. To achieve their ultimate goal, enterprises should first increase the selling price of products or lower their cost. Product sales prices cannot directly depend on the wishes of enterprises. After all, they change in the market according to the law of supply and demand. Expenses are formed within joint-stock companies. Control of their level depends on the enterprise's management. Currently, it is time to improve the calculation of production costs and use advanced management methods.

Development of International Entrepreneurship Based on Corporate Accounting and Reporting According to IFRS
Advanced Series in Management, Volume 33B, 41–46
Copyright © 2024 Dono A. Sativaldiyeva, Nargiza A. Khaydarova and Ibrokhimjon U. Tursunaliev
Published under exclusive licence by Emerald Publishing Limited
ISSN: 1877-6361/doi:10.1108/S1877-63612024000033B006

Keywords: Strategic accounting; production costs; cost; cost management; classification of costs; cost accounting system; the cost of resources

JEL Codes: M4; M41

Price, quality, and time are three crucial criteria that economic analysis has recently highlighted as being crucial to a company's success in the face of intense competition. The globe still has trouble integrating sustainable corporate practices; sustainability data integration is still insufficient. Manufacturers have not performed particularly well since they must deal with heightened competitiveness, which is strongly influenced by globalization and the rapid advancement of technology. Blue Scope and other industrial businesses must ensure that their goods are of the highest quality, delivered on time, inventive, and cost-effective to operate (Mack & Khare, 2016).

Financial management, cost management, and strategic management are intertwined in the complex process known as strategic cost management. This process entails reducing expenses and getting financial resources ready to take the desired strategic market position in an affordable way. Cost management and business plan alignment are essential requirements for businesses in the current difficult economic climate. Long-term improvements, influence on people, and integration with the whole business plan are becoming more important than the conventional strategy of only reducing costs in the short term.

The strategic cost management method offers a convincing and effective answer for improving cost management in industrial organizations, promoting sustainable development, and developing integrated systems. Organizations can significantly improve their decision-making processes and gain a distinct competitive advantage in today's quickly changing business environment by successfully tackling cost stickiness and assiduously monitoring product life cycles. Adopting this strategic paradigm enables businesses to successfully traverse the obstacles posed by global competition, quickly adapt to changing consumer needs, and build a solid basis for long-term success and increased profitability (Henri et al., 2016). Companies are well-positioned to improve resource usage, drive operational efficiency, and make wise strategic decisions through the implementation of strategic cost management, resulting in long-term success and progressive growth in the fiercely competitive business climate.

METHODOLOGY

The research effort employed data collection, observational, and grouping methodologies.

In connection with the research question, the information from the State Statistics Committee of the Republic of Uzbekistan, "Uzmetkombinat" JSC, library catalogs, and internet resources available in Uzbekistan are used. The authors also used official reports, information-analytical bulletins, academic articles, internet resources, and databases of international organizations.

All manufacturing sectors seek ways to reduce costs by implementing cutting-edge cost management strategies. To be more competitive, they must control expenses while simultaneously enhancing efficiency. Manufacturing and other costs should be controlled using an industrial cost accounting system. Industrial firms (e.g., Blue Scope) might employ a variety of cost management strategies. Some of them are overall quality management, life cycle costing, target costing, the just-in-time method, material requirement planning, enterprise resource planning, and activity-based costing.

More than 75% of firms in the nation and more than 65% of industrial organizations employ target costing. The production costs of a certain product with a specific function and quality to make a specific profit at its predicted selling price are determined using the structured approach known as target costing (Gupta, 2009; Hansen et al., 2007).

Life-cycle costing differs from standard costing methods in that it provides frequent profitability reports (e.g., monthly, quarterly, and annual reports). It focuses more on monitoring expenses and income on a certain product across a product base throughout time (Elhwaity, 2013).

RESULTS AND DISCUSSION

Costs are categorized in management accounting in accordance with the management's goals and objectives. In casual conversations, business executives from various types of businesses commonly express concern that management never has enough information about total costs. As a result, companies utilize management accounting, which enables them to collect cost data from the various data sources within the company and further evaluate these costs using a number of layouts and structures.

Throughout the world, the theory and practice of cost management have evolved and improved, including absorption costing, direct costing, standard costing, and other ways of managing them.

The method of cost calculation that will be used during the computation process must be chosen carefully. The calculating approach combines a number of strategies and procedures to estimate the cost of particular commodities produced by business units while considering the particulars of technological conversions and processes. Drury claims that because each customer's order is distinct and necessitates a different labor, material, and overhead cost, the cost distribution for each individual customer's order is an integral aspect of the cost-generating process in the order calculation system. When similar products are produced in series and in a predetermined order through each stage of production, this method of process-based production cost estimation is applied. These industries include (not limited to) those in the chemical, cement, oil refining, paint, and textile sectors. Considering departures from and modifications to current standards, the real cost of production is calculated:

$$Ca = Nc \pm D \pm Ch,$$

where: Ca – actual cost of production, Nc – standard costs, D – deviations from standard costs, Ch – changes in standard costs.

We may calculate the production's actual cost using this method without having to wait until the conclusion of the reporting period. By affecting how costs are created within the current process, this enables us to manage costs.

The industrial companies in the Republic of Uzbekistan currently employ the direct costing method, which separates expenses into variable and fixed costs.

The various cost kinds stated in the table can also be computed in accordance with the steps taken during production. Given the circumstances of the planned economy, there was no need for the cost of goods to be set by the steps of the production process. According to Table 1, the majority of costs belonged to cost of goods sold (COGS) at 63.86% in 2019;

Table 1. Cost Allocation of "Uzmetkombinat" in Thousands UZS.

	Indicators	2019		2020	
		Sum	%	Sum	%
1	Cost of goods sold	1,216,623	63.86	4,128,260	81.97
2	Sales expenses	32,634	1.71	39,990	0.79
3	Administrative costs	78,899	4.14	177,992	3.53
4	Income tax	4,942	0.26	71,006	1.41
5	Financial expenses	352,415	18.50	239,805	4.76
6	Other expenses	219,668	11.53	379,202	7.53
	Total	1,905,181	100	5,036,255	100

	Indicators	2021		2022	
		Sum	%	Sum	%
1	Cost of goods sold	5,629,728	79.08	5,920,909	71.52
2	Sales expenses	40,445	0.57	37,875	0.46
3	Administrative costs	270,575	3.80	326,349	3.94
4	Income tax	290,918	4.09	226,605	2.74
5	Financial expenses	343,203	4.82	1,074,917	12.99
6	Other expenses	543,913	7.64	691,456	8.35
	Total	7,118,782	100	8,278,111	100

Source: Developed by the authors based on Financial Statements of Uzmetkombinat.

this contribution increased with some fluctuations in the following three years, reaching 71.52% in 2022. The figures for administrative costs and income tax were less than 5% in four years. With regard to financial expenses, the share decreased considerably from 18.5% in 2019 to 4.76%, before showing a dramatic growth to almost 13% in 2022. In contrast, the lowest proportion of total costs belonged to sales expenses, less than 2% in four years. Between 2019 and 2022, the share of other expenses decreased from 11% to 7.5%, prior to increasing slightly to 8.35% in 2022.

To calculate the gross profit margin, we gathered some data about net sales and cost of goods sold for the years from 2019 to 2022. Then, we subtracted the cost of goods sold from net sales and divided by net sales.

Gross profit margin = (net sales − cost of goods sold)/net sales:
Gross profit margin$_{2019}$ = (1,799,607–1216,623)/1,799,607 = 0.32 or 32%.
Gross profit margin$_{2020}$ = (5,260,718–4128,260)/5,260,718 = 0.215 or 21.5%.
Gross profit margin$_{2021}$ = (8,352,753–5629,728)/8,352,753 = 0.326 or 32.6%.
Gross profit margin$_{2022}$ = (8,384,683–5920,909)/8,384,683 = 0.293 or 29.3%.

As can be seen from the calculations, the gross profit margin percentage was 32% in 2019. After a considerable decrease of 9% in 2020, the gross profit margin then increased to 32.6% in the following year. Furthermore, this rate indicated 29.3% in 2022, meaning that the company netted 32.6 sums from each sum of sales generated.

To describe the relationship between assets and liabilities, the authors calculated and analyzed the current ratio:

Current Ratio = Current Assets/Current Liabilities:
Current Ratio$_{2019}$ = 1,242,655/738,052 = 1.68.
Current Ratio$_{2020}$ = 2,482,132/1,305,619 = 1.90.
Current Ratio$_{2021}$ = 5,936,665/3,498,015 = 1.70.
Current Ratio$_{2022}$ = 6,607,404/3,624,351 = 1.82.

The data show that current assets and current liabilities increased year by year.

The current ratio of "Uzmetkombinat" grew yearly, meaning the company's assets increased more than liabilities to cover its debts.

"Uzmetkombinat" produces many various products every year. We selected four of them, namely enamelware, thermal insulation materials, products from copper and its alloys, and ferrosilicon, and analyzed the growth rate and profitability of these goods.

It is apparent from Table 2 that the net revenue and gross profit of these four products increased by 33% and 49% between 2021 and 2022, respectively.

Net revenue of enamelware increased by 24%. However, gross profit decreased by 128%. Profitability also declined.

Net revenue and gross profit of thermal insulation materials grew, meaning that the profitability of this product also increased in the given two years.

While the net profit of products from copper and its alloys grew from 234 to 326 billion sums, the rate of gross profit decreased by 6 billion sums from 2021 to 2022. As there was a decrease in gross profit, the profitability of these products also declined from 24% in 2021 to 12% in 2022.

Net revenue and gross profit rose considerably in the given years. Interestingly, the profitability percentage also grew from 0% to 80%.

Table 2. Profitability Analysis of Four Different Products in 2021 and 2022.

Name	2021	2022	Growth Rate, %
Enamelware			
Net revenue, billion sums	91	113	24%
Gross profit, billion sums	−4	−10	128%
Profitability	−5%	−9%	–
Thermal Insulation Materials			
Net revenue, billion sums	85	103	22%
Gross profit, billion sums	20	39	101%
Profitability	33%	70%	–
Products from Copper and Its Alloys			
Net revenue, billion sums	234	326	39%
Gross profit, billion sums	45	39	−13%
Profitability	24%	12%	–
Ferrosilicon			
Net revenue, billion sums	31	46	48%
Gross profit, billion sums	0	21	–
Profitability	0%	80%	–
All			
Net revenue, billion sums	441	588	33%
Gross profit, billion sums	61	89	49%

Source: Developed by the authors based on Financial Statements of Uzmetkombinat.

In the author's opinion, it is necessary to take the following actions to ascertain and analyze the price structure of the product quality improvement:

- To keep an eye on the dynamics of the cost-cutting plan's implementation.
- To pinpoint the causes of the cost shift and accurately pinpoint the variables that influence it, namely the impact of quality on quantity.
- To study the costs associated with raising the caliber of particular product categories.
- To look for ways to save expenses and increase product quality.
- To create ideas with a scientific foundation incorporated into the product's cost to improve the product's (work's and service's) quality, the organization of costs for production and sale, and the formation of financial results resulting from the industry's features.

CONCLUSION

For companies wanting to enhance decision quality, obtain a competitive edge, boost firm profitability, and maintain organizational viability, strategic cost management has developed into a valuable instrument. Therefore, this research aimed to investigate how organizational sustainability as a result of supply chain management (SCM) may be affected by decision quality, competitive advantage, and firm profitability. Components of SCM include cost driver analysis, value chain analysis, and study of strategic positioning. In this research, the sample data from "Uzmetkombinat" JSC are used as a sample analysis. The research findings showed that value chain analysis and strategic positioning analysis significantly improved the quality of decisions, competitive advantage, firm profitability, and organizational sustainability. Cost driver study also considerably boosts organizational sustainability, corporate profitability, and competitive advantage. Additionally, corporate profitability and organizational sustainability are greatly enhanced by decision effectiveness and competitive advantage. Company profitability has a substantial positive impact on organizational sustainability.

The use of strategic cost management techniques aids in boosting and sustaining competitiveness in the iron and steel sector. By improving pricing efficiency and cutting costs, it helps draw in more new clients while keeping existing ones. Using the technique of strategic cost management, it is possible to enhance the product continuously to boost the profitability of the firm and the company's market share globally. Increasing and expanding the competitive advantage of the product by reducing the cost of manufacturing processes is one of the most important strategic lines of defense against market competition.

REFERENCES

Elhwaity, A. B. (2013). *Strategic cost management to maximize the value of the organization and its competitive advantage: Applied study at industrial companies at Gaza strip.* Islamic University of Gaza.

Financial Statements of Uzmetkombinat. (2019, 2020, 2021, 2022). https://www.uzbeksteel.uz/korporativnoe-upravlenie/raskritie-informacii/godovoy-otchet/5215. Accessed on 15 September 2023.

Gupta, K. P. (2009). *Cost management: Measuring, monitoring and motivating performance.* Global India Publications.

Hansen, D., Mowen, M., & Guan, L. (2007). *Cost management: Accounting and control.* Cengage Learning.

Henri, J.-F., Boiral, O., & Roy, M.-J. (2016). Strategic cost management and performance: The case of environmental costs. *The British Accounting Review, 48*(2), 269–282. https://doi.org/10.1016/j.bar.2015.01.001

Mack, O., & Khare, A. (2016). Perspectives on a VUCA world. In O. Mack, A. Khare, A. Krämer, & T. Burgartz (Eds.), *Managing in a VUCA world* (pp. 3–19). Springer. https://doi.org/10.1007/978-3-319-16889-0_1

FORECAST SCENARIOS OF THE DEVELOPMENT OF AGRICULTURAL INSURANCE IN UZBEKISTAN BASED ON ECONOMETRIC MODELS AGAINST THE BACKGROUND OF CLIMATE CHANGE

Aktam U. Burkhanov, Akram A. Yadgarov and Malika S. Tugizova

Tashkent State University of Economics, Uzbekistan

ABSTRACT

Natural disasters and human-made events occurring against the background of global climate change are directly causing an unexpected financial recession in agriculture. From this point of view, agricultural insurance is of special importance in financially mitigating the damage caused by climate change. The research analyzed the forecast parameters by selecting the amount of precipitation and the factors affecting cotton crop insurance, which is considered one of the agricultural crops. The research discusses the effective utilization of agricultural insurance opportunities in compensation for damage from climate change and the development of forecast development scenarios based on using econometric models in this direction. The authors explore the importance of further improving insurance protection measures in the future based on projection scenarios developed up to 2028 for crop and livestock insurance in agricultural insurance activities.

Keywords: Climate change; crop insurance; climate action; insurance organizations; forecast; scenarios

JEL Codes: G22; O13; Q54

Unexpected natural disasters and human-made events are increasing. The occurrence of natural disasters against the background of global climate change and the annual increase

Development of International Entrepreneurship Based on Corporate Accounting and Reporting According to IFRS
Advanced Series in Management, Volume 33B, 47–53
Copyright © 2024 Aktam U. Burkhanov, Akram A. Yadgarov and Malika S. Tugizova
Published under exclusive licence by Emerald Publishing Limited
ISSN: 1877-6361/doi:10.1108/S1877-63612024000033B007

in financial losses as a result of human-made and unexpected natural disasters create considerable economic and social problems. The emergence of food security problems, mainly due to climate change, is attracting the attention of the world community and researchers. It is also threatening international insurance organizations.

Particularly, $105 billion was covered by global insurers due to the emergence of climate change risks. To mitigate the negative impact of natural hazards on food security in the agricultural sector and eliminate losses in agricultural crops and livestock, it is recommended to continue scientific research in the field of agricultural insurance.

It is inappropriate to conclude that global climate change will not affect or bypass Uzbekistan. It is desirable for every country to widely implement effective financial mechanisms against natural disasters and expected economic losses. In fact, developing measures to prevent and mitigate climate change and eliminate climate change damages is urgently important.

Agriculture will not produce the expected result. Climate change directly causes the incapacity to supply the population with agricultural goods, leading to food shortages and malnutrition.

Global climate change negatively affects agriculture in all countries. Therefore, the climate changes occurring in Uzbekistan directly affect agricultural activities. The lack of expected results in agriculture impacts all types of production enterprises.

Forecast scenarios of agricultural insurance development in Uzbekistan are not based on econometric models against the background of climate change, which is explained by the fact that its methodological and practical aspects have not been studied as an independent research object.

To eliminate these problems, it is necessary to perform the following tasks:

- To study methodological bases of agricultural insurance as a financial lever for mitigating climate change.
- To study the criteria for the effective use of financial mechanisms to mitigate climate change based on agricultural insurance.
- To develop forecast scenarios for developing agricultural insurance based on econometric models analysis of strategic aspects.

LITERATURE REVIEW

Many researchers (Biglari et al., 2019; Cannon et al., 2020; John et al., 2019; Jorgensen et al., 2020; Zhang et al., 2019) study the problems of climate change and how to assess its damages and mitigate the situation through insurance.

Livestock network of Uzbekistan to ensure the implementation of the mentioned normative-legal documents adopted on the development of the livestock network requires the relevance of insurance protection, which can also ensure the needs of the population in food supply (Yadgarov & Rakhimov, 2021).

Researchers in this field consider the methodological foundations for developing direct insurance activity, the importance of theoretical and practical approaches to insurance under various risk conditions, specific aspects of factors affecting insurance, and the prevention of financial losses based on various production facilities. Uzbek economists also study issues of agricultural development based on using econometric models (Saidova et al., 2023).

METHODOLOGIES

The emergence of environmental risks will directly affect all types of production and service sectors. Environmental hazards directly caused by climate change will not fail to affect agricultural activities. The development of the gross insurance system provides financial support to agricultural enterprises as a financial lever that mitigates climate change in agriculture.

The development of the agricultural insurance system has an important financial significance – it is a mechanism that provides compensation to the enterprise for material and financial losses caused by climate change, which is subject to various environmental risks. During the research, the authors developed forecasting scenarios based on econometric models, with a comparative analysis of the state of insurance of agricultural crops and livestock of agro-industrial sectors.

ANALYSIS AND RESULTS

The Republic of Uzbekistan is located in a dangerous agricultural zone. In some cases, the occurrence of large losses due to water shortages and other natural disasters considerably affects the activities of representatives of the agricultural sector.

It is important to study the state of the insurance system of the agro-industrial complex and forecast its future development. The authors used data on 13 regions of the Republic of Uzbekistan (except the city of Tashkent) for 2011–2021. In the livestock insurance model, the size of the insurance premium was selected as a dependent variable (Uzagrosugurta JSC, n.d.).

The economic literature has produced scientific findings on the negative impact of reduced precipitation on livestock production. Therefore, the annual average amount of precipitation was chosen as the independent variable, assuming that the increase in the amount of precipitation increases livestock production and, as a result, decreases the demand for insurance.

The "Fixed-effect panel threshold" model was used for cotton crop insurance in agriculture. According to this model, the studied phenomena are divided into several regimes. The coefficients of variables depending on the regime are different for each regime. The "Threshold" variable defines the mode change interval. The equation of the "Threshold" model is expressed as follows.

$$\gamma_{it} = \mu + X_{it}(q_{it} < \gamma)\beta_1 + X_{it}(q_{it} \geq \gamma)\beta_2 + u_i + e_{it}$$

in this q_{it} – "threshold" variable, γ – the equation β_1 and β_2 threshold parameter separating two modes with a coefficient, u_i – parameter individual effect, and e_{it} – model error.

In the model, income from insurance premiums was taken as a dependent variable. Insurance coverage paid one year ago, the natural logarithm value of per capita income one year ago, and the amount of hail during the reporting period are independent variables independent of the regime. Insurance tariff rates, rainfall on cotton in the reporting year, and the variable "Threshold" are independent variables dependent on the regime. In other words, when building the model, the authors assumed that cotton crop insurance providers make decisions according to the climatic characteristics of their operating regions and that the natural events of the previous year are important (Table 1).

The annual average precipitation one year ago is significant at a 95% confidence interval in the insurance decisions of cotton growers (Table 2).

Table 1. Single Threshold Detection Result (With 95% Accuracy).

Model	Threshold	Lower Limit	Upper Limit
Th-1	20.634	20.485	22.379

Source: Compiled by the authors based on Uzagrosugurta JSC (n.d.).

Table 2. Threshold Impact Assessment Result.

Threshold	RSS	MSE	Fstat	Prob	Crit10	Crit5	Crit1
Single	5.56e08	4.63e06	23.30	0.020	16.010	19.140	26.271

Source: Compiled by the authors based on Uzagrosugurta JSC (n.d.).

Data on 13 regions of the republic (except Tashkent) were used to construct the model in 2011–2021. The number of observations was 130; the values (lags) of some variables were obtained one year ago (Table 3).

The results show that last year's increase in insurance coverage by 1,000 sums will increase the income from insurance activities by 369 sums in the reporting year. The increase in the annual average amount of precipitation in the last year by 1 mm will cause the insurance income to decrease by 303.2 million sums (Table 4).

Table 3. Model Description.

Fixed-effects (within) regression	The number of observations	130
Group variable: Region	Number of groups	13
R^2: within = 0.4394 between = 0.0103	Number of observations per group	
Overall = 0.2329	Minimum	10
	Average	10
	Maximum	10
	$F(8.109)$	10.68
corr(u_i, X_b) = −0.5633	Prob > F	0.0000

Source: Compiled by the authors based on Uzagrosugurta JSC (n.d.).

Table 4. Model Coefficientients Assessment Results.

Income	Coefficient	t	$P > t$	95% Confidence Interval	
Cover[$t - 1$]	0.369*** (0.079)	4.67	0.000	0.212	0.525
ln(income[$t - 1$])	922.544 (547.147)	1.69	0.095	−161.884	2,006.973
Rain[$t - 1$]	−303.244*** (67.757)	−4.48	0.000	−437.536	−168.952
Hail	12.153(18.766)	0.65	0.519	−25.039	49.346
Rate Range					
Mode 1	1,759.561** (626.942)	2.81	0.006	516.9819	3,002.14
Mode 2	1,951.057*** (467.365)	4.17	0.000	1024.755	2,877.359
Precipitation Interval					
Mode 1	−8.821 (114.046)	−0.08	0.938	−234.856	217.214
Mode 2	281.092*** (60.673)	4.63	0.000	160.839	401.344
Constant	−13,240.23* (5,527.269)	−2.40	0.018	−24,195.1	−2,285.36
F test: $F(12, 109) = 2.07$ Prob > F = 0.0249					

Source: Compiled by the authors based on Uzagrosugurta JSC (n.d.).

Note: Standard error is given in parentheses. Accuracy rate: ***99.9%, **99%, * 95%, 90%

That is, the amount of rainfall in oil-rich areas encourages cotton growers to become participants in insurance activities. A 1% change in tariffs increases the insurance income by 1759.6 million sums in the regions where the first regime applies and by 1951.1 million sums in the regions where the second regime applies. The research developed three different scenarios of the forecast parameters of insurance premiums in the Republic of Uzbekistan until 2028. Data from 1997 to 2021 were used to develop forecast parameters. Income was transferred to the prices of 2021 based on the consumer price index and expressed in natural logarithm values (Table 5).

When checking the difference in the data compared to the previous years by giving a value of 0 to the parameter, the test of stationarity is satisfied.

The dotted blue line shows the significance threshold for each lag. There is no significant correlation after lag 1. Hence, this test confirms that the data are stationary because most past observations are unrelated to future values. Given this, the forecast parameters are nonstationary; 95% confidence intervals were developed (Fig. 1).

The regression equation of the autoregressive integrated moving average (ARIMA) forecast model is expressed as follows:

$$Y_t = c + \varphi_1 y_{dt-1} + \varphi_p y_{dt-p} + \ldots \theta_1 e_{t-1} + \theta_q e_{t-q} + e_t$$

where:

Y_t – the forecast value of the factor at time t.
φ, θ – model parameters.
e – model error.
c – constant number (constant).

Table 5. Stationarity (Dickey–Fuller) Test Results.

				Confirmed Hypothesis	
Database	Dickey–Fuller Test	Parameter	p Value	95% Interval	90% Interval
Insurance proceeds	−3.51	0	0.063	Nonstationary	Stationary
Difference (insurance proceeds)	−8.00	0	0.01	Stationary	Stationary

Source: Compiled by the authors based on Uzagrosugurta JSC (n.d.).

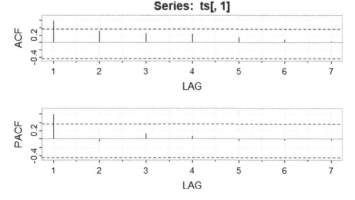

Fig. 1. Time Series Correlogram. *Source:* Developed by the authors.

p – the order of AR part.
q – order of part MA.
d – differences.

Considering this, the negative effects of various economic shocks on the forecast were prevented by attaching quality parameters (dummy variables) to the time scales.

DISCUSSION

In the first scenario, insurance premium income has a slow growth trend, increasing 1.76 times in 2026 compared to 2021 and 1.78 times compared to 2028.

According to the second scenario, the income of insurance premiums has an average growth trend. The amount of income will increase 2.74 times in 2026 compared to 2021 and 3.53 times by 2028.

According to the third scenario, the income from insurance premiums tends to grow rapidly. The amount of income will increase 4.22 times in 2026 compared to 2021 and 5.55 times by 2028.

Achieving realistic and optimistic scenarios requires several measures, considering the following recommendations:

• Establishing effective cooperation between the public and private sectors in agricultural insurance. In this regard, it is appropriate to adapt the experience of the United States, the most developed country in agricultural insurance, to Uzbekistan. Subsidized agricultural insurance in the United States is administered by the Risk Management Agency. Also, insurance products are offered by private insurance companies developed by the agency. However, the insurance services are accredited for the right to work under the subsidized insurance program. Insurers are required to reinsure part of the risks through the state reinsurance fund. Nevertheless, they bear most of the responsibility for making payments. Terms of insurance products are strictly regulated.
• Increasing the variety of insurance products. For example, more than 100 insurance products are offered for crop and animal insurance in Spain.

CONCLUSION

The authors developed the following conclusions:

• Decrease in insurance premiums.
• Decrease in profitability in the livestock sector due to the decrease of vegetation in pastures every year.
• Existing cattle is a motivating factor for insurance. In this situation, insurance companies should try to retain their potential customers and develop mechanisms to encourage them by providing discounts when they increase the volume of livestock insurance.

According to our calculations based on the models, the high probability of livestock deaths, plant and livestock diseases, and damage from natural disasters affecting the agricultural insurance sector indicate a lack of insurance knowledge and a low confidence level among agricultural workers. Thus, it is advisable for insurance companies to organize short-term training for representatives of the agricultural sector, promote the results of their activities, and further develop advertising.

In the regions of Bukhara, Navoi, Khorezm, and the Republic of Karakalpakstan, where the amount of precipitation is less than the threshold value (20.6 mm), the insurance income decreases directly with the increase in the amount of precipitation.

Therefore, it is appropriate to stratify cotton insurance tariffs by region, dividing regions into two groups. The first group should include the Republic of Karakalpakstan, Bukhara, Navoi, and Khorezm Regions. The second group should include Andijan, Fergana, Jizzakh, Namangan, Kashkadarya, Samarkand, Syrdarya, Surkhandarya, and Tashkent Regions.

REFERENCES

Biglari, T., Maleksaeidi, H., Eskandari, F., & Jalali, M. (2019). Livestock insurance as a mechanism for household resilience of livestock herders to climate change: Evidence from Iran. *Land Use Policy, 87*, 104043. https://doi.org/10.1016/j.landusepol.2019.104043

Cannon, C., Gothamb, K. F., Lauve-Moonc, K., & Powers, B. (2020). The climate change double whammy: Flood damage and the determinants of flood insurance coverage, the case of post-Katrina New Orleans. *Climate Risk Management, 27*, 100210. https://doi.org/10.1016/j.crm.2019.100210

John, F., Toth, R., Frank, K., Groeneveld, J., & Müller, B. (2019). Ecological vulnerability through insurance? Potential unintended consequences of livestock drought insurance. *Ecological Economics, 157*, 357–368. https://doi.org/10.1016/j.ecolecon.2018.11.021

Jorgensen, C. L., Termansenb, M., & Pascual, U. (2020). Natural insurance as condition for market insurance: Climate change adaptation in agriculture. *Ecological Economics, 169*, 106489. https://doi.org/10.1016/j.ecolecon.2019.106489

Saidova, M., Yadgarov, A., Kodirova, D., Turdialiev, J., & Embergenova, G. (2023). Econometric analysis of the influence of climate characteristics on the ecological condition of soils and the productivity of agricultural crops. *E3S Web of Conferences, 377*, 03017. https://doi.org/10.1051/e3sconf/202337703017

Uzagrosugurta JSC. (n.d.). *Annual reporting data.* https://www.agros.uz/ru/interaktive_service/. Accessed on 1 December 2023.

Yadgarov, A., & Rakhimov, A. (2021). Reforms on the development of the livestock sector and insurance protection in Uzbekistan. *E3S Web of Conferences, 244*, 12012. https://doi.org/10.1051/e3sconf/202124412012

Zhang, Y.-Y., Ju, G.-W., & Zhan, J.-T. (2019). Farmers using insurance and cooperatives to manage agricultural risks: A case study of the swine industry in China. *Journal of Integrative Agriculture, 18*(12), 2910–2918.

METHODOLOGY FOR ASSESSING THE ECONOMIC SUSTAINABILITY OF INDUSTRIAL ENTERPRISES

Aktam U. Burkhanov, Abdumalik M. Kadirov, Bunyod Usmonov and Jahonmirzo Z. Nizomiddinov

Tashkent State University of Economics, Uzbekistan

ABSTRACT

The research studies the issues of ensuring the economic sustainability of chemical industry enterprises based on financial and economic management. This chapter explores the theoretical and methodological aspects of appraising the economic stability of industrial enterprises. The authors presented a unique view on the essence of economic stability and clarified the interpretation of the economic sustainability of enterprises from the perspective of the influence of factors of the external and internal environment. The authors devised an innovative approach to appraising the economic stability of industrial enterprises using integral differential equations derived from regression analysis. The advantage of existing methods in the proposed assessment methodology is that it is possible to see the only clear expression of the comprehensive evaluation of weight values by calculating the main internal (quantity of product sales, employee efficiency, material and technical resources, sales worth, and equity) and external factors (social elements, market demand, inflation, variations in exchange rates, infrastructure, regulation of legislation, etc.).

Keywords: Industrial enterprise; economic stable; quantity; quality indicators; methodology; scale; integral

JEL Codes: L53; L65; M21; Q01

The global chemical industry is an intricate and significant component of the worldwide economy and supply chain. Chemical production entails converting raw materials (e.g., fossil fuels, water, minerals, metals, etc.) into a myriad of products essential to contemporary living. In 2021, the collective revenue of the global chemical industry surpassed $4.7 trillion (Statista, 2023). In 2021, the primary regions dominating the chemical market include Asia–Pacific,

Development of International Entrepreneurship Based on Corporate Accounting and Reporting According to IFRS
Advanced Series in Management, Volume 33B, 55–65
ISSN: 1877-6361/doi:10.1108/S1877-63612024000033B008

Western Europe, Eastern Europe, North America, South America, the Middle East, and Africa. During the Fourth Industrial Revolution, chemical industrial enterprises have been transforming into a new system.

In the developed countries of the chemical industry of the world, this network includes general chemical products, printing inks, hygiene products, soap and cleaning mixtures, adhesives, paints and coatings, pesticides and other types of agricultural chemicals, chemical fertilizers, synthetic rubber and fibers, plastic materials and resins, and ethyl alcohol. Research is also conducted on inorganic chemical compounds (e.g., methanol, ethylene oxide, and propylene oxide), along with technological investigations into expansion. Extensive scientific studies (Qurbanov & Isaev, 2017; Tulueva, 2014) cover topics such as stimulating the economy of chemical industry enterprises, updating the chemical network, incorporating market mechanisms into management, and creating organizational and economic mechanisms to ensure the stability of these enterprises. Furthermore, exploration encompasses scientific, methodological, and practical aspects, employing advanced approaches to securing the economic stability of chemical enterprises. Financial and economic management is one of the relevant scientific directions.

LITERATURE REVIEW

The problem of economic stability is studied in the works of B. Venturi, P. Gerstner, F. Lightner, S. Posani, L. Abalkina, I. Aleshina, A. Borodina, E. M. Korotkova, D. Kovaleva, T. Sukhorukova, Z. V. Korobkova, A. D. Sheremet, Y. Schumpeter, Yu. V. Maslenco, N. A. Kulbaka, and other Western and Uzbek scientists.

The problems of economy and finance and economic stability of industrial enterprises were researched by local economic scientists, including E. A. Akramov (2003), N. M. Maxmudova (Egamberdiyev & Maxmudova, 2018), A. M. Kadirov (2023), M. A. Ikramov (Ikramov & Avulchaeva, 2011), R. I. Nurimbetov (Nurimbetov & Akhmedov, 2008), M. A. Makhkamova (2004), A. U. Burkhanov (Burkhanov, 2020; Burkhanov et al., 2023), E. X. Mahmudov (2004), A. Ortikov, and J. Nosirov (Nosirov et al., 2023).

Despite the scale of scientific research, activities conducted in this area involve methodological approaches to modernize and diversify enterprises in the tangible sectors of Uzbekistan's economy, as well as active liberalization of the economy, rapid integration of the world economy, and assessment and analysis of the level of economic stability of industrial enterprises in the post-COVID-19 period.

Based on the analysis carried out based on existing research, it has been observed that there is no standardized framework that includes clear definitions for economic stability, dominance in competition, and competitiveness. There is a lack of a unified classification system for internal and external factors that impact the stability and competitiveness of enterprises. Additionally, there is no universally agreed-upon methodological approach for evaluating the relationship between economic stability and competitiveness. Quantitative assessments are not commonly conducted. Moreover, there is a notable absence of a formulated methodology for managing economic stability. The highlighted theoretical and practical challenges concerning the economic sustainability of enterprises underscore the significance of this research. E. M. Korotkov (1998), D. Kovalev and T. Sukhorukova (1998), Z. V. Korobkova (2005), A. D. Sheremet (2008), B. Usmonov (2023), J. A. Schumpeter, and others, such as those mentioned by Schumpeter (1998), frequently link the economic sustainability of a business to its financial health. Many economists argue that the enterprise's stability depends on the economic resources at its disposal and the influence of various destabilizing factors in the external environment. For instance, according to N. A. Kulbaka (2002) and A. U. Burkhanov (Burkhanov & Mansur qizi, 2021), economic stability is marked by a uniformly balanced condition of economic resources.

According to O. N. Zaitsev, this pertains to enterprises that can operate efficiently and exhibit continuous progress, even in situations with a negative impact from the external environment (Zaitsev, 2007). As per the scientist's viewpoint, financial stability signifies a consistent excess of revenue over costs, promoting the uninterrupted progression of production and product realization. This forms a foundational component of the enterprise's economic stability. Nevertheless, economic stability is a holistic concept of wide importance. It necessitates a connection with a competitive environment and competitiveness, involving not just the condition of the enterprise's economic resources but also multiple aspects of its functioning, such as innovation, technical and technological elements, production organization, and management systems. The author offers a clear interpretation of the economic stability of enterprises. According to his viewpoint, the economic stability of an enterprise is its capacity to function and progress in a state of equilibrium or near balance, even when influenced by factors from the external and internal environments. Additionally, the author introduces his unique perspective on the essence of economic stability.

RESULTS

It is crucial to pay attention to M. G. Efimova's research model for establishing a comprehensive methodology to evaluate the economic stability of industrial enterprises, illustrating the extent of factors influencing economic stability (Efimova, 2022). The author assesses the enterprise's economic stability by examining the level and magnitude of its capital. The established model reveals the possible detrimental effects of economic, social, political, and legislative factors that may unfavorably impact the economic and financial activities of the enterprise, resulting in instability and imbalance. The authors assess the probability dependence of the obtained indicator on the change in the parameters included in this model. The author notes, "Addressing this issue requires dividing the entire time interval obtained for analysis by the number of ranges. At each point in time, a random variable, i.e., the indicator 'cost of an industrial enterprise' [C0; C1], characterizes the zone of steady state of this system."

$$P(CO_t \leq \overline{C_t} \leq CI_t) = \Phi\left(\frac{CI_t - \overline{C_t}}{\sigma}\right) - \Phi\left(\frac{CO_t - \overline{C_t}}{\sigma}\right)$$

where:

P – probability.
CO_t – "in the stable state of the system, the enterprise has a minimum (sheep) limit of value."
CI_t – "in the stable state of the system, the enterprise is the maximum (upper) limit of the value."
$\overline{C_t}$ – "random value of the enterprise value at the t-the moment of time."
Φ – "LaPlace function."
σ – "mean quadratic deviation of a random C value."

The advantage of this model is that it is effective in solving many problems that arise in the management of industrial enterprises, particularly in the constant analysis of market conjuncture and timely detection and prevention of all kinds of risks associated with the influence of the external environment. It is crucial to make prompt management decisions when analyzing the economic stability of an industrial enterprise and plan and predict the influence of factor components on the industrial enterprise.

Subsequently, the authors explore the model introduced by V. V. Volkov and T. A. Khudyakova, which utilizes a comprehensive approach to calculate the economic stability indicator using gravity coefficients (Volkov & Khudyakova, 2022).

The authors consider the economic stability of industrial enterprises in relation to four factors that directly impact the financial and economic activities of such enterprises: (1) operational stability, (2) financial stability, (3) social stability, and (4) governmental stability. The authors propose the following model of economic stability:

$$\begin{cases} Y_{\text{econ.}} = k_1 * Y_{\text{oper}} + k_2 * Y_{\text{fin}} + k_3 * Y_{\text{soc}} + k_4 * Y_{\text{GR}} \\ k_1 + k_2 + k_3 + k_4 = 1 \end{cases}$$

where:

k_1, k_2, k_3, k_4 – "Weight coefficients reflecting the degree of significance of this type of stability for a particular enterprise."

The authors define their own methods for assessing the operational sustainability of an industrial enterprise, considering the profitability ratio of product sales (R) and profit from operational activities (R). V. V. Volkova and T. A. Khudyakov noted that industrial enterprises develop over time; they are indicators of stability and dynamic development. Thus, the operationality indicator should be calculated as follows:

$$Y_{\text{oper}} = \sqrt[3]{\frac{\text{PR}_{\text{fact}}}{\text{PR}_{\text{plan}}} * \frac{R_{\text{(pn)fact}}}{R_{\text{(pn)plan}}} * \frac{\text{EVA}_{\text{fact}}}{\text{EVA}_{\text{plan}}}}$$

where:

Y_{oper} – operational stability.
PR – profit from operational activities.
$R_{\text{(pn)}}$ – sales profitability.
EVA – added economic value.

A new scale of economic sustainability has been developed:

- High level of economic sustainability – $Y_{\text{oper}} > 1$.
- Higher-than-average level of economic sustainability – $0.8 \leq Y_{\text{oper}} \leq 1$.
- Middle level of economic sustainability – $0.5 \leq Y_{\text{oper}} < 0.8$.
- Lower level of economic sustainability – $0.3 \leq Y_{\text{oper}} < 0.5$.
- Critical level of economic sustainability – $Y_{\text{oper}} < 0.3$.

This model of economic stability assessment shows the current state of economic and financial activity of an industrial enterprise, identifies diverse forms of enterprise stability, and pinpoints areas of concern that require management intervention to address the model's challenges.

Another interesting approach is the Russian researcher belonging to V. A. Tulueva. The author develops a model based on integral criteria. The model also identifies indicators belonging to the first group as normative criteria and those in the second group as non-normative criteria. The first group of normative indicators encompasses the following criteria:

- Improvement 1 – "the value of the N1 indicator is in the normal range. There is a positive trend in the change of indicator. The value of the O1 indicator is beyond the recommended range. However, there is a tendency to improve."
- The value of a stable 2 – "the value of the N2 indicator is within the recommended limits. The trend indicates their stability. The value of the O2 indicator is stable and is outside the recommended standard range of values."
- Violation 3 – "N3 indicator is within the recommended limits, but the trend indicates deterioration. The value of the O3 indicators is beyond the norm. There is a tendency to deteriorate."

The author places non-normative indicators in the second group: "base period trend and current period trend." The author expertly receives the score assessment. That is, the indicators reveal the extent of the impact of various factors on the financial and economic operations of the enterprise. Two scales are suggested. The first one is for the indicators in the first group. Another one is for those in the second group. The author devises a framework for evaluating the enterprise's economic stability levels. Consequently, rapid assessment criteria are derived, where a higher level in the framework signifies a swift evaluation; a lower level indicates a comprehensive assessment of the enterprise's economic stability level.

The model of the level of economic stability of the enterprise is as follows:

$$
\begin{aligned}
y = {} & \frac{1}{n_1} * \sum_{i=1}^{n_1} x_i * a_1 + \frac{1}{n_2} * \sum_{i=1}^{n_2} x_i * a_2 + \frac{1}{n_3} * \sum_{i=1}^{n_3} x_i * a_3 \\
& + \frac{1}{n_4} * \sum_{i=1}^{n_4} x_i * a_4 + \frac{1}{n_5} * \sum_{i=1}^{n_5} x_i * a_5,
\end{aligned}
\tag{1}
$$

where:

he – "assessment of the economic stability of the enterprise."

n_j – "j the number of important indicators obtained during the influencing selection with a score equal to the module, j = 1, 2, 3, 4, 5."

x_n – "digital evaluation of an individual indicator influencing economic stability, derived in accordance with the scale."

The model of V. A. Tulueva shows an integral assessment of the level of economic stability, which can change over time depending on the external and internal environment. The model considers the factors of the industrial enterprise's production environment.

Thus, the authors examined three models for evaluating economic stability from various authors. M. G. Efimova highlights the degree of influence of factors on economic stability. The advantage of this model is that it is effective in solving many problems arising in managing industrial enterprises, particularly, in the constant analysis of market conjuncture, early identification and prevention of various risks related to production, external environmental impact, and timely implementation of management decisions based on the analysis of the economic stability of industrial enterprises planning and forecasting the impact of factor components on an industrial enterprise. V. V. Volkov and T. A. Khudyakova proposed a comprehensive method for evaluating economic stability, utilizing weighted coefficients to determine the stability indicator. This model of economic stability assessment shows the current state of economic and financial activity of industrial companies. V. A. Tulueva's approach to evaluating the economic stability of enterprises involves identifying different forms of stability and pinpointing areas that require managerial attention. Tulueva adopts an intriguing method by developing a model that incorporates integral criteria. The model classifies indicators into two groups: normative criteria and non-normative criteria. By providing an integral assessment of economic stability levels, Tulueva's model acknowledges the dynamic nature of these levels over time depending on the external and internal environment. The model considers the complex of factors of the industrial enterprise's production environment.

In this chapter, the authors aim to create an innovative approach for appraising the economic stability of industrial enterprises, encompassing a comprehensive consideration of the primary factors influencing these economic entities. It is crucial to highlight that the principal internal factors impacting the economic stability of industrial enterprises include the volume of product sales, labor productivity of employees, material and technical equipment, cost of sale, and equity. The authors also note that the influence of external factors on economic stability is of particular importance, particularly social factors (consumer demand for industrial products), economic factors (inflation, exchange rate fluctuations, etc.), infrastructure, legislative regulation, etc.

V. A. Tulueva employs a method for appraising the economic stability of businesses that entails recognizing diverse stability types and highlighting specific managerial focal points. Tulueva employs an engaging strategy by constructing a model inclusive of integral criteria, categorizing indicators into normative and non-normative criteria groups. Tulueva's model offers a comprehensive evaluation of economic stability levels and recognizes the evolving nature of these levels over time. To achieve this, the authors construct a block diagram illustrating the influence of various factors on the economic stability of industrial firms. This schematic representation serves as a model depicting the formation of factors and their relationships (Fig. 1).

The block diagram represents a collection of logical, coherent, and interconnected factors designed to ascertain the extent of their impact on the economic stability of industrial enterprises.

When formulating an innovation model, the authors utilize the coefficient method to measure the financial metrics of an industrial enterprise, with a specific emphasis placed on evaluating indicators related to financial stability and profitability. It is important to mention that the profitability indicator of an industrial enterprise mirrors the ratio's extent.

The solvency of an industrial enterprise is reflected in its economic stability, which encompasses financial capacity and internal funding sources. To calculate economic stability, the authors present an algorithm that considers factor criteria. This entails the use of mathematical tools, primarily integral differential equations. The application of these equations follows a specific formula:

$$y' = f(x,y) \text{ under the initial conditions: } x = x_0 \text{ and } y = y_0.$$

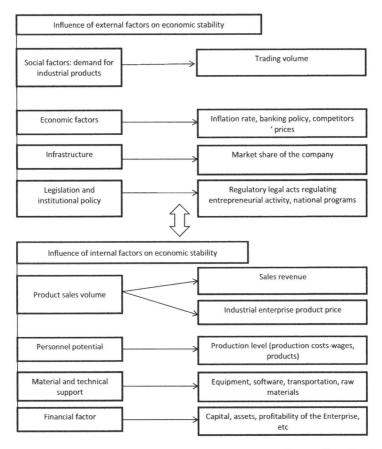

Fig. 1. Drawing of the Influence of Factors on the Economic Stability of Industrial Enterprise. *Source:* Created by the authors.

Let us consider s_1, s_2, s_3, and s_4 as coefficient criteria for financial indicators s_p factors x_1, x_2, x_3, and x_4. Let us imagine a series in which x_n is presented as internal factors affecting the economic stability of industrial enterprises y_1, y_2, y_3, y_4, and y_n (Vygodsky, 2002).

Then, using the regression order of the equation, we present our own formula that shows the sequential effects of the factor indicators:

$$\sum_{i=1^n}^{n} xy = c_0 + yx_1((x - x_1)^1 * (y - y_1))^1 + c_{n_1}$$

$$\sum_{i=1^n}^{1n} x_1y_1 = c_1 + y_1x_2((x - x_2)^2 * (y - y_2))^2 + c_{n_2}$$

$$\sum_{i=1^n}^{2n} x_2y_2 = c_2 + y_2x_3((x - x_3)^3 * (y - y_3))^3 + c_{n_3}$$

$$\sum_{i=1^n}^{3n} x_3 y_3 = c_3 + y_3 x_4 ((x - x_4)^4 * (y - y_4))^4 + c_{n_4}$$

$$\sum_{i=1^n}^{4n} x_4 y_4 = c_4 + y_4 x_5 ((x - x_5)^5 * (y - y_5))^5 + c_{n_5}$$

$$\sum_{i=1^n}^{5n} x_5 y_5 = c_5 + y_5 x_6 ((x - x_6)^6 * (y - y_6))^6 + c_{n_6}$$

$$\sum_{i=1^n}^{nn} x_{n+1} y_{n+1} = c_{n+1} + y_n x_{n+1} ((x - x_{n+1})^{n+1} * (y - y_{n+1}))^{n+1} + c_{n(n+1)}$$

In this case, we change the equation in the first order. For each factor, it is crucial to compute its level concerning the total sum of factors, resulting in the following changes, as a result of which the proportion criteria for assessing further economic stability is indicated:

$$\sum_{i=1^n}^{nn} x_{n+1} y_{n+1} = \left(c_0 + y x_1 (xy - xy_1 - x_1 y + x_1 y_1)^1 + c_{n1} \right)^1$$

$$+ \left(c_1 + y x_2 (xy - xy_2 - x_2 y + x_2 y_2)^2 + c_{n2} \right)^2$$

$$+ \left(c_2 + y x_3 (xy - xy_3 - x_3 y + x_3 y_3)^3 + c_{n3} \right)^3$$

$$+ y x_4 \left((xy - xy_4 - x_4 y + x_4 y_4)^4 + c_{n4} \right)^4$$

$$+ y x_5 \left((xy - xy_5 - x_5 y + x_5 y_5)^5 + c_{n5} \right)^5$$

$$+ \cdots + y x_{n+1} \left((xy - xy_{n+1} - x_{n+1} y + x_{n+1} y_{n+1})^{n+1} + c_{nn+1} \right)^{n+1}$$

In terms of the second order, we convert to the equation:

$$\sum_{i=1^n}^{nn} x_{n+1} y_{n+1} = c_{n0} \frac{yx}{\sum_{n=1}^1 y} + + c_{n2} \frac{x_2 y_2}{\sum_{n=2}^2 y} + c_{n3} \frac{x_3 y_3}{\sum_{n=3}^3 y} + c_{n4} \frac{x_4 y_4}{\sum_{n=4}^4 y}$$

$$+ c_{n5} \frac{x_5 y_5}{\sum_{n=5}^5 y} + c_{n_1} + n \frac{x_{n+1} y_{n+1}}{\sum_{n=1}^{n+1} y}$$

We adopt a model to evaluate the impact of factors on economic stability, defining the impact of external and internal factors on the economic and financial activities of the enterprise:

$$\sum_{i=1^n}^{nn} x_{n+1} y_{n+1} = c_{n_1} + n \frac{x_{n+1} y_{n+1}}{\sum_{n=1}^{n+1} y}$$

The formula for assessing the economic sustainability of an enterprise will have an appearance on it:

$$\Theta Y = \sum_{i=1^n}^{nn} c_{xy_1 + n}$$

This model illustrates the extent to which external and internal factors impact the enterprise's operations. The advantage of this model is that it considers the conditions that create all factors indicating the impact index. The second positive point lies in determining the problematic factors and reducing the enterprise's economic stability.

DISCUSSION

Therefore, the authors developed a model for assessing the economic stability of industrial enterprises, measured according to the defined scale as detailed in Table 1.

The strong economic stability evident in industrial enterprises indicates the positive impact of external and internal factors. It underscores the significant production and financial capabilities of the enterprise, accompanied by heightened financial stability and profitability in production.

This elevated overall economic status signifies the favorable production potential of the industrial enterprise, positive outcomes from specific factors, favorable production profitability, and a solid financial position.

The average economic stability of industrial enterprises suggests a generally satisfactory condition of the enterprise. It mirrors the combined impact of specific factors, encompassing positive and negative effects, the latter serving as indicators of areas requiring attention or presenting challenges for the enterprise. These problem areas affect the enterprise's operations, underscoring the need for management attention to address and rectify shortcomings. The overall average level emphasizes the importance of strategic management in maintaining and improving the enterprise's performance.

A diminished economic stability level points to reduced profitability, diminished financial stability, and discontent with the financial and production capacity of the enterprise. This threshold also indicates the unfavorable consequences of various factors on the potential of the industrial enterprise. When economic stability reaches a crucial point, it signifies the enterprise's vulnerability to bankruptcy. This is marked by negative profitability, increased dependence on external financing, indicating a complete reliance on external creditors, and inadequate internal funding to fulfill obligations and debts.

Table 1. Enterprise Economic Stability Assessment Scale.

Degrees	Assessment
High	More than 0.9
Higher than average	From 0.7 to 0.9
Average	From 0.5 to 0.7
Low	From 0.1 to 0.5
Critical	Negative

Source: Created by the authors.

CONCLUSION

The authors devised an innovative approach to appraising the economic stability of industrial enterprises using integral differential equations derived from regression analysis. These equations are crafted to formulate a relationship that captures changes in individual factors concerning the overall factor set. The inventive methodology for evaluating economic stability elucidates the extent to which external and internal factors impact the economic efficiency of an industrial enterprise. Specifically, if a factor exerts a low influence, measures should be devised to enhance it by implementing strategies to improve (e.g., the demand for industrial products through marketing initiatives, pricing adjustments, and contractual terms). In cases where the factor's influence is moderate, optimization measures targeting specific processes that mitigate the assessment of economic stability become imperative.

REFERENCES

Akramov, E. A. (2003). *Analysis of the financial condition of enterprises*. Finance.

Burkhanov, A. U. (2020). Assessment of financial security of investment funds. *Journal of Advanced Research in Dynamical and Control Systems, 12*(5), 293–300. https://doi.org/10.5373/JARDCS/V12I5/20201717

Burkhanov, A. U., & Mansur qizi, M. E. (2021). The ways for improvement of investment strategy in the period of digital economy. In *ICFNDS 2021: The 5th International Conference on Future Networks & Distributed Systems* (pp. 655–662). Association for Computing Machinery. https://doi.org/10.1145/3508072.3508202

Burkhanov, A. U., Tursunov, B., Uktamov, K., & Usmonov, B. (2023). Econometric analysis of factors affecting economic stability of chemical industry enterprises in digital era: In case of Uzbekistan. In *Proceedings of ICFNDS '22: The 6th International Conference on Future Networks & Distributed Systems* (pp. 484–490). Association for Computing Machinery. https://doi.org/10.1145/3584202.3584274

Efimova, M. G. (2022). Actualization of the issue of the influence of uncertainty of environmental factors on the cost of an industrial enterprise from the point of view of economic sustainability. *Science Time, 1*, 171–179.

Egamberdiyev, R. I., & Maxmudova, N. M. (2018). Strengthening of macroeconomic stability in the country to maintain high growth is one of the most important areas of its strategy. *Theory and Practice of Contemporary Science, 1*(31), 805–807.

Ikramov, M. A., & Avulchaeva, F. (2011). Trends in the development of foreign economic activity. *Economic Revival of Russia, 2*, 25–28. https://cyberleninka.ru/article/n/tendentsii-razvitiya-vneshneekonomicheskoy-deyatelnosti. Accessed 26 October 2023.

Kadirov, A. (2023). Theoretical and methodological foundations of ensuring financial and economic stability of enterprises. *E3S Web of Conferences, 402*, 08005. https://doi.org/10.1051/e3sconf/202340208005

Korobkova, Z. V. (2005). Sustainable development of industrial enterprises in a globalized economy. In V. V. Titov & V. D. Markova (Eds.), *Improvement of institutional mechanisms in industry: Collection of scientific papers* (pp. 90–101). Institute of Economics and Industrial Engineering, Siberian Branch of RAS.

Korotkov, E. M. (1998). *Anti-crisis management: Textbook*. Infra-M.

Kovalev, D., & Sukhorukova, T. (1998). Economic security of the enterprise. *The Economy of Ukraine, 5*, 48–52.

Kulbaka, N. A. (2002). *The essence and factors of economic stability of the enterprise*. Donetsk National Technical University.

Mahmudov, E. X. (2004). *Enterprise economy*. TDIO.

Makhkamova, M. A. (2004). *Formation of organizational and economic mechanism of innovation activity management at industrial enterprises of the Republic of Uzbekistan*. Synopsis of Dissertation of Doctor of Economic Sciences.

Nosirov, J., Uktamov, K., Xabibullayev, D., & Mirolimov, M. (2023). Ensuring the financial stability of insurance companies in the innovative development of the economy. *E3S Web of Conferences, 402*, 08007. https://doi.org/10.1051/e3sconf/202340208007

Nurimbetov, R. I., & Akhmedov, S. I. (2008). *Development management: Tutorial*. Interpretation.

Qurbanov, Z. N., & Isaev, F. I. (2017). Analysis of indicators of economic stability. *Economics and Innovative Technologies, 1*, 321–328.

Schumpeter, J. A. (1998). *History of economic analysis* (Transl. from English). Economic School.

Sheremet, A. D. (2008). *Complex analysis of economic activity: Textbook*. Infra-M.

Statista. (2023). Chemical industry worldwide – Statistics & facts. https://www.statista.com/topics/6213/chemical-industry-worldwide. Accessed 26 October 2023.

Tulueva, V. A. (2014). Methodological aspects of assessing the economic stability of an enterprise under the influence of internal and external factors. *Journal of Economic Studies*, *4*(14). https://myeconomix.ru/articles/predprinimatelstvo/metodicheskie-aspekty-otsenki-ekonomicheskoy-ustoychivosti-predpriyatiya-pod-vliyaniem-vnutrennikh-i/. Accessed 26 October 2023.

Usmonov, B. (2023). The impact of the financial ratios on the financial performance. A case of Chevron Corporation (CVX). In Y. Koucheryavy & A. Aziz (Eds.), *Internet of things, smart spaces, and next generation networks and systems*. Springer. https://doi.org/10.1007/978-3-031-30258-9_28

Volkov, V. V., & Khudyakova, T. A. (2022). An integrated method for assessing the economic sustainability of industrial sector enterprises. *Bulletin of the South Ural State University. Series: Economics and Management*, *16*(3), 58–65. https://doi.org/10.14529/em220307

Vygodsky, M. Ya. (2002). *Handbook of higher mathematics*. Astrel Publishing House.

Zaitsev, O. N. (2007). *Assessment of economic sustainability of industrial enterprises*. Synopsis of Dissertation of Candidate of Economic Sciences. Pacific State University.

EVALUATION OF EFFICIENCY OF CAPITAL MANAGEMENT IN JOINT-STOCK COMPANIES IN THE CHEMICAL SECTOR: THE CASE OF UZBEKISTAN

Bunyod Usmonov

Tashkent State University of Economics, Uzbekistan

ABSTRACT

The research is devoted to the theoretical foundations of capital management efficiency based on the existing management problems in joint-stock companies. The author develops conclusions and recommendations for improving the efficiency of capital management. The research analyzes the capital management status of a joint-stock company using indicators that show the enterprise's capital efficiency, the seasonality of the chemical industry, low profitability, high turnover of working capital, and other peculiarities. The methodology presented in this research allows chemical enterprises to assess capital efficiency. In this research, the author created a regression model based on the financial data of enterprises, approaching the existing methodology in the world, and analyzed the specific situation that affects the growth of enterprise assets. According to the six-year financial data for "Farg'onaazot" Joint Stock Company (JSC) and "Bekabadcement" JSC, the author concludes that the ratio for the last three years shows a satisfactory level in the remaining indicators despite recording a good result, indicating that capital management is not reasonable. The practical significance of this research is that the results obtained will serve to improve the financial management of enterprises in the chemical industry.

Keywords: Chemical enterprises; evaluation; capital; ROA; ROE; ROS; ROCE; profitability; efficiency; coefficient

JEL Codes: G31; G32; G51

The chemical industry gives great opportunities for humanity. Therefore, the fact that the chemical industry spends a huge amount of capital to produce such a variety of products

Development of International Entrepreneurship Based on Corporate Accounting and Reporting According to IFRS
Advanced Series in Management, Volume 33B, 67–74
Copyright © 2024 Bunyod Usmonov
Published under exclusive licence by Emerald Publishing Limited
ISSN: 1877-6361/doi:10.1108/S1877-63612024000033B009

and ensure its efficient utilization indicates the relevance of this research (Vanitha & Selvam, 2010). P. L. Short (2009) noted that the expansion and development of chemical companies depends on how much debt is obtained or how much investment is received by the company. Sato (2012) studied process of effective capital management in enterprises and justified importance of capital efficiency the need to develop a budget plan based on investment flows and further strategic plans. The fact is that a sharp increase in investment or total debt can lead to the company's bankruptcy, reflecting the need to optimize budget planning (Ayneshet, 2019).

The world's scientists researched financial stability, particularly when investigating LyondellBasell Industries and researching the effects of its financial indicators and net profit reduction (Borhan et al., 2014). This research shows that establishing a correct distribution of leverage and profitability coefficients makes it possible to prevent climate change and efficiently use financial resources. In the conditions of COVID-19, this encourages the author to delve deeper into the processes involved in the effective capital management of chemical companies.

LITERATURE REVIEW

Corporate capital management issues are an important conceptual and empirical part of financial management, and scholars have conducted research in this area in various ways. According to Sunday (2011), increasing the efficiency of capital in joint-stock companies is important for solvency and its liquidity. His research has shown that ensuring the financial stability of joint-stock companies has improved their financial reporting and control system, effective organization of their funds management, and continuous growth and solvency.

Islam et al. (2018) studied effective capital management by profitability indicators of nine selected pharmaceutical companies in Bangladesh. During the research, they used financial data of all nine companies from 2011 to 2015 and applied the Pearson correlation matrix and multiple regression analysis to find the relationship and impact of capital.

According to Alipour (2011), the capital management of joint-stock companies serves to increase its profitability and provides a great opportunity for shareholders to invest in the process by reducing receivables. Ganesan (2007) argues that increasing capital management efficiency is about minimizing the demand for working capital and maximizing potential returns. Leland (1994) also cited his findings related to capital on a company's capital efficiency.

F. Modiglian and M. H. Miller studied the effective assessment of capital structure and value. They explained the principles of capital formation. According to scientists, the definition of capital structure and its effective assessment relies on effective capital management and capital structure, excluding factors such as taxes, revenues, bankruptcy, unstable capital markets, and inflation, which are factors affecting the real economy (Modigliani & Miller, 1958). The theory of F. Modilyan and M. Miller considers a number of issues in determining the rational composition of capital, particularly the relationship between the composition of debt capital and private capital. F. Modilyan and M. Miller draw several conclusions on determining the value of a company's capital and its effective management, considering effective management of a company's capital, including capital value, company profit, and company value.

According to the research of S. C. Myers and N. S. Majluf, retained earnings, private equity, and debt capital serve as indicators in determining the value of a company's capital and its effective management (Myers & Majluf, 1984).

Owolabi and Alu (2012) showed that working capital with multiple components affects different levels of a company's performance when each component is compared separately. When these components are combined simultaneously, the effect is relatively low. Nevertheless, economists provided recommendations for capital efficiency, which allows companies to adequately plan and control their activities, consider financial principles, and use business analysts in decision-making. In turn, this demonstrates the importance of capital efficiency.

Another foreign economist, R. Braille, argues that in corporate finance, the corporation uses a method of financing its assets consisting of capital, debt capital, or a combination of securities, which reflects the results of effective capital management (Brailey & Myers, 2015). At this point, according to Damodaran (2012) and Akinlo (2012), effective management by the companies' managers could create profits.

During 10 years of observation, Othuon et al. (2021) found that the manufacturing sector of Kenya has undergone declining growth due to the poor financial performance of the coffee industry sector. The author conducted a study using multivariate regression analysis. According to this study, return on assets (ROA) can be improved by reducing the period of accounts payable and current ratio. The study found that capital management has a negative impact on the ROA of the Kenyan coffee industry. Thus, by managing capital effectively and increasing the current ratio, it is possible to lengthen the period of average payment and simultaneously give the opportunity to raise the return payable. Speaking of capital control, Yin et al. (2022) note that reducing control on capital and improving capital flow channels can cause potentially unfavorable ramifications of short-term capital flight.

According to Cardot-Martin et al. (2021), who investigated the effectiveness of capital in the banking sector, banking crises can be avoided by using capital ratios, as is evident in the EU between 1998 and 2017. These measures have demonstrated unfavorable effects on the possible occurrence of banking crises. The result indicates that outliners can be confidently excluded, and various control variables for banking, financial, and macro-economic risks can be included. The probability of a crisis is almost always negatively impacted by the bank's regulatory capital to Risk Weighted Assets (RWA). However, the bank capital to total assets ratio is comprised of approximately 10% or 12%.

The research of Rey-Ares et al. (2021) on controlling better capital management in 377 Spanish companies over nine years found that the capital of these companies can be at an optimal level when increasing sales by balancing receivables. These would correlate with profitability and investment of the company in inventory.

From the general perspective of Dhole et al. (2019), effective capital management would have problems with financial constraints, which is depicted as an example of Australian companies. According to them, the effectiveness of capital management would have better results with lower financial constraints in companies. However, it could affect future share prices negatively, weakening a company at a significant level. Thus, effective capital management is crucial to avoid financial constraints (Borhan et al., 2014; Burkhanov & Mansur qizi, 2021; Usmonov, 2023; Burkhanov et al., 2023; Eshov, 2020).

METHODOLOGY

This research uses econometric methods. Correlation-regression analyses were performed using the following models:

$$d_{\mathrm{p}} = \frac{\sum(y_{t+1} + y')^2}{\sum y_t^2}$$

$$b = \frac{\sum\left(x - \bar{x}\right)\left(y - \bar{y}\right)}{\sum\left(x - \bar{x}\right)^2}$$

$$SE(b) = \frac{s_{\mathrm{res}}}{\sum\left(x - \bar{x}\right)^2}$$

$$s_{\mathrm{res}}^2 = \frac{\sum(y - Y)^2}{(n - 2)}$$

$$b + / - t_{0.05}SE(b)$$

The resulting model of regression ($F_{\mathrm{est}} = 5.355$) is statistically significant.

RESULTS

Improving the efficiency of capital use of a joint-stock company in the chemical industry can be done in the following options:

H1. In industrial companies, ROA ratios are influenced by Return On Equity (ROE), Return On Sales (ROS), equity ratio, and Return On Capital Employed (ROCE) only by debt-to-equity and capitalization ratios.

H2. ROA coefficients in chemical companies in the form of joint-stock companies differently affect ROE, ROS, ROCE, and debt-to-equity, equity, and capitalization ratios.

The author investigates the two largest chemical enterprises in 2015–2020 (Bartik et al., 2020; Statistics Agency, 2023; Uzkimyosanoat, 2023; World Health Organization, 2020). In international practice, there are several specific indicators and models of management of companies (Table 1).

Based on the correlation matrix, an arbitrary variable with a dependent variable has a direct or inverse correlation (mostly equal to 0.99). However, the author constructs the regression equation of only statistically significant factors.

According to the regression analysis, both factors have a *p*-value less than 0.05, which is statistically significant. Thus, while other factors remain unchanged, an increase in ROE per unit in "Farg'onaazot" JSC increases the ROA by 1.86. An increase in ROS per unit in the same enterprise reduces the ROA value by 1.23. We can see this visually in the SEM

Table 1. Indicators in the Analysis of the Profitability of JSC "Farg'onaazot".

Indicators	ROA	ROE	ROS	Debt-to-Equity (*D/E*)	Equity Ratio	Capitalization Ratio	ROCE
Variables	Y_1	X_4	X_2	X_3	X_4	X_5	X_6

Source: Compiled by the author.

model. The regression model of profitability indicators of "Farg'onaazot" JSC is as follows:

$$Y = 1.86x_1 - 1.23x_2 + 0.5932 \tag{1}$$

To continue this research, the author considers the impact of other factors on the ROE value of "Farg'onaazot" JSC. According to the regression analysis, both factors have a *p*-value less than 0.05, which is statistically significant. Hence, increasing the debt-to-equity ratio by one unit in "Farg'onaazot" JSC reduces the ROA value to 5.24 while other factors remain unchanged. An increase in ROCE per unit in this enterprise increases the ROA value to 73.06. The regression equation would be as follows:

$$Y = -5.24x_3 + 73.06x_6 + 2.6224 \tag{2}$$

Table 1 analyzes the profitability of "Farg'onaazot" JSC from 2015 to 2020. In 2015, all indicators showed a negative result (0.02%); equity was 0.13%; the return on sales was 0.08%. In 2016, the ROA ratio was stable. This figure increased to 0.04% in 2017 and reached 0.44% in 2018. Significant increases were recorded between 2019 and 2020, at 9.9% and 17.6%, respectively.

As a result of the decrease in 2016 compared to 2015, it amounted to 0.04%. In 2017, it improved to 0.09%. In 2018, there was a slightly positive result: the ratio increased to 0.6%. From 2019 to 2020, it was 14.2% and 22.1%, which is almost 15 and 23 times higher than in 2018. The return on sales ratio decreased by 0.02%–0.06% in 2016 and increased by 0.04%–0.1% in 2017. By 2018, this figure increased eight times compared to 2017, reaching 0.8%. This ratio was 13.3% in 2019 and 19.2% in 2020.

The financial leverage ratio fell from 4.53 in 2015 to 0.74 in 2016 as a result of a sharp decline of 6.1 times. In 2018, this ratio was 0.94. In 2020, it decreased by almost four times to 0.25. In 2018–2019, this coefficient was observed to be 0.48 and 0.42, respectively. The financial leverage ratio of "Farg'onaazot" JSC significantly decreased and became less than one, indicating that part of the company's profits was lost due to debt. To prevent this and increase the efficiency of capital management, an increase in equity and a proportionate reduction in debt reflects a prudent level of capital management for a publicly traded company.

The equity ratio changed from 0.19 in 2015 to 0.79 in 2020. In 2016–2017, these figures were 0.57 and 0.51. In 2018–2019, they were 0.67 and 0.70, respectively. "Farg'onaazot" JSC shows that it is stable and self-financing. The capitalization ratio (CR) was 0.59 in 2015 and 0.16 as a result of a 3.75-times decrease by the end of 2020. Additionally, the excessively low level of this ratio indicates the lack of capital management efficiency of this joint-stock company.

The ROCE ratio has hardly increased over the years: 0.002 in 2015 and 0.0015 in 2016. Although this figure rose slightly in 2017, it decreased by nearly four times to 0.012.

However, the value of this indicator has increased from 0.12 in 2019 to 0.22 in 2020. The analysis of "Bekabadcement" JSC based on its financial performance is performed below.

Based on the financial statements of "Bekabadcement" JSC, the author got a correlation matrix. Only the regression equation of statistically significant factors was formed. According to the regression analysis, both factors have a *p*-value less than 0.05, which is statistically significant. Thus, without changing other factors, a one-point increase in the debt-to-equity ratio in "Bekabadcement" JSC will reduce ROA by 97.82. Increasing the CR by one point will reduce ROA by 143.64. An increase in ROCE by one point will increase the value of ROA to 10.22.

The regression equation is as follows:

$$Y = -97.82x_3 + 143.64x_5 + 41.28x_6 + 10.229 \tag{3}$$

The ROA of "Bekabadcement" JSC in 2015 was 0.37. It has exhibited high volatility for several years. In particular, it was 10.29 in 2016 and 2.24 in 2017. By 2020, its volume was 19.68. However, the ROA ratio has not changed.

The financial leverage ratio was observed to decline from 2015 to 2020, from 0.67 in 2015 to 0.24 in 2020. If this ratio is greater than 1, then the company's assets are financed by creditors. When this ratio is less than 1, the company finances its assets with its own funds. In this regard, the results of the financial leverage ratio of "Bekabadcement" JSC show that the company finances its assets by directing own funds, which shows low efficiency of capital management in this company.

In 2015, the equity ratio was 0.6. by 2020; it saw an increase of 34% and 0.8. The average growth for 2016–2018 was 9.4%. Therefore, considering that this ratio of "Bekabadcement" JSC is higher than 0.5, the company can provide more financing from its own funds than from borrowed funds. Capitalization dropped significantly, from 0.3 in 2015 to 0.15 in 2020, illustrating a doubling reduction. Simultaneously, during 2016–2018, it also recorded a significant decrease, falling from 0.18 to 0.05. The ROCE ratio was 0.3 in 2015. This indicator did not fall below 0.5 over the next two years. It declined sharply over the remaining years, reaching 0.068 in 2019 and 0.27 in 2020.

DISCUSSION

The research had two objects: "Farg'onaazot" JSC and "Bekabadcement" JSC. On an example of "Farg'onaazot" JSC, we see that the relationship of ROE with ROS was relatively negative. These variables are the most impactful factors regarding the company's effective capital.

In "Bekabadcement" JSC, the main negative impact on ROA was made by the debt-to-equity ratio. CR also affected the ROA. To sum up, profitability ratios are accosted for as the key factors that highly influence the effective capital management of both objects. CR is the most impactful variable that affects the company's capital negatively. Thus, an increase in profitability will contribute to efficiency gains. An increase in ROE and ROCE ratios would have a positive relationship with the ROA of both companies. Thus, both companies should manage their assets and liabilities wisely to sustain effective capital management. Furthermore, companies are encouraged to fully utilize their assets rather than buying new ones, which can result in higher total debt and overall costs. Companies may grow the profit gains and reduce total expenses by implementing recommendations.

CONCLUSIONS

Using regression analysis, the author proved that ROA coefficients in enterprises of the chemical industry (JSC) influence ROE, ROS, ROCE, and debt-to-equity, equity, and CRs differently (hypothesis H_2 is proven).

According to the six-year financial data for "Farg'onaazot" JSC and "Bekabadcement" JSC, the ratio for the last three years shows a satisfactory level in the remaining indicators despite recording a good result, which indicates that capital management is not reasonable. On this basis, the author provides the following recommendations:

- It is necessary to replace a certain amount of long-term borrowed financial resources with short-term borrowed resources.
- The amount of equity and debt capital should be organized in direct proportion to each other based on international experience while ensuring rational management of capital of joint-stock companies by increasing the net profit of the joint-stock company.
- It is necessary to effectively maximize the capital capacity of the enterprise by utilizing all assets of the company in the enterprise rather than buying new assets and increasing the liabilities of the company.

REFERENCES

Akinlo, O. O. (2012). Effect of working capital on profitability of selected quoted firms in Nigeria. *Global Business Review, 13*(3), 367–381. https://doi.org/10.1177/097215091201300301

Alipour, M. (2011). Working capital management and corporate profitability: Evidence from Iran. *World Applied Sciences Journal, 12*(7), 1093–1099.

Ayneshet, A. (2019). The effect of working capital management on profitability: The case of selected manufacturing and merchandising companies in Hawassa city administration. *Research Journal of Finance and Accounting, 10*(1), 51–85. https://doi.org/10.7176/RJFA/10-1-07

Bartik, A. W., Bertrand, M., Cullen, Z., & Stanton, C. (2020). The impact of COVID-19 on small business outcomes and expectations. *PNAS, 117*(30), 17656–17666. https://doi.org/10.1073/pnas.2006991117

Borhan, H., Naina Mohamed, R., & Azmi, N. (2014). The impact of financial ratios on the financial performance of a chemical company: The case of LyondellBasell Industries. *World Journal of Entrepreneurship, Management and Sustainable Development, 10*(2), 154–160. https://doi.org/10.1108/WJEMSD-07-2013-0041

Brailey, R., & Myers, S. (2015). *Principles of corporate finance* (Transl. from English) (7th ed.). Olimp-Business; Troika Dialog. (Original work published 2003).

Burkhanov, A. U., & Mansur qizi, M. E. (2021). The ways for improvement of investment strategy in the period of digital economy. In *Proceedings of the ICFNDS 2021: The 5th International Conference on Future Networks & Distributed Systems* (pp. 655–662). Association for Computing Machinery. https://doi.org/10.1145/3508072.3508202

Burkhanov, A. U., Tursunov, B., Uktamov, K., & Usmonov, B. (2023). Econometric analysis of factors affecting economic stability of chemical industry enterprises in digital era: In case of Uzbekistan. In *Proceedings of the ICFNDS '22: The 6th International Conference on Future Networks & Distributed Systems* (pp. 484–490). Association for Computing Machinery. https://doi.org/10.1145/3584202.3584274

Cardot-Martin, R., Labondance, F., & Refait-Alexandre, C. (2021). Capital ratios and banking crises in the European Union. *International Economics, 172*, 389–402. https://doi.org/10.1016/j.inteco.2021.07.003

Damodaran, A. (2012). *Investment valuation: Tools and techniques for determining the value of any asset* (3rd ed.). Wiley.

Dhole, S., Mishra, S., & Pal, A. M. (2019). Efficient working capital management, financial constraints and firm value: A text-based analysis. *Pacific-Basin Finance Journal, 58*, 101212. https://doi.org/10.1016/j.pacfin.2019.101212

Eshov, M. (2020). Influence assessment of enterprise management value based on coefficients methods under the risk conditions. *Advances in Mathematics: Scientific Journal, 9*(9), 7573–7598. https://doi.org/10.37418/amsj.9.9.104

Ganesan, V. (2007). An analysis of working capital management efficiency in telecommunication equipment industry. *Rivier Academic Journal*, *3*(2), 1–10. https://studylib.net/doc/10281286/an-analysis-of-working-capital-management-efficiency-in-t.... Accessed on 26 October 2023.

Islam, R., Hossain, M. E., Hoq, M. N., & Alam, M. M. (2018). Impact of working capital management on corporate profitability- Empirical evidence from pharmaceutical industry of Bangladesh. *International Journal of Economics and Finance*, *10*(9), 136–144. https://doi.org/10.5539/ijef.v10n9p136

Leland, H. E. (1994). Corporate debt value, bond covenants, and optimal capital structure. *The Journal of Finance*, *49*(4), 1213–1252. https://doi.org/10.1111/j.1540-6261.1994.tb02452.x

Modigliani, F., & Miller, M. H. (1958). The cost of capital, corporation finance and the theory of investment. *The American Economic Review*, *48*(3), 261–297. https://www.jstor.org/stable/1809766. Accessed on 26 October 2023.

Myers, S. C., & Majluf, N. S. (1984). Corporate financing and investment decisions when firms have information that investors do not have. *Journal of Financial Economics*, *13*(2), 187–221. https://doi.org/10.1016/0304-405x(84)90023-0

Othuon, D. O., Gatimbu, K. K., Musafiri, C. M., & Ngetich, F. K. (2021). Working capital management impacts on small-scale coffee wet mills' financial performance in eastern Kenya. *Heliyon*, *7*(9), e07887. https://doi.org/10.1016/j.heliyon.2021.e07887

Owolabi, S. A., & Alu, C. N. (2012). Effective working capital management and profitability: A study of selected quoted manufacturing companies in Nigeria. *Economics and Finance Review*, *2*(6), 55–67.

Rey-Ares, L., Fernández-López, S., & Rodeiro-Pazos, D. (2021). Impact of working capital management on profitability for Spanish fish canning companies. *Marine Policy*, *130*, 104583. https://doi.org/10.1016/j.marpol.2021.104583

Sato, Y. (2012). Optimal budget planning for investment in safety measures of a chemical company. *International Journal of Production Economics*, *140*(2), 579–585. https://doi.org/10.1016/j.ijpe.2012.05.030

Short, P. L. (2009). Debt threatens LyondellBasell: Restructuring measures under consideration include possible Chapter 11 bankruptcy protection. *Chemical & Engineering News*, *87*(1), 1–2.

Statistics Agency. (2023). Statistics agency under the president of the Republic of Uzbekistan. www.stat.uz. Accessed on 26 October 2023.

Sunday, K. J. (2011). Effective working capital management in small and medium scale enterprises (SMEs). *International Journal of Business and Management*, *6*(9). https://doi.org/10.5539/ijbm.v6n9p271

Usmonov, B. (2023). The impact of the financial ratios on the financial performance. A case of Chevron Corporation (CVX). In Y. Koucheryavy & A. Aziz (Eds.), *Internet of things, smart spaces, and next generation networks and systems* (pp. 333–344). Springer. https://doi.org/10.1007/978-3-031-30258-9_28

Uzkimyosanoat. (2023). *State joint stock company "Uzkimyosanoat"*. www.uzkimyosanoat.uz. Accessed on 26 October 2023.

Vanitha, S., & Selvam, M. (2010). Financial performance of Indian manufacturing companies during pre and post merger. *International Research Journal of Finance and Economics*, *20*(12), 7–35.

World Health Organization. (2020, October 13). *Impact of COVID-19 on people's livelihoods, their health and our food systems*. https://www.who.int/news/item/13-10-2020-impact-of-covid-19-on-people's-livelihoods-their-health-and-our-food-systems. Accessed on 26 October 2023.

Yin, Z., Peng, H., Xiao, W., & Xiao, Z. (2022). Capital control and monetary policy coordination: Tobin tax revisited. *Research in International Business and Finance*, *59*, 101514. https://doi.org/10.1016/j.ribaf.2021.101514

AGRICULTURAL INSURANCE PROTECTION AND FOOD SECURITY IN THE FACE OF GLOBAL CLIMATE CHANGE

Aktam U. Burkhanov[a], Akram A. Yadgarov[a], Munisa E. Saidova[b] and Malika S. Tugizova[a]

[a]Tashkent State University of Economics, Uzbekistan
[b]Tashkent State Agrarian University, Uzbekistan

ABSTRACT

Global climate change threatens world food security. This research raises the issues of priority agricultural development, increasing agricultural production, and expanding the insurance coverage of the industry. The authors propose to implement insurance activities further to prevent the effects of climate change and economic support in the emphasized advancement of food production in agriculture. The research relies on direct comparative analysis, statistical and economic analysis, and monographic observational data. To conduct deep research, the authors apply analysis and synthesis. The authors also use the questionnaire methods across the country and organization, monographic research, and other methods. Furthermore, the authors used international normative documents, research of scientists in scientific periodicals, and data from official websites. The authors conclude that to protect agricultural insurance and ensure the continuous development of agriculture, it is advisable to transition from administrative methods to the following recommendations for insurance against various financial and natural losses that may arise in agriculture due to the vagaries of nature. It is also recommended to introduce a mechanism of state subsidies to compensate for the costs and improve the efficiency of insurance agents in the insurance activities of agricultural enterprises.

Development of International Entrepreneurship Based on Corporate Accounting and Reporting According to IFRS
Advanced Series in Management, Volume 33B, 75–79
Copyright © 2024 Aktam U. Burkhanov, Akram A. Yadgarov, Munisa E. Saidova and Malika S. Tugizova
Published under exclusive licence by Emerald Publishing Limited
ISSN: 1877-6361/doi:10.1108/S1877-63612024000033B010

Keywords: Financial losses; natural losses; administrative methods; development of agriculture; insurance activities; agriculture

JEL Codes: G22; Q14

Global climate change and its impact on food insecurity are increasing global concerns. In this respect, studying such issues has interested the world community. The fact that globalized food shortages continue to shake the countries poses specific and contradictory challenges for different nations. In the conditions of scarcity of food resources, along with health protection and comprehensive social protection of the population, it is necessary to ensure food security.

The influx of scarce food resources into Uzbekistan also negatively affects the activities of various production and service enterprises. It has also influenced the rise in food prices, which provide basic needs in some areas while posing specific risks, mainly in terms of food supply to the population. Simultaneously, the sharp decline in employment and the emergence of unemployment had a considerable influence on the social security of citizens, who do not have a stable source of income.

Nowadays, it is time to deeper improve insurance mechanisms to develop agriculture and solve food safety problems.

LITERATURE REVIEW

Various scholars conducted research in the field of global climate change (Cai & Song, 2017; Du et al., 2014, 2015; Farzaneh et al., 2017; Ginder et al., 2009; Just et al., 1999; Sherrick & Barry, 2004; Wang et al., 2023). Moreover, the economists from Uzbekistan also conducted many works that contributed to the balance of the economy with the optimal use of agricultural mechanisms. The works of A. Yadgarov (Yadgarov, 2020; Yadgarov & Rakhimov, 2021) and others greatly influenced and contributed to the development of this field.

METHODOLOGY

It is proposed to further implement insurance activities for preventing the effects of climate change and economic support in the emphasized advancement of food production in the agricultural sector. The research relies on direct comparative analysis, statistical and economic analysis, and monographic observational data. To conduct deep research, the authors applied analysis and synthesis. The authors also use the questionnaire methods across the country and organization, monographic research, and other methods. Furthermore, the authors used international normative documents, research of scientists in scientific periodicals, and data from official websites.

RESULTS

When the threat of food scarcity is prevalent and food scarcity is growing worldwide, it is challenging to guarantee that the scarce food resources will not affect the economy of Uzbekistan. It is crucial to develop measures to prevent the transmission of a pandemic in the face of scarce food resources, mitigate and repair the damage to the country's economy, and deal with the looming crisis.

Sharp exchange rate fluctuations are very good for countries exporting food products created in agriculture to guarantee food security. It allows them to sell their products at a higher price and make more profit. In turn, it creates a high risk for food-importing countries, creating a serious threat to food security policies in these countries.

In March 2020, the national currencies of Argentina, India, Japan, Russia, and Kazakhstan, which are members of Asia-Pacific Economic Cooperation (APEC), fluctuated sharply against the US dollar.

France planned to direct up to $50 billion directly into the country's economy (France 24, 2020b) to prevent the economic catastrophe associated with the COVID-19 pandemic aid for large and small businesses. Moreover, the country plans to address social insurance and unemployment benefits and provide assistance to the most severely impacted sectors of the economy (e.g., the aviation and tourism industries) (France 24, 2020a; Ministry for Europe and Foreign Affairs [France], 2020). The UK government has also introduced a number of tax incentives to help large and small businesses in the face of a crisis that could occur in the context of scarce food resources. The UK government has allocated significant funds in direct financial aid to help the economy emerge from this crisis (Brien & Keep, 2023).

Due to the scarce food resources, the German government has also decided to implement more than 750 billion euros ($808 billion) in stimulus measures to prevent the economic crisis (Nienaber, 2020). The German government has also set a target of 156 billion euros from the emergency budget, which will be used mainly to support large and small businesses and the banking and financial system, ensure social protection for the less fortunate, and advance the health system (Nienaber et al., 2020).

To decrease the impact of scarce food resources and fight the crisis, the Japanese government has implemented a $1 trillion incentive program. These funds will be provided mainly through direct payments to the population, delays in tax and social insurance payments for enterprises, increased unemployment and social security benefits, economic and social incentives, and the introduction of tax benefits.

To prevent the impact of the pandemic on the economy of the neighboring Kyrgyz Republic, the government decided to provide social support, food security, and some tax benefits and incentives for businesses. The International Monetary Fund (IMF) has pledged $120.9 million to help Kyrgyzstan fight the scarce food.

According to the decree, the Republican Anti-Crisis Commission was established to mitigate the effects of the scarce food resources and the global crisis in different segments of the economy. It was decided to establish the Anti-Crisis Fund. Additionally, 10 trillion sums were allocated to the fund from the state budget. The funds will be directed mainly to combat the spread of natural disasters related to agriculture and support entrepreneurship and employment, including the implementation of infrastructure projects, ensuring the sustainable operation of economic sectors, and expanding social support.

Predicting the damage that scarce food resources could do to agriculture is challenging.

At the global level, the spread of the scarce food resources adversely affects agriculture in all countries. Therefore, in the epidemiological situation of Uzbekistan, it is necessary to protect the process from various hazards. This process currently places a great responsibility on the insurance companies in the country. It is recommended to offer dependable insurance services. In this regard, the country is actively working to provide insurance coverage for the lives and assets of businesses and the populace (Table 1).

Table 1. Research Data.

Years	Insurance Contracts	Insurance Liability (Million UZS)	Insurance Premiums (Million UZS)	Paid Insurance Compensation (Million UZS)
2012	37,443	608,121.1	8,590.9	2,934.2
2013	25,429	683,868.4	9,672.3	2,798.2
2014	28,291	1,188,823.5	13,263.4	4,901.6
2015	33,960	1,350,386.1	18,862.7	7,777.0
2016	58,048	1,917,389.7	45,609.3	15,441.2
2017	53,658	1,928,357.9	37,041.3	73,864.4
2018	58,561.0	3,017,441.0	58,927.9	46,081.5
2019	100,640.0	6,636,621.0	120,359.1	77,283.3
2020	11,180	1,602,156.0	57,598.6	44,683.9
2021	405	192,126.0	2,058.1	7,819.7

Source: Created by the author based on Uzagrosugurta JSC (n.d.).

DISCUSSION

Natural and spontaneous hazards in agriculture seriously affect agricultural activities and cause economic losses. In 2012, the number of contracts concluded with risks at the republican level was 37,443. As of the end of 2021, this number decreased to 405 (Uzagrosugurta JSC, n.d.). Notably, the financial backing provided by joint stock company (JSC) "Uzagrosugurta" is a crucial factor in supporting agricultural enterprises.

Overall, ensuring the population's access to a diverse array of agricultural products and sustaining the country's needs calls for the continued advancement of insurance protection to avert food insecurity. From the author's perspective, it is necessary to ensure the evolution of financial mechanisms that alleviate and stimulate economic crises within the realm of agriculture.

Timely insurance of the agricultural sector against various unexpected natural disasters and natural calamities will ensure the economically stable operation of agricultural enterprises, protect the country's food security, and expand opportunities to export agricultural products to foreign markets.

CONCLUSION

To ensure agricultural insurance protection and continuous development of agriculture, it is expedient to transition from administrative methods to insurance against various financial and natural losses that may occur in agriculture due to natural vagaries. It is also recommended that a mechanism of state subsidies be introduced to compensate for the costs. Moreover, it is necessary to improve the efficiency of insurance agents in the insurance activities of agricultural enterprises.

REFERENCES

Brien, P., & Keep, M. (2023, September 12). *Public spending during the COVID-19 pandemic.* House of Commons Library. https://researchbriefings.files.parliament.uk/documents/CBP-9309/CBP-9309.pdf. Accessed on 1 December 2023.

Cai, J., & Song, C. (2017). Do disaster experience and knowledge affect insurance take-up decisions? *Journal of Development Economics*, *124*, 83–94. https://ink.library.smu.edu.sg/lkcsb_research/6506/. Accessed on 1 December 2023.

Du, X., Hennessy, D. A., & Feng, H. (2014). A natural resource theory of U.S. crop insurance contract choice. *American Journal of Agricultural Economics*, *96*(1), 232–252. https://doi.org/10.1093/ajae/aat057

Du, X., Ifft, J., Lu, L., & Zilberman, D. (2015). Marketing contracts and crop Insurance. *American Journal of Agricultural Economics*, *97*(5), 1360–1370. https://doi.org/10.1093/ajae/aav024

Farzaneh, M., Allahyari, M. S., Damalas, C. A., & Seidavi, A. (2017). Crop insurance as a risk management tool in agriculture: The case of silk farmers in northern Iran. *Land Use Policy*, *64*, 225–232. https://doi.org/10.1016/j.landusepol.2017.02.018

France 24. (2020a, July 9). France pledges 15 billion euros in aid for aviation sector. https://www.france24.com/en/20200609-france-pledges-15-billion-euros-in-aid-for-aviation-sector. Accessed on 1 December 2023.

France 24. (2020b, March 18). Fearing coronavirus recession, France announces €45 billion in business aid. https://www.france24.com/en/20200318-fearing-a-recession-sparked-by-coronavirus-france-announces-45-billion-euros-in-business-aid. Accessed on 1 December 2023.

Ginder, M., Spaulding, A. D., Tudor, K. W., & Winter, J. R. (2009). Factors affecting crop insurance purchase decisions by farmers in northern Illinois. *Agricultural Finance Review*, *69*(1), 113–125. https://doi.org/10.1108/00021460910960507

Just, R. E., Calvin, L., & Quiggin, J. (1999). Adverse selection in crop insurance: Actuarial and asymmetric information incentives. *American Journal of Agricultural Economics*, *81*(4), 834–849. https://doi.org/10.2307/1244328

Ministry for Europe and Foreign Affairs [France]. (2020, April 24). Press release: Measures to support restaurants, cafés, hotels and businesses in the tourism, events, sport and culture sectors. https://www.diplomatie.gouv.fr/en/coming-to-france/coming-to-france-your-covid-19-questions-answered/coronavirus-statements/article/measures-to-support-restaurants-cafes-hotels-and-businesses-in-the-tourism. Accessed on 1 December 2023.

Nienaber, M. (2020, March 24). Germany launches 750 billion euro package to fight coronavirus. *Reuters*. https://www.reuters.com/article/idUSKBN21A2XQ/#:~:text=BERLIN%20(Reuters)%20%2D%20Germany%20on,the%20first%20time%20since%202013. Accessed on 1 December 2023.

Nienaber, M., Hansen, H., & Kraemer, C. (2020, March 21). Germany prepares 150 billion euro emergency budget in coronavirus package. *Reuters*. https://www.reuters.com/article/us-germany-debt-idCAKBN2180KV/. Accessed on 1 December 2023.

Sherrick, B. J., & Barry, P. J. (2004). Factors influencing farmers 'crop insurance decision. *American Journal of Agricultural Economics*, *86*(1), 103–114.

Uzagrosugurta JSC. (n.d.). *Annual reporting data*. https://www.agros.uz/ru/interaktive_service/. Accessed on 1 December 2023.

Wang, W., Jiang, H., Shoukat, A., & Usmanovich, B. A. (2023). Quantifying the impact of green growth and digital transformation on health: New insights from Asian economies. *Environmental Science and Pollution Research*, *30*, 107624–107633. https://doi.org/10.1007/s11356-023-29595-2

Yadgarov, A. (2020). International insurance market and experience of foreign countries in agricultural insurance. *Economics and Innovative Technologies*, *2020*(2), 16. https://uzjournals.edu.uz/iqtisodiyot/vol2020/iss2/. Accessed on 1 December 2023.

Yadgarov, A. A., & Rakhimov, A. S. (2021). Reforms on the development of the livestock sector and insurance protection in Uzbekistan. *E3S Web of Conferences*, *244*, 12012. https://doi.org/10.1051/e3sconf/202124412012

RUSSIA'S PERSPECTIVES IN THE GLOBAL OUTSOURCING SERVICES MARKET

Irina N. Belova, Alexey V. Groshev and Elena A. Egorycheva

RUDN University, Russia

ABSTRACT

Due to global systemic changes, the Brittle Anxious Nonlinear Incomprehensible (BANI)-world model has been formed since 2020, which greatly affects the world economic model. To overcome the main challenges, developing countries have to solve the tasks of their sustainable development and flexibility and transparency of various management methods at the microlevel. Outsourcing is regarded as one of such tools. Understanding the origins and development trends of outsourcing services makes it possible to effectively implement the tasks set for business in today's realities and contribute to the development of entrepreneurship and the economy of a country, making the system more sensitive and responsive. This research provides an overview of the development of the market for outsourcing services in Russia based on general information about the global market for outsourcing services and the current trends in Russia. The authors described the main milestones in the history of the formation of the outsourcing market in Russia, which influenced the formation of the main current features of the outsourcing services market. The authors also identified the main problems of the market for outsourcing services in Russia and highlighted the main directions for developing outsourcing.

Keywords: Russia; outsourcing; outsourcing services; business efficiency; prospects of outsourcing services; outsourcing market problems

JEL Codes: F01; F15; O24; Q43

According to the World Bank's January 2023 report, economic growth is expected to decline to 1.7% in 2023. Simultaneously, a sharp decline in the pace of economic development will affect about 95% of the economies of developed countries and about 70% of emerging and developing economies (International Bank for Reconstruction and Development, 2023).

Development of International Entrepreneurship Based on Corporate Accounting and Reporting According to IFRS
Advanced Series in Management, Volume 33B, 81–89
Copyright © 2024 Irina N. Belova, Alexey V. Groshev and Elena A. Egorycheva
Published under exclusive licence by Emerald Publishing Limited
ISSN: 1877-6361/doi:10.1108/S1877-63612024000033B011

In the context of the economic downturn, which will be observed in 2023 and beyond, the issue of maintaining competitiveness and reducing transaction costs is being acutely raised for businesses of various levels (Abramova, 2016). One of the ways to solve this problem is the consolidation of the business structure through the integration and formation of vertical, horizontal, and diversification types of companies. Thus, as a rule, the company turns into a full-cycle company, producing a product and providing a service to the market. The second way to solve this problem is based on the introduction of an outsourcing mechanism, which is a mechanism for distributing business functions to other organizations with a certain set of competencies.

The desire to successfully conduct business and increase competitiveness makes companies look for new ways and forms of business organization and management. Outsourcing is one of these forms.

It has always made sense to outsource only those processes and services that are not the main activity of the company and its key competence because the provision of the company's business processes to third-party performers is associated with considerable risks, including the following:

- It is impossible to outsource any tasks that are not specified in the contract to the involved specialist.
- There may be difficulties with the introduction of a freelancer in the company's specifics.
- It is impossible to personally select and bring in people who will work on the outsourced project.
- In case of limited supply on the market, outsourcers may provide low-quality services or overcharge.
- There may be downtime due to waiting for a freelance specialist.
- The risk of the wrong choice of transferred processes (transfer to external contractors of those processes that are categorically not suitable for this) provokes an additional risk of loss of competitive advantages by the company.
- Lack of a clear legal framework.
- The risk of difficulties in terminating the outsourcing contract.
- The difficulty of choosing an organization.

If there are many risks, then it is better to refuse outsourcing. To minimize risks, it is worthwhile to conduct a thorough analysis of all indicators and decide whether outsourcing is rational.

It has always made sense to outsource only those processes and services that are not the company's main activity and its key competence.

In addition to simple and fairly easily scalable services (e.g., cleaning), to reduce the cost of outsourcing, it has always been advisable to outsource professional services for which the company does not have enough competencies or services that require competencies that are long and expensive to develop and maintain at the average market level. Examples of such professional services are accounting, human resources (HR), and design.

The most popular tasks to transfer in information technology (IT) outsourcing are as follows:

- Software development, including mobile applications.
- Services of providers and data centers.
- Infrastructure and database administration.
- Maintenance of workstations.

Another popular area of cooperation under the outsourcing model has been and remains the maintenance of a wide variety of infrastructure and equipment. This is the maintenance of cash registers, security equipment, equipment and GPS monitoring systems/Global Navigation Satellite System (owned by Russian Federation) (GLONASS), office equipment, and medical equipment. A large block is also related to the operation of commercial real estate.

However, outsourcing has almost always been the prerogative of large businesses due to the tasks being solved and financial opportunities. Medium and small businesses continued to operate full function and process.

Foreign experts confirm that companies with fewer than 50 employees are less likely to resort to outsourcing. In turn, enterprises with more than 50 employees are much more likely to seek help from other organizations. To a greater extent, this is a consequence of the low financial and managerial literacy of small business representatives.

As a result, many full-cycle software developers have appeared, even for those goods and services that are not key for their business and in which they have never had competencies. Lockdowns and the transition to a remote work format increased the trend of "everything is at home" in terms of IT outsourcing and the demand for IT specialists as full-time employees. Thus, small and medium businesses continued to believe that it was cheaper to develop their accounting system and keep an HR specialist on staff.

Simultaneously, the demand for other services was growing. In recent years, external maintenance of infrastructure and equipment has shown a small growth. According to MAGRAM market research, the total volume of the Russian recruitment, staffing, and outsourcing market increased by 8.8% and amounted to 288.3 billion rubles in 2020 (Achaz, 2021).

METHODOLOGY

The research provides an overview of the development of the market for outsourcing services in Russia based on general information about the global market for outsourcing services and the current trends in Russia. The research defines the main milestones in the history of the formation of the outsourcing market in Russia, which influenced the formation of the main current features of the market for outsourcing services. The authors identified the main problems of the outsourcing services market in Russia and outlined the main directions for the development of outsourcing.

The methodological basis of the research is formed by a combination of various widely used methods. When carrying out the research, the authors focused on the principle of scientific objectivity. The authors applied a comparative method, statistical approach, and system approach so as to fully describe the research topic.

The authors used various research methods, including search, systematization, evaluation, and structural and dynamic analysis of outsourcing market indicators, to characterize Russia's peculiarities.

RESULTS

Outsourcing became popular in international business practice in the late 1980s. In Russia, outsourcing became popular much later, in the 1990s. The basis for its development in Russia was a change in the political system and the provision of the opportunity to enter the market of the first foreign companies. Automated management systems and the internet served as the basis for the development of financial outsourcing in Russia (Laktionova, 2012).

The main difficulty for Western companies to enter the Russian market by providing outsourcing services was the lack of a legislative framework and the use of European and Russian standardization documents. Thus, the introduction of the concept of "Borrowed labor" in the Labor Code of the Russian Federation in 2016, as well as amendments to the Civil Code of the Russian Federation, served as an impetus for expanding the scope of outsourcing services and their application area (Russian Federation, 1994, 2001).

The formation of legal acts, the development of globalization, and the openness of the economies of countries allowed Russia to quickly expand and develop the outsourcing mechanism (Kurbanov & Plotnikov, 2013). Over the past 20 years, certain global trends, such as the shift of secondary business functions from developed countries to emerging markets and developing economies in the outsourcing market, have been formed (Peshkova et al., 2016).

The United States, Canada, and Western Europe were the leaders in the consumption of business process outsourcing services in 2020. Outsourcing is one of the important parts of Japanese business practice. These countries are characterized by a wide range of outsourced functions. In Russia, the leading outsourced functions are IT and HR (Nepochatykh, 2020; Perepechaeva & Simonenko, 2012). The Russian IT services market has not stopped growing even during the COVID-19 pandemic and is at a pace ahead of the world. The research company Gartner predicted a growth of 9% in 2021 and 7% in 2022. According to TAdviser, the volume of the Russian IT services market increased by 15% by the end of 2021, exceeding the mark of 485 billion rubles (TAdviser, 2020).

The outsourcing market is growing annually and will continue to grow. For example, according to Grand View Research forecasts, business process outsourcing alone will exceed $400 billion by 2027; it means that IT outsourcing will grow by an average of 4% in the next 2–3 years (Grand View Research, 2023).

Simultaneously, it is impossible to give any relevant forecasts for the whole world, especially for Russia, given the current events. Nevertheless, it is possible to identify what business processes and services are advisable to outsource now.

Such a wide application of outsourcing, particularly in IT services, is justified by its number of advantages, including the following:

- Business processes optimization.
- Concentration of efforts on the main activity without noncore areas.
- Operational support for the safe operation of the organization's information systems.
- Reduction of financial costs for building and maintaining the organization's IT infrastructure (Russoft, 2022).

India was the leader in outsourcing in 2020. Currently, India is being hampered by new players, such as Bangladesh, which, thanks to the available internet in cities and many qualified specialists, has already become the second largest number of freelancers in the world, accounting for 16% of their total number. According to this indicator, Bangladesh is still inferior to India (24%) but ahead of the United States (12%). Russia occupies the 12th place in this market with a share of about 1% (TAdviser, 2020).

In the current situation, it is quite challenging to make an unambiguous conclusion about the position of the Russian market in the world market. Many Russian companies have changed their Russian jurisdiction to a foreign one, and some have left the market.

According to the rating of the International Association of Outsourcing Professionals (IAOP) presented in Table 1, although Russian companies are marked on the world market, only two companies entered the rating in 2022 (Russoft, 2022).

In 2022, entrepreneurial activity around the world faced new challenges and realities characteristic of the Brittle Anxious Nonlinear Incomprehensible (BANI) world. According to Deloitte, every second manager considers it possible to outsource certain functions. The distribution of functional responsibilities is shown in Fig. 1. Additionally, the last two years have been unusual in terms of growth: more than 75% of managers reported that their organizations received income and growth, and every fourth reported significant growth of more than 10% with the introduction of outsourcing in the company (Mirigos, 2022).

The established supply environment has huge opportunities for expanding innovation and competitiveness in the market for outsourcing companies and the development of this direction. Simultaneously, for each direction and country, there is a certain pool of problematic issues, including for the Russian Federation, requiring prompt intervention from the internal restructuring of existing business processes and the need for intervention at the level of state regulation and support.

The outsourcing market in Russia is still in its infancy in many areas. The first reason for this is the difficulty of retaining employees in small companies. There are cases when big businesses hired specific specialists and offered them salaries with a coefficient of "3" to the average. Second, the market had no opportunities for active development and growth in some areas, including IT outsourcing.

Table 1. Russian Companies in the Rating of the Best of the Global Outsourcing (the Global Outsourcing 100) in 2020–2022.

№	Company Name	2020	2021	2022
1	Artezio	Rising Star	Rising Star	–
2	Auriga	Rising Star	Rising Star	Rising Star
3	First Line Software	Rising Star	Rising Star	Rising Star
4	ICL Services	Leader	Leader	Leader
5	SimbirSof	Rising Star	Leader	–
6	Reksof	–	Leader	–

Source: Compiled by the authors based on the 19th Annual RUSSOFT Study (Russoft, 2022).

Fig. 1. Distribution of Functional Responsibilities. *Source:* Compiled by the authors based on Deloitte Global Outsourcing Survey 2022 (Mirigos, 2022).

On the other hand, the vast majority of companies that are given the maintenance of equipment and infrastructure in all industries are surprisingly immature in terms of managerial and financial skills.

The problem also lies in the fact that representatives of the IT outsourcing market and service companies for equipment and infrastructure maintenance do not understand the requests of large organizations in terms of quality assurance and business continuity.

Thus, according to the results of industry survey of integrators servicing transportation satellite monitoring systems, only 60% of companies have all customer requests forwarded to technical support (Okdesk, 2020). The requirements of the Service Level Agreement (SLA) are controlled by slightly more than 20% of companies. As a result, almost 58% of companies have customers who refuse their services several times a year due to poor service (Okdesk, 2020).

Business owners turn to outsourcing when they need to stay competitive or scale quickly. The strategic advantage of outsourcing is that the company's management can use all time resources available to focus on key business processes. When choosing a contractor, a businessman is only interested in the cost and quality of services because all responsibility, including financial risks, is shifted to outsourcing partners.

The factors determining the global development of the logistics outsourcing market are as follows:

• Globalization of the world economy. The trend of the global division of labor and the territorial expansion of networks of interaction between manufacturers and suppliers has led to the rapid development of interregional and international cooperation. As a result, the distribution networks of the world's largest enterprises entered new markets, which greatly complicated the logistics flow. That is why logistics outsourcing is the only way to effectively manage international cooperation for enterprises that are not experienced in it.

• Differentiation of demand. Many businesses operate in a competitive environment where efficient logistics management is key to maintaining competitive advantage. Logistics outsourcing makes it possible to meet the growing demands of buyers for the delivery of orders, increases inventory turnover, and maintains a balance between costs and the quality of the service provided without the need to invest in creating their own logistics department.

• Outsourcing as a business model of an enterprise. Logistics outsourcing contributes to the successful development, implementation, and subsequent management of the enterprise's business model by directing resources to the main activity.

• Logistics providers can provide all the logistics resources necessary for the development without additional investments for the successful implementation of the main activity. Additionally, the logistics provider can often track market changes and support the requirements of the integration process, which is beneficial for the enterprise.

DISCUSSION

Currently, when using outsourcing functions in Russia, the following problems arise, which have developed historically and given the specifics of 2022:

- The lack of a regulatory legal framework for the formation of responsibility for the leakage of confidential information and fixed control methods (Trofimova & Budagov, 2021).
- Restriction on the use of foreign outsourcing companies.
- Search for a bona fide service provider in the domestic market and the absence of a single database of verified suppliers.
- Training of professional personnel for Russian outsourcing companies and professional managers for the selection of outsourcing services.
- The lack of unified economic models for the formation of a balanced assessment of financial and organizational costs arising in the process of outsourcing.

CONCLUSION

However, the current situation will make it possible to restart the outsourcing market in Russia. First, it will be possible to restart IT outsourcing and the maintenance market for various equipment and infrastructure, including the operation of commercial real estate. There are at least several reasons for this.

Given the uncertainty in the medium term, the suspension of some projects, and the need to reduce costs, it is likely that the demand for IT specialists will decrease for some time, which is evidenced by the latest labor market research. According to HeadHunter, the number of vacancies in the IT sector decreased by a quarter by the end of March, and the number of resumes increased by 15% (Yasakova, 2022).

This situation will push companies to more actively use outsourcing in IT, at least until the situation with the planning horizon becomes clearer for at least 2–3 years.

The tendency to outsource even more noncore business processes in the near and medium term will grow due to the following reasons:

- The need to reorient costs to key business areas.
- The importance of retaining key employees to ensure the smooth functioning of these areas.

Additionally, some projects, including development, will be put on pause even for large companies in the near future.

On the other hand, there is a renewed trend toward allocating entire departments to optimize costs and the desire to make the receipt of specific services as transparent as possible. This primarily concerns IT departments, which are divided into separate legal entities with the transition to full-fledged service relations.

Another reason for the growing demand for outsourcing, primarily in the maintenance of equipment, will be the reduction of budgets and the inability to purchase new equipment due to sanctions, restrictions, or destruction of supply chains. The trend of the next 2–3 years for many companies will be associated with extending the life of a particular equipment.

This is confirmed by the research of more than 4000 companies servicing medical equipment (Okdesk, 2023). According to this research, 70% of respondents faced the problem of shortage of spare parts. Despite possible difficulties, 85% of respondents believe that the contracts will be fulfilled. In the comments to the question, some respondents explained that there would be no difficulties because spare parts are not included in the contract price. Another option is that it will be proposed to conclude additional agreements with changing the conditions just for the replacement and maintenance of spare parts.

Small businesses will suffer more than others in the current situation. These businesses have no "safety cushion" and opportunity to continue inventing something new in all aspects of their activity. Organizations that want to get out of the current storm will have to focus entirely on the core business and abandon unrelated expenses. On the one hand, together with the automation of processes, this should allow the companies to survive and become more efficient. On the other hand, it will also generate demand for outsourcing in the regions.

The current situation and the growth of requests from large businesses should finally force companies providing professional services to think about the quality of their provision processes. The latter is inextricably linked with their automation and the need to work on SLA, which are dictated by the customer.

In the Russian market of automation of service provision processes, including field service, there are currently unique domestic solutions available even to microbusinesses.

ACKNOWLEDGMENTS

This paper has been supported by the RUDN University Strategic Academic Leadership Program.

REFERENCES

Abramova, A. E. (2016). Outsourcing as a management tool during economic downturns. *Symbol of Science: International Scientific Journal, 5–2*(17), 239–240.

Achaz. (2021). Market for recruitment, provision of personnel and outsourcing 2020. https://achaz.ru/news/news_detail_18_836/. Accessed on 15 October 2023.

Grand View Research. (2023). *Business process outsourcing market size, share & trends analysis report by service type (customer services, finance & accounting), by end-use (IT & telecommunication, BFSI), by region, and segment forecasts, 2023–2030.* https://www.grandviewresearch.com/industry-analysis/business-process-outsourcing-bpo-market. Accessed on 15 October 2023.

International Bank for Reconstruction and Development. (2023). *Who we are.* https://www.worldbank.org/en/who-we-are/ibrd. Accessed on 25 March 2023.

Kurbanov, A. H., & Plotnikov, V. A. (2013). *Outsourcing: History, methodology, practice.* Infra-M.

Laktionova, O. E. (2012). Genesis of outsourcing of corporate finance management functions. *Current Issues in Economic Sciences, 26,* 243–248.

Mirigos. (2022). *Deloitte Global Outsourcing Survey 2022.* https://www.mirigos.com/deloitte-2022-global-outsourcing-survey-insights/. Accessed on 16 April 2023.

Nepochatykh, O. Y. (2020). Socio-economic policy measures adjustment methodology taking into account an indicative approach. *Bulletin of the Academy of Knowledge, 40*(5), 311–317. https://doi.org/10.24412/2304-6139-2020-10635

Okdesk. (2020). *Service among integrators of satellite monitoring and transport.* https://okdesk.ru/uploads/gps-smt_research_2020.pdf. Accessed on 15 October 2023.

Okdesk. (2023). *Service and repair of medical equipment in conditions of disruption of supply chains.* https://okdesk.ru/uploads/okdesk-research-med-equipment-2023.pdf. Accessed on 15 October 2023.

Perepechaeva, E. S., & Simonenko, E. S. (2012). Assessment and management of competitiveness of an industrial enterprise. *Proceedings of the Southwestern State University, 5–2*(44), 298–306.

Peshkova, T., Konik, N. V., Efimova, S., & Rytik, S. (2016). *Outsourcing.* Scientific book.

Russian Federation. (1994). *The Civil Code of the Russian Federation (part one)* (November 30, 1994 No. 51-FZ (as amended December 29, 2017). https://www.consultant.ru/document/cons_doc_LAW_5142/. Accessed on 15 March 2023.

Russian Federation. (2001). *Labor Code of the Russian Federation* (December 30, 2001, as amended February 5, 2018 No. 197-FZ). Moscow, Russia. https://www.consultant.ru/document/cons_doc_LAW_34683/. Accessed on 15 March 2023.

Russoft. (2022, December 2). *The 19th Annual Russoft Study.* https://russoft.org/analytics/19-e-ezhegodnoe-issle-dovanie-russoft-2022-rossijskaya-softvernaya-otrasl. Accessed on 11 April 2023.

TAdviser. (2020, May 5). *The global IT outsourcing market grew by 13% over the year.* https://www.tadviser.ru/index.php/. Accessed on 15 March 2023.

Trofimova, N. N., & Budagov, A. S. (2021). Advantages and disadvantages of outsourcing of key business processes of an enterprise in modern conditions. *Bulletin of the Altai Academy of Economics of Law, 12–1,* 169–174.

Yasakova, E. (2022, April 4). In Russia, the number of vacancies in the IT sector has decreased, and the number of resumes has increased. *RBC Daily.* https://www.rbc.ru/technology_and_media/04/04/2022/6249af479a 79478e68d160ac. Accessed on 15 October 2023.

TÜRKIYE IN THE WORLD TEXTILE MARKET: TRENDS AND PROSPECTS

Olga B. Digilina and Elza R. Gasimova

RUDN University, Russia

ABSTRACT

The research aims to identify the importance of the Republic of Türkiye in the global textile market. The research methodology is based on basic methods of scientific cognition, such as analysis, synthesis, deduction, and induction. From the particular methods used, it is worth highlighting the applicable comparison method. During the research, the authors carried out a content analysis, mainly of scientific works by Turkish scientists and news from the Turkish media. The research object is the global textile industry market. Nowadays, Türkiye faces damaged industrial buildings and an acute labor shortage. The country will need to spend a lot of time and efforts to restore its former production capacity in economically important regions, which will affect the country's export potential. COVID-19 has greatly affected the state of various sectors of the economy; the global textile market is no exception. Unlike other sectors of the economy, the global textile market recovered quickly; by 2021, it had regained its production capacity. In turn, Türkiye was even able to exceed its exports and increase its role in the world market. The country did not have time to reach new heights: on February 6, 2023, several powerful earthquakes occurred in economically important provinces of Türkiye. Most of them are provinces of the expensive the Southeastern Anatolia Project (GAP) project, where 60% of the cotton of all Türkiye is produced, and the population mainly works in the textile industry.

Keywords: Türkiye; international trade; textile industry; world competition; COVID-19; Gaziantep–Kahramanmaras earthquakes

JEL Codes: F18; F63; P52; Q53; Q54

The textile trade has been of great importance in the life of humankind since ancient times. Being one of the first and leading branches of the economy, the textile industry occupies a leading position in the light industry. The changes that have occurred under the influence of globalization have led to the fact that the production of textile product has shifted from

Development of International Entrepreneurship Based on Corporate Accounting and Reporting According to IFRS
Advanced Series in Management, Volume 33B, 91–97
ISSN: 1877-6361/doi:10.1108/S1877-63612024000033B012

developed Western countries toward developing ones. Developed countries have become more specialized in producing expensive and branded textiles, which helps them compete with developing countries in the Asian region. Sufficiently affordable prices for textile products, an increase in the standard of living of consumers, and the dominance of so-called fast fashion have led to high consumption. In recent years, materials in the textile industry have become increasingly synthetic. The process of manufacturing and using such a textile product has a negative impact on the environment. About 70%–80% of textile industry products end up in landfill without a chance for recycling, after which the soil receives a large dose of toxic substances. As a result, humanity is faced with pollution of water bodies and a huge amount of unprocessed waste from the textile industry. The consequences of such consumption can be quite deplorable.

COVID-19 also left an important mark on the textile industry, where manufacturers faced shortages of raw materials and disruption in supply chains. The COVID-19 pandemic has also changed people's tastes and preferences. Consumers began to think about their excessive consumption, preferring to make informed purchases without excess and unnecessary environmental harm. In this context, in the new world of the post-COVID-19 era, eco-textiles and the production of organic cotton as the main raw material of the eco-industry are gaining special importance. India, Türkiye, China, and Kyrgyzstan are the main countries producing organic cotton on the world market. This research aims to identify the importance of Türkiye in the global textile market.

MATERIALS AND METHOD

The research methodology is based on basic methods of scientific cognition, such as analysis, deduction, and induction. From the practical methods used, it is worth highlighting the applicable comparison method. During the research, the authors carried out content analysis, mainly of scientific works of Turkish scientific and Turkish media news. The 10 leading countries' exporters of the textile industry, as well as their share in the world market, are identified (Table 1). The statistical base of the study is the World Trade

Table 1. Top 10 Exporters of the Global Textile Market, 2021 (Billion Dollars).

Exporters	Value	Share in World Exports/Imports		Annual Percentage Change			
	2021	2005	2010	2021	2019	2020	2021
China	146	20.2	30.4	41.4	1	29	−6
EU	73	32.5	25.3	20.9	−6	−3	14
Extra-EU exports	25	11.3	9.0	7.2	−6	−9	16
India	22	4.1	5.1	6.3	−5	−12	48
Türkiye	15	3.5	3.5	4.3	−1	−1	30
USA	13	6.1	4.8	3.7	−3	−15	15
Vietnam	11	0.4	1.2	3.2	10	8	14
Pakistan	9	3.5	3.1	2.6	−4	−8	29
Republic of Korea	9	5.1	4.3	2.5	−7	−15	12
Chinese Taipei	9	4.8	3.8	2.4	−8	−17	21
Japan	6	3.4	2.8	1.8	−2	−14	11
Above 10	313	83.5	84.5	89.0	–	–	–

Source: Compiled by the authors based on World Trade Organization (2022).

Organization (WTO) Report Trade Statistical Review (World Trade Organization, 2022). A special report issued after the earthquake in Kahramanmaras and Hatay (Presidency of Strategy and Budget, 2023), which occurred in 2023, was considered and used separately.

The current state of the world textile market, as well as the Turkish textile market, are studied in the works of Abbate et al. (2023), Bayraktar and Seker (2022), Bulur et al. (2022), Cinar et al. (2023), Çubukcu et al. (2021), Diyrik and Baykal (2022), Dolzhenko (2021), Gürsoy et al. (2023), Guresci (2021), Halife (2022), Karabay and Sariçoban (2021), Lagâri et al. (2021), Ozudogru (2021), Pak et al. (2021), Pal et al. (2021), Puig et al. (2022), Savinov and Dolzhenko (2023), Zengin and Sekmen (2023), and Tokel et al. (2022).

RESULT

The period from 2019 to 2020 was remembered for sharp declines in indicators. By 2021, the global textile market managed to restore export and import potential. China has been a leader in the global textile market for many years. In 2021, China's export of textile amounted to $146 billion, with a share of 41% of total world textile exports (Statista, 2022). As can be seen from the data presented in Table 1, the EU and extra-EU also play an important role in the textile industry as exporters and importers. Countries such as India, Pakistan, and Türkiye distinguished themselves in 2021 exports and were able to perform quite well. The United States is more of an importer in the textile world than an exporter. Their share of imports is 10.2%, which makes $40 billion for 2021 (World Trade Organization, 2022).

Türkiye and other countries have managed to give back to the consequences of the COVID-19 pandemic. In the global textile market, Türkiye ranks fifth in exports and ninth in the import market. In 2021, the volume of textile exports amounted to $15 billion, with a share of 4.5% of total world textile exports. In the textile world, Türkiye occupies a rather honorable position where it seeks to increase its export potential.

There are more than 40,000 textile firms located in the territory of Türkiye; about 4 million workers work in the textile industry. The use of high-tech equipment and the availability of qualified workers makes Turkish textile products demanded and affordable for consumers on the world market. The reason for this effect is the unification of many manufacturers into holdings, where everything for the production process is made in one factory (from threads to finished products). Such independence from external factors increases the country's competitiveness in the global textile market. The main countries importing textile products from Türkiye are Germany, Spain, and the United Kingdom.

Fig. 1 shows selected cities with a high density of jobs in the textile industry and workers insured for them in the form of circles. Consequently, the following cities can be distinguished: Istanbul, Bursa, Tekirdag, Gaziantep, Kahramanmaras, Adana, Kayseri, Denizli, Usak, and Izmir. The share of three cities (Istanbul, Gaziantep, and Bursa) accounts for almost 80%–85% of total textile production. Accordingly, the labor force is concentrated mainly in these important cities for production.

On February 6, 2023, several powerful earthquakes in economically important provinces of Türkiye shocked the whole world. The earthquakes immediately affected three regions: the Mediterranean, Eastern Anatolian, and Southeastern Anatolian. Eleven provinces of Türkiye were mainly affected by the earthquakes: Kahramanmaras, Gaziantep, Adana, Kilis, Hatay, Adiyaman, Sanliurfa, Malatya, Osmaniye, Elazig, and Diyarbakir.

Fig. 1.   Map of Türkiye by the Density of Jobs in the Textile Industry. *Source:*
Compiled by the authors based on Ministry of Industry and Technology of the Republic of
Türkiye (2021).

For the first time after the earthquakes, the production capacity of these territories was
literally paralyzed. Labor is of key importance for production in textile enterprises.
Nowadays, Türkiye is faced with a shortage of labor; about 50% of workers are absent
from their workplaces due to various causes of the consequences of a natural disaster. It is
worth noting the population's morale because many have lost people close to them and
have been wounded. Most of those who could enter production have no roof over their
heads and are forced to live with their families in prepared tents of the rescue forces.
Türkiye has focused all its power on the affected provinces to return people to their usual
lives. Entire residential blocks are being practically rebuilt, and industrial buildings are
being restored.

    Five of the affected provinces are located in the economically important region of
Türkiye, where the GAP project is located. Founded on November 6, 1989, the 34-year-old
GAP project includes all provinces of the Southeastern Anatolian region. As a result of
large-scale investments, the export potential of the region has grown more than 25 times
compared to 2000. For the textile industry, the value of the GAP project lies in the production of 60% of the country's cotton on these lands. The territorial proximity of factories
to the main raw materials of the textile industry is another advantage of the textile industry
of Türkiye.

    One of Türkiye's main trends in recent years has been the tendency to produce
ecologically correct cotton, the so-called organic cotton. This interest is provoked by the
interest of brands and retailers in Turkish organic cotton, which, at an affordable price,
shows high-quality of raw materials. In the post-COVID-19 era, such interest will increase
even more. The textile industry begins to cause environmental damage to nature, already
in the process of producing raw materials. Today's global trends show that only 1%–2% of
cotton grown worldwide is organic.

    The differences in the cultivation and processing of cotton in organic and traditional
industries are sharply different. At the stage of seed selection, the chosen production path
already becomes clear. In organic production, only genetically unmodified cotton seeds are
selected, and the fertilizers used are on natural origin without chemical composition. Toxic
substances such as insecticides and pesticides are not used to control pests and fungi; they
are replaced by different types of traps. Harvesting is also different in the case of organics;
it is exclusively manual harvesting. Further raw material processing is harmless for nature,
the producer, and the consumer. After all, during traditional cotton production, workers

are often poisoned by the toxic agents used in the workplace, a couple with a fatal outcome.

To confirm the fact of compliance with all environmental requirements, international compliance standards issued by independent commissions have been introduced. The main ones are "Global Organic Textile Standard" (GOTS), "Oeko-Tex Standard 100," and "NATURTEXTILE IVN zertifiziert BEST." Türkiye is one of the largest producers of organic cotton in the world (Common Objective, 2021; FAO, 2018). The leading Turkish manufacturers of eco-textiles are "OrganicEra," "Ucak Tekstil," "Polen Tekstil," "Simurg Tasarim Textile Co Ltd," and "Zirve Tekstil."

Cotton is an important fiber in the textile industry. However, the current traditional methods of production are fraught with environmental hazards. The first-ever global analysis of climate risks for cotton production describes how cotton production by traditional methods contributes to climate change. The risk of global warming, erosion of the topsoil, and water pollution with toxic chemicals suggest that the traditional cotton production and textile industry requires radical changes.

DISCUSSION

This scientific study examines the two main existing problems related to the textile industry of the Republic of Türkiye. The first problem related to the global problem of environmental pollution from the textile industry and the risks associated with it have already been studied in depth by many scientists; we already have a fairly expanded concept of the causes and consequences of this problem. However, the second earthquake-related problem is very recent and has not been practically considered in the scientific world. In this research, the authors tried to reveal the current difficult state of the textile industry in Türkiye. They listed the provinces and their importance for this industry. They gave the expected forecasts about the prospects of Türkiye in the world textile market, which they noticed in the process of studying the problem. The results obtained can give an approximate picture of the development of the Turkish textile industry for the next few years.

CONCLUSIONS

China's export potential compared to other countries, including Türkiye, is quite impressive. China remains the main competitor for Türkiye in the global textile market. With an export volume almost 10 times greater than that of Türkiye, China firmly holds the leading position in its hands. Given the rapid trend in increasing the importance of the Republic of Türkiye in the global textile market, it can be concluded that in the coming years, the country will be able to overtake the volume of exports of India, which is not much inferior according to 2021. Moreover, an increase in consumer demand for eco-friendly textile products will open up new opportunities for the country's industrial sector.

Nowadays, Türkiye is faced with damaged industrial buildings and an acute shortage of labor. The country will need to spend a lot of time and effort to restore its former production capacity in economically important regions, which will affect the country's export potential.

REFERENCES

Abbate, S., Centobelli, P., Cherchione, R., Nadeem, S. P., & Riccio, E. (2023). Sustainability trends and gaps in the textile, apparel, and fashion industries. *Environment, Development and Sustainability*. https://doi.org/10.1007/s10668-022-02887-2

Bayraktar, N., & Seker, A. (2022). The power of Turkey in textile export and the dimension of competition with China. *PressAcademia Procedia*, *15*, 54–58. https://doi.org/10.17261/Pressacademia.2022.1577

Bulur, M., Özceylan, E., & Çetinkaya, C. (2022). A study to measure the economic effects of COVID-19 on the textile industry: Comparative evidence from Bursa and Gaziantep. *Journal of Turkish Operations Management*, *6*(2), 1172–1183. https://doi.org/10.56554/jtom.1127585

Cinar, N. E., Abbara, A., & Yilmaz, E. (2023). Earthquakes in Turkey and Syria—Collaboration is needed to mitigate longer terms risks to health. *BMJ*, *380*, 559. https://doi.org/10.1136/bmj.p559

Common Objective. (2021, December 1). *Cotton and sustainable cotton: Key world commodity*. https://www.commonobjective.co/article/cotton-and-sustainable-cotton-key-world-commodity#:~:text=India%20(50%20percent)%2C%20China,of%20global%20organic%20cotton%20production. Accessed on 10 April 2023.

Çubukcu, F., Turkmen, A., & Emsen, Ö. S. (2021). Export oriented or import substitution effects of foreign direct capital investments – A research on Turkish textile industry. *Gaziantep University Journal of Social Sciences*, *20*(4), 1647–1668. https://doi.org/10.21547/jss.907372

Diyrik, B., & Baykal, E. (2022). A qualitative study about internationalization of Turkish textile & clothing industries. *Fibres and Textiles*, *29*(3), 8–21. https://doi.org/10.15240/tul/008/2022-3-002

Dolzhenko, I. B. (2021). Impact of COVID-19 pandemic on international trade in textiles and apparel. *International Journal of Humanities and Natural Sciences*, *1–2*(52), 89–93.

FAO. (2018). *Development of organic agriculture in Central Asia: Proceedings of the international conference*. FAO. https://www.fao.org/3/i8685en/I8685EN.pdf. Accessed on 10 April 2023.

Guresci, E. (2021). A study on the sericulture in Turkey. *ISPEC Journal of Agricultural Sciences*, *5*(4), 890–902. https://doi.org/10.46291/ISPECJASvol5iss4pp890-902

Gürsoy, S., Zeren, F., Kevser, M., Akyol, G., & Tunçel, M. B. (2023). The impact of 2023 Turkey earthquake on Istanbul stock market: Evidence from Fourier Volatility Spillover test. *Social Sciences Research Journal*, *12*(1), 98–105. https://www.researchgate.net/publication/369334694_The_Impact_of_2023_Turkey_Earthquake_on_Istanbul_Stock_Market_Evidence_from_Fourier_Volatility_Spillover_Test. Accessed on 12 April 2023.

Halife, H. (2022). Competitiveness analysis of textile industry of Turkey: Revealed comparative advantage approach. *International Journal of Global Business and Competitiveness*, *17*, 25–30. https://doi.org/10.1007/s42943-022-00062-y

Karabay, G., & Sariçoban, K. (2021). Research on competitiveness in technical textiles: Comparison of countries having the lion's share of technical textile world exports and Turkey. *Fibres and Textiles in Eastern Europe*, *29*(6), 22–31. https://doi.org/10.5604/01.3001.0015.2718

Lagâri, E. C., Erzurumi, A. M., & Tomur, B. F. (2021). Strategic planning and crisis management in textile sector in Turkey. *Journal of Strategic Management*, *5*(4), 1–12. https://doi.org/10.53819/81018102t4023

Ministry of Industry and Technology of the Republic of Turkey. (2021). *Textile apparel and leather goods sectors report 2021*. https://rizetso.org.tr/wp-content/uploads/2022/04/Tekstil-Hazir-Giyim-ve-Deri-Urunleri-Sektorleri-Raporu-2021.pdf. Accessed on 10 February 2023.

Ozudogru, T. (2021). Cotton production economy in the world and Turkey. *Journal of Textiles and Engineer*, *28*(122), 149–161. https://doi.org/10.7216/1300759920212812208

Pak, S., Altilgan, T., & Kanat, S. (2021). Analyzing competitiveness of Denizli home textile sector. *Industria Textila*, *72*(4), 378–387. https://doi.org/10.35530/IT.072.04.1805

Pal, U., Rycerz, A., & Linares, Á. (2021). *Physical climate risk for global cotton production: Global analysis*. WTW. https://www.wtwco.com/en-EG/Insights/campaigns/cotton-2040#analysis. Accessed on 17 February 2023.

Presidency of Strategy and Budget. (2023). *Kahramanmaras and Hatay earthquake report 2023*. https://www.sbb.gov.tr/wp-content/uploads/2023/03/2023-Kahramanmaras-ve-Hatay-Depremleri-Raporu.pdf. Accessed on 10 April 2023.

Puig, F., Cantarero, S., & Verdone, F. (2022). Coronavirus versus the textile industry: Cluster lessons for future challenges. *Fashion and Textiles*, *9*, 10. https://doi.org/10.1186/s40691-021-00284-3

Savinov, Y. A., & Dolzhenko, I. B. (2023). Trends in international textile trade in the post-COVID era. *Russian Foreign Economic Bulletin*, *2*, 102–112. https://doi.org/10.24412/2072-8042-2023-2-102-112

Statista. (2022). China's share of global textile export value in selected years between 2000 and 2021. https://www.statista.com/statistics/1204126/china-share-of-global-textile-exports/. Accessed on 10 April 2023.

Tokel, D., Dogan, I., Hocaoglu-Ozyigit, A. & Ozyigit, I. I. (2022). Cotton agriculture in Turkey and worldwide economic impacts of Turkish cotton. *Journal of Natural Fibers*, *19*(15), 10648–10667. https://doi.org/10.1080/15440478.2021.2002759

World Trade Organization. (2022). *World Trade Statistical Review 2022*. WTO. https://www.wto.org/english/res_e/booksp_e/wtsr_2022_e.pdf. Accessed on 2 March 2023.

Zengin, M., & Sekmen, M. (2023). Trends and future perspective of occupational accidents in the Turkish textile industry between 2011–2020. *Journal of Textile and Engineer*, *30*(129), 61–70. https://doi.org/10.7216/teksmuh.1272286

CHINA IN THE RUSSIAN AUTOMOTIVE MARKET

Daria S. Sokolan and Nikolay D. Keosya

RUDN University, Russia

ABSTRACT

The research aims to assess the Russian automobile market before and after the imposition of sanctions, analyze the positions of Chinese automobile brands in the Russian market, and assess trends and prospects for the development of China's presence in this segment. The authors use the statistical method and the method of comparative analysis to determine the position of Chinese automakers in the Russian automotive market. The research determines that most Western and Japanese brands left the Russian market due to the strengthening of sanctions in 2022. Due to problems in the supply of components and spare parts, most of the Russian automotive market was filled with Chinese automobile companies planning to expand their presence. This research examines the trend of the presence of Chinese automobile brands in the automotive industry of Russia. Under sanctions, the economy of the Russian Federation is forced to look for other opportunities to develop technology and production. The relevance of this topic is due to the significant role of the automotive industry in the economy of any country, as well as the importance of this industry for the employment of the able-bodied population. To achieve this goal, the authors formulated the tasks to assess the automotive market before and after the imposition of sanctions, to analyze the Chinese automotive market, and to assess the prospects for its development in Russia.

Keywords: Automotive; automakers; sanctions; automotive market; market share; premium cars; car dealer

JEL Codes: G01; L9; Q24

After the sanctions were imposed, the economy of the Russian Federation adapted to the new conditions on the world market and opened up new opportunities for the development of automotive production. Considering the significant role of the automotive industry in the country's economy, the employment of the working population, the creation of new production technologies and their optimization, and the creation of joint factories with

Development of International Entrepreneurship Based on Corporate Accounting and Reporting According to IFRS
Advanced Series in Management, Volume 33B, 99–106
Copyright © 2024 Daria S. Sokolan and Nikolay D. Keosya
Published under exclusive licence by Emerald Publishing Limited
ISSN: 1877-6361/doi:10.1108/S1877-63612024000033B013

foreign countries and manufacturers, the impact of sanctions entails significant changes in all processes related to the production and development of the automobile.

The research aims to investigate the Russian automotive market before and after the introduction of sanctions, determine the position of Chinese manufacturers in the Russian automotive market, and assess trends and prospects for the development of China's presence in this market.

METHODOLOGY

During the research, the authors used general scientific methods, a method for analyzing a large amount of statistical data, and a graphical method for systematizing data on the automotive industry and visualizing the results. Additionally, the authors used the data grouping method. A statistical method and comparison were used to determine the importance of China in the automotive industry of the Russian Federation. For the study, the author used the works of Russian authors and statistical data from several Russian analytical agencies.

RESULTS

Many foreign brands left Russia or suspended car sales to the Russian market in 2022. Their share in the Russian market is now increasingly occupied by Chinese companies. Many of them are developing specific plans to expand penetration into the Russian market for 2023 and beyond.

In the early 2000s, the purchasing power of the population in Russia increased compared to the purchasing power in the 1990s. In the 1990s, Russian companies were the main producers in the automotive industry of Russia; such plants as Volga Automobile Plant (VAZ), Gorky Automobile Plant (GAZ), Ulyanovsk Automobile Plant (UAZ), and *Kamskiy* Automobile Plant (KAMAZ) operated successfully. The main competitors of the Russian automotive industry were foreign cars that were in use and brought mainly from Europe and the United States for the central and western parts of Russia. The eastern part of Russia mainly brought cars from Japan due to its territorial proximity and low prices. In July 2002, the government signed a concept for the development of the domestic auto-motive industry until 2010 (Juraev et al., 2022). The main goal of this concept was the integration of the Russian automotive industry into the global automotive industry, including the production of equipment that meets international safety and environmental standards. The concept also meant the development of the automotive industry with the participation of foreign capital and gradual integration into the world market.

In October 2002, measures were taken for imported foreign cars older than 7 years. The measures implied an increase in the tariff on these cars, which led to an increase in demand for new cars. These measures allowed the government to open the Russian market for the world's leading manufacturers at the beginning of the 2000s and increase the demand for new cars manufactured in Russia. Having limited the pressure on the market with used foreign cars, the government adopted an "Industrial assembly" concept. Industrial assembly meant a localization of 30% of production and included processes such as welding, body painting, and various car assembly operations. In the 2000s, fac-tories of automobile concerns (e.g., Volkswagen, Skoda, BMW, Ford, Renault, and Toyota) were opened in Russia. Since 2002, the production of foreign cars has begun to grow. The Renault–Nissan–Mitsubishi alliance has signed an agreement with the Russian company AvtoVAZ LLC on the joint use of the concern's production facilities.

The appearance of Chinese manufacturers on the territory of the Russian Federation has led to the emergence of new major players in the automotive market. In the early years of the emergence of Chinese companies, it cannot be called significant or significant for the market. The share of Chinese cars in 2007 was 3.1%. This was a year before the global financial crisis. By 2010, the share was reduced to 1%. The price of Chinese brand cars was significantly higher than their closest competitors. However, this factor could not influence the choice of consumers for several reasons. The first reason is distrust of new car brands. The second reason is the lack of a well-established spare parts supply system. The third reason is the lack of an established warranty service.

In 2014–2015, there was an increase in competition among automobile manufacturers. Rising prices, the emergence of new models from major market players, the formation of consumer preferences, competition between sellers, the fight for customers, new loyalty programs, and the development of car loans led to a difficult environment for Chinese companies. In such a strong competition, the Ford company left the market in 2018. The lack of consumer demand and high prices for cars led to the company's withdrawal from the Russian market. In a highly competitive environment, customer loyalty is a key factor for growth.

In 2019, the global automotive industry was affected by the crisis associated with the spread of COVID-19, which led to massive morbidity and mortality, causing a partial or, in some cases, complete shutdown of production in the automotive and other industries.

As a result of the demand for computers, televisions, and game consoles, noted during the COVID-19 pandemic, when most enterprises and firms transferred workers to a remote type of work, there was a crisis of semiconductors that are used not only in home appliances and computers but also for car electronics control units and software security.

The main problem with the shortage of microchips was a state of trade confrontation between the United States and China. Thus, the US authorities imposed restrictions on the Chinese manufacturer Semiconductor Manufacturing International (SMIC), which was a leader in the production of microelectronics, particularly semiconductors. A ban was imposed on the export of the company's products, which included restrictions on the purchase of equipment and the sale of chips for American companies.

The vacant place in the American market was taken by Taiwan Semiconductor Manufacturing (TSMC), which is also engaged in the production of semiconductors and is the main competitor of SMIC, which led to a change in supply chains, which, in turn, affected the availability of the chips themselves.

Companies engaged in the production of computer equipment (e.g., Huawei) and companies engaged in the production of cars were ready for problems with the absence and complication of the delivery of semiconductors and made purchases of equipment in advance, which led to a shortage of semiconductors with increasing demand and declining production.

In 2020, due to the limited number of semiconductors and the problem with their delivery and transportation, many companies limited their production capacities, and new market leaders appeared in the face of Chinese companies.

The first half of 2022 was a period of great trials for the Russian automotive industry. Due to the sanctions imposed by the West, the import of certain automotive components was directly prohibited, and the supply of others became impossible due to the disruption of logistics chains (Belov & Karpova, 2022).

Table 1. Russian Car Market in January 2023 – Data on Brands.

No.	Car Brand	January, 23		January, 22		Changes, %
		Amount	Proportion, %	Amount	Proportion, %	
1	LADA	17,635	38.99	16,210	18.86	8.8
2	CHERY	5,518	12.2	2,699	3.14	104.4
3	HAVAL	4,116	9.1	2,842	3.31	44.8
4	GEELY	3,465	7.66	1,766	2.06	96.2
5	KIA	2,295	5.07	11,745	13.67	−80.5
6	EXEED	1,807	4	436	0.51	314.4
7	HYUNDAI	1,542	3.41	8,967	10.43	−82.8
8	OMODA	1,187	2.62			
9	TOYOTA	992	2.19	6,501	7.57	−84.7
10	RENAULT	714	1.58	8,921	10.38	−92
11	MITSUBISHI	666	1.47	2,068	2.41	−67.8
12	YAZ	647	1.43	1,211	1.41	−46.6
13	VOLKSWAGEN	557	1.23	3,574	4.16	−84.4
14	BMW	369	0.82	2,236	2.6	−83.5
15	SKODA	367	0.81	4,170	4.85	−91.2
16	MAZDA	354	0.78	1,990	2.32	−82.2
17	MERCEDES-BENZ	327	0.72	1,985	2.31	−83.5
18	JAC	307	0.68	69	0.08	344.9
19	CHANGAN	297	0.66	232	0.27	28
20	GREAT WALL	268	0.59	27	0.03	892.6
21	NISSAN	241	0.53	3,113	3.62	−92.3
22	AUDI	151	0.33	680	0.79	−77.8
23	LEXUS	111	0.25	638	0.74	−82.6
24	FAW	98	0.22	53	0.06	84.9
25	LAND ROVER	93	0.21	380	0.44	−75.5
	Total for Russia	*45,231*	*100*	*85,392*	*100*	*−47.4*

Source: Compiled by the authors based on Loboda (2023).

According to Table 1, Lada retained first place with dynamics of 8.8% and a share of 39% (Loboda, 2023). The other former leaders continue to fall: Kia became fifth, Hyundai – seventh, Toyota – ninth, and Renault – tenth. Most likely, their situation will not get any better.

There are now three Chinese brands in the top 5 and five Chinese brands in the top 10. Four more brands managed to break into the top 25. All companies recorded sales growth except Omoda (perhaps because these machines began to be sold in Russia only at the end of 2022). Chery, with its sub-brands, has already acquired a share of 18.8%. This is almost half of all sales of Chinese cars in January (Timerkhanov, 2023a).

In the model standings, the traditional leaders are several Lada models. The main Chinese bestseller of 2022 – Chery Tiggo 7 Pro – retains its status now not only among "compatriots" but also among all foreign cars. Geely Coolray also made its way into the top 5. Next on the list are almost all Chinese cars. The first car not from Russia or China in the top 25 – the Kia Sportage crossover – takes 15th place.

According to data from the Russian analytical agency "Autostat," which you can see on Fig. 1, sales of passenger cars of Chinese brands in Russia increased sharply from

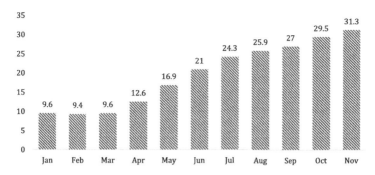

Fig. 1. Dynamics of Growth of the Share of Sales of Chinese Automakers in the Automotive Market of Russia. *Source:* Compiled by the authors based on Analytical Agency Autostat (n.d.).

8,235 units in January 2022 to 16,138 units in November 2022 (the market share increased from 9.6% to 31.3%). The best-selling brands were Haval, Chery, and Geely (Timerkhanov, 2023a).

After February 2022, the majority of Western automakers occupying a significant share of the Russian market (Renault, Mercedes, BMW, Toyota, and others) ceased their activities in Russia (Belov & Karpova, 2022).

In the near future, if Western brands do not return, Chinese sales could account for 35% of all car sales in Russia. In monetary terms, this share may exceed 40% of what is projected to be 1.5 trillion rubles in the market in 2023.

During 2023, Chinese automakers based in Russia intend to release a series of premium cars. Many car factories in Russia will also return to work after several months of downtime due to uncertain market conditions.

According to an analytical note by Silk Road Briefing, leading Chinese companies are developing particular plans to increase their presence in the Russian market for the period up to 2025 and beyond. The rapid departure of major European original equipment manufacturers (OEMs) has led to the conclusion of deals in which competitors can buy up production capacity at low prices, which has led to a large number of mergers and acquisitions.

Of Russia's sectors, the automotive industry was the most affected by the sanctions imposed against the country. By the end of 2022, production recovered slightly as Russian factors adapted to the new realities. However, production remains lower by more than 60% year-on-year.

Kaliningrad Avtotor, which previously assembled BMW, Hyundai, and Kia, has signed an agreement with new partners – with strong rumors about the Chinese manufacturers DongFeng and BAIC. Details are expected in the second quarter of 2023. The company has already started the test assembly of new cars.

The Chinese manufacturer Chery has already established itself well in Russia and is going to announce expansion plans this year. From January 1, sales of the Chery Tiggo 7 Pro Max, an upgraded version of the popular crossover, will begin in Russia.

This car will have a modified appearance and interior, more options, the same powertrain, and only front-wheel drive. However, they also promise a more powerful engine and an all-wheel drive transmission later this year.

With the Arrizo 8 sedan, Chery plans to enter a new market segment and start selling a hybrid with a gasoline engine and two electric engines in Russia.

Exeed, the premium brand of Chery, is also planning a complete update of the model range. This will include a completely new model of 2023 – a coupe – a different crossover, presented in China under the name Yaoguang. This is the first model on a modernized platform and in a new brand style.

The third Chinese car company in Russia is Geely, which has recertified the long-awaited Monjaro crossover, which should go on sale in Russia at the beginning of the year.

For a medium-sized car, a two-liter turbo motor (238 hp) is provided, paired with an eight-speed automatic. Monjaro is planned to be imported from China. Inexpensive Geely Emgrand 7 sedans will be assembled in Belarus for the Russian market.

Other brands that have not previously been active in the Russian market are also becoming more active.

Changan is a state-owned automobile manufacturer headquartered in Jiangbei, Chongqing. Founded in 1862, it is the oldest automaker in China. In the second half of 2022, the company increased its presence in the Russian market by introducing its Uni-K crossover. At the end of 2022, the company began selling restyled versions of its CS55 Plus and CS35 Plus crossovers.

Another novelty on the Russian market is the Chinese Livan, the heir to the once-popular Lifan, which went bankrupt and was reacquired after Geely acquired the company.

Currently, the first model of the brand is undergoing certification for Russia. This is a small crossover X3 Pro with a 1.5-liter engine with a power of 113 hp, which is equipped with a manual gearbox or variator.

In 1958, Hongqi released the first car produced in China. This car was assembled entirely by its own production forces in China. FAW Group Corp. Ltd. owns Hongqi. This company plans to produce premium-class cars; two models have already received certificates in Russia. The first model is a large (5,137 mm) premium sedan H9. It is planned to supply a basic car with a two-liter engine (245 hp), a robotized gearbox, and rear-wheel drive to Russia. Simultaneously, a more expensive version with an elongated wheelbase and a V6 engine is available in China. This is a medium-sized Hongqi HS5 crossover with a two-liter engine, a six-speed automatic, and all-wheel drive. Hongqi cars will be distributed by FAW Eastern Europe, which already supplies FAW vehicles.

DISCUSSION

According to Fig. 2, in sales of new cars, domestic brands today occupy 41%, Chinese – 38%, Korean – 9%, European and Japanese – 6% each, and American – less than 1%. Most likely, the ratio of Russian and Chinese brands will remain approximately at a comparable level until the end of the year (Government of the Russian Federation, 2002).

Chinese cars surpassed Russian sales in the last week of the winter month. From February 20 to February 26, Russians purchased 4,663 new Chinese passenger cars, which corresponds to 41.6% of the total volume. The second place is occupied by domestic cars (4,552 units) with a share of 40.7%.

According to forecasts of the results of 2023, the share of Chinese cars sold in Russia will increase. In January, cars from China occupied about 60% of the Moscow and St. Petersburg markets. The positive dynamics of the sale of Chinese cars remained in

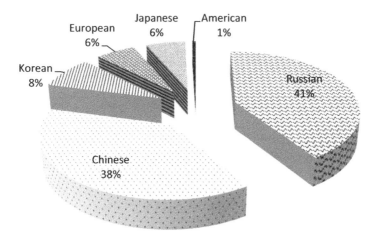

Fig. 2.   Structure of the Russian Automobile Market at the Beginning of 2023. *Source:*
Compiled by the authors based on Timerkhanov (2023b).

February 2023: in the last week of the month, Russians purchased 4,663 new cars from China, which accounted for almost 42% of all sales. However, these cars are presented in one-piece copies and are usually made to order by specific customers. Therefore, despite the fact that Russians spent about 112 billion rubles on the purchase of new cars in January 2023, most of them went to purchase Chinese cars.

Experts do not exclude that cars hailing from China may eventually gain superiority in the market of Russia, even over the products of the Russian automotive industry.

The share of Chinese cars in the market is growing and will continue to increase. In fact, they occupy the niche that was vacated by manufacturers from countries that supported anti-Russian sanctions. Chinese cars are quite competitive in price and quality, which allows them to displace Russian manufacturers who are now experiencing difficulties with components. Korean manufacturers, who did not leave the Russian market, are also strengthening their positions.

Brands from Europe, Japan, and other countries that supported the sanctions against the Russian Federation will continue to remain outsiders. However, thanks to parallel imports, their presence in the Russian car market will remain.

On the one hand, Russian conveyors will increase the pace (some, like LADA Vesta NG, will launch again). On the other hand, Chinese brands will continue to expand the range, including through the budget segment of sedans. Brands not previously presented in the Russian Federation should be connected to this. At the end of January, according to "Autostat," domestic brands occupied 41% of new car sales, Chinese – 38%, Korean – 9%, European and Japanese – 6% each, and American – less than 1%. Chinese brands are interested in increasing their sales in the Russian Federation, as well as in bringing new brands to the Russian market.

Sales volumes of Chinese cars on the Russian market in 2023 increased from 10% to 38%, including due to the departure of European brands. In the future, manufacturers from China plan to increase their presence in Russia. Demand for European, Korean, and Japanese cars will continue. It is expected that their supplies will increase to some extent due to parallel imports. Nevertheless, there will be a shortage of cars of some foreign brands. The share of American cars in the Russian Federation previously did not exceed 1%. Thus, there are no significant changes in this segment. There are offers on the market of new cars that were not there before. Sales of electric vehicles increased by 33% compared to 2021 and amounted to 3,000 units. Simultaneously, the share of electric cars in the Russian Federation accounts for 0.5% of the total volume of the car market. In Moscow, this figure reaches 1%. Sales of electric vehicles are expected to grow. From 2025, automakers plan to supply more than 50,000 electric cars per year to the Russian market. Additionally, there is an increase in demand for crossovers in Russia. The market may also expand due to the supply of cars from Iran. In 2022, a new trend has emerged – the service life of cars with mileage presented by official dealers has exceeded 7 years.

CONCLUSION

Thus, it was determined that due to the withdrawal from the Russian automotive market in 2022 of many foreign brands, as well as problems with the supply of components and spare parts that arose as a result of increased sanctions, Chinese car companies are rapidly entering their place, planning to increase their presence in up to 50% of the Russian automotive industry in the near future. However, Russia should be careful with Chinese brands because the further increase in the share of Chinese brands will lead to an increase in the industry's dependence on China. Against this background, the Russian auto industry will suffer. Russia needs to promote the idea of car joint ventures with Chinese brands.

REFERENCES

Analytical Agency Autostat. (n.d.). *Official website.* https://китайскиеĸавтомобилиħрф/2023/02/03/rossijskij-avtorynok-v-yanvare-2023/. Accessed on 10 April 2023.

Belov, A. S., & Karpova, E. G. (2022). Consequences of anti-Russian sanctions for the domestic automotive market. *Theory and Practice of Social Development, 12*(178), 16–20. https://doi.org/10.24158/tipor.2022.12.1

Government of the Russian Federation. (2002). *Order "On approval of the concept for the development of the Russian automobile industry" (July 16, 2002 No. 978-r).* https://base.garant.ru/184706/. Accessed on March 5 2023.

Juraev, A. D., Sklyar, V. D., & Yankovsky, P. S. (2022). Economic sanctions of 2022 against Russia: Decisions taken, consequences and prospects. *Economy and Business: Theory and Practice, 6–1*(88), 133–136. https://doi.org/10.24412/2411-0450-2022-6-1-133-136

Loboda, V. (2023, February 2). *The market of new passenger cars in January 2023. Top 25 makes and models.* Analytical Agency Autostat. https://www.autostat.ru/press-releases/53779/. Accessed on 10 April 2023.

Timerkhanov, A. (2023a, January 11). *In 2022, Russians purchased a record number of Chinese cars.* Analytical Agency Autostat. https://www.autostat.ru/news/53574/. Accessed on 10 April 2023.

Timerkhanov, A. (2023b, February 27). *Chinese cars became the most popular in the Russian Federation in the last week of February.* Analytical Agency Autostat. https://www.autostat.ru/news/53976/. Accessed on 10 April 2023.

MARKETING EFFECTIVENESS OF RUSSIAN COMMERCIAL BANKS: METHODOLOGICAL APPROACHES AND QUANTITATIVE METRICS

Natalya I. Bykanova

Belgorod State National Research University, Russia

ABSTRACT

The research aims to determine the directions for developing marketing strategies of state commercial banks based on quantitative metrics for evaluating the effectiveness of the marketing activities of banks adapted for the banking sector. During the research, the author applied the methods of terminological, structural, and logical analysis, analogy, synthesis, system analysis, methods of generalization and grouping, table and graphic methods, economic and statistical methods, and methods of dynamic and logical analysis. The result of this research is the systematization of existing theoretical and methodological approaches to calculating the effectiveness of marketing activities in a bank, as well as the calculation of the author's methodology for assessing the main, innovative, and total effectiveness of marketing activities in leading Russian banks. The methodology for assessing the quantitative indicators of a bank's marketing effectiveness has been improved, which consists of the indicators of the effectiveness of fixed costs for marketing in the bank and considers unforeseen expenses caused by the bank's innovative activity related to challenges of time and digital transformation.

Keywords: Banking marketing; commercial bank; marketing activities; marketing strategy; marketing effectiveness; banking market

JEL Codes: M31; G21; F63; J15; J61; O15

Marketing effectiveness is a fundamental indicator of the activities of commercial banks, showing the degree of achievement of the goals set for the marketing service. Marketing is undoubtedly an essential area of the bank's strategic management because suitable marketing activities may increase its competitiveness in the market, enlarge market share,

Development of International Entrepreneurship Based on Corporate Accounting and Reporting According to IFRS
Advanced Series in Management, Volume 33B, 107–113
ISSN: 1877-6361/doi:10.1108/S1877-63612024000033B014

expand the client base, and form a positive image and reputation for the bank. Therefore, effectiveness is a defining characteristic of all processes occurring in the bank.

The marketing effectiveness of a commercial bank should be assessed through the prism of consumer satisfaction. Thus, the evaluation should be subject to their reactions and actions under the influence of marketing activities. The bank's marketing activity is obliged to ensure the constant sale of bank products, its gradual increase, and stimulation of frequency and size of the sale. On this basis, the bank will be able to increase sales volumes and improve the economic indicators of its economic activity.

MATERIALS AND METHODS

To form theoretical and methodological aspects regarding the research object, the author used the analogy method (to identify general characteristics of marketing activities in the views of various authors) and the synthesis method (to identify distinctive characteristics in the definitions of the definition of marketing activity). Using the system analysis method, the work substantiates a conceptual approach to developing banks' marketing activities. To display quantitative indicators of the activities of commercial banks in Russia for a certain period, the author applied the grouping method. To justify changes in these indicators, the author used the generalization method. Consequently, tabular and graphical methods were used to visually express the results obtained. The economic-statistical method and the method of dynamic analysis made it possible to assess the effectiveness of the marketing activities of leading banks in the Russian Federation.

The information basis for the research includes textbooks, monographs, manuals of foreign and Russian researchers on the issue, statistical reporting, and financial results of banks for 2018–2022. The author processed data processing using advanced information technology and Microsoft Word and Excel software.

Marketing effectiveness is an indicator showing the ability of marketing activities to provide a continuous process of the reproduction of demand for goods and services at a given level of marketing costs. To determine the marketing effectiveness of Russian commercial banks, it is advisable to refer to the works of Russian and foreign scientists on this issue that are available at https://figshare.com/ with the identifier https://doi.org/10.6084/m9.figshare.24424615.

The analysis of the above concepts regarding the content of the definition of the effectiveness of an organization's marketing activities has shown a lack of unity of views in the scientific literature. The lack of development of classification criteria for marketing effectiveness in relation to banking activities indicates the difficulty of determining the quantitative effect as a result of marketing activities.

RESULTS

Based on the conducted research on determining approaches to evaluating bank marketing, we can say that quantitative indicators of marketing activities are currently the most used criteria for marketing effectiveness in Russian practice.

Based on the methodology of Jeffrey (2013), the author proposed an adapted methodology for calculating quantitative indicators of the effectiveness of marketing activities in a bank. Quantitative indicators of the bank's marketing effectiveness are available at https://figshare.com/ with the identifier https://doi.org/10.6084/m9.figshare.24424729.

The main feature of the author's methodology, which complements existing methods for assessing quantitative indicators of the effectiveness of marketing activities, is that, unlike in other organizations, in a bank, it is necessary to consider not only fixed marketing costs but also unforeseen ones. The author defines unforeseen costs as additional costs that the bank must incur in connection with the overall digital transformation (i.e., the costs of innovation and its positioning).

Consequently, to assess the marketing approaches of doing banking business, it is advisable to assess the effectiveness of the marketing expenses of Russian banks. This will help determine the amount of marketing spending by banks and how this affects the attractiveness and profitability of their products and services. Let us present the initial statistical data regarding the activities of banks in 2018–2022 in Table 1.

DISCUSSION

Using formulas for calculating the effectiveness of the marketing activities in the bank from the table available at https://figshare.com/ with the identifier https://doi.org/10.6084/m9.figshare.24424729 and data from Table 1, let us calculate the effectiveness indicators of the marketing activities of the three analyzed banks and present them in Fig. 1.

The activities of public joint stock company (PJSC) Sberbank are focused on innovative development in the digital environment, which is accompanied by innovative marketing activities regarding the development and growth of the number of components of the marketing mix from 4 Ps to 12 Ps. Ef_{BMAm} is a low-component marketing mix oriented within the 4 Ps, which has relatively low success rates. This circumstance is confirmed by the bank's high activity in promoting its products and services (Ef_{BMAin} – effectiveness of the innovative bank's marketing activities), which generates significant profit for the bank. The sum of the indicators of effectiveness of the main and innovative bank's marketing activities makes up the Ef_{BMA} indicator (total marketing effectiveness), which is characterized by the high efficiency of funds spent on marketing during 2018–2021.

However, the events of 2022 significantly affected the bank's financial condition. Despite the leading position of PJSC Sberbank in marketing activities, it is characterized by a negative indicator Ef_{BMA}, which is equal to $-77,054.97$ billion rubles. This means that the bank's expenses on marketing in 2022, which is 10 billion rubles, have not led to the expected results. Nevertheless, the effectiveness of the innovative bank's marketing activities (Ef_{BMAin}) has a positive result of 74,274.19 billion rubles even in this period.[1]

The analysis of PJSC Sberbank shows that its marketing strategy focused on innovative development and a multicomponent complex will contribute to maintaining and preserving the bank's position in the banking sector of Russia and increasing its financial performance.

VTB Bank (Foreign Trade Bank – in Russian, VTB) (PJSC) is the leader in the amount of marketing expenses, which amounted to 22.6 billion rubles in 2022 (Central Bank of the Russian Federation, 2022b). Unlike PJSC Sberbank, the activity of VTB Bank (PJSC) is focused not on the financial supermarket but on the main banking activity, which is the development of banking products and services (Buryak et al., 2023). This is confirmed by

---

[1] Data are calculated by the author based on the methodology of M. Jeffrey. Quantitative indicators of the bank's marketing effectiveness are available at https://figshare.com/ with the identifier https://doi.org/10.6084/m9.figshare.24424729. Data from the Central Bank of the Russian Federation (2022a, 2022d) were used for the calculation.

Table 1. Initial Data of Leading Banks for Assessing the Marketing Effectiveness in 2018–2022, Billion Rubles.

Bank	Year	$V_{p/s}^{bp}$	$V_{p/s}^{ep}$	$\Delta V_{p/s}$	Total Assets at the End of the Period	C_{MA}	C_{wf}	C_{BMA}	$V_{p/s(in)}$	$C_{m.res.}$	$C_{str.}$	C_{MC}	Marketing Costs (C_{BMA} + $C_{m.res.}$ + $C_{str.}$ + C_{MC})
Sberbank	2018	23,633,271.4	27,132,447.2	3,499,175.8	27,356,547.2	2.33	0.94	3.27	224,100	0.46	0.17	0.8	4.7
	2019	27,356,547.2	28,697,097.2	1,340,550	28,973,297.2	2.98	1.03	4.01	276,200	0.52	0.17	0.9	5.6
	2020	28,973,297.2	34,689,086.6	5,715,789.4	35,037,786.6	2.06	1.51	3.57	348,700	0.48	0.14	1.11	5.3
	2021	35,037,786.6	38,552,335.2	3,514,548.6	38,812,535.2	5.8	1.4	7.2	260,200	0.756	0.224	1.42	9.6
	2022	38,812,535.2	37,674,539.9	−1137995.3	37,858,739.9	6.1	1.42	7.52	184,200	0.86	0.184	1.436	10
VTB Bank	2018	9,353,664.7	13,775,289.4	4,421,624.7	13,832,231.4	4.04	0.56	4.6	56,942	2.3	0.8	3.1	10.8
	2019	13,832,231.4	14,425,365.1	593,133.7	14,483,875.1	4.64	0.7	5.34	58,510	2.6	0.96	3.4	12.3
	2020	14,483,875.1	16,789,483.7	2,305,608.6	16,860,503.7	4.9	0.7	5.6	71,020	3.1	1.1	5.2	15
	2021	16,860,503.7	19,455,385.5	2,594,881.8	19,531,685.5	7.02	0.66	7.68	76,300	3.2	1.32	4.8	17
	2022	19,531,685.5	19,101,605.3	−430080.2	19,152,805.3	9.61	0.93	10.54	51,200	4.1	1.56	6.4	22.6
Rosselkhozbank	2018	3,117,836.2	326,946.2	−2790890	327,767.205	1.12	0.1	1.22	821	0.5	0.08	0.2	2
	2019	327,767.205	3,297,073.4	2,969,306.2	3,297,821.4	0.96	0.08	1.04	748	0.42	0.1	0.14	1.7
	2020	3,297,821.4	3,840,583.35	542,761.95	3,841,315.35	1.08	0.06	1.14	732	0.31	0.03	0.12	1.6
	2021	3,841,315.35	4,142,305.9	300,990.55	4,142,947.9	0.86	0.08	0.94	642	0.28	0.03	0.2	1.45
	2022	4,142,947.9	4,243,192.1	100,244.2	4,243,815.1	0.859	0.081	0.94	623	0.25	0.03	0.18	1.4

Source: Compiled by the author based on Banki.ru (2023), Central Bank of the Russian Federation (2022a, 2022b, 2022c, 2022d), and Vaganova et al. (2019).

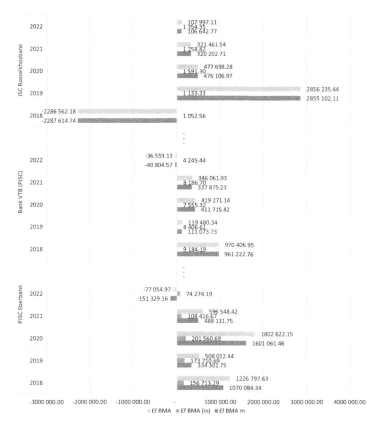

Fig. 1. Dynamics of Indicators of Marketing Effectiveness of PJSC Sberbank, of Bank VTB (PJSC), of JSC Rosselkhozbank for 2018–2022, Billion Rubles. *Source:* Calculated and built by the author.

the high efficiency of marketing expenses for developing core and innovative activities and increasing the elements of the marketing mix to 8 Ps. The dynamics of VTB Bank (PJSC) marketing performance indicators are as follows. The Ef_{BMAin} indicator (effectiveness of the innovative bank's marketing activities) of VTB Bank (PJSC) has a positive trend without a jump effect. Only the results of 2022 show some decrease. The result of such marketing strategy of VTB Bank (PJSC) is approximately equal performance of the Ef_{BMAm} indicator (effectiveness of the main bank's marketing activities) and the Ef_{BMA} indicator (total effectiveness of the bank's marketing activities) throughout 2018–2022. A significant decline in these indicators is observed in 2019 and 2022. The bank has a high development potential despite the restrictions on its activities due to sanctions. The forecasted results of the financial activity of VTB Bank (PJSC) for 2023 and 2024 will have positive dynamics at the level of 2021 (Tokareva, 2023) due to the bank's chosen policy focused on banking business and marketing strategy, focused on innovation in the field of promotion of banking products and services, unlike PJSC Sberbank, which has refocused its activities as a credit institution to a financial supermarket.

As for JSC Rosselkhozbank, the conservative marketing strategy and the low-component marketing mix in the bank leads to a reduction in marketing costs and the effectiveness of marketing activities in general. Thus, since 2019, the effectiveness of the main bank's marketing activities (Ef_{BMAm}) in JSC Rosselkhozbank has been declining; the effectiveness of the innovative bank's marketing activities (Ef_{BMAin}) has slight fluctuations.

As a result, the financial condition of JSC Rosselkhozbank, which occupies one of the leading positions in the Russian banking sector, is provided only by the specialization of the bank, state support, and expensive transactions with certain bank customers in the field of its specific activity.

However, if JSC Rosselkhozbank would pay more attention to marketing research and promotion of its products and services not only in the areas of its specialization (an example is 2018–2019 when the bank was one of the first to offer the refinancing service to legal entities and individuals, which contributed to the growth in the effectiveness of the bank's marketing activities (Ef_{BMA}) from 2,286,562.18 billion rubles in 2018 to 2,856,235.44 billion rubles in 2019), then its position in the rating of Russian banks would have increased significantly.[2]

CONCLUSION

Based on the assessment of the effectiveness of the marketing activities of leading Russian banks, the author can conclude that the marketing strategies of credit organizations of various types are quite effective. The considered banks use different strategies for doing banking business. However, each bank shows a positive effect, not counting the difficult events of 2022, which became a turning point in the functioning of the economy not only for Russia but for the whole world (Jeffrey, 2013, p. 80). However, observing the effect shown by the activities of banks in the context of digital transformation in promoting innovative and main banking products and services, the author can say that the subsequent stages of the development of the banking market and the economy as a whole are capable of achieving the same performance results and even more.

The marketing strategies of PJSC Sberbank and VTB Bank (PJSC) are considered the most effective in promoting their products and services among target customers and building strong relationships with them. The analyzed banks have a strong marketing strategy based on understanding the needs of their customers and building strong relationships with them. Banks also focus on building trust with their customers by providing quality customer service, transparent pricing, and customer-centric business models. Banks focus on innovation, digitization, personalization, customer experience, diversification, integration with third-party services, security, and competition.

REFERENCES

Banki.ru. (2023). *Bank rating*. https://www.banki.ru/banks/ratings/. Accessed on 16 March 2023.

Buryak, A. S., Bykanova, N. I., Biryukov, V. V., & Volkova, S. S. (2023). The use of digital technologies in the marketing activities of banks. *Economics of Sustainable Development*, *1*(53), 79–83.

Central Bank of the Russian Federation. (2022a). *Report of PJSC Sberbank*. https://cbr.ru/finorg/foinfo/reports/?ogrn=1027700132195. Accessed on 16 March 2023.

Central Bank of the Russian Federation. (2022b). *Report of VTB Bank (PJSC)*. https://cbr.ru/finorg/foinfo/reports/?ogrn=1027739609391. Accessed on 16 March 2023.

---

[2]Data are calculated by the author based on the methodology of M. Jeffrey. Quantitative indicators of the bank's marketing effectiveness are available at https://figshare.com/ with the identifier https://doi.org/10.6084/m9.figshare.24424729. Data from the Central Bank of the Russian Federation (2022c, 2022d) were used for the calculation.

Central Bank of the Russian Federation. (2022c). *Report of JSC Rosselkhozbank*. https://cbr.ru/banking_sector/ credit/coinfo/a2022/?regnum=3349. Accessed on 16 March 2023.

Central Bank of the Russian Federation. (2022d). *Statistical indicators of the banking sector of the Russian Federation*. https://cbr.ru/statistics/bank_sector/review/. Accessed on 16 March 2023.

Jeffrey, M. (2013). *Data-driven marketing: The 15 metrics everyone in marketing should know* (P. Mironov, Transl. from English). MIF. (Original work published 2010).

Tokareva, A. (2023). VTB forecasts bank profits in 2024 at the level of 2021. *Frank Media*. https://frankmedia.ru/. Accessed on 16 October 2023.

Vaganova, O. V., Bykanova, N. I., Mityushina, I. L., Mohanad, A.-S., & Salim, R. (2019). Introduction of the latest digital technologies in the banking sector: Foreign experience and Russian practice. *Humanities and Social Sciences Reviews*, 7(5), 789–796. https://doi.org/10.18510/hssr.2019.7599

METHODS FOR ASSESSING THE ECONOMIC SECURITY OF ENTERPRISES: THE EXAMPLE OF THE TEXTILE INDUSTRY IN UZBEKISTAN

Aktam U. Burkhanov, Bobir O. Tursunov and Khonzoda M. Shamsitdinova

Tashkent State University of Economics, Uzbekistan

ABSTRACT

This chapter assesses the economic security of enterprises on the example of the textile industry of Uzbekistan. The authors considered the ways to identify new textile enterprises in Uzbekistan and studied the issues related to the enterprises' financial security. The process of index formation and its dependence on the initial data is also of interest. Given that the level of receivables turnover is gradually decreasing, we can assume that the company's customers will accumulate late payments and return them near the end of the financial year. This situation can increase liquidity indicators, which shows the low efficiency of the system for managing accounts with customers and the lack of working money during the financial year. This hypothesis is also confirmed by the decrease in the capital ratio during the period analyzed. The proposed methodology was tested in the automated Microsoft Excel, which made it possible to quickly and efficiently form the final calculated indicator. In addition, this methodology allows users to expand the range of inputs and double-check other factors depending on market conditions.

Keywords: Macro- and micro-factors; financial security of enterprises; textiles; economic standards; criteria; methods; financial coefficient; indicators

JEL Codes: L16; L53

The global recession is affecting the financial stability of business entities in various directions. The global economy shrank by 3.27% in 2020 compared to 2019, bringing the most significant loss since World War II (Statista, 2023; Zumbrun, 2020). Additionally,

Development of International Entrepreneurship Based on Corporate Accounting and Reporting According to IFRS
Advanced Series in Management, Volume 33B, 115–122
Copyright © 2024 Aktam U. Burkhanov, Bobir O. Tursunov and Khonzoda M. Shamsitdinova
Published under exclusive licence by Emerald Publishing Limited
ISSN: 1877-6361/doi:10.1108/S1877-63612024000033B015

there has been extensive research on assessing financial risks, their risk reduction, the decline in share prices on the stock market, and the conceptual aspects of the strategic management of the enterprise.

LITERATURE REVIEW

The world's top universities, research institutions, and prestigious international financial and credit organizations, including Harvard University, World Bank, IMF, Multilateral Investment Guarantee Agency, and Eurostat, conduct research based on the British standard BS 31100:2008 developed by Ernst & Young, KPMG, and Deloitte.

In Uzbekistan, research is being conducted in certain priority areas to improve the theoretical, methodological, and economic-legal base (Rangel, 2019). Economic development is reflected in the fundamental and practical projects of the Institute of Forecasting and Macroeconomic Research under the Ministry of Employment and Poverty Reduction of the Republic of Uzbekistan.

Some authors (Kiss et al., 2019; Marshall, 1996; Mill, 1981) have extensively explored the theoretical underpinnings of ensuring the financial stability of companies and their gradual improvement. S. M. Amanda (2017), S. Ahmad, de Goede (2010), Santiago Moral-Garcia, W. Zeng, and other scientists researched problems related to financial security, financial security risks, and methods to prevent them.

Economists and scientists from the CIS also study the considered issues, including the works of K. Senchagov and I. Lebedev (2008); G. E. Krokhicheva et al. (2017).

The authors use the method of the analysis of financial risks using the Monte Carlo model based on mutual cooperation with shareholders.

Uzbek scholars, including N. Jumaev (Jumaev et al., 2020), D. Rakhmonov and A. Burkhanov (Burkhanov & Mansur qizi, 2021; Burkhanov et al., 2022), and H. P. Abulkasimov (2006), explored the challenges of providing economic administration.

Indicators of an enterprise's financial stability are gathered when formulating procedures for evaluating its financial security. Different economists from around the world take different stances on how to evaluate an enterprise's financial security. The scientific literature offers methodical techniques for figuring out one's level of financial security.

For example, T. M. Gladchenko advocates the indicator approach, which, according to the author, consists of comparing the actual values of financial security indicators with the threshold values of indicators of this level. Many foreign economists represent financial security through financial stability (Tagkalakis, 2014).

Raul Fernandez et al. (2021) identified threats to the country's financial sector. They studied the influence of sources of financial risk, such as financial fraud, failures in the payment system, and money laundering as indicators. They considered the relationship with financial market risk, stock market volatility, sovereign risk, and exchange rate volatility.

G. C. Montes, M. Valladares, and C. O. de Moraes (2021) analyzed the factors affecting the financial security of Brazilian banks. It is investigated that the state of sovereign credit news (rating change, outlook, and credit control) of credit rating agencies (CRAs) affects banks in the form of credit risk and solvency risk. It modifies credit risk (credit reserves) and solvency risk (capital buffer) guaranteed by Brazilian banks. It was scientifically proven that improving Brazil's sovereign risk causes banks to reduce their protection against financial risks (credit reserves) and capital levels, which can threaten financial stability (Fernandez et al., 2021).

Rubio-Misas studied global factors affecting the financial stability of a large insurance company. The study found differences in resilience between insurance companies and traditional insurers and that ownership concentration affects firms' exposure to risk. According to the research results, companies with a more concentrated ownership structure tend to show a lower level of financial stability (Rubio-Misas, 2020).

P. Wanke and others evaluated 124 banks (2004–2013) based on accounting and financial indicators that reflect the bank's production process and activities. According to the results obtained from the models proposed by them, it is influenced differently by socioeconomic and business-related variables (Wanke et al., 2020).

A group of Chinese researchers evaluated Chinese mining companies. According to their results, there is a correlation between climate change and the financial performance of mining companies. Because mining companies with different types of resources are differently sensitive to climate change risks, climate change risks have positive and negative effects on mining companies. According to the researchers, in response to the threat of climate change, mining companies should actively implement low carbon strategies and actively disclose emission information to improve brand value and create new competitive advantages for long-term development. Researchers have tried to evaluate quantitative and qualitative indicators in their scientific work (Sun et al., 2020).

The information above shows that the financial stability of an organization can be evaluated by different indications that must be obtained depending on the unique characteristics of each region and industry. Numerous scholars investigated the macro and microelements that directly and indirectly influence financial stability and security. We believe it is reasonable to calculate internal environmental elements using their indicators in the financial report, as well as external environmental indicators that directly impact the firm's financial stability through expert surveys (Burkhanov et al., 2022).

ANALYSIS AND RESULTS

Therefore, we can provide a questionnaire for an expert assessment of the impact of external risks by researching and supporting the primary external variables of financial security.

The enterprise's management may supplement the list of listed criteria by considering the development of the industry or business area and its unique characteristics. Top managers can complete this questionnaire directly, or it can be given to relevant experts. As a result of filling it, a grade from 5 to 50 points is formed.

It is difficult to quantify this indicator. Therefore, we think that the presence of illegal businesses and corruption in the country can serve as a factor in reducing the level of general financial security.

Proponents of self-reliant growth argue that external financing should be minimized and companies should avoid debt, interest payments, and costs associated with debt service. On the other hand, some people believe it is necessary to use their own money and the money of other people. Furthermore, the existence of outside funding sources suggests that the company attracts investors and has additional development potential. It is critical to maintain a positive dynamic of financial stability indicators. Although the precise coefficient values vary depending on the business type, low profitability is typical of textile businesses. In this regard, the predominant focus of existing methodologies is on analyzing complex financial and economic variables.

The standards and uppermost values of the indicators of financial security provoke intense debate (Burkhanov et al., 2022).

It should be emphasized that it is challenging to condense the block of risk assessment indicators into precise single-digit indicators.

Let us say $x_j, j = \overline{1,m}$ are initial indicators. For their comparison, each indicator x, $\overline{x}_j$ $_j$ is normalized. That is, $0 \leq 1$ should be included in the interval, where $\overline{x}_j = 1$ corresponds to the optimal (or high) value of this indicator, and $\overline{x}_j = 0$ corresponds to an unacceptable value. Thus, $\overline{x}_j$ is a normalized value that can be considered as an indicator.

After the indicators are normalized, the integral index (the indicator) is calculated. This index is calculated as a sum of normalized values using weighting coefficients.

That is, if x_{ij} is the value in a certain period of time $j = 1, ... ,; i = 1, ..., n$ (e.g., n years), then the integral indicator (index) of a linear function can be of the following form:

$$I = \sum_{i=1}^{n} \sum_{j=1}^{m} k_j \overline{x}_{ij}, \tag{1}$$

where:

k – the weighting coefficient for the indicator that determines the j-indicator on the integral index in the i-period;

$\overline{x}_{ij}$ – normalized values of indicators.

If the value of all parameters is optimal (high), the calculated index is 1. If the obtained index is 0, the financial security is tight.

In this method, there is a way to normalize the indicators at the manager's discretion. There are five main statistical methods:

(1) Method of mathematical statistics. It is used in stimulating studies (an increase in all indicators leads to an improvement in the condition of the entire system).
(2) Method of nonmonotonic dependencies. In this case, the optimal value of the studied indicator is in the range from the lowest to the highest.
(3) Limit value method, that is, there can be several optimal values at different limits.
(4) Medical-biological method (specific to the study of living beings and organic compounds).
(5) Vector method (specific to the study of mechanical sets).

Particularly, the normalization of indicators according to the method of mathematical statistics:

$$\overline{x}_i = \frac{x_i - x_{min}}{x_{max} - x_{min}}, i = \overline{1,n}, \tag{2}$$

Normalization of indicators according to the method of nonmonotonic dependencies:

$$\overline{x}_i = 1 - \frac{|x_i - x_{onm}|}{max\{(x_{max} - x_{opt}), (x_{opt} - x_{min})\}}, i = \overline{1,n}, \tag{3}$$

$$x_{ij(risk)} = Z_q / E_q \tag{4}$$

where:

$x_{ij(risk)}$ – an estimate given to a certain level of volatility; Z_q – damage that can be seen in case of failure; E_q – the probability of failure.

After that, it is possible to normalize the value assigned to each level of volatility according to the chosen method for quantitative indicators. Then, it will be possible to form the matrix integral index. For this purpose, it is possible to determine how much each evaluation element deviates from the average absolute indicator (using normalized values):

$$\Delta \overline{x_{ij}} = \overline{x_{ij}} - \overline{x_{ijca}} \tag{5}$$

where: $\overline{x_{ijca}}$ – the normalized value of each component of the method.

The next step is to determine the number of cases where the normalized indicator deviates positively from the average value and when it deviates negatively. A positive deviation will appear m_i for each coefficient, and a negative deviation will appear m_i for each coefficient m_j:

$$y_{ij} = m_i / m_j \tag{6}$$

We use the following matrix:

$$I = \begin{bmatrix} y_{11} & \cdots & y_{1n} \\ \vdots & \ddots & \vdots \\ y_{m1} & \cdots & y_{nm} \end{bmatrix} \tag{7}$$

The main advantage of the presented method is its ease of use. It does not require special software and can be performed using Microsoft Excel or Libre Office tools. However, financial-analytical tools (e.g., Finansist software) can form a primary database. Another advantage of the developed method is the possibility of obtaining a comparable index for different enterprises.

Based on this information, we calculate financial indicators. Microsoft Excel makes it possible to write a formula for each indicator and perform additional calculations for the first year of statistical observation. The next step is to determine the minimum and maximum values for all financial ratios based on classical standards and laws of formal logic. For example, the level of profitability cannot be lower than 0 (if the activity is unprofitable, it is not appropriate to calculate its value). All ranges are set for similar points.

After that, we can proceed to the standardization of indicators according to the method of mathematical statistics according to the following formula:

$$\overline{x_i} = \frac{x_i - x_{min}}{x_{max} - x_{min}}, i = \overline{1, n}, \tag{8}$$

where:

n – data volume (the number of indicators) or time series points;

$\overline{x_i} = 0$ when $x_i = x_{min}$;
$x_i = 1$ when $x_i = x_{max}$.

We determine the weighting coefficients for each component of the calculation. Weighting coefficients are set by an expert method. That is, each user of the financial security assessment methodology can adapt them for their own enterprises with their own help. To simplify the calculations and ensure reliability, the authors set equal weighting factors for all 12 indicators: $1/12 = 0.08333333....$

We can define the index as the following linear function:

$$I = \sum_{i=1}^{n} \sum_{j=1}^{m} k_j \overline{x_{ij}}$$

The obtained values indicate a significant level of financial security related to the large number of liabilities exceeding the company's equity, as well as harmful activities.

Participating in the calculation of the index of the external environment in which textile enterprises operate makes it possible to determine its importance in relation to the economy and its position in the market. In this case, the range of the index value is from 0 to the maximum year of statistical observation; in our case, it is 10. Accordingly, the calculation form is converted to a matrix form, as a result of which the result is presented not by calculation period but by one index for each period.

The research evaluated the financial *security* of 28 textile enterprises belonging to the association "Uztokimaliksanoat" (Table 1).

Table 1. Evaluation Results.

Enterprises/Years	2016	2017	2018	2019	2020
"BIRYUZA GROUP" LLC	0.36	0.62	0.77	0.82	1.33
"BETLIS TEXTILE" LLC	0.16	0.18	0.19	0.20	0.24
"NAMANGAN TOKAMACHI" LLC	-	-	0.32	0.49	0.53
"SIRDARYA BEST FASHION" LLC	0.04	0.02	0.03	0.01	0.03
"UZTEX TASHKENT" LLC	0.87	1.12	0.56	0.41	0.89
LUKBO TEXTILE LTD	0.18	0.25	0.68	0.37	1.24
"ELEGANT GARMENT TEXTILE" LLC	0.71	0.55	0.63	0.47	0.45
OOO "KUVA TEXTILE" LLC	0.43	0.13	0.74	0.81	0.86
"SATISFIED QUALITY" LLC	0.11	0.15	0.16	0.11	0.08
"BONITO GROUP" LLC	0.60	0.07	0.31	0.24	0.29
"KOBOTEX" LLC	0.15	0.39	0.41	0.17	1.17
IFTIKHOR CLOTHING INDUSTRY LLC	0.12	0.19	0.26	0.45	0.68
"BETLIS TEXTILE" LLC	0.33	0.46	0.89	0.71	0.68
"KHORAZM TEX" LLC	0.17	0.45	0.46	0.39	0.33
"PLATINUM-TEXTIL" LLC	0.89	0.90	1.12	0.56	0.85
"URGANCH BAXMAL" LLC	0.16	0.26	0.44	0.32	0.70
"SHAYHONTOHUR TEXTILE" LLC	0.36	0.55	0.87	0.48	0.51
"PRONTO TEXTILE GROUP" LLC	0.49	0.77	0.65	0.38	0.42
"PAPFEN FOREIGN ENTERPRISE" LLC	0.65	0.73	0.91	0.42	0.94
"SPACE-LUXE" LLC	0.41	0.07	0.16	0.39	0.28
"OKTOSH TEXTILE" LLC	0.08	0.63	0.82	0.38	1.60
"LOTUS TEXTILE" LLC	0.60	0.54	0.79	0.93	0.64
"DAKA-INTEX" LLC	0.78	0.25	0.40	0.17	0.55
"ART SOFT TEX SPINNING" LLC	0.19	0.30	0.38	0.89	0.96
"AMUDARYOTEX" LLC	0.08	0.11	0.49	0.22	1.41
"AMINA GOLD INVEST" LLC	0.71	0.68	0.60	0.39	0.41
"KONIMEXTEX" LLC	0.33	0.56	0.89	0.52	0.77
"OK SAROY TEXTILE" LLC	0.14	0.88	1.12	1.54	1.91

Source: Calculated by the authors.

The analyzed enterprises should focus their efforts on strengthening the internal components of their financial security.

DISCUSSION

Based on the assessment given by the experts during the research, the authors developed the scale to assess the level of financial security in textile enterprises, considering the nature of the network (Table 2). The upper and lower limits of the evaluation criteria (linear matrix values (0-0.22) – "high risk," (0.23-0.51) – "moderate risk," (0.52-0.80) – "stable," (0.81-0.99) – "moderately safe," and (above 1) – "absolutely safe").

When determining the upper and lower limits of the criteria for evaluating internal and external environmental factors, the threshold values were determined by evaluating the linear matrix values of 28 textile enterprises. This sample set allows us to make inferences about the main set, as the state of representativeness is preserved.

For the last seven years, the index of the financial security assessment matrix for the company "Sirdarya Best Fashion" LLC was 4.183898701. That is, it is almost an average indicator due to the stability of the external environment. Due to the stability, safety, and prospects for the enterprise, the index value of "Sirdarya Best Fashion" LLC for 10 years was 3.034381027. Accordingly, the managers of the analyzed enterprises should focus their efforts on strengthening the internal components of their financial security.

CONCLUSION

The process of index formation and its dependence on input data is of particular interest. Given that the level of receivables turnover is also gradually decreasing, we can assume that the company's customers will accumulate the amount of late payments and return them near the end of the financial year. This situation can cause an increase in liquidity indicators, which indicates the low efficiency of the system for managing accounts with customers and the lack of working money during the financial year. This hypothesis is also confirmed by the decrease in the capital ratio during the analyzed period.

The proposed methodology was tested in the automated Microsoft Excel, which made it possible to quickly and efficiently form the final calculated indicator. Additionally, this methodology gives users the opportunity to expand the range of input data and double-check other factors depending on market conditions.

Table 2. Upper and Lower Limits of Criteria for Evaluating Internal and External Environmental Factors.

Scale	The Content of the Assessment
0–0.22	High risk
0.23–0.51	Moderate risk
0.52–0.80	Stable
0.81–0.99	Moderately safe
>1	Absolutely safe

Source: Calculated by the authors.

REFERENCES

Abulkasimov, H. P. (2006). *Economic security*. Academy.

Amanda, S. M. (2017). Perpetual anarchy: From economic security to financial insecurity. *Finance and Society*, *3*(2), 188–196. https://doi.org/10.2218/finsoc.v3i2.2578

Burkhanov, A. U., & Mansur qizi, M. E. (2021). The ways for improvement of investment strategy in the period of digital economy. In *Proceedings of the ICFNDS 2021: The 5th International Conference on Future Networks & Distributed Systems* (pp. 655–662). Association for Computing Machinery. https://doi.org/10.1145/3508072.3508202

Burkhanov, A. U., Tursunov, B., Uktamov, K., & Usmonov, B. (2022). Econometric analysis of factors affecting economic stability of chemical industry enterprises in digital era: In case of Uzbekistan. In *Proceedings of ICFNDS '22: The 6th International Conference on Future Networks & Distributed Systems* (pp. 484–490). Association for Computing Machinery. https://doi.org/10.1145/3584202.3584274

de Goede, M. (2010). Financial security. In J. P. Burgess (Ed.), *The Routledge handbook of new security studies* (pp. 100–109). Routledge.

Fernandez, R., Guizar, B. P., & Rho, C. (2021). A sentiment-based risk indicator for the Mexican financial sector. *Latin American Journal of Central Banking*, *2*(3), 100036. https://doi.org/10.1016/j.latcb.2021.100036

Jumaev, N. Kh., Rakhmanov, D. A., & Azimova, D. M. (2020). *Public debt of Uzbekistan and economic globalization*. Innovative Development Publishing House.

Kiss, M., Breda, G., & Muha, L. (2019). Information security aspects of Industry 4.0. *Procedia Manufacturing*, *32*, 848–855. https://doi.org/10.1016/j.promfg.2019.02.293

Krokhicheva, G. E., Arkhipov, E. L., Bazdikyan, M. Yu., & Istomin, A. V. (2017). Identification of risky situations in the system of economic security. *Internet Journal "Naukovedenie"*, *9*(4), 1–8. https://naukovedenie.ru/PDF/95EVN417.pdf. Accessed on October 26, 2023.

Lebedev, I. (2008). *Methods of minimizing financial risks while ensuring the economic security of metallurgy enterprises (Dissertation of Candidate of Economic Sciences)*. Financial Academy Under the Government of the Russian Federation.

Marshall, A. (1996). *Principles of economics: in 3 volumes (Transl. from English)* (Vol. 1). Western economic thought. (Original work published 1890).

Mill, J. S. (1981). *Principles of political economy: in 3 volumes (Transl. from English)*. Progress. (Original work published 1848).

Montes, G. C., Valladares, M., & de Moraes, C. O. (2021). Impacts of the sovereign risk perception on financial stability: Evidence from Brazil. *The Quarterly Review of Economics and Finance*, *81*, 358–369. https://doi.org/10.1016/j.qref.2021.06.010

Rangel, A. (2019). Why enterprises need to adopt 'need-to-know' security. *Computer Fraud & Security*, *2019*(12), 9–12. https://doi.org/10.1016/S1361-3723(19)30127-7

Rubio-Misas, M. (2020). Ownership structure and financial stability: Evidence from Takaful and conventional insurance firms. *Pacific-Basin Finance Journal*, *62*, 101355. https://doi.org/10.1016/j.pacfin.2020.101355

Statista. (2023). Growth of the global gross domestic product (GDP) from 1980 to 2022, with forecasts until 2028. https://www.statista.com/statistics/273951/growth-of-the-global-gross-domestic-product-gdp/. Accessed on October 26, 2023.

Sun, Y., Yang, Y., Huang, N., & Zou, X. (2020). The impacts of climate change risks on financial performance of mining industry: Evidence from listed companies in China. *Resources Policy*, *69*, 101828. https://doi.org/10.1016/j.resourpol.2020.101828

Tagkalakis, A. O. (2014). Financial stability indicators and public debt developments. *The Quarterly Review of Economics and Finance*, *54*(2), 158–179. https://doi.org/10.1016/j.qref.2013.12.005

Wanke, P., Tsionas, M. G., Chen, Z., & Antunes, J. J. M. (2020). Dynamic network DEA and SFA models for accounting and financial indicators with an analysis of super-efficiency in stochastic frontiers: An efficiency comparison in OECD banking. *International Review of Economics & Finance*, *69*, 456–468. https://doi.org/10.1016/j.iref.2020.06.002

Zumbrun, J. (2020, May 10). Coronavirus slump is worst since Great depression. Will it be as painful? *The Wall Street Journal*. https://www.wsj.com/articles/coronavirus-slump-is-worst-since-great-depression-will-it-be-as-painful-11589115601. Accessed on October 26, 2023.

PART 2

INTERNATIONAL EXPERIENCE IN THE DEVELOPMENT OF TRADE COOPERATION AND INTERNATIONAL ENTREPRENEURSHIP

IMPACT OF THE REGIONAL COMPREHENSIVE ECONOMIC PARTNERSHIP ON SINO–JAPANESE TRADE

Zhang Xiao and Roman V. Manshin

RUDN University, Russia

ABSTRACT

On January 1, 2022, the Regional Comprehensive Economic Partnership (RCEP) officially came into force. It was implemented in six ASEAN countries and four non-ASEAN countries (China, Japan, New Zealand, and Australia) as the world's largest free trade agreement (FTA) and the first direct free trade area agreement between China and Japan, indicating that the agreement to develop China–Japan FTA relations has borne brand new results. It will be the first time China signs an FTA with the world's top 10 economies. In the context of global de-internationalization, unilateralism, and trade protectionism, as well as the adoption and implementation of various restrictions on international trade by some countries to strengthen their capacity to protect the market economy, the RCEP is an important activity for the major economies in the Asian region to actively seek change in the face of the crisis. Under the RCEP, China and Japan have reached agreements on bilateral trade in commodities, trade in services, and rules of origin, all of which will jointly promote trade between China and Japan. Analyzing the current trade situation between China and Japan, this chapter discusses the impact that the entry into force of the RCEP may have on bilateral trade between China and Japan. Moreover, this chapter provides suggestions for further developing Sino–Japan trade for reference.

Keywords: Regional Comprehensive Economic Partnership (RCEP); Sino–Japanese trade in goods; trade in services; current trading situation; free trade zone (FTZ); bilateral trade

JEL Codes: F02; F10; F13; F15; F18; F53

The countries that are members of the Regional Comprehensive Economic Partnership (RCEP) actively completed domestic approval procedures within a year of signing the

Development of International Entrepreneurship Based on Corporate Accounting and Reporting According to IFRS
Advanced Series in Management, Volume 33B, 125–134
Copyright © 2024 Zhang Xiao and Roman V. Manshin
Published under exclusive licence by Emerald Publishing Limited
ISSN: 1877-6361/doi:10.1108/S1877-63612024000033B016

agreement. By January 1, 2022, the RCEP had officially entered into force in six ASEAN countries and in China, Japan, New Zealand, and Australia. South Korea entered the agreement on February 1, 2022. Malaysia entered on March 18, 2022. The remaining three countries will enter the agreement after completing the internal approval process. According to the agreements reached by member countries, the main achievements of the RCEP in the area of trade are reflected in the following aspects.

The first aspect is greater liberalization of trade in goods. Once the RCEP agreement enters into force, more than 90% of goods in the region will eventually be subject to a zero tariff. For key products, zero tariffs will be achieved immediately after the agreement enters into force, or the tariff will be reduced to zero within 10 years, benefiting businesses and consumers in the region and each member country within a short period and facilitating trade exchanges. Regarding China and Japan's commitments to reduce tariffs on commodities, 24.9% of tariff lines imported by China into Japan will be immediately zeroed out in the year of the agreement's entry into force; 55% of tariff lines exported from China to Japan will be zeroed out on a tariff-by-tariff basis. Ultimately, it is planned that China will impose a zero tariff on 86% of its imports from Japan, and Japan will impose a zero tariff on 88% of its imports to China. China and Japan will mutually reduce tariffs in a number of areas, such as machinery and electrical appliances, light industry and textiles, automobiles and auto parts, and trade goods, thus achieving a higher degree of trade liberalization.

The second aspect is related to rules of cumulation of origin. The content of the cumulative rules of origin is that the raw materials of other RCEP countries can be calculated cumulatively to determine the origin eligibility and meet the origin criteria with a value added of 40% of final products, making it relatively more convenient for them to enjoy tariff preferences. After the entry of the RCEP into force, initial countries subject to the rules of origin of the ASEAN-Japan Free Trade Agreement (FTA) and other measures, such as local production of products, can directly benefit from Japan's duty-free treatment. For example, many Chinese knitwear enterprises in ASEAN countries that invest in knitted garment factories must also invest in knitted fabric production to benefit from Japan's duty-free regime. Following the entry of the RCEP into force, imported fabrics from China that are processed into garments in ASEAN countries and then exported to Japan can also enjoy a duty-free regime. Aggregate rules of origin encourage the use of intermediate goods in the region, which helps reduce production costs for relevant enterprises through rules of origin, which, in turn, will encourage relevant Chinese enterprises to export to Japan.

The third aspect is trade facilitation in commodities. RCEP countries have agreed on several high-level rules to facilitate commodity trade, including simplifying complex customs procedures and improving and rationalizing common standards and technical norms for inspection and quarantine between China and Japan. Implementing these new rules will reduce the cost of trade inconvenience between the two countries in the region to a certain extent and improve the competitiveness of products in both regions, which will benefit enterprises and consumers.

Finally, trade in services is to be facilitated. The RCEP divides the services trade liberalization regime into positive and negative lists. All 15 RCEP parties have made liberalization commitments that exceed those of the World Trade Organisation (WTO) and their respective original "10 + 1" FTAs. Except for Laos, Cambodia, and Myanmar, other ASEAN members have increased the number of service sectors in the RCEP to more than 100. China's commitment to open a positive list reached the highest level among all existing FTAs. In addition to about 100 sectors in the WTO, it added 22 new sectors, such as R&D, management consulting, manufacturing-related services, and air transportation. The country raised the level of commitments in 37 sectors, such as finance, law, construction, and maritime transportation. Japan has the highest level of liberalization, with overall full liberalization in areas such as computer services, environmental services, tourism services, entertainment and culture, and sports, giving full national treatment to member countries. The RCEP aims to create a fairer and more open competitive environment for financial services by promoting the interconnection of telecommunications infrastructure and fair competition in the telecommunications market and, through a range of measures, helping professionals to practice more easily in other member countries and facilitating trade in services in related areas.

MATERIALS AND METHODS

The current state of Sino–Japanese trade is explored in the works of Du and Liu (2021) and Zhao (2019).

The impact of RCEP on Sino–Japanese trade is studied in the works of Chen (2021), Pang et al. (2019), Qin (2022), M. Xu (2021), and G. Xu and Liu (2021).

Using survey and data study methods, the authors studied and analyzed the status of Sino–Japanese trade in recent years. The research objects are China and Japan.

RESULTS

Sino–Japanese Trade at a High Level

Due to the effects of the COVID-19 pandemic, Japan's economy has been severely curtailed, and its total trade with the United States, ASEAN, and the EU has declined by more than double digits. As shown in Fig. 1, Sino–Japanese trade is growing against the trend. China has been Japan's top trading partner for five consecutive years. In 2021, Japan will become China's fourth-largest trading partner after ASEAN, the EU, and the United States. According to statistics, in the first three quarters of 2021, bilateral trade between China and Japan increased by more than 20% compared to the same period in 2020. From January to November 2021, the total trade volume between China and Japan amounted to $339.8 billion, up 18.9% year-on-year (GAC of China, 2023). Total annual trade reached a record high of $371.4 billion, up 17% year-on-year. In the face of the

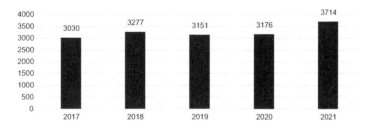

Fig. 1.   Total Bilateral Trade Volume Between China and Japan, 2017–2021. *Source:* Compiled by the authors based on General Administration of Customs People's Republic of China (GAC of China, 2023).

COVID-19 pandemic and the unpredictable political environment abroad, the development of bilateral trade between China and Japan has shown high resilience and potential (GAC of China, 2023).

Analysis of Commodity Trade Structure Between China and Japan

Zero tariffs are introduced in various areas to facilitate the restructuring of bilateral trade in goods. On China's side, the cost of importing goods from Japan will be significantly reduced after the RCEP comes into effect. First, these changes are to be seen in the field of electronic machinery and equipment, which will account for 44.66% of China's total industrial imports in 2020. Japanese machinery and equipment is an important item of Sino–Japanese trade due to its advanced technology and branding effect. Zero tariffs will be introduced on spare parts and components such as loudspeakers, digital images, and memory cards once the RCEP enters into force. Additionally, once the agreement enters into force, tariffs for household appliances and other electrical household goods will also be significantly reduced. Rates for appliances and other electrical household goods have also dropped significantly since the agreement came into effect. Before the RCEP came into force, China and Japan had their advantages in the electronics sector. Japan held a leading position in the Chinese market due to its technological and brand advantages. In turn, China has gained a foothold in the Chinese and Japanese markets due to its advantage of cheap labor. Under the RCEP, significant tariff reductions have also weakened the economic advantages of China's electronics industry and forced Chinese enterprises to face fiercer market competition in this area. From another perspective, it is also an opportunity to develop Chinese enterprises under the RCEP, which can strengthen cooperation with Japan in the high-tech electronics industry, accelerate the development of domestic production technology and industrial upgrading, and promote the adjustment of the trade structure in goods. Second, as for nonelectric machinery, electrical machinery, and transportation goods, China's total exports to Japan accounted for 43.5% in 2019. These areas of trade in goods are an important component of Sino–Japanese trade in goods, an important tool for realizing China's technological products as part of the "go-won" strategy. After the RCEP came into effect, Japan granted a 100% zero tariff in these areas, which significantly reduced the cost of Chinese machinery and vehicles to enter the Japanese market, enhanced the competitiveness of Chinese products in the market, and expanded the market scale. As for agricultural products, Japan's tax rate range on Chinese products will be reduced from 221.1% to 55.7% (UN Comtrade Database, n.d.), an unprecedented range of tax cuts. Compared to China, Japan imposes higher tariffs on China in agricultural products, especially dairy products and cereals, which are 89.3% and 34.6% in 2020 (UN Comtrade Database, n.d.). After the RCEP came into force, China seized the opportunity to boost its agricultural exports to Japan, increase the number of agricultural products traded, and improve the structure of agricultural trade.

Cooperation in technical fields contributes to the diversification of the commodity structure. In 2017, China's top five imports from Japan were as follows (in descending order):

(1) machinery, mechanical appliances, electrical equipment, tape recorders, and other goods and spare parts;
(2) chemicals and related industrial products;
(3) vehicles, aircraft, ships, and related transportation equipment;
(4) optical, photographic, and medical equipment and other precision instruments;
(5) precious metals.

By 2021, China's top five imports from Japan will be in the following order:

(1) machinery, mechanical appliances, electrical equipment, tape recorders, and other goods and spare parts;
(2) chemicals and related industrial products;
(3) optical, photographic, and medical equipment and other precision instruments;
(4) precious metals;
(5) vehicles, aircraft, ships, and related transportation equipment.

For imports of the first two categories, positions were unchanged. Vehicles, aircraft, ships, and related transportation equipment fell two places. China's imports from Japan are concentrated in the field of medium- and low-tech goods; the top five goods accounted for more than 85% of China's total imports from Japan and remained largely stable. As for China's exports to Japan, the top five products in rank order in 2017 include the following:

(1) machinery, mechanical appliances, electrical equipment, tape recorders, and other goods and spare parts;
(2) textile raw materials and textile products;
(3) weapons, ammunition parts, and accessories;
(4) non-precious metal products and chemicals;
(5) related industrial products.

The top five products in rank order in 2021 include the following:

(1) machinery, mechanical appliances, electrical equipment, tape recorders, and other products and spare parts;
(2) textile raw materials and textile products;
(3) parts and accessories for arms and ammunition;
(4) precious metals;
(5) products of chemical and related industries.

The types of commodities did not change between 2017 and 2021 in terms of export destinations. However, the share of trade volume of the top five commodities in total export trade decreased from 73.11% to 68.07%. China's exports to Japan have become more diversified and dispersed. After the RCEP comes into force, China will be able to strengthen the development of bilateral trade in labor-intensive goods and in medium-, low-, and high-tech areas, improve the technological level of its industries and the technological content of its products through investment cooperation and technology diffusion and other economic effects, and promote cooperation in the field of high technology to promote the diversification of commodity structure.

The effects of intraregional cooperation contribute to improved trade patterns. China and Japan can strengthen cooperation and improve the structure of trade in goods through direct tariff concessions under the RCEP and realize the adjustment of China's merchandise trade structure through the "China – RCEP countries – Japan" trade transfer effect, which will adjust the structure of bilateral trade between China and Japan.

Bilateral Trade Competition Between China and Japan Gradually Increases

At the beginning of trade between China and Japan, China and Japan mainly engaged in interindustry trade due to the large difference in industrial level between the two countries. With the development of Chinese technology, trade between China and Japan gradually shifted from interindustry trade to intra-industry trade; the nature of trade between the two countries changed from complementary to competitive. Comparing the commodity trade data between China and Japan in recent years, the authors found that the two major categories of Chinese exports to Japan and the two major categories of Japanese imports to China in recent years are exactly the same, namely electrical appliances, electronic equipment, nuclear reactors, boilers, and machinery.

Gap Between China and Japan in Trade in Services Gradually Narrowing

Let us compare the structure of services exports by industry between China and Japan in 2021. China's transportation exports account for 32.4% of total trade services exports, compared to 15% in Japan. Tourism accounts for 3.0% of China's share, compared to 2.9% in Japan. They are followed by knowledge-intensive services trade sectors. China's share of exports in the construction sector is 7.4%, compared to Japan's 4.9%. China's share of insurance services is 1.4% compared to 1.3% in Japan. China's share of financial sector exports is 1.3%, compared to 8.1% in Japan. The share of China in royalties for intellectual property rights is 3.4%, compared to 28.5% in Japan. The share of China in telecommunications and computer and information services is 19.6%, compared to 6.3% in Japan. Other business services account for 19.6% in China and 28.0% in Japan; personal cultural and leisure services account for 0.4% in China and 1.1% in Japan. Competitive industries in China are mainly construction and telecommunications, computer and information services, and other business services. In turn, competitive industries in Japan are mainly transportation, construction, patent and licensing services, and government services (UN Comtrade Database, n.d.).

DISCUSSION

Thus, the development of bilateral trade between China and Japan has shown high resilience and potential in the face of the COVID-19 pandemic and the unpredictable political environment overseas. Electronic and electrical appliances and machinery products have always been leading Japanese imports of Chinese goods. After the RCEP takes effect, China will impose zero tariffs on imports of most products immediately or within the 11th year, which promotes Japan's exports from these products, expanding the range of its advantages, increasing national income, making it possible to take full advantage of the complementary effects of the Sino–Japanese industrial chain, and promoting the improvement of the industrial chain structure. Simultaneously, lower tariffs help purchase manufacturing products at lower prices, thereby expanding the effect of trade transfers, reducing international spending, and balancing the balance of payments. Second, concerning apparel and other cotton and synthetic fiber products, Japan's initial tariffs of 5%–15% were reduced year after year; zero tariffs were reached in the 17th year after the RCEP went into effect. As the textile and apparel industry is labor-intensive, these goods account for a high share of total Japanese imports, mainly due to Japan's relatively high-labor costs. With the implementation of RCEP, Japan will be able to purchase these goods at lower prices; the volume of imports will increase, contributing to changes in

Japan's import structure. As for agricultural products, China will apply zero tariffs to 83.8% of Japanese agricultural products under the RCEP, significantly improving the status quo of high-trade barriers between the two countries on agricultural products. This will significantly improve the high-trade barriers between the two countries. This will encourage Japan to increase its agricultural exports to China and strengthen technical cooperation between the two countries in agricultural products to achieve the modernization of commodity trade patterns and industrial development patterns.

In fact, China and Japan imported goods from both sides. In descending order of size of the top 10 categories of goods, most industrial goods and chemical products match in six categories; they are indispensable in the field of science and technology. Although the current situation is such that China and Japan will maintain vertical intra-industry trade relations for some time, it is reasonable to believe that, along with the narrowing gap between the scientific, technological, and economic levels of China and Japan, the trend of economic isomorphism between the two countries will continue increase, leading to increased competition in bilateral trade.

Trade in services also plays an important role in bilateral trade. With the development of China's economy, the economic structures of China and Japan are gradually converging. China also pays increased attention to the development of trade in services. Initially, the trade in services between China and Japan was in a state of complementarity. Nowadays, it has turned into a state of complementarity and competition. The gap in trade in services between China and Japan is gradually narrowing. As trade in services has become increasingly important, competition in trade in services between the countries has also become more intense. Nevertheless, there is still a gap between China and Japan in some sectors of trade in services.

CONCLUSION

Impact of RCEP on Trade in Goods

It is possible to capitalize on the trade potential of textile and apparel and light industrial products. Japan is currently China's third-largest export market for textile and apparel products. According to Chinese customs statistics, from January to September 2021, China's exports of textile and apparel products to Japan reached $14.15 billion, accounting for about 6.5% of the total exports of these products. Tariffs on textile and apparel products, such as silk fabrics, cotton fabrics, and synthetic fiber products, will be proportionately reduced yearly; finally, zero tariffs will be reached in the 16th year of the agreement.

Exports of Chinese toys, bags, plastic products, and other goods to Japan will also be subject to tariff reductions. Japan is China's fourth-largest toy export market; once the RCEP agreement comes into effect, the prices of most of these products will decrease yearly for 11–16 years to eventually reach zero tariffs. After the United States and the EU, Japan is China's third-largest export market for handbags and leather goods. As of January–September 2021, China's exports of handbags and leather goods to Japan amounted to $1.84 billion, accounting for about 8.5% of the total exports of such goods. The current tariff rate on most of these goods is 8%; the tariff is expected to be reduced to zero after 21 annual tariff reductions. Once the RCEP takes effect, major plastic goods exported from China to Japan will be reduced from 3.9% to zero tariffs after 11 annual tariff reductions. In general, the period of tariff reduction on Chinese textile, garment, and light industrial products exported to Japan is generally long. The short-term effect is limited. In the long run, it will be beneficial to the stable development of bilateral Sino–Japan trade.

Electronic devices and mechanical goods will always be in the mainstream trade. Under the RCEP, China is committed to further reducing tariffs on such goods. In the first year of the agreement, China will impose a zero tariff on electronic appliances such as amplifiers, digital video disks, and memory. In 11 and 21 years after the agreement enters into force, China will impose a zero tariff on inverters and rice cookers, respectively. Although China and Japan did not have a duty-free plan for appliances and electrical household goods, they made a plan to reduce the tariff substantially; in the year of the tariff reduction, the tariff was reduced from a higher tariff of 20%–30% to a lower tariff of 8%. Although China is still weaker than Japan in terms of product design and technology creation, it has taken full advantage of its demographic dividend. It has an edge in producing labor-intensive goods such as machining and assembly, which local consumers like in the Japanese market because of their high cost and significant global market share. RCEP has increased the competitiveness of Japanese high-tech industrial products in China by competing with some Chinese goods. Overall, imports and exports of such products between China and Japan are more complementary; electronic goods will likely maintain healthy competition. With regard to machinery products, China's external investment in machinery and equipment has declined due to trade frictions between China and the United States, resulting in a significant decline in Japan's exports to China and even double-digit declines in trade in some machinery products. For the Japanese side, most electronic appliances and machinery imported into China have zero tariffs; the tariff rate for goods that have not yet reached zero tariffs will decrease yearly until the zero-tariff coverage level is raised to 98%.

The automotive supply chain and industrial supply chain are integrated in East Asia. In terms of the automotive industry, in 2018, China announced that tariffs on cars and auto parts imported from Japan were 15% and 6%, respectively, and the RCEP agreement is in line with tariff levels on all types of goods, while China promises that 65% of tariff lines on parts will be in line with tariff levels on all types of goods. Imports from Japan will be reduced to zero. On the Japanese side, due to imports of Chinese vehicles, especially passenger cars, many do not participate in tariff reduction, or the tariff reduction cycle is long (it is expected to take 15–20 years to reduce the level). Thus, the volume of vehicle imports will not be significant in the short term. In the long run, China's annual tax cuts on Japanese imports of auto parts will help increase the dividends brought by the RCEP to the auto industry, which will significantly integrate the auto supply chain and industry chain in East Asia and reduce the production costs of the auto industry, especially the entire auto industry, while the number of imported cars from Japan will not increase significantly in the short run, which also leaves a pause for the development of China's auto industry.

Impact of the RCEP on Trade in Services

Japan adopts a negative list model for trade in services. In contrast, China is expected to introduce a negative list by 2028. Japan is categorized as an RCEP country with a high level of liberalization of trade in services, which allows for the entry of most trade in services. China has also achieved the highest level of liberalization under the FTA and has committed to further expanding the level of liberalization under the RCEP. China promised Japan to expand access to Japanese financial, real estate, and services for older people. In turn, Japan has made commitments to China's transportation, real estate, and financial sectors to open up at a higher level. Thus, the level of trade in services between China and Japan will have more room for development.

Policy Proposals on Sino–Japan Trade Policy in the RCEP Context

It is necessary to strengthen political ties and reduce trade friction. Contemporary economic and trade relations between countries and political relations can no longer be accurately separated; good or bad political relations have a greater or lesser impact on economic trade between the two countries. For economic and trade relations between China and Japan to develop in a favorable direction, political issues must be China's primary concern. It is not difficult to analyze the history of economic and trade development between China and Japan and find that each rise and fall is closely related to political changes and deterioration. Therefore, China and Japan should continue strengthening political ties and engaging in political diplomacy and historical issues that may affect Sino–Japanese trade détente. The Taiwan issue should be handled properly and carefully. Simultaneously, China and Japan have long had good bilateral trade coordination and negotiation mechanisms. Nevertheless, both countries should consider the overall situation and maintain a friendly trade cooperation mechanism to minimize trade friction.

It is also necessary to accelerate the establishment of a free trade zone (FTZ). The signing of the RCEP agreement removes some obstacles to negotiating an FTA between China, Japan, and South Korea. However, the main obstacle to an FTA between China, Japan, and South Korea is the political relationship between China, Japan, and South Korea and the interference of the United States. Establishing a FTZ between China and Japan is reasonable; the two countries should also actively pursue Sino–Japanese FTA negotiations, which benefits both countries. China and Japan should try to exclude external adverse factors led by the United States Japan has a policy of political dependence on the United States and economic dependence on China. Japan can make limited concessions. China should be responsible for a major power to support the process and handle the pressure from the United States.

REFERENCES

Chen, Zh. (2021). The impact of RCEP on Sino-Japanese trade and related suggestions [RCEP 对中日贸易的影响及相关建议]. *China Economic and Trade Guide [中国经贸导刊]*, 7, 70–72. https://oversea.cnki.net/kcms/detail/detail.aspx?dbcode=CJFD&filename=ZJMD202107021&dbname=CJFDLAST2021. Accessed on March 20, 2023.

Du, R., & Liu, K. (2021). The current situation, problems and countermeasures of China-Japan bilateral trade [中日双边贸易的现状、问题与对策]. *China Economic and Trade Guide [中国经贸导刊]*, 3, 27–30. https://chn.oversea.cnki.net/KCMS/detail/detail.aspx?dbcode=CJFD&dbname=CJFDLAST2021&filename=JMDL202103010&uniplatform=OVERSEA&v=g09f64yByawUQZXZfGj4Zuvo7bEA2MHyk4F-0HA3PQf8hahwhPK4Xy8NnfkFII1h. Accessed on March 22, 2023.

General Administration of Customs People's Republic of China (GAC of China). (2023). Total bilateral trade volume between China and Japan in 2017–2021. General Administration of Customs of China. http://stats.customs.gov.cn. Accessed on March 21, 2023.

General Administration of Customs People's Republic of China (GAC of China). (n.d.). Customs statistics. General Administration of Customs of China. http://stats.customs.gov.cn. Accessed on March 22, 2023.

Pang, T., Liu, J., & Bailu. (2019). Analysis of Sino-Japanese trade commodity structure and its influencing factors [中日贸易商品结构及其影响因素分析]. *Inner Mongolia Science and Technology and Economy [内蒙古科技与经济]*, 11, 31–33. https://chn.oversea.cnki.net/KCMS/detail/detail.aspx?dbcode=CJFD&dbname=CJFDLAST2019&filename=NMKJ201911015&uniplatform=OVERSEA&v=7tAgCjBfknrxI8UkDm6NTObNKsKhcpF-yrzipaZOEeATRVZV6E4STaMGlFZ3nLZV. Accessed on March 20, 2023.

Qin, H. (2022). Talking about the far-reaching impact of RCEP [浅谈 RCEP 的深远影响]. *Ningbo Communication [宁波通讯]*, 3, 36–37. https://doi.org/10.16710/j.cnki.cn33-1272/d.2022.03.014

UN Comtrade Database. (n.d.). Trade data. UN Comtrade database. https://comtradeplus.un.org/. Accessed on March 21, 2023.

Xu, M. (2021). What does RCEP bring to Sino-Japanese trade in goods? Taking textile and garment and light industry as examples [RCEP 为中日货物贸易带来什么？以纺织服装和轻工为例]. *Import and Export Manager [进出口经理人]*, *11*, 45–47. https://chn.oversea.cnki.net/KCMS/detail/detail.aspx?dbcode=CJFD&dbname=CJFDLAST2022 &filename=SJJD202111018&uniplatform=OVERSEA&v=8EoKPhX54nrsDCdwJvhdjDLLjUfXxy1 Q1YJRuIU66mAPQJoVSYGwEFcC4U6w6Wgt. Accessed on March 20, 2023.

Xu, G., & Liu, Y. (2021). RCEP China's auto product tax reduction and its impact on auto consumption [RCEP 中国 汽车产品降税情况及对汽车消费的影响分析]. *Automobile and Parts [汽车与配件]*, *4*, 33–35. https://chn.o-versea.cnki.net/KCMS/detail/detail.aspx?dbcode=CJFD&dbname=CJFDLAST2021&filename=QCPJ2021 04042&uniplatform=OVERSEA&v=Ire6_YB153JTMY3cWcpNLNXAAjN01JsV_KWexElEnHFLTgJyy 1F3h11BXInquxWsK. Accessed on March 20, 2023.

Zhao, K. (2019). Research on the current situation and development trend of Sino-Japanese trade [中日贸易现状及发展 趋势研究]. *China Foreign Investment [中国外资]*, *22*, 13–14. https://chn.oversea.cnki.net/KCMS/detail/detai-l.aspx?dbcode=CJFD&dbname=CJFDLAST2020&filename=WQZG201922010&uniplatform=OVERSE A&v=GPYQh1m_erZKnYQwORLFte_68RFpUh2Pr2K2rHGt8qvQppvzyGr1W28l4h_oegII. Accessed on March 22, 2023.

CHINESE INVESTMENTS IN TAJIKISTAN: CONTRIBUTION TO ACHIEVING TRANSPORT AND LOGISTICS SYSTEM DEVELOPMENT GOALS

Inna V. Andronova and Gulsher A. Qalandarshoev

RUDN University, Russia

ABSTRACT

This chapter focuses on Chinese investments in Tajikistan's transportation and logistics infrastructure. This chapter studies the role and place of Chinese investments in the development of the transport and logistics infrastructure of Tajikistan, the country's exit from the transport and communication deadlock, and the transformation of Tajikistan into a transit country of the Central Asian region. The research raises the issues of the economic efficiency of these investments. The authors apply general scientific methods. Statistical and comparative methods are used to examine the investment cooperation between China and Tajikistan. Compared to other strategic partners of Tajikistan, China greatly contributes to the development of the Tajik economy and ranks first in the list of major investors. Chinese investment in transport made it possible to logistically connect Tajikistan to four neighboring countries through roads and railroads built and reconstructed by Chinese investors and companies. According to the analysis of the research topic, the effective use of Chinese investments for repairing and reconstructing the transport infrastructure of Tajikistan is important for improving the country's transport and logistics system. The two neighboring countries are using economic mechanisms to increase the effectiveness of direct financing by the Chinese government and private companies for transport projects to help Tajikistan overcome its communication isolation and become a transit country in the Central Asian region. This chapter analyzes the experience of successful transport projects with Chinese investments. The analysis showed that Chinese investments in transport have played a key role in improving Tajikistan's economic and social environment.

Development of International Entrepreneurship Based on Corporate Accounting and Reporting According to IFRS
Advanced Series in Management, Volume 33B, 135–142
Copyright © 2024 Inna V. Andronova and Gulsher A. Qalandarshoev
Published under exclusive licence by Emerald Publishing Limited
ISSN: 1877-6361/doi:10.1108/S1877-63612024000033B017

Keywords: Tajikistan; China; Chinese investments; transportation infrastructure; long-term loans; grants

JEL Codes: F21; F32; F50; H54; O18; O53; R42

The Republic of Tajikistan is a small agrarian-industrial country in Central Asia, with 93% of its territory occupied by mountains. Geographically, the country has no access to sea routes and is remote from large world markets, which limits the competitiveness of the national economy. Tajikistan's trade and economic relations with the outside world are carried out mainly through land transportation routes. In this regard, the Government of Tajikistan pays special attention to constructing and reconstructing roads and railroads. In 2016, the Government of Tajikistan adopted an important document for the country's economic and social development for the next 15 years – the National Development Strategy of the Republic of Tajikistan for the period up to 2030 (National Development Strategy of the Republic of Tajikistan, 2016). According to this program, four strategic goals are set to develop the economy and improve the welfare of the country's population, one of which is to get out of transport and communication isolation and become a transit country. According to the program, the following main activities are planned to achieve the set goal:

(1) construction and modernization of transport and logistics infrastructure;
(2) development of transport provision of industrial regions in the country;
(3) construction of transport transit corridors;
(4) development of a network of airports, small and medium aviation, etc.

Considerable investments are required to achieve this goal.

Faced with economic problems after the civil war of the 1990s, Tajikistan received economic and humanitarian support from its main economic partners. China, which is now Tajikistan's strategic partner, paid great attention to providing investments and soft loans for developing real sectors of the Tajik economy even in the early years of economic cooperation. The neighboring country saw its interest in this cooperation. Nevertheless, the analysis shows that Tajikistan also benefited from these investments.

To achieve common goals, cooperation between Tajikistan and China on attracting Chinese investment is being developed at the bilateral level and within the framework of regional integration groups such as the Shanghai Cooperation Organization. The first investments that China offered to Tajikistan were for transport projects and the development of the logistics system, which are analyzed in this research.

This research aims to analyze Chinese investments in the transport infrastructure of Tajikistan and study their economic significance, for which the following tasks are set:

• to present statistics on the volume of Chinese investments in the economy of Tajikistan;
• to provide information on implemented transport projects using Chinese investments;
• to examine the economic significance of Chinese investment in the country's transportation infrastructure;
• to assess the current and prospective state of cooperation in attracting and effectively utilizing Chinese financing for developing Tajikistan's transport and logistics system.

MATERIALS AND METHODS

The basis for analyzing the attraction of Chinese investments and their effective use for developing the economy of Tajikistan and its transport infrastructure was formed by the works of such researchers as R. K. Alimov (2015, 2023), R. M. Aminjanov, R. M. Babajanov, and A. L. Alimov (Aminjanov et al., 2019), R. Dj. Haydarov (2019), E. P. Ionova (2019), P. Krasnopolsky (Kassenova, 2009), G. Maitdinova (2021), G. Rasulov and M. G. Rasulov (2020), O. M. Sharapov (2020), and M. S. Sodikov (2021).

During the research, the authors used the research works of Tajik, Russian, and other foreign scientists and researchers. For a detailed study of the empirical material on this topic, the authors also used statistical data from the State Committee on Investments and State Property Management of the Republic of Tajikistan, the National Bank of Tajikistan, the Ministry of Transport of the Republic of Tajikistan, and other relevant agencies of the country.

When reviewing scientific papers on the selected topic, the authors used general scientific methods, including analysis, synthesis, generalization of statistical data, and comparison. Content analysis was used when working with media materials. During the analysis, the authors paid special attention to the form of attracting Chinese investments in transport infrastructure.

RESULTS

Investment cooperation between Tajikistan and China began only in the second half of the 2000s. From 2007 to 2021, Tajikistan's economy attracted foreign investment worth $11.01 billion. China is the main investor in the Tajikistan' economy during this period and is at the top of the list of major investors. China accounts for $3.2 billion or 29.5%. Second place after China is occupied by another strategic partner of Tajikistan – Russia with $1.6 billion (15.0%). The United Kingdom and the United States are in third and fourth places with $714.6 million (6.5%) and $712.8 million (6.4%), respectively (Fig. 1).

Of the Chinese investment attracted during the considered period, 63.3% was direct investment, and 36.6% was other investment. During the studied period, portfolio investments were only attracted in 2020 and amounted to $75.6,000 (State Committee on Investments and State Property Management of the Republic of Tajikistan, 2023).

Compared to other major strategic partners of Tajikistan, Chinese investments are attracted mainly in the form of direct investments. Energy, transportation, and industry

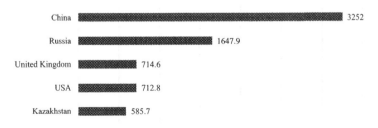

Fig. 1.   Top 5 Investor Countries in the Economy of Tajikistan in 2007–2021, $ mln.
Source: Compiled by the authors based on State Committee on Investments and State Property Management of the Republic of National Bank of Tajikistan (2023).

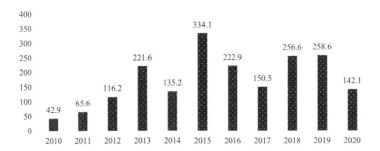

Fig. 2. China's FDI Inflow in Tajikistan for 2010–2020, $ mln. *Source:* Compiled by the authors based on Annual Statistical Collections (2001–2021).

are the main sectors for attracting these funds. According to Fig. 2, Chinese direct investment inflows were several times lower in 2020 than in 2015 (Annual Statistical Collections, 2001–2021). However, due to the documents signed between the two countries and planned investment projects, more Chinese direct investment inflows into the economy of Tajikistan are expected in the coming years.

Within the framework of bilateral meetings between the leaders of Tajikistan and China, agreements on economic and technical cooperation were concluded, under which China offered grants to Tajikistan to develop the country's economy. For example, based on the Agreement between the governments of the two countries, China provided Tajikistan with a grant of 300 million yuan in 2014. In 2017 and 2019, agreements were signed between the Governments of Tajikistan and China to grant assistance to Tajikistan for its economic development.

China began investing in Tajikistan's economy in 2005 through grants and nonrefundable aid and, since 2006, in the form of soft loans. The main lender is the Export–Import Bank of China, which offers soft loans in US dollars or Chinese yuan. The main attraction of these loans for Tajikistan is their annual interest rate, which is 1.5%–2%. The term of the loans offered is up to 25 years, of which 5–11 years is considered a grace period (Aminjanov et al., 2019).

Attracting Chinese investment for constructing and reconstructing transportation infrastructure in Tajikistan is of interest to both countries. Along with the fact that China considers Tajikistan as a market for its industrial goods and an important destination for investment, Tajikistan is also of great importance to China as a transit country, including for the realization of the "One Belt One Road" project. Tajikistan may be important for developing the southern part of the Silk Road. Given the insecurity of the neighboring country of Afghanistan, access to Pakistan and Iran via Tajikistan is currently considered difficult for China. China and Tajikistan would benefit from realizing this project because it could be one of the ways to diversify communication routes (Haydarov, 2019).

Although Tajikistan is not directly involved in implementing the large Chinese project, there is a clear Chinese interest in implementing small and large transport infrastructure projects in Tajikistan, which is done for the prospect of other Chinese projects. Tajikistan and China are linked by air and road. However, as Sharapov emphasizes, "... construction of a railroad is not excluded, which is important for both countries. This will allow Tajikistan to reduce its dependence on other countries for transportation and will allow China to increase exports of its products and find new opportunities for the development of the Silk Road project" (Sharapov, 2020).

China primarily considers its economic interests in financing transportation projects in Tajikistan. Tajikistan is a transit corridor for China's access to Central Asian countries and, thus, the market of European countries. On the initiative of the Asian Development Bank, the Regional Economic Cooperation Development Program was adopted, which is an important document for integrating Central Asian countries. Under this program, six transit corridors have been developed, four of which pass through Tajikistan's territory. For China, two of these four corridors are important. Corridor No. 2 connects China to other Central Asian countries and Turkey via Tajikistan. Corridor No. 5 connects China to Central and South Asian countries (Sodikov, 2021). Therefore, China's interest in investing in Tajikistan's transportation and logistics infrastructure is growing annually.

Next, the authors provide specific examples of successfully implemented projects in the field of transport and logistics with the use of Chinese investments. The role of these projects in Tajikistan's way out of communication isolation and their significance for developing the Tajik economy are discussed.

In 1996, a temporary border crossing Kulma-Karasu was opened on the Tajik–Chinese border after a bilateral agreement was signed. In 2001, the parties settled the existing border problems and signed an intergovernmental protocol, greatly expanding cooperation in the following years. On May 25, 2004, a checkpoint was opened at the Kulma Pass for the transportation of goods. This checkpoint plays a major role in smooth trade and economic interaction between the two countries (Alimov, 2015). These were the first steps toward Tajikistan's access to the border areas of China and, through China, to the countries of South and North Asia.

With the increase in Tajik–Chinese trade turnover, there was a need to increase the checkpoint's capacity. In 2011, the Parties signed an Agreement on transferring the checkpoint to year-round operation and giving it the status of an international one. The Dushanbe-Khorog-Kulma Road became a transit road linking China with other Central Asian countries through Tajikistan's territory (Alimov, 2015). The opening of the checkpoint has increased trade turnover between Tajikistan and China several times. Until 2004, Tajik–Chinese trade turnover averaged $10 million; within a year after the opening of the checkpoint, the turnover increased 10 times. Nowadays, this checkpoint is fully operational; according to experts, 30–35 cargo containers pass through it daily.

China plays a major role in reconstructing roads of international importance, one of which is the Dushanbe-Kulma road (from the capital of Tajikistan to the border with China). This road is of international importance; it connects cities and districts of Southern Tajikistan with the Badakhshan Autonomous Region (BAR) and reaches the Karakoram highway (Maitdinova, 2021). A total of $51.6 million was allocated for the full and quality completion of the repair and reconstruction of the Dushanbe-Dangara section of this road, of which $49 million were allocated by the Export–Import Bank of PRC and $2 million by the Government of Tajikistan.

Another such transportation infrastructure funded by China is the Dushanbe-Khujand-Chanak highway. The highway runs along the Dushanbe-Khujand-Chanak highway (from the capital of Tajikistan to the Uzbekistan border in the north). Reconstruction of this 355 km road continued between 2006 and 2013. The full and quality completion of the reconstruction work required a total of $304.5 million, of which $281.1 million (92.3%) was a loan from the Export–Import Bank of China. On this road, 5.2 km long Shahriston and 1 km long Dusti tunnels, 39 small and large bridges, and 6 km of avalanche protection structures have been built. After the commissioning of these projects, the journey between the country's south and north has been reduced by 4–5 hours, and an annual connection to the northern regions up to the border of Uzbekistan is ensured.

In 2006, with financial support from China, the construction of the Ozodi Tunnel (formerly called Shar-Shar) began, which is located 47 kilometers from the country's capital, on the Dushanbe-Kulyab highway. Construction lasted three years and raised $38 million, of which about $30 million was a grant from China. On both sides, 5 km long access roads and a 180 m long bridge have been built. The commissioning of this tunnel has reduced the road's length between the capital and the city of Kulyab (southern Tajikistan) by 7 km; the travel time was reduced by 40 minutes, which positively affected the population's socioeconomic life (Kassenova, 2009).

The Khatlon Tunnel (formerly called Chormagzak) is another project implemented by a Chinese company with a length of 4.4 km as part of the repair and modernization of the Dushanbe-Vahdat-Kulyab road, which reduced the distance between Dushanbe and Kulyab (Khatlon Region) by 100 km. The total cost of this project amounted to about $70 million.

In addition to financing road construction and reconstruction projects in Tajikistan, Chinese companies are also involved in the construction of railroads. In 2016, the Vahdat-Yavan section of the Dushanbe-Bokhtar railroad was put into operation, the construction of which was completed by China Railway Construction Company. The Export–Import Bank of China provided a $68 million loan for its construction. This 40.7 km section connects the capital of Tajikistan with the Khatlon Region. This railroad has three tunnels with a total length of 3.6 km and eight bridges with a total length of 683 meters. The Vahdat-Yavan section contributed to the integration and development of the central, southern, and eastern regions of Tajikistan and solved the problems of internal rail transit in Tajikistan. Prior to the construction of this section, Tajikistan's railroads were divided into three separate parts. The Vahdat-Yavan road has connected almost all free economic zones and increased Tajikistan's trade turnover with neighboring countries (G. Rasulov & M. G. Rasulov, 2020). This road is currently used for passenger and freight transportation.

In recent years, cooperation between Tajikistan and China in implementing other transportation projects has increased. The Kulyab-Muminabad highway, located in the country's southern part, has been repaired and upgraded with a nonrefundable grant from China Road in 2019–2021. The section where restoration work was carried out is 35 kilometers long. The total cost of this project was $19 million. This section plays a major role in connecting Dushanbe to cities and districts in the eastern part of the country and to China.

In July 2022, China Road and Bridge Corporation (CRBC) started overhauling the transportation artery connecting the districts of the BAR with China. Repair and reconstruction are planned for the Kalai Khumb-Wanch section up to the Roushan district boundary (Ionova, 2019). According to Tajikistan's Ministry of Transport, a $230 million grant from China is planned for this project, which will also be used to build two new tunnels (3.4 km and 1.8 km) on this section, which will reduce the length between the districts from 109 to 90 kilometers. To fully reconstruct the Dushanbe-Khorog-Kulma Road in the BAR, the reconstruction of the road is divided into three separate parts, given its geographical location. It is planned to attract $200 million to reconstruct the second part of Rushan-Khorog (163 km long) and $567 million for the third part of this road (395 km long) to the border with China. China technically supports implementing these projects, which are important for linking China's western regions, especially the Xinjiang Uygur Autonomous Region, with Central Asian countries, and offers long-term loans and grant aid.

In the same year, an agreement was signed with the Chinese company China Railway Wuju Corporation (Group) on the construction of four road sections in northern Tajikistan with a total length of 51.2 km within the framework of the project of the Fourth Phase of the Program "Improvement of Regional Roads in Central Asia" for the amount of $56.6 million. Under this project, 11 new bridges with a total length of 444.2 meters will be constructed (Ministry of transport of the Republic of Tajikistan, 2023).

DISCUSSION

The Government of Tajikistan always welcomes China's financial and technical support to achieve its strategic goal. At the 2019 "One Belt One Road International Forum," President of the Republic of Tajikistan Emomali Rahmon noted, ".... we pay great attention to developing and implementing joint infrastructure regional projects. In this regard, we are interested in implementing projects for the construction of the 'China-Tajikistan-Uzbekistan' and 'China-Tajikistan-Afghanistan' highways" (Haydarov, 2021). The leadership of Tajikistan proposed adding these two projects to the "One Belt One Road" initiative. It was noted that Tajikistan supports the China-Kyrgyzstan-Uzbekistan railroad project and is ready to join this project.

This major project can help Tajikistan to solve important issues of the country's development, primarily economic development. This project must play a big role in realizing one of the main goals of Tajikistan until 2030 – getting out of the communication deadlock and becoming a transit country. The construction of railroads across the Tajik border has been discussed for many years by experts from both sides. So far, due to the lack of a particular program, these projects remain at the level of negotiations. Some experts believe that China will use all its financial and technological potential to fully implement its initiative. In the future, it is not ruled out to start implementing the China-Kyrgyzstan-Tajikistan-Afghanistan-Iran railroad, which will seriously boost the industrialization of the country's southern regions.

CONCLUSION

In general, the analysis has shown that the importance of Chinese investments in the development of Tajikistan's transport infrastructure and logistics system, bringing the country out of communication isolation and turning the country into a transit territory of Central Asia, is increasing annually. With financial and technical assistance, highways of international importance passing through the territory of Tajikistan have been reconstructed, including the following:

- Dushanbe-Khorog-Kulma highway connected the regions of Tajikistan with the communications system of Western China (repair and reconstruction work is ongoing);
- Dushanbe-Khujand-Chanak highway (Uzbekistan border);
- Dushanbe-Jirgatal-Sary-Tash highway (Kyrgyz border);
- four tunnels (out of five tunnels built in Tajikistan);
- Vahdat-Yavan section of the Dushanbe-Bokhtar railroad, etc.

These projects have improved intra-republican transport connections and expanded trade cooperation between Tajikistan and neighboring countries. They serve as an important part of transport projects of regional importance.

Cooperation in the field of transport between Tajikistan and China continues to this day. The parties use all opportunities to achieve common goals. The prospects of this cooperation are constantly discussed within the framework of bilateral meetings. Currently, contracts and agreements have been concluded between Tajikistan and Chinese companies for the repair and construction of roads and railroads; construction work is underway in various regions of Tajikistan. In the near future, it is necessary to deepen the pairing of the National Development Strategy of the Republic of Tajikistan for the period up to 2030 with the Chinese government's programs in the field of transport.

REFERENCES

Alimov, R. K. (2015). The role of China in Tajikistan's way-out from transport deadlock. *China in World and Regional Politics. History and Modernity*, *20*(20), 292–305.

Alimov, R. K. (2023). Tajikistan and China: From the first steps towards each other to all-weather friendship and comprehensive strategic partnership. *Russian China Studies Scientific Journal*, *1*(2), 150–166. https://doi.org/10.48647/ICCA.2023.26.85.008

Aminjanov, R. M., Babajanov, R. M., & Alimov, A. L. (2019). Investment activity of the Republic of Tajikistan within the initiative's framework "One belt – One way." *Economics of Tajikistan*, *2*, 71–81.

Annual statistical collections "Foreign economic activity of the Republic of Tajikistan", editions 2001-2021 years. Dushanbe.

Haydarov, A. R. (2021). Cooperation between Tajikistan and China in the framework of the "Belt & Road" initiative as a factor in achieving the country's strategic goals. *The Republic of Tajikistan on the way of implementing development goals* (Materials of the republican scientific-practical conference dedicated to the 30th anniversary of the independence of the Republic of Tajikistan) (pp. 252–259).

Haydarov, R. Dj. (2019). Significance of the Chinese initiative the "Belt and Road Initiative" for Tajikistan. *Proceedings of the Institute of Philosophy, Political Science and Law named after A. Bahovaddinov of the Academy of Sciences of the Republic of Tajikistan*, *2*, 162–166.

Ionova, E. P. (2019). Tajikistan in the orbit of interests of China and Russia. *Russia and New States of Eurasia*, *3*(44), 107–120. https://doi.org/10.20542/2073-4786-2019-3-107-120

Kassenova, N. (2009). China as an emerging donor in Tajikistan and Kyrgyzstan. *Russie.Nei.Visions*, *36*, 1–29. https://www.ifri.org/sites/default/files/atoms/files/ifrichinacentralasiakassenovaengjanuary2008.pdf. Accessed on April 2, 2023.

Maitdinova, G. (2021). Bilateral Tajik-China relations in the polycentric world formation. *Post-Soviet Research*, *4*(4), 255–264.

Ministry of transport of the Republic of Tajikistan. (2023). *Signing of the contract for the construction of four sections of roads in the Sughd region*. Dushanbe.

National Development Strategy of the Republic of Tajikistan. (2016). Dushanbe. p. 96.

Rasulov, G., & Rasulov, M. G. (2020). China's import substituting investments in the economy of the Republic of Tajikistan. *Economics of Tajikistan*, *1*, 208–215.

Sharapov, O. M. (2020). Priority vectors of strategic partnership of Tajikistan and China at the present stage: Problems and prospects. *Proceedings of the Institute of Philosophy, Political Science, and Law named after A. Bahovaddinov of the Academy of Sciences of the Republic of Tajikistan*, *1*, 117–121.

Sodikov, M. S. (2021). Prospects for implementing the transit potential of the Republic of Tajikistan in the framework of the SCO. *Economics of Tajikistan*, *3*, 249–257.

State Committee on Investments and State Property Management of the Republic of Tajikistan. (2023). Statistics of foreign investments. *Information on the inflow of foreign investment into the economy of the Republic of Tajikistan in 2021* (p. 11).

CHINESE MULTINATIONALS IN KAZAKHSTAN: TRENDS AND PERSPECTIVES

Natalia A. Volgina and Li Dingbang

RUDN University, Russia

ABSTRACT

In recent decades, with China's "Go Global" and "Belt and Road" strategies, Chinese multinational corporations (MNCs) have been provided with a new development direction. This chapter aims to identify the features of the entry of Chinese multinationals into Kazakhstan and analyze their characteristics in terms of investment attractiveness and location advantages. The basic method for evaluating the characteristics of the development of Chinese MNCs in Kazakhstan is a statistical analysis based on UNCTADstat. Based on the analysis, the authors conclude that although China has many MNCs, their rate of transnationality and competitiveness index are far behind those of European and American ones. The number of Chinese multinational companies investing in Kazakhstan (1,234 companies) ranks third in the number of foreign companies in the country. Chinese multinationals investing in Kazakhstan are mainly concentrated in Xinjiang because it borders Kazakhstan and has geographical and cultural advantages. China's direct investment in Kazakhstan covers a wide range of industries, including agriculture, animal husbandry, planting, construction, mining, transportation and communication, hotel and catering industry, trade and auto repair industry, etc. However, most registered enterprises are engaged in developing and utilizing energy fields in Kazakhstan.

Keywords: Multinational corporations (MNCs); China; Kazakhstan; "Belt and Road," Foreign Direct Investment (FDI); Transnationality Index (TNI); Corporate profits

JEL Codes: F21; F23; F43; F51; F60

After the reform and opening up, Chinese multinational corporations (MNCs) began to extend their capital growth, raw material sources, and markets for their products to foreign

Development of International Entrepreneurship Based on Corporate Accounting and Reporting According to IFRS
Advanced Series in Management, Volume 33B, 143–150
Copyright © 2024 Natalia A. Volgina and Li Dingbang
Published under exclusive licence by Emerald Publishing Limited
ISSN: 1877-6361/doi:10.1108/S1877-63612024000033B018

countries. In 2013, with the "Belt and Road" strategy, Chinese MNCs' investment in Central and South Asia gradually increased. The development of Chinese MNCs in the regions along the "Belt and Road" promotes the infrastructure construction of the regions and countries along the routes and the development of the local economy. It also provides new ways for China to solve the problems of excess foreign exchange reserves, over-capacity, and energy security.

Kazakhstan is one of the five Central Asian countries with the strongest economy, relatively stable political situation, high openness to the outside world, and good invest-ment environment and policies. The country has close economic and trade cooperation with China. This chapter aims to identify the factors influencing the entry of Chinese MNCs into Kazakhstan and analyze their characteristics from the perspective of the investment industry and location advantages.

METHODOLOGY

The academic literature on the development of Chinese multinational companies in Kazakhstan is quite extensive. The most significant are works of such authors as Liu & Yang (2014), Gelvig (2020), Yermekbayev, Sarybayev, and Suriguga (2022), and others.

Currently, international direct investment can be analyzed using various statistical databases, including UNCTADstat, the World Bank FDI database, Chinese and Kazakh national databases, and government information. The choice of the statistical base for the study depends on research goals, scope, countries, and regions coverage. Regardless of the database chosen, the main indicators of the development of Chinese multinational com-panies in Kazakhstan are as follows:

- Foreign Direct Investment (FDI) reflects economic investments made by investors to gain lasting benefits in another economy;
- Transnationality Index (TNI) is used to assess the scale and degree of foreign activity of MNCs;
- Corporate Profit refers to the difference between the income and expenses of a company or business over a certain period.

Based on these indicators, the authors assess the extent of the development of Chinese multinational companies in Kazakhstan.

RESULTS

Overseas Development of Chinese MNCs

The direct evidence of the development of MNCs is the outward FDI flows. The scale of outward investment by Chinese MNCs has been increasing since the reform and opening up. In 2021, China's outward FDI flows as a developing country reached \$145.19 billion, making it the fourth largest outward investor in the world. Figure 1A, which supports the findings of the study, is available at https://figshare.com/with an identifier https://figshare.com/articles/figure/China_s_Outbound_Investment_Flows_after_Reform_and_Opening_docx/23723979.

Chinese MNCs' outbound investments are mainly concentrated in Asia, Europe, and Latin America. After China proposed the "Belt and Road" strategy in 2013, which was officially implemented in 2015, the share of Chinese investment in Asia has grown rapidly at a faster rate than in other regions. Figure 2A, which supports the findings of the study, is available at https://figshare.com/with an identifier https://figshare.com/articles/dataset/Regional_Segmentation_of_China_s_outbound_investment_flows_2015-2020_docx/2372 4039.

As shown in Figure 2A, from 2015 to 2020, the share of Asia in China's foreign investment is as follows:

- $108.37 billion in 2015 (74.4% of the total investment in the same year);
- $130.27 billion in 2016 (66.4% of the total investment in the same year);
- $110.04 billion in 2017 (69.5% of the total investment in the same year);
- $105.51 billion in 2018 (73.8% of the total investment in the same year);
- $110.84 billion in 2019 (81.0% of the total investment in the same year);
- $112.34 billion in 2020 (73.1% of the total investment in the same year) (Ministry of Commerce of the People's Republic of China, 2015–2020).

By the end of 2021, the five industries and fields with the most concentrated Chinese investment in Asia are rental and business services (42.7%), wholesale and retail trade (15.4%), finance (11.9%), manufacturing (7.7%), mining (5%), and other (17.3%). Table 1A, which supports the findings of the study, is available at https://figshare.com/with an identifier https://figshare.com/articles/dataset/Industrial_distribution_of_China_s_direct_investment_stock_in_Asia_by_the_end_of_2021_docx/23724750.

The TNI is used to assess the scale and degree of foreign activity of MNCs. The higher the TNI, the higher the degree of internationalization of the enterprise. In 2021, China was listed 10th among the world's top 100 nonfinancial multinational companies. The average TNI was 30.67% in 2021, while 75 European and American countries were listed in the same period with an average TNI of 66.11%. Compared with the multinational companies in European and American countries, the level of transnational operation of Chinese multinational companies is still very low. Table 2A, which supports the findings of the study, is available at https://figshare.com/with an identifier https://figshare.com/articles/dataset/Top_100_multinationals_by_2021_TNI_Comparison_docx/23725050.

The 2022 Fortune 500 MNCs' data includes 145 Chinese companies, with an average profit margin of 4.71% and an average profit margin of 12.11% for MNCs in developed countries (Fortune 500, 2022). Chinese MNCs still have a big gap with European and American countries in terms of international competitiveness and profitability (Table 3A).

Chinese Multinational Companies in Kazakhstan

"Doing Business 2020 report" published by the World Bank (2019) shows that Kazakhstan ranks 25th in the world in terms of doing business. "The Global Competitiveness Report 2022," published by the World Economic Forum (2022), shows that Kazakhstan ranks 43rd in global competitiveness. Thus, Kazakhstan has a relatively favorable business environment.

"The number of Chinese multinational companies in Kazakhstan is rather numerous, and the Statistical Committee of Kazakhstan reported that, as of March 1, 2020, the total number of Chinese companies operating in Kazakhstan was 1,234, up 27% year-on-year from 972 at the end of 2019" (Consulate General of the People's Republic of China in Almaty, 2020)." Of these, 1,197 are small, 15 are medium-sized, and 22 are large enterprises. By industry, there were 461 wholesale and retail trade companies, accounting for

37.4%. Additionally, 168 companies in construction, 96 in mining, 81 in manufacturing, 76 in science and technology, 33 in finance and insurance, and 161 in other types of services ranked third in Kazakhstan, after Russia (7,396) and Turkey (2,440).

The sources of enterprises investing in Kazakhstan are relatively concentrated, mainly in the Xinjiang Uygur Autonomous Region, which is related to the fact that Xinjiang is adjacent to Kazakhstan and the two places have similar cultures, customs, etc.

The sectoral distribution of Chinese direct investments in Kazakhstan is very wide, involving agriculture, animal husbandry, plantation, construction, mining, transport and communication, services, hotels and restaurants, trade and car repair, etc. However, most enterprises registered in Kazakhstan are engaged in developing and utilizing the energy sector. Large state-owned oil and energy enterprises include CNPC, Sinopec, CNOOC, and other large petrochemical enterprises and energy companies (e.g., Xinjiang Dashami Jilin Chemical Co).

Characteristics of Chinese MNCs' Investments in Kazakhstan: Industry and Share

As shown in Fig. 1, after 2012, the investments of Chinese TNCs in Kazakhstan have a clear fluctuating trend. The reasons for such changes are directly related to the industries in which China invests in Kazakhstan.

From the perspective of industry distribution, Chinese investment and joint project investment contracts in Kazakhstan amounted to $34.93 billion in 2005–2019, of which 70% of the funds went to the energy sector ($24.28 billion), followed by the chemical industry ($3.7 billion), transportation ($3.7 billion), and metal processing ($2.3 billion) (China Council for The Promotion of International Trade, 2020). Figure 3A, which supports the findings of the study, is available at https://figshare.com/with an identifier https://figshare.com/articles/dataset/Sectoral_distribution_of_Chinese_investments_in_Kazakhstan_2005-2019_docx/23 724060.

Chinese investments in Kazakhstan are mainly focused on energy chemicals. The changes in the international energy market significantly impact Chinese investments in Kazakhstan. When energy prices increase, Chinese investments in Kazakhstan grow, and vice versa (Fig. 2). This explains the fluctuating changes in Chinese investments in Kazakhstan since 2013.

To address the negative impact of Chinese investments in Kazakhstan in sectors that are mainly focused on energy and chemical industries, Chinese outward investments are also gradually adjusting their investment strategy and increasing investments in other sectors.

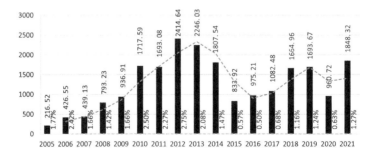

Fig. 1.   Total of Chinese FDI Inflows to Kazakhstan ($ million). *Source:* Compiled by the authors based on National Bank of Kazakhstan (2023).

Fig. 2. Comparison of China's Direct Investment in Kazakhstan and the Annual Average Price of Oil in 2005–2021. *Source:* Compiled by the authors based on West Texas Intermediate (2023).

According to the results of 2021, investments in agriculture, forestry, and fisheries increased 2.8 times; investments in professional, scientific, and technical activity increased 2.6 times; investments in information and communication increased 80.1%; investments in electricity supply increased 68.3%. Investments in manufacturing also increased significantly.

Other Major Investors in Kazakhstan

According to the data of the National Bank of Kazakhstan (2023), the Netherlands ranked first in the list of investments in Kazakhstan with a total amount of $6.999 billiNational Bank of Kazakhstan (2023) on in 2021 (29.4% of total FDIs in Kazakhstan in 2021). The United States occupied second place with $2.807 billion in investments (12%). Switzerland took third place with $2.698 billion (11.3%). These three countries have invested more than 50% of the total direct investments in Kazakhstan. Russia occupied fourth place with an investment of $1.9 billion (8%). The fifth place was occupied by Chinese investments of $1.848 billion (6%). European and American countries are still the main countries of investment in Kazakhstan. They are constantly expanding their investments in the country. In terms of trends, the change in investment in Kazakhstan is largely consistent across countries, increasing and decreasing at the same time. Figure 4A, which supports the findings of the study, is available at https://figshare.com/with an identifier https://figshare.com/articles/dataset/Total_investment_nflows_of_foreign_direct_investors_to_the_Republic_of_Kazakhstan_2005-2021_docx/237 24075.

Table 4A, which supports the findings of the study, is available at https://figshare.com/with an identifier https://figshare.com/articles/dataset/Total_FDI_inflows_to_Kazakhstan_from_foreign_direct_investors_by_resident_economic_activity_2017-2021_docx/23725659. As can be seen from Table 4A, mining, manufacturing, trade, auto repair, finance and insurance, transportation, and warehousing are the main sectors of foreign investment, accounting for 34.7% (97.2 million USD), 33.9% (53.3 million USD and 41.6 million USD), 13.8% (38.7 million USD), 5.8% (16.2 million USD), and 3.6% (10.1 million USD). However, FDI is constantly shifting to nonresource fields (i.e., other fields than mineral extraction).

Although China is increasing its investment in Kazakhstan, there is still a big gap between China and the main investors in Kazakhstan.

DISCUSSION

Chinese multinational companies have rapidly developed in recent years. The transnational competitiveness and influence of Chinese enterprises are constantly increasing. However, there is still a big gap compared with developed countries. For example, although China has more multinational companies in the Fortune 500 and Global 100 nonfinancial multinational companies lists, its profitability and multinational companies' competitiveness index have a big gap compared to developed countries.

The share of Chinese multinational companies in Kazakhstan still has a gap compared to European and American countries. Among the top five countries investing in Kazakhstan as of 2022, European countries invested a total of $11.597 billion, accounting for 49.4% of Kazakhstan's foreign investment flow; the United States invested $2.807 billion (12%); and China invested $1.848 billion (6%). The investment sectors are mainly concentrated in energy, chemical, transportation, metal processing, and other industries. It should be noted that 80% of China's investments are concentrated in the energy and chemical sectors, which makes the share of China's investments in Kazakhstan vulnerable to the international energy market, which can change simultaneously with the increase or decrease in energy prices.

CONCLUSION

This chapter aimed to identify the factors influencing the entry of Chinese MNCs into Kazakhstan and analyze their characteristics in terms of investment sectors and location advantages.

The authors conclude that the main factors for the entry of Chinese MNCs into Kazakhstan are as follows:

• Kazakhstan's proximity to Xinjiang and its high location advantage;
• Kazakhstan is located in an important position in China's "Belt and Road" development map and is an important platform for China's westward development;
• Kazakhstan is rich in natural resources, with large reserves of oil, natural gas, and mineral resources, which are of great significance in helping to solve China's energy security problems.

DATA AVAILABILITY

Figure 1A: Data on China's Outbound Investment Flows after Reform and Opening, which supports the findings of the study, is available at https://figshare.com/with an identifier https://figshare.com/articles/figure/China_s_Outbound_Investment_Flows_after_Reform_and_Opening_docx/23723979.

Figure 2A: Data on Regional Segmentation of China's outbound investment flows, 2015–2020, which supports the findings of the study, is available at https://figshare.com/with an identifier https://figshare.com/articles/dataset/Regional_Segmentation_of_China_s_outbound_investment_flows_2015-2020_docx/23724039.

Figure 3A: Data on Sectoral distribution of Chinese investments in Kazakhstan, 2005–2019, which supports the findings of the study, is available at https://figshare.com/with an identifier https://figshare.com/articles/dataset/Sectoral_distribution_of_Chinese_investments_in_Kazakhstan_2005-2019_docx/23724060.

Figure 4A: Data on Total investment inflows of foreign direct investors to the Republic of Kazakhstan, 2005–2021, which supports the findings of the study, is available at https://figshare.com/with an identifier https://figshare.com/articles/dataset/Total_investment_inflows _of_foreign_direct_investors_to_the_Republic_of_Kazakhstan_2005-2021_docx/23724075.

Table 1A: Data on Industrial distribution of China's direct investment stock in Asia by the end of 2021, which supports the findings of the study, is available at https://figshare.com/with an identifier https://figshare.com/articles/dataset/Industrial_distribution_of_China_s_direct_investment_stock_in_Asia_by_the_end_of_2021_docx/23724750.

Table 2A: Data on Top 100 multinationals by 2021 TNI Comparison, which supports the findings of the study, is available at https://figshare.com/with an identifier https://figshare.com/articles/dataset/Top_100_multinationals_by_2021_TNI_Comparison_docx/23725050.

Table 3A: Data on Revenues of the Fortune 500 Companies, 2022, which supports the findings of the study, is available at https://figshare.com/with an identifier https://figshare.com/articles/dataset/Revenues_of_the_Fortune_500_Companies_2022_docx/23725428.

Table 4A: Data on Total FDI inflows to Kazakhstan from foreign direct investors by resident economic activity, 2017–2021, which supports the findings of the study, is available at https://figshare.com/with an identifier https://figshare.com/articles/dataset/Total_FDI_inflows_to_Kazakhstan_from_foreign_direct_investors_by_resident_economic_activity_2017-2021_docx/23725659.

REFERENCES

China Council for The Promotion of International Trade. (2020). Business Environment Guidelines for Enterprises' Overseas Investment Countries (Regions)-Kazakhstan 2020. https://www.ccpit.org/image/1/4af03bb9f9f149c4bddefb4f24b1cd5c.pdf. Accessed on March 18, 2023.

Consulate General of the People's Republic of China in Almaty. (2020, April 11). Economic and trade news. http://almaty.china-consulate.gov.cn/jmxx/202005/t20200519_4699973.htm. Accessed on March 19, 2023.

Fortune 500. (2022). *Ranking.* https://fortune.com/ranking/fortune500/2022/search/. Accessed on March 19, 2023.

Gelvig, S.. (2020). China-Kazakhstan economic cooperation and "one belt, one road" initiative. *European Journal of Economics and Management Sciences.* №2. https://cyberleninka.ru/article/n/china-kazakhstan-economic-cooperation-and-one-belt-one-road-initiative. Accessed on March 16, 2023.

Liu, W., & Yang, J. (2014). Analysis of the current situation and problems of China's direct investment in Kazakhstan. http://www.oyjj-oys.org/UploadFile/Issue/vaook2z1.pdf. Accessed on March 16, 2023.

Ministry of Commerce of the People's Republic of China. (2015). *2015 Statistical Bulletin of China's Outward Foreign Direct Investment.* https://fdi.mofcom.gov.cn/resource/pdf/2019/12/28/6106dd33a9934d1eb6b4226049e1922c.pdf. Accessed on March 18, 2023.

Ministry of Commerce of the People's Republic of China. (2016). *2016 Statistical Bulletin of China's Outward Foreign Direct Investment.* http://images.mofcom.gov.cn/fec/201711/20171114083528539.pdf. Accessed on March 18, 2023.

Ministry of Commerce of the People's Republic of China. (2017). *2017 Statistical Bulletin of China's Outward Foreign Direct Investment.* http://images.mofcom.gov.cn/hzs/201810/20181029160118046.pdf. Accessed on March 18, 2023.

Ministry of Commerce of the People's Republic of China. (2018). *2018 Statistical Bulletin of China's Outward Foreign Direct Investment.* http://fec.mofcom.gov.cn/article/tjsj/tjgb/201910/20191002907954.shtml. Accessed on March 18, 2023.

Ministry of Commerce of the People's Republic of China. (2019). *2019 Statistical Bulletin of China's Outward Foreign Direct Investment.* http://images.mofcom.gov.cn/hzs/202010/20201029172027652.pdf. Accessed on March 18, 2023.

Ministry of Commerce of the People's Republic of China. (2020). *2020 Statistical Bulletin of China's Outward Foreign Direct Investment.* https://www.gov.cn/xinwen/2021-09/29/5639984/files/a3015be4dc1f45458513ab39691d37dd.pdf. Accessed on March 18, 2023.

National Bank of Kazakhstan. (2023). Direct investments according to the Republic of Kazakhstan's balance of payments data. https://www.nationalbank.kz/en/news/platezhnyy-balans-vn-sektora. Accessed on March 20, 2023.

West Texas Intermediate. (2023). *WTI oil futures.* https://ru.investing.com/commodities/crude-oil. Accessed on March 20, 2023.

World Bank. (2019, October 24). Doing Business 2020. https://archive.doingbusiness.org/en/reports/global-reports/doing-business-2020. Accessed on March 16, 2023.

World Economic Forum. (2022, January 11). Global Risks Report 2022. https://www.weforum.org/reports/global-risks-report-2022/. Accessed on March 17, 2023.

Yermekbayev, A. S., Sarybayev, M., & Suriguga, C. (2022). China-Kazakhstan Strategic Partnership and Bilateral Economic Cooperation CAA 1 2022. 10.52536/CAA. https://www.researchgate.net/publication/359772600_China-Kazakhstan_Strategic_Partnership_and_Bilateral_Economic_Cooperation_CAA_1_2022. Accessed on March 16, 2023.

MUTUAL BENEFITS OF ECONOMIC COOPERATION BETWEEN EAEU COUNTRIES AND TURKEY: POTENTIAL PRACTICE AREAS OF COOPERATION IN THE CONTEXT OF THE REGIONAL ECONOMIC INTEGRATION PROCESS

Inna V. Andronova and Nurselen T. Yildirim

RUDN University, Russia

ABSTRACT

Regional economic integrations bring many economic benefits to member countries. In international competition, there are integrations that make it easier for countries to reach their goals and attract attention with their effectiveness today. The Eurasian Economic Union (EAEU) is one of the main important regional economic integrations. This chapter details the relations Turkey can establish with the EAEU by considering the import and export data between Turkey and Russia. The research of recent data will discuss how Turkey's trade relations with Russia strengthen the EAEU and what kind of relationship will be possible in the future, considering commercial and economic integrations that are already included, as well as geographical and historical elements. This chapter will assess the potential relationship that can be established with the EAEU, given the strengthening of trade ties between Turkey and Russia. This chapter highlights the alternatives for the harmonization of Turkey's potential cooperation with the EAEU, which is planning a development strategy.

Keywords: EAEU; Turkey; Russia; integration; Central Asia; economic geography

JEL Code: F15

In this globalized world, strengthening relations with regional powers is a prerequisite for being progressive and strong in international competition. It is crucial to consider which

Development of International Entrepreneurship Based on Corporate Accounting and Reporting According to IFRS
Advanced Series in Management, Volume 33B, 151–158
Copyright © 2024 Inna V. Andronova and Nurselen T. Yildirim
Published under exclusive licence by Emerald Publishing Limited
ISSN: 1877-6361/doi:10.1108/S1877-63612024000033B019

status (i.e., member country, observer, inter-country integration, preferential trade agreement, etc.) will be robust and strategic in the established relationship. This chapter focuses on the positivity created by the trade cooperation between Russia and Turkey for the Eurasian Economic Union (EAEU). The authors discuss the status with which Turkey can establish relations with the EAEU. This chapter discusses how Turkey, which has relations with the EAEU, will establish a connection with the association as a result of these positive trade relationships. This chapter also emphasizes the effects of Russia's membership in the EAEU and the increasing Turkish–Russian trade relations in 2021–2022 on this relationship.

MATERIALS AND METHOD

The relations of the EAEU, a global actor, are examined by I. V. Andronova (2016), S. V. Bazavluk et al. (2022), A. Yalcinkaya and M. Guzel (2021), G. Denizci and M. Marangoz (2019), and F. S. Bahsi Kocer and K. Gokten (2021).

Regional economic integration is one of the most important concepts that promotes economic growth, increases job opportunities, and increases international solidarity, especially through regional proximity. Compared to bilateral trade and economic agreements, regional economic integrations facilitate holistic understanding. Countries cluster by taking into account their commercial, economic, and even political, social, and cultural interests. It supports global economic stability. Establishing a free trade area aims to remove obstacles such as tariffs and quotas. Creating a common market increases the international mobility of production factors such as labor, capital, and natural resources. Consolidating monetary and social policies provides financial ease, leading to a strong position in international competition. Economic integrations reduce costs and increase competition by providing greater market access and resource sharing.

B. Balassa (1976) describes economic integration as a process and as a situation. According to B. Balassa (1976), integration as a process means taking measures to eliminate discrimination between economic units belonging to different national states. Integration as a situation means the absence of various types of discrimination between national economies.

Therefore, there are many elements to be considered in regional economic integration. We can limit and define these elements within the framework of Turkey and the EAEU. The first issue that needs to be paid particular attention to and examined is the economic and commercial relations between Turkey and Russia, which are getting stronger daily. The boundaries of the relationship with the EAEU, with which Turkey maintains primary commercial relations and is a member, are important. The political, cultural, geographical, commercial, and economic relations of the EAEU and Turkey should be evaluated considering all these balances and borders. As S. V. Bazavluk et al. (2022) said, the Russian geopolitical concept of Eurasianism, with all its changes and modifications, remains very powerful, dominant, and alive in historical and cultural, academic, national, political, and ideological debates and discourses. For this reason, it would be the right step to start monitoring the relationship between the EAEU and Turkey, considering the factors between Turkey and Russia.

The importance of this chapter is that it makes it easier for us to discuss and understand how Turkey can establish a balance between the two integrations.

The chapter first details, through data, the bilateral economic and commercial cooperation and cooperation areas between Turkey and the EAEU. This chapter considers bilateral import and export dynamics and lists product and service groups. It also details strong product groups. The authors discuss the effects of EAEU member countries' relations with Europe and America on commercial and economic cooperation with Turkey and product groups. The academic studies elaborate on Turkey's role in the EAEU development strategy and how it can be included in this strategy. Using ongoing examples, the authors collected data on member countries and provided concretizations in the qualitative analysis.

The most important point that needs to be considered is the economic and trade relationship between Turkey and Russia. There are also serious economic interests between EAEU countries and Turkey. The economic relationship between Turkey and Russia, affected by periodic events, has always maintained its win-win policy. The problems between the two countries become ignored after a certain period due to economic interests.

RESULTS

Russia is the world's most important supplier of raw materials in oil, natural gas, mineral resources, agriculture, and forestry. According to A. Yalcinkaya and M. Guzel (2021), the future of the European Economic Area (EEA), especially its superiority in fossil fuels, is closely linked to global developments in energy and agriculture, especially from raw materials, such as natural gas, hard coal, iron and steel products, petroleum and its products, oilseeds, grain, and vegetable oils, which are the main groups of goods exported to Turkey. While Russia's export volume in 2020 was 16th in the world with approximately $337.1 billion, with the influence of the rising trend in commodity prices, Russia's export volume increased to $492.3 billion in 2021, ranking 13th in the world. Its relationship with Turkey also has a huge share in this rising export volume because the export rate with Turkey has also increased. While Russia's mineral resource exports to Turkey were 44.70% in 2020, they grew by 6.8% in volume, reaching 51.50% in 2021. While Russia's exports to Turkey in agricultural raw materials were 16.57% in 2020, it has a growth volume of 6.41%, reaching 22.98% in 2022. There is also visible growth in metal products and chemical products (Russian Foreign Trade, 2021; Turkish Statistical Institute, 2022).

The main goods and products exported from Turkey to Russia are machinery parts and equipment, food products, textiles, and shoes. There is a growth in the export volume of these goods in 2021 compared to 2020. For example, machinery parts and equipment increased from 29.79% in 2020 to 32.31% in 2021 (2.52%).

Other data to look at are the rate of imports from EAEU countries to Turkey and the rate of imports from Russia to Turkey in the same group of goods. The reason we examine these two values is that it shows how big a role Russia plays in Turkey's trade volume with EAEU countries.

The significance of the EAEU market for Turkey lies in the fact that there are 68 commodity items in Turkish exports with the share of EAEU countries exceeding 50% of total exports of these commodity items, seven items – 100%, 20 commodity items – 80%–90% of total exports of these goods. The indication of the Russian Federation has the largest specific weight in all commodity categories. For example, the rate of oil and oil products imports from EAEU countries to Turkey is close to the rate of imports from Russia to Turkey.

F. S. Bahsi Kocer and K. Gokten (2021) note that the difference in the economic development levels of the EAEU member countries, which is important for the union's future, is a significant problem. While Russia accounts for more than 80% of the EAEU's GDP, Belarus has a slice of 3% (Russian Foreign Trade, 2021; Turkish Statistical Institute, 2022).

In 2021, imports of oil and petroleum products from the EAEU to Turkey amounted to 39%, of which 38% came from Russia. Imports of aluminum from the EAEU to Turkey were 36%, of which 29% came from Russia. What is clear is that the relationship between Turkey and Russia actually shapes the relations with the EAEU. Additionally, Turkey exports not only common items with Russia but also different product and commodity groups to the EAEU countries. For the commercial relationship between Turkey and the EAEU to be strong, it is important to trade in different types of goods. However, the large commodity groups that exist and are traded regularly between Russia and Turkey are of primary importance in examining the relationship between the EAEU and Turkey. To understand the commercial importance of the EAEU for Turkey, it is important to start examining the commercial relations between Russia and Turkey. There are 72 more commodity items where the share of the EAEU countries exceeds 50%, for example, 95% of all imported fertilizers, 75% of wheat, 99% of coal, 100% of nuclear reactors and parts of nuclear reactors, 89% of vegetable oils, 100% of timber, 100% of cobalt ores and concentrates, 98% of precious metal ores and concentrates, etc. The EAEU countries have significant potential in developing agriculture. Russia and Kazakhstan are among the top 10 world leaders in grain exports. Thanks to regional integration, the production potential and production factors of these countries, which are pioneers in the field of agriculture, will continue to provide permanent positive progress through integration (Russian Foreign Trade, 2021; Turkish Statistical Institute, 2022).

In 2021, Turkey took the 10th place on the list of the largest exporters of goods to Russia. However, due to the sanctions imposed by Europe and America in 2022, the rate of exports to Russia, one of the top 10 European countries, decreased significantly. Turkey has skipped Italy, Poland, Japan, the Netherlands, France, and the United States on this list. Due to the Ukraine–Russia military operation that started in 2022, Turkey–Russia trade volume has increased even more. Being Russia's trading partner, Turkey has risen even higher in the ranking of exporting countries to Russia. The import and export rate with Western countries has decreased due to sanctions. However, since the demand for goods and products supplied from the West did not decrease, their substitutes were met from Turkey. Since substitutes for goods and product groups coming from Europe are supplied from Turkey, the ongoing commercial partnership with Russia has grown rapidly in recent years. For this reason, no matter what happens in history, both countries want to maintain a win-win policy toward each other. Permanent commercial and economic relations are indispensable for both countries; their volume must be increased.

There are also serious economic interests between EAEU countries and Turkey. Affected by periodic events, the economic relationship between Turkey and Russia has always maintained its win-win policy. All problems between the two countries become ignored after a certain period due to economic interests. I. V. Andronova (2016) said Russia is an integrating power in the EAEU.

Looking at the economic and trade data between Turkey and Russia for 2021, we point out that the relationship between the two countries based on the adopted policies is an unbreakable bond. The reason why 2021 is an important date in the relationship between these two countries is the changing balances in the world economy (especially in the EU and the United States) and the intensification of the problems between Russia and Ukraine that have been ongoing since 2014. In its win-win policy, it keeps strong commercial relations between the two countries, which will produce holistic positive results. The Russian Federation accounts for most of the trade volume of the EAEU. For this reason, any commercial relationship between Turkey and Russia indirectly affects the EAEU.

The data in Fig. 1 and Fig. 2 attempt to express the volume of Turkey's commercial relations with Russia and the EAEU. The slight difference between the columns also reflects Russia's role in the EAEU (Russian Foreign Trade, 2021; Turkish Statistical Institute, 2022).

If we examine Turkey's import dynamics to EAEU countries in Fig. 2, Russia plays the most important role in Turkey's cooperation with the EAEU (Russian Foreign Trade, 2021; Turkish Statistical Institute, 2022).

In line with this result, we can state that any agreement that Turkey makes with the EAEU will, in a way, be made with Russia. Russia's power and dominance in the EAEU are unlike the role played by any other European country in the EU. There are social,

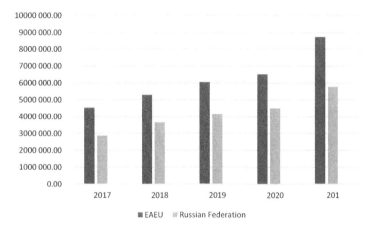

Fig. 1. Dynamics of Turkey's Exports to the EAEU Countries (1000 $). *Source:* Compiled by the authors based on data from the Russian Foreign Trade (2021) and Turkish Statistical Institute (2022).

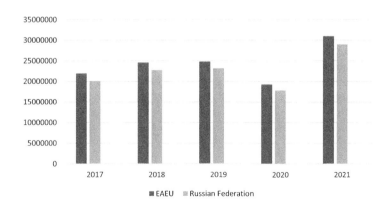

Fig. 2. Dynamics of Turkey's Imports to the EAEU Countries (1000 $). *Source:* Compiled by the authors based on data from the Russian Foreign Trade (2021) and Turkish Statistical Institute (2022).

geographical, and historical reasons (Soviet period) why Russia comes to the fore regarding unity. For example, G. Denizci and M. Marangoz (2019) said that Turkey is the only country for the EAEU countries to access the south and open to the sea.

It plays a vital role in activating the gates. EAEU countries are critically important in diversifying Turkey's foreign trade market and developing strategic cooperation.

DISCUSSION

To summarize, with the examined data, the authors stated that Turkey's relationship with Russia is indispensable. This relationship is important for the two countries, the EAEU, the EU, and other Western countries.

By looking at Turkey's relations with Russia, we can indicate which elements are important between Turkey and the EAEU.

Regional integrations enable cooperation with third countries, making common goals more effective globally. Collaborations within the integration increase economic convenience and facilitate the achievement of the planned targets. In fact, transparent and regular negotiations should be held to help develop trade and economic cooperation between Turkey and the EAEU, as well as to identify and eliminate trade barriers.

The observer state status that the EAEU currently maintains can be one of the fields of cooperation that can be made with Turkey. They may be authorized, if necessary, to form subcommittees and working groups to resolve individual problems. For example, observer states in the EAEU have been the Republic of Cuba, the Republic of Moldova, and the Republic of Uzbekistan. According to Article 109 of the EAEU, Turkey may be eligible for observer country status (Eurasian Economic Commission, 2018).

Due to Turkey's geographical location, its relations with the EAEU are mutually important. What will make the relationship between Turkey and the EAEU stronger than the country's status is a free trade agreement or preferential trade agreement.

A free trade agreement or preferential trade agreement could be concluded between the EAEU and Turkey, which would be more comprehensive than the status of an observer country. A preferential trade agreement exists between Turkey and Azerbaijan (World Trade Organization, 2020). The difference between the preferential trade agreement and the free trade agreement is that the agreements are made for more specific goods. What we emphasize here is that Turkey can make this agreement with the EAEU. In this way, conflicting interests of the EU, Turkey, and the EAEU can be prevented. The idea of regional order and unity targeted by regional economic integration is supported and does not raise any questions. The competitive value of the goods is preserved.

Turkey's relationship with the EU should be carefully examined when deciding which of these two types is more appropriate. Because of the initiatives to be granted to Turkey or the terms of the agreement to be achieved, it must not create a bridge between the EU and the EAEU. If such a situation is caused, regional economic integration will deviate from its goals, and price competition in trade will be disrupted.

CONCLUSION

In this process, if one of the application areas can be evaluated in a real position, the EAEU will get closer to the future development strategy and reach the goals in more areas (EFSD, 2022). The existence of a new country that will provide new foreign economic activities will strengthen the place of integration in international competition. These economic benefits and application possibilities should be explained to the countries and included in cooperation most effectively. It is necessary to consider some points when deciding which of the listed and discussed application areas (observer country status, free trade agreement, or preferential trade agreement) is reasonable. For mutual cooperation to be more holistic and effective, the specific and basic trends that need to be considered should be as follows:

- a unified foreign trade policy (a unified customs and tariff regulation and a unified system of nontariff regulation);
- a unified system of technical regulation;
- coordinated industrial policy, agro-industrial policy, and macroeconomic policy;
- the EAEU establishes common markets for energy resources, transport services, single transport space, medicines, medical equipment, etc;
- participate in the work of the Eurasian Economic Commission (EEC) to develop trade and economic cooperation, develop technical, customs, sanitary, and phytosanitary regulations, discuss other issues in the Commission's work area, and promote dialogue and collaboration in the area of mutual interest of the observer state and member states.

It is necessary to provide macroeconomic regulations. In this process, audit procedures should be arranged in accordance with international procedures and implemented realistically. Trade and investment statistics should be reviewed. Objective assessments should be made on negative data. Tariff and nontariff arrangements should not be ignored while making logistics and customs arrangements. The rate of labor migration in the employment rate should not be underestimated. Intellectual property rights should be discussed. In the age of developing technology, all arrangements should be compatible with the current period.

The envisaged cooperation will bring the mentioned economic and commercial benefits. The union participants should discuss economic benefits and implementation possibilities transparently and regularly. Ensuring the most effective cooperation will strengthen the economic and commercial relations between Turkey and Russia. Moreover, the conceptual and purposeful integrity of regional economic integration will be strengthened by Turkey's relationship with the EAEU and will positively affect the world economy in terms of goods, services, and capital.

REFERENCES

Andronova, I. V. (2016). Eurasian Economic Union: Opportunities and barriers to regional and global leadership. *International Organisations Research Journal, 11*(2), 7–23. https://doi.org/10.17323/1996-7845-2016-02-07

Azerbaijan and World Trade Organization. (2020). A preferential trade agreement between Azerbaijan and Turkey has entered into force. https://wto.az/en/article/a-preferential-trade-agreement-between-azerbaijan-and-turkey-has-entered-into-force/80. Accessed on March 15, 2023.

Bahsi Kocer, F. S., & Gokten, K. (2021). Eurasian Economic Union: Formation, potential and limitations. *Academic Review of Economics and Administrative Sciences, 14*(4), 1468–1485. https://doi.org/10.25287/ohuiibf.932656. Accessed on March 15, 2023.

Balassa, B. (1976). Types of economic integration. In F. Machlup (Ed.), *Economic integration: Worldwide, regional, sectoral* (pp. 17–40). Palgrave Macmillan. https://doi.org/10.1007/978-1-349-02571-8_2

Bazavluk, S. V., Kurylev, K. P., & Savin, L. V. (2022). Eurasianism, Eurasian Economic Union and multipolarity: Assessments of foreign experts. *Vestnik RUDN. International Relations, 22*(1), 30–42. https://doi.org/10.22363/2313-0660-2022-22-1-30-42

Denizci, G., & Marangoz, M. (2019). Trade between Eurasian Economic Union member countries and Turkey. *Eurasian Journal of International Studies*, 7(16), 414–431. https://doi.org/10.33692/avrasyad.543822

Eurasian Economic Commission (EEC). (2018). Observer state status at the EAEU. https://eec.eaeunion.org/en/comission/department/dep_razv_integr/mezhdunarodnoe-sotrudnichestvo/o-statuse-gosudarstva-nablyuda-telya.php. Accessed on March 15, 2023.

Eurasian Fund for Stabilization and Development (EFSD). (2022). *The Eurasian Fund for Stabilization and Development 2022–2026 strategy (Approved by the EFSD Council on 31 May 2022 No. 78.)*. EFSD. https://efsd.org/upload/iblock/d77/EFSD_strategy_General_ENG.pdf. Accessed on March 15, 2023.

Russian Foreign Trade. (2021). Report on foreign trade between Russia and Turkey in 2021; exports, imports. https://russian-trade.com/reports-and-reviews/2022-02/torgovlya-mezhdu-rossiey-i-turtsiey-v-2021-g/. Accessed on March 15, 2023.

Turkish Statistical Institute. (2022). Foreign trade statistics, March 2022. https://data.tuik.gov.tr/Bulten/Index?p=Foreign-Trade-Statistics-March-2022-45538&dil=2. Accessed on March 2, 2023.

Yalcinkaya, A., & Guzel, M. (2021). Eurasian Economic Union, Belt-Road, TRACECA, and New Silk Road as examples of regionalization. *International Journal of Afro-Eurasian Research*, 6(12), 100–124. https://dergipark.org.tr/en/pub/ijar/issue/64457/937162. Accessed on March 15, 2023.

IMPROVEMENT IN THE ECONOMIC INTEGRATION MECHANISMS IN THE CURRENT CONTEXT OF TRADE RELATIONS BETWEEN CUBA AND RUSSIA

Mireya Jay Alcántara

RUDN University, Russia

ABSTRACT

This chapter aims to improve the mechanisms of economic integration between Russia and Cuba. The methodology used by the author in this chapter is mainly composed of the method of historical-comparative, inductive, and analytical-synthetic analysis. The author used the existing information on the internet and other analyzed references. Additionally, the author qualitatively analyzed the opinions of various experts and drew conclusions. Regional integration is examined conceptually as a basis for a better understanding of integration processes. The research provides historical data after including Cuba in the Council for Mutual Economic Assistance (CMEA), considering this structure as the first one with characteristics of an economic integration structure. Next, the author considered the post-Soviet stage until the present. Statistical data according to the Observatory of Economic Complexity (OEC) summary are provided. These data correspond to the periods from 2018 to 2021 and show the statistics of exports, imports, and other important indicators between the two countries. Based on the analysis, it is necessary to update the integration mechanisms to reduce tariff rates, promote free trade between the two countries, and increase the participation of Russian companies in the Mariel Special Development Zone (ZED Mariel), Havana, Cuba.

Development of International Entrepreneurship Based on Corporate Accounting and Reporting According to IFRS
Advanced Series in Management, Volume 33B, 159–165
Copyright © 2024 Mireya Jay Alcántara
Published under exclusive licence by Emerald Publishing Limited
ISSN: 1877-6361/doi:10.1108/S1877-63612024000033B020

Keywords: Integration; economy; Russia; Cuba; Council for Mutual Economic Assistance (CMEA); globalization

JEL Codes: F00; F10; F15; O10; R01

In today's world, new alliances are being formed that seek to unify blocks by crossing the barriers imposed by globalization and the unipolar world where the rich are getting richer and the poor are getting poorer. These blocks of different levels of development, social and economic patterns, and geopolitical and geographical scenarios use new technologies to strengthen regional integration structures. This process constitutes a paradigm that is already seeing positive results in the growth of many countries.

Husillos Vidic (2020) considers economic integration as the process of unification of economic policies and the elimination of economic barriers between two or more countries. The objective of economic integration is to create broader economic spaces in which the advantages of international trade can be taken advantage of, such as increasing specialization or increased productivity.

This type of alliance requires development and cooperation agreements between the participating countries and the political will of their governments. It modifies the external economic relations of the countries and requires great coordination of their economic policies. Economic integration is also expressed at the level of regional integration infrastructures. Although this research does not deal with this topic itself, it is important to guide the concept of regional integration.

When we think of infrastructures for regional integration or integration between countries in general, the first thing that comes to mind is a large-scale project with a high budget (Rodriguez Molina, 2020). We think of financing in terms of a complex cooperation structure between countries, the period of preparation and maturation of which requires a complex institutional and financial framework. To the extent that we delve into the countries' export value chains, we see that the ramifications of the effects of regional integration go beyond even this type of physical infrastructure with an international vocation. Quantitatively analyzing the impact of a project at the regional level requires an adequate approximation of the social benefits and costs of the projects. For this reason, the study of changes in economic surpluses in a project of regional scope must consider all countries involved.

In summary, regional integration is understood as the process in which a group of countries gradually coordinate or merge their economic policies over time. It seeks to overcome (by mutual agreement) the barriers that divide the member countries to manage shared resources and assets jointly.

According to Malamud (2011), regional integration is based on regional agreements that improve cooperation and eliminate barriers to exchanging goods, services, capital, and people. It also includes coordination, convergence, and deep integration initiatives on political, environmental, and educational issues.

The Cuba–Russia alliance, taken in the strategic and economic context, has been structured since Soviet times as an alliance of cooperation. Despite having gone through some pause periods, it is no different. We could even say that in recent years, this alliance has been strengthened through some agreements in various sectors (social, economic, and political) with positive results for both countries.

The cooperation mechanisms have been modified according to each stage and category. Nevertheless, they have always been based on mutual aid for the economic strengthening of both countries. Russia (formerly the Soviet Union) has been Cuba's most important strategic partner throughout its history.

MATERIALS AND METHOD

Economic integration is studied in the works of Coll Morales (2020), Duque and Noroño (2019), Husillos Vidic (2020), Leidys Ramos (2019), Lipkin (2019), Malamud (2011), Marin Alvarez (2022), Rodriguez Molina (2020), Richard, Charles Wyplosz, Willem Molle, Jacques Pelkmans, Miroslav N. Jovanović, Frank McDonald, Stephen Dearden, Robert Barrass, and Shobhana Madhavan.

The process of economic integration between Cuba and Russia is evident from the creation of the Council for Mutual Economic Assistance (CMEA).

The CMEA was an economic cooperation organization formed around the USSR in 1949 by various socialist countries whose objectives were to promote trade relations between member countries in an attempt to counteract the international economic organizations of the capitalist economy.

The CMEA members divided the work between the different countries, creating zones that produce raw materials, the steel industry, the petrochemical industry, etc., to which production quotas and prices were set, in exchange for military protection and fuel. Its phase of greatest international expansion coincided with the 1970s when it controlled 10% of world merchandise traffic.

The CMEA was formed based on achieving an economic integration or coordination plan among its member countries. Particularly, the planning economies were reflected among its members. On itself, the organization did not possess supranational authority to decide and implement. The decisions came from higher levels that jumped any influence of the markets and the private initiative. Another particularity that identified this integration group was that its recommendations could only be implemented with the full concurrence of interested members and did not affect those who were not interested or, in some way, did not assume these recommendations.

As noted above, most of CMEA's foreign trade was a state monopoly, which placed several barriers between a producer and a foreign customer.

In trade between CMEA members, the Soviet Union used to provide raw materials, and Central and Eastern European countries provided finished equipment and machinery. The three underdeveloped members of the CMEA had a special relationship with the other seven. CMEA gained disproportionately more politically than economically from its heavy contributions to the underdeveloped economies of these three countries.

According to Coll Morales (2020), the organization tried to organize production by zones for processing raw materials, developing industry, and ensuring the collectivization of agriculture. In this sense, the well-known Soviet five-year plans were applied, aimed at promoting and controlling all production. Some plans represented 40% of production.

A new stage in the development of the 29th socialist economic integration of the CMEA member countries was the adoption of the Comprehensive Program for the Scientific and Technological Progress of the CMEA countries until the year 2000, which defined the scientific, technical, and economical tasks in the field of atomic energy, integrated automation and digitization, and other areas of scientific and technological progress.

During this period, and thanks to this integration model, Cuba developed many production sectors, such as mechanized agriculture, metallurgy, transportation, and education; generally, a substantial growth in the country's gross domestic product was noted (Lipkin, 2019). For its part, Russia had imports of metals, agro-industrial products, and others.

The training of Cuban professionals in the countries belonging to the block, as well as their exchange, was an important result of this alliance.

Over the years, after the dissolution of the USSR and the European socialist bloc, it became necessary to restructure the economic integration models between Cuba and Russia from the late 1990s and over the course of the years 2000 to date.

The necessary updating and strengthening of the cooperation and integration mechanisms between the two countries in the post-Soviet era and the recent entry into the digital era, to deal with globalization and strong sanctions and the commercial economic blockade (in the case of Cuba) in which the United States and its European allies have involved both countries, is a current issue on the bilateral economic agenda.

According to Leidys Ramos (2019), Cuba and Russia are currently promoting a constant process of updating bilateral economic ties in areas such as energy, metallurgy, the automotive, railway and aviation sectors, agriculture, and the biopharmaceutical industry, among many others.

Although contacts between the two countries began to resume in 1995–2000, strategic alliances were not established until the 2004–2014 phase, as from that point on, Russia's positions on the international stage once again began to largely coincide with Cuba's.

In 2014, the visit of Vladimir Putin, President of Russia, marked the beginning of a new stage in relations, marked by the cancellation of 90% of the Cuban debt with Russia, which included obligations contracted with the former USSR and amounted to $35.2 billion. The 10% that Cuba had to pay would be invested in the country in social and economic development projects of mutual interest.

Since then, Cuba and Russia have collaborated on energy, transportation, metallurgical, science, technology, and environmental projects.

In the 2019 Observatory of Economic Complexity (OEC) Russia–Cuba report, Cuba exported $18.4 million to Russia. The main products that Cuba exported to Russia are Rolled Tobacco; Hard Liquor; Vaccines, blood, antisera, toxins and cultures; Gold; Crustaceans; Coffee. During the last 23 years, Cuban exports to Russia have decreased at an annualized rate of 12.1%, from $354 million in 1996 to $18.4 million in 2019. In 2019, Russia exported $285 million to Cuba. There were no major exports from Russia to Cuba in 2019. During the last 23 years, Russia's exports to Cuba have decreased at an annualized rate of 1.93%, from $446 million in 1996 to $285 million in 2019.

In 2018, Russia exported $10 million worth of services to Cuba, with Other Business Services ($6.9 million), Insurance Services ($2.4 million), and Transportation ($400 million) being the largest in terms of value.

Although the advances in economic-commercial relations between Russia and Cuba are notable, evidenced in other scientific research, it is necessary to review the integration mechanisms and establish new guidelines that benefit both countries.

According to the theory of economic integration, its degree is determined by various categories, which are defined as follows:

• preferential trade zone;
• free trade zone (e.g., Andean Pact);
• customs union (e.g., Cartagena Agreement);
• common market (e.g., Andean Community);

- economic and monetary union, which supposes a common market, a single currency, and a certain uniformity in terms of economic policies;
- Complete economic integration. There is the unification of policies, merging the economies, and adopting common plans. There is a monetary, fiscal, social, service unification, etc. This leads to the creation of a supranational authority whose decisions fall on the member countries.

However, in dynamics, the integration mechanism goes beyond the purely economic and begins to play a predominant role in politics and defense, which eventually boils down to the actual or legal creation of supranational countries, when nation-states "give in" part of their sovereignty to the new supranational country.

In this sense, the economic members can be constituted as follows:

- tariff preference;
- free trade zone;
- customs union;
- economic and monetary union common market; monetary union;
- free movement of people (visa is not required); customs control is not required;
- political union;
- agreement on defense matters.

According to a World Trade Organization (WTO) compliant article, tariffs are the "customs duties applied to merchandise imports" (i.e., a type of tax on goods and services that enter a country in a certain way).

Although there are several types of tariffs, the most common is the one that is calculated as a percentage of the product's value, also known as ad valorem. In the case of Russia, this percentage was 30% in 2019 for Cuban merchandise (e.g., lobsters, crustaceans, milk and cream, yogurt, fresh cheese, and natural honey).

For its part, Cuba does not establish a fixed percentage; it rather varies depending on the product (Marin Alvarez, 2022). The island's commodities are ethyl alcohol and brandy, poultry, water with and without added sugar, nonalcoholic beer, soft drinks, and malt beer.

On the other hand, Cuba has been developing efforts regarding regional economic integration. An example of this is the Mariel Special Development Zone (ZED Mariel) (ZED Mariel, 2023).

The ZED Mariel is an area in Cuba where foreign investment is encouraged.

The ZED Mariel, founded in November 2013 with an extension of 465.4 square kilometers, reported 63 approved businesses from 21 countries until 2022 and generated 10,532 direct jobs.

In this area, Cuba encourages foreign investment with tax incentives such as tax exemptions on repatriation of capital, labor, contribution to local development, imports on the investment process and on profits for the first 10 years and 12% after that. The ZED Mariel is divided into the following sectors:

- A – industrial and logistics activities;
- B – industrial;
- C – industrial and tourist;
- D and E – livestock and forestry;

- F – agricultural and extractive activities;
- G – industrial, extractive, and livestock activities;
- H – tourism and agriculture.

   The special zone is presented as a project aimed at attracting national and foreign investments with the main goal of increasing the production of goods and services with high added value, using knowledge based on innovations, as well as the application of environmentally friendly technologies, creating industrial clusters that implement import substitution, export promotion, and the creation of new sources of employment as an economic policy.

   It is considered one of the most complex works that has been carried out in Cuba. The future container terminal is the beginning of the country's first ZED and is destined to become the main entry and exit door for Cuban foreign trade.

   However, interesting and debatable is the fact that Russia currently has only one presence in the ZED Mariel.

   Russia has an important place as a commercial partner in the National Plan for the Economic and Social Development of the Island until 2030. The active participation in the editions of the International Fair of Havana confirms the interest of investors in strengthening the integration between both countries.

   Russia currently contributes to the development of Cuba through various projects, especially in energy, industry, telecommunications, agriculture, and land, rail, and civil aviation transportation. The efforts with this nation also include the renewal and expansion of the production of steel and laminates, the evaluation of geological resources and the prospects for the development of oil deposits in the northern strip of the country, the investment of about one billion euros until 2030 to improve road capacity and revive the railway system, the loan of $150 million for agriculture and housing construction, and cooperation in the biopharmaceutical industry, creation of companies, and production and extension of the visa exemption period to three months.

RESULTS

The research has provided a series of historical data and has concluded that these mechanisms must continue to be updated regarding tariff reductions and free trade. It is necessary to promote the more active participation of Russian companies in the ZED Mariel to achieve greater economic independence from the globalized world and strengthen economic-commercial relations between both countries. Thus, a more current tariff preference mechanism could be a proposal to consider.

DISCUSSION

The economic integration processes between Cuba and Russia have allowed these nations to be more united on trade and economic issues, which has been of great benefit. Other lines that can be considered in a future Russian investment on the island would be energy, mining, agricultural industry, finance, tourism, metallurgy, science, and construction.

CONCLUSION

According to Duque and Noroño (2019), the commercial exchange in the world has always existed, and countries and organizations have constantly commercialized. The traditional paradigms have been undertaken for decades, instituting guidelines for behaviors and corporate, organizational, and family relationships, translating into a way of being, developing, and relating. The change of models with globalization has instituted other technical, economic, social, and environmental archetypes. These changes have forced organizational management to enter complex contexts, provide the internationalization of capital, and assume the challenge of betting and positioning in expanded markets, defining conditions and behaviors on organizational and cultural schemes.

Economic integration is one of the most powerful mechanisms to face the globalized world in times of digital economy. Cuba and Russia have starred in one of the most important scenarios in this area, from including Cuba in the CMAE to the most current integration projects between both countries.

It is important to emphasize the role that each integration process plays for each nation or country and to know the different guidelines to be followed in the establishment of this kind of system in the legal, political, social, economic, commercial, and strategic fields, creating conditions favorable to each country participating in these integration processes. Additionally, rules of nondiscrimination are established. In accordance with this principle, tariffs and other rules should apply between the participating countries.

REFERENCES

Coll Morales, F. (2020, April 1). COMECON. *Economipedia.* https://economipedia.com/definiciones/comecon.html. Accessed on March 31, 2023.

Duque, A. E. A., & Noroño, J. G. (2019). Regional integration as a mechanism of Latin American sustainable development: Ontological point of view. *Organizational Sapienza, 6*(11), 101–141.

Husillos Vidic, M. (2020, May 1). Economic integration. *Economipedia.* https://economipedia.com/definiciones/integracion-economica.html. Accessed on March 31, 2023.

Leidys Ramos, G. (2019, December 3). Why are relations with Russia at the best moment of the last 20 years? *Granma.* https://www.granma.cu/mundo/2019-12-03/por-que-las-relaciones-con-rusia-estan-en-el-mejor-momento-de-los-ultimos-20-anos-03-12-2019-00-12-53. Accessed on March 31, 2023.

Lipkin, M. (2019). The Council for Mutual Economic Assistance and the existing trends in study of the 20th century: Towards the 70th anniversary of CMEA. *St. Petersburg Slavic and Balkan Studies, 2*(26), 56–66. https://doi.org/10.21638/11701/spbu19.2019.204

Malamud, A. (2011). Concepts, theories and debates on regional integration. *North America, 6*(2), 219–249. http://www.scielo.org.mx/scielo.php?script=sci_arttext&pid=S1870-35502011000200008&lng=es&tlng=es. Accessed on March 31, 2023.

Mariel Special Development Zone (ZED Mariel). (2023). Summary. https://cel-logistica.org/wp-content/uploads/2020/03/Resumen-ZED-Mariel.pdf. Accessed on March 31, 2023.

Marin Alvarez, O. (2022, March 4). The economic relations between Russia and Cuba, explained. *Periodismo de Barrio.* https://periodismodebarrio.org/2022/03/las-relaciones-economicas-entre-rusia-y-cuba-explicadas/. Accessed on March 31, 2023.

Rodriguez Molina, R. (2020, June 5). What are we talking about when we talk about regional integration? https://blogs.iadb.org/transporte/es/de-que-hablamos-cuando-hablamos-de-integracion-regional/. Accessed on March 31, 2023.

FOREIGN ECONOMIC POTENTIAL OF THE REPUBLIC OF CHAD IN THE SYSTEM OF THE AFRICAN CONTINENT: PROBLEMS AND SOLUTIONS

Abdoulaye M. Hassane, Diana M. Madiyarova and Ousman N. Mahamat Nour

RUDN University, Russia

ABSTRACT

This chapter aims to analyze and evaluate the economic potential of Chad within the African continent, identify the challenges faced by the country, and propose potential solutions. The authors used a combination of qualitative and quantitative research methods. Relevant data is collected from reliable sources such as government reports, international organizations, research institutes, and academic studies, including data on Chad's GDP, trade flows, foreign direct investment (FDI), infrastructure, human capital, and natural resources.

The Republic of Chad is an agrarian country where the prosperity of 55% of the population depends on the development of agriculture, mainly livestock. Although rich in natural resources, Chad is one of the poorest countries in the world. Several investment projects have recently appeared in this country, which will help reduce the population's poverty in the future. The growth rate of Chad's economy lags behind that of the population. Foreign assistance is needed to solve the identified problem. With regard to the investment projects that have become more active this year, it would be unnecessary to be dizzy with success because they are still unable to break the established way of life. The Republic of Chad is situated in Africa and is considered one of the largest countries in the continent. The country has no access to the sea.

Development of International Entrepreneurship Based on Corporate Accounting and Reporting According to IFRS
Advanced Series in Management, Volume 33B, 167–172
ISSN: 1877-6361/doi:10.1108/S1877-63612024000033B021

Keywords: Economy; agriculture; foreign trade; export; import; problems and solutions

JEL Codes: Q18; Q13; Q17; O13; O55

The Republic of Chad has a tremendous opportunity to boldly embark on a new path or develop its economy to a new level to embrace the latest technologies, deepen regional integration, develop the country's trade, and have innovative partnerships with other countries. Investment security is especially relevant for the African continent, which today has the youngest population in the world. Simultaneously, there are several serious problems in the field of human capital development in Africa.

Since Idriss Deby Itno took over the leadership of the Republic of Chad in 1990, consistent structural changes have been carried out in Chad to modernize the country's economy; a program of privatization of state enterprises (companies) is being implemented.

Investments are a condition for the development of developing economies. Having an inefficient economy, the Republic of Chad has a large amount of natural resources, which makes it possible to count on the investment activity of the developed countries. Over the past few years, African countries have made encouraging progress in implementing Agenda 2030; Agenda 2063, according to the UN.

This chapter aims to analyze and evaluate the economic potential of Chad within the African continent, identify the challenges faced by the country, and propose potential solutions.

MATERIALS AND METHODS

The research methods include a content analysis of economic methods and open sources of information – data from the internet, including data from the Ministry of Economy of the Republic of Chad, the World Bank, various expert communities, and scientific works of economic experts.

RESULTS

The Republic of Chad is one of the agricultural countries in Africa. However, the country is rich in natural resources. Recently, several investment projects have emerged in this country, which will help reduce the population's poverty in the long run. Chad is a very eclectic state in national and legal terms. It has a population of Muslims (Sunni, Hanafi, and Shafi'i madhhabs in the north) and Christians (Catholics and, to a lesser extent, Protestants). The legal system is also mixed, including elements of customary law.

In terms of demography, Chad is a very young country. Most of the population are young people (less than 25-years old); they make up about 67.2% of the population. The average life expectancy is low. The population density by African standards is also low due to the predominance of desert landscapes. The overall literacy rate is only 22.3% (as of 2018). Like many African countries, the Republic of Chad has rich natural resources such as oil, salt, copper, sand, gum arabic, sesame, natron and spirulina (blue algae), etc. Agriculture and oil have so far been the backbone of the country's economy. The discovery and production of crude oil in the southern region of the country since 2013 has made

Chad an oil exporter and an Organization of the Petroleum Exporting Countries (OPEC) member. The decline in crude oil prices sent the country into a two-year recession in 2016–2017 and the debt crisis. GDP growth turned positive again in 2018 thanks to oil and cotton production. However, the country has achieved an average annual GDP growth of only 0.4% over the past five years.

The volume of foreign trade turnover of the Republic of Chad amounted to $7,128.0 million in 2019 – the beginning of 2020. The country's exports amounted to $4,053 million. Imports amounted to $3,075 million. Chad exports oil (up to 90% of the value of exports; mainly to the United States), livestock (to Nigeria), gum arabic (fourth place in the world; to European countries – France, Germany, the United Kingdom, etc.), and cotton (to France, the Netherlands, etc.). As of 2019, the main purchases of products and goods produced in the Republic of Chad are the United States (58.5% of the cost), India (13.3%), and Japan (11.3%).

The country also imports machinery and equipment, including oil-producing, consumer goods, and food. The main suppliers are France (16.5%), China (14.2%), and Cameroun (11.0%), which supplied food to Chad in 2019 (World Bank, 2023). At the beginning of the 20th century, foreign trade policy in Chad underwent several changes. Protectionism, which had a different character and a different meaning, became its characteristic sphere again. Goods were subject to high duties not because their production in the country is poorly developed but to prevent foreign goods from entering the domestic market and provide support for the country's industry and high prices (African Development Bank, 2023).

In 2020, the GDP in Chad increased to $13.0 billion. The maximum volume was $13.94 billion, and the minimum was $3.1 billion. The total percentage of GDP in the above-mentioned year was divided among three sectors of the economy – agriculture, industry, and services – 46.83%, 15.96%, and 43.58%, respectively (Chad: Share of economic sectors in the gross domestic product [GDP] from 2011–2021, 2023).

Table 1 shows data indicating various aspects of economic growth in Chad within two decades (2001–2020). There is a tendency that the level of the population's prosperity depends mainly on agriculture and oil production. For example, oil exploitation in Chad within 2003–2011 directly related to the increase of the population wellbeing from 0.596 to 0.616 (Gadom et al., 2018). Nowadays this tendency is preserved.

Table 1. Indicators of the Economic Development of the Republic of Chad in %.

Indexes	2001	2005	2010	2017	2018	2020
GDP growth	1.0	1.2	−1.1	0.9	1.1	1.3
GDP growth per capita	0.2	0.4	−1.8	0.6	0.5	1.0
Labor cost	4.2	5.4	3.4	−6.2	0.2	−1.2
Labor productivity	2.9	4.0	3.3	8.7	4.0	4.2
Employment growth	1.7	−1.9	−1.8	−0.7	−0.3	−0.1
Unemployment rate	5.5	7.7	8.9	9.6	9.4	10.3
Prices	3.5	5.1	4.5	2.7	1.8	1.6
Public debt in % of GDP	41.1	44.1	48.2	50.0	54.1	60.0
Balance of current items of the balance of payments in % of GDP	−1.0	−1.0	−7.0	−1.0	−9.0	−8.0

Source: Compiled by the author based on data by Global Economy – World Bank (n.d.) and CIA World Factbook (2022).

In 2022, according to Exchange Portal "Take-Profit" (2023), GDP data were the following: GDP volume was 12.7 billion dollars, annual GDP growth – 2.4% (which is noticeably higher than in 2020), GDP per capita amounted to 590 dollars whereas GDP per capita PPP (purchasing power par) amounted to 1,413 dollars.

According to Table 2, the proportion of the country's population is very dependent on the development of agriculture, which ranks first with 57%, overtaking such sectors as industry, transport, and tourism. The second place goes to industries with 18%.

Currently, the exploitation of African countries, including the Republic of Chad, is still being carried out through the penetration of transnational companies into their economies and their economic dictate, which is based on the huge external debt of these countries; military pressure is not excluded. The economic activity of foreign companies or monopolies in the Republic of Chad is selective – they open their enterprises in locations rich with natural resources, a cheap labor market, and where low wages go well with the presence of disciplined and easily trained workers.

The Republic of Chad has trade relations with many countries of the world. Russia is one of these countries with which Chad has diplomatic relations (though with a small share). In 2021, according to Britannica, the following countries imported to Chad: China – 28.3%, the United States – 3.2%, France – 6.4%, and other countries including Russia, Turkey, the Netherlands, and Germany – more than 50%. In terms of export, the main countries where goods were exported in 2021 were distributed in the following ratio: Germany – 35.5%, United Arab Emirates – 25.4%, Taiwan – 15.5%, etc. (Britannica, 2021).

In 1970–2020, Chad's GDP at current prices increased by $10.8 billion (five times more) to $11.2 billion, a change of $1.3 billion due to a population growth of 15.5 million people, as well as by $9.5 billion thanks to an increase in GDP per capita by $581. In 2024, GDP is expected to grow 3.7% mostly by the further development of the oil sector (African Development Bank, 2023).

The research shows that the development of the economy as a whole and the sector of the external economy is influenced by the following factors:

- geographical remoteness from the main transport and trade flows;
- lack of access to the sea;
- underdeveloped infrastructure;
- political instability, world conflicts, fluxes of refugees;

Table 2. The Structure of Chad's GDP by Industry. Data for 2022 According to the Resource Report for Selected Countries and Subjects.

Areas	Share in GDP, %
Agriculture	57
Industry	18
Tourism	10
Transport	3
Others	12
Total	100

Source: Compiled by the author based on CIA World Factbook (2022, pp. 1142–1170), Statista (2023), and AfDB, OECD, UNDP, & UNECA (2012).

- the presence of remnants of the "ways of the past centuries." In the country, especially in areas remote from large cities, there is still a feudal, patriarchal system and even covert trade in human resources, including minors;
- natural disasters, such as drought, which adversely affect the development of agriculture as a fundamental sector of the economy (Ortiz, 2022).

DISCUSSION

To make a discussion, it is necessary to understand the above results. From this part, we can say that the main problem for Chad is the external debt – this country is one of 13 African countries (27 globally) that in February 2023 were considered as at high debt risk – which practically does not decrease: it amounted to 2/5 of the annual gross production of goods and services in the country at the end of the 20th century. That is why, Chad's government spends almost all assistance received from other countries to pay interest and other obligations on external debt (AUC/OECD, 2018).

Simultaneously, these countries point to their experience; their reasoning is aimed at logic based on practical experience and the past colonial experience of this country and other countries with a similar development history that preserved even at the second decade of the 21st century – in 2011, 38% of Chad's popularity lived in rather poor conditions, starving, not getting the medical care they needed. Moreover, in 2016 this country was ranked as 135 of 136 possible as the less open economy in the world. However, for the past five or six years, Chad has been proving that its economic and social development is paying off (Ortiz, 2022). Moreover, the Government has outlined further plans to strengthen the country's position in the global market.

The Government of Chad has identified the following promising areas of action:

- continuation of the policy of development of the agricultural sector, increasing the level of food and nutrition security;
- further promotion and protection of the rights of women and youth;
- strengthening democracy, rational management, and enhancement of the state's role;
- strengthening environmental protection;
- strengthening peace, unity, and national concord;
- strengthening the fight against poverty, social inequality, and social exclusion;
- support for the system of basic social services and its further development.

CONCLUSION

Having considered foreign trade policy, Chad's economic reforms, and all the pros and cons, the authors can conclude that the Republic of Chad belongs to developing countries. Chad exports petroleum, fish, meat, hides, livestock, salt, gum arabic, and caustic soda. The country imports industrial and medical equipment, petroleum products, vehicles, and foodstuffs. The main trading partners are France, the United States, India, Portugal, Spain, Russia, Cameroon, Nigeria, Zaire, and Gabon.

The importance of external economic relations for the economic development of the Republic of Chad is determined by this ambition and by the fact that the development of the economic situation of the country makes its external trade relations play an important role. This importance for the development of foreign economic relations depends not only on the fact that the main turnover of wealth takes place in foreign trade but also on the fact that the development of trade processes depends to a greater extent on the development of foreign trade.

For the Republic of Chad, the general patterns of the development of foreign economic trade also apply to the countries of the developing world. However, foreign trade has certain peculiarities, especially compared to trade in developed countries, for example, the lack of internal savings, the need to use external financing, etc.

From an economic point of view, the mentioned characteristics in the trade and external economic relations of developing countries are typical of the export and import activities of the Republic of Chad and contribute to attracting external financing for external economic activities.

REFERENCES

AfDB, O. E. C. D., UNDP, & UNECA. (2012). Republic of Chad – African Economic Outlook 2012. https://www.afdb.org/fileadmin/uploads/afdb/Documents/Publications/Chad%20Full%20PDF%20Country%20Note.pdf. Accessed on July 7, 2023.

African Development Bank. (2023). Chad Economic Outlook. In *African Economic Outlook 2023*. Abidjan, Côte d'Ivoire. https://www.afdb.org/en/countries/central-africa/chad/chad-economic-outlook. Accessed on July 7, 2023.

Britannica. (2021). Chad: Finance and trade. https://www.britannica.com/place/Chad/Finance-and-trade. Accessed on July 7, 2023.

CIA World Factbook. (2022). Economy of Chad. https://archive.org/details/cia-world-factbook-2022-2023/page/n1169/mode/2up. Accessed on July 7, 2023.

Exchange Portal "Take-Profit". (2023). Chad's GDP: Volume, growth rate, structure. https://take-profit.org/statistics/gdp/chad/. Accessed on July 7, 2023.

Gadom, D. G., Kountchou, A. M., & Araar, A. (2018) *The impact of oil revenues on wellbeing in Chad*. https://www.cambridge.org/core/journals/environment-and-development-economics/article/impact-of-oil-revenues-on-wellbeing-in-chad/946CAE7A9A35C606DD4DCAEF5E6B7E23. Accessed on July 7, 2023.

Ortiz, A. (2022). CHAD: Socio-Economic Country Profile (Infographic). *Global CAD* https://globalcad.org/en/2022/07/14/chad-profile-infographic/. Accessed on July 7, 2023.

Statista. (2023). Chad: Share of economic sectors in the gross domestic product (GDP) from 2012 to 2022. https://www.statista.com/statistics/529370/share-of-economic-sectors-in-the-gdp-in-chad/. Accessed on July 7, 2023.

World Bank. (2023). Chad Overview: Development news, research, data. https://www.worldbank.org/en/country/chad/overview. Accessed on July 7, 2023.

World Bank. (n.d.). Official website. http://www.worldbank.org. Accessed on July 7, 2023.

ASSESSMENT OF SOCIOECONOMIC EQUALIZATION OF REGIONS OF THE KYRGYZ REPUBLIC BY GRP PER CAPITA IN THE SUSTAINABLE DEVELOPMENT CONTEXT

Alina S. Alymkulova, Ainura J. Murzataeva, Ainura K. Kydykbayeva, Almagul T. Attokurova and Tolonbek Sh. Abdyrov

International University of the Kyrgyz Republic, Kyrgyzstan

ABSTRACT

This chapter focuses on the problem of socioeconomic development of the Kyrgyz Republic's regions based on the analysis of the gross regional product per capita in all regions and determines the need for interregional alignment in the sustainable development context. The subject of this research is the issue of interregional inequality. This chapter aims to study and develop proposals for the socioeconomic alignment of the regions of the Kyrgyz Republic in the sustainable development context. The methodological basis of this chapter is based on economic and mathematical methods of data processing and the method of scientific analysis, including statistical data analysis. The authors propose measures to reduce the socioeconomic differentiation of the regions of the Kyrgyz Republic. The relevant state bodies in the development of regional socioeconomic programs can use the recommendations and conclusions of this chapter. The scientific value of the publication is that its results can be used in further research on territorial alignment.

Development of International Entrepreneurship Based on Corporate Accounting and Reporting According to IFRS
Advanced Series in Management, Volume 33B, 173–179
ISSN: 1877-6361/doi:10.1108/S1877-63612024000033B022

Keywords: Region; sustainable development; gross regional product; regional alignment; interregional inequality; socioeconomic alignment

JEL Code: R130

The relevance of this research lies in the fact that in economic terms, there is a similarity in
the development of the Kyrgyz Republic to global trends, which consists of increasing
interregional central-peripheral differences and strengthening financial and industrial
concentration in strong regions. This situation disrupts the socioeconomic balance in the
country, increases migration outflows, and skews economic development toward financial
centers. It is important to note that the situation with the central-peripheral inequality is
observed not only on the country's scale but also within the regions, at the level of regional
centers, and Aiyl-Okmotu.

In this regard, the regional policy of the Kyrgyz Republic in the sustainable development context should be aimed at improving the population's standard of living and the
welfare of citizens living in the country's regions, reducing the disparity of regions in terms
of subsidies. To achieve this goal, the Presidential Decree "On further measures to improve
the administrative-territorial structure and development of the regions of the Kyrgyz
Republic" (October 18, 2022 No. 350) introduces a Regional Policy Concept for
2023–2027, the main areas of which are a new system of planning and development of the
regions, socioeconomic growth. (Cabinet of Ministers of the Kyrgyz Republic, 2022;
President of the Kyrgyz Republic, 2022). Activities aimed at the integrated development of
growth reference points (urbanization) and policy support for the regions are also
considered a priority.

Spatial inequality is the result of unbalanced regional policies in the demographic,
sociocultural, economic, and environmental sectors. Solving this problem requires a
comprehensive approach and a close interrelation of political, cultural, socioeconomic,
and psychological factors. The concept of spatial justice is that all citizens, regardless of
where they live, are entitled to the same level of quality of life (Boyne & Powell, 1991).
Achieving spatial justice by smoothing out interregional disparities should become a priority of state policy.

Recent scientific research of Kyrgyz and foreign scientists pay much attention to
various aspects of the problems of socioeconomic alignment of regions and reduction of
interregional inequality. Clearly, the solution to the problems mentioned above in the
context of balanced and sustainable development requires a combination of legal, economic, and political levers of action (Novkovska, 2017).

However, it should be noted that an important role is given to economic regulation.
This part of the budget policy lies at the core point relevant to the reduction of interregional inequality.

Thus, the formation of a resource base in the form of a regional financial fund for
adjusting the directions of socioeconomic development based on the identified regional
imbalances is studied in the works of Kovarda (2018) and Moroshkina (2018).

The relationship between the alignment of regions with their sustainable development is
directed by the study of Shedko (2014). According to this study, the region's sustainable
development is the result of a combination of various factors of the region that affect all
aspects of local functioning and development.

The problems of regional policy associated with the reduction of donor regions and the
increase in recipient regions that survive on budget transfers are the subject of the work of

researchers, namely, Zubarevich (2020), Kolodina (2019), Shevchenko and Sergeicheva (2020), Menshikova (2010), Poluyanova (2020), and others. These researchers generally believe that constant budget transfers that equalize grants to recipient regions lead to the fact that their attitude toward other strong regions becomes somewhat dependent, and the reduction of interregional imbalance only by such measures leads to deterioration in the socioeconomic situation in the country.

The tasks of reducing regional disproportions are discussed in the works of Abdyrov (2017), Toktogulov (Abdyrov & Toktogulov, 2017), Sayakbaeva (Sayakbaeva et al., 2018), Murzataeva (Sayakbaeva et al., 2018), Kydykbaeva (2019), Alymkulova (2012), Kemeldinova (Alymkulova & Kemeldinova, 2016), and others.

However, this does not mean that subsidized regions do not need to allocate budgetary funds. The state should continue to provide them with balanced support by allocating subsidies. These funds must be targeted. That is, the government should implement a strategy to equalize subsidized regions and increase their indicators to the maximum level. It is also necessary to strengthen the role of transfer instruments in the processes of convergence of financial support for the sustainable development of the country's regions.

MATERIALS AND METHOD

To quantify the inequality of the regions, it is necessary first to determine regional indicators of socioeconomic development. The authors chose gross regional product per capita as the calculation indicator. The research is based on data from the National Statistical Committee of the Kyrgyz Republic (n.d.). The study period covers 2016–2021.

The authors apply the method of assessing interregional inequality. Criteria such as the scale, structure, and dynamics of inequality are studied (Maslikhina, 2013). Thus, based on this systematization, they can be divided into three groups according to the above three criteria.

There are quite a lot of evaluation methods. In this research, the authors use Theil's index (Theil, 1967) and Atkinson's index (Atkinson, 1970) because they make it possible to determine the scale, dynamics, and structure of inequality.

Dispersion indicators (variance, mean square deviation, and variation coefficient) are also studied. Although these indicators do not consider such a significant factor as population size, they make it possible to conduct a statistical analysis of the indicator.

The main advantage of using Theil's index lies in the fact that it makes it possible to assess the indicator for each region separately (e.g., its decomposability throughout the whole distribution scale).

$$I_T = \frac{1}{N} \sum_{i=1}^{N} \left(\frac{x_i}{x_A} * ln \frac{x_i}{x_A} \right) \tag{1}$$

$$I_{MLD} = \frac{1}{N} \sum_{i=1}^{N} ln \frac{x_i}{x_A} \tag{2}$$

where I_T – first Theil's index, I_{MLD} – second Theil's index or mean log deviation (MLD), N – the number of observations (regions), x_i – the value of x-indicator for i-region, x_A – the average value of totality. The value of the index will be equal to 0 under the absolute equality of regions on x-indicator, whereas the value will increase up to $\ln (x_i/x_A)$ under the absolute inequality.

MLD is the measure of income inequality. MLD is equal to zero when all have the same income and takes more positive values when incomes become unequal.

$$
I_A = \begin{cases} 1 - \left(\frac{1}{N} \sum_{i=1}^{N} \left(\frac{x_i}{x_A} \right)^{1-\varepsilon} \right)^{\frac{1}{1-\varepsilon}}, \varepsilon \neq 1 \\ \\ 1 - \prod_{i=1}^{N} \left(\frac{x_i}{x_A} \right)^{\frac{1}{N}}, \ \varepsilon = 1 \end{cases}
\tag{3}
$$

where I_A – Atkinson's index, N – the number of observations (regions), x_i – the value of x-indicator for i-region, x_A – the average value of totality, ε – parameter, reflecting the attitude of the society to inequality. The value of the index will be equal to 0 under the absolute equality of regions as of x-indicator; in the same manner, the value will increase up to $\ln (x_i/x_A)$.

RESULTS

First, it is necessary to analyze the main statistical characteristics. Next, we need to calculate the coefficient of variation (CV) for GRP per capita, which will be the basis for conducting a graphical analysis of the CV = f(t) function.

Table 1 shows that all statistical characteristics of the indicator had a positive trend. For example, the minimum value of the indicator for six years increased by 15,600 soms, the maximum value – by 85,800 soms, the average value – by 112,222.2 soms, and the median – by 31,800 soms. However, the growth of the CV between 2016 and 2019 indicates an increase in inequality between regions of the Kyrgyz Republic, which is caused by socioeconomic circumstances falling in this time interval. The decrease in the dynamics of CV from 2019 to 2021 suggests σ-convergence and an increase in the growth rate of convergence.

Table 1. Dynamics of Dispersion Indicators, the Theil Index and the Atkinson Index for GRP per Capita for 2016–2021.

	2016	2017	2018	2019	2020	2021
Minimum value, soms	28,000.0	31,100.0	34,800.0	35,300.0	37,000.0	43,600.0
Maximum value, soms	181,000.0	196,800.0	220,200.0	230,900.0	212,000.0	266,800.0
Average value, soms	80,422.2	87,366.7	90,133.3	96,988.9	94,377.8	112,222.2
Median, soms	59,800.0	63,900.0	59,200.0	64,000.0	66,400.0	114,000.0
Standard deviation	49,722.2	54,383.9	60,660.6	66,761.9	61,690.4	70,604.1
coefficient of Variation (CV)	0.6183	0.6225	0.6730	0.6883	0.6537	0.6291
Theil's index (T)	0.1577	0.1612	0.1798	0.1897	0.1724	0.1594
Indicator normalization, 1-ε-T	0.1459	0.1489	0.1645	0.1728	0.1584	0.1473
Atkinson's index (IA)	0.1493	0.1535	0.1635	0.1729	0.1577	0.1486

Source: Authors' calculations based on National Statistical Committee of the Kyrgyz Republic (n.d.).

During the studied period, the values of Theil's and Atkinson's indexes for individual regions are similarly duplicated. Thus, the Batken, Osh, Jalal-Abad, Naryn, and Talas Regions have the least value. Moreover, relatively prosperous regions include Osh city, the Chui Region, and the Issyk-Kul Region. The undisputed leadership belongs to the capital of the Kyrgyz Republic – Bishkek.

Based on this analysis, we can note that there is a meaningful divergence in the growth rates of GRP per capita in 2016–2019, that is, a period of divergence and its subsequent stabilization until 2021. The trend of Theil's and Atkinson's indexes coincides. From 2016 to 2019, there was an increase in regional disparities. In subsequent years, due to the budget equalization of the regions, there is some smoothing of interregional differences.

Thus, we arrive at the following result:

(1) Regions with above-average GRP per capita are as follows:
   • Regions of maximum influence on inequality: Bishkek and the Issyk-Kul Region (2016); Bishkek (2017–2021);
   • Regions of minimal influence on inequality: Osh city and the Chui Region (2016); Osh city, the Issyk-Kul Region, and the Chui Region (2017–2018); Osh city and the Issyk-Kul Region (2019–2020); Osh city, the Issyk-Kul Region, the Talas Region, and the Chui Region (2021);
(2) Regions with below-average GRP per capita are as follows:
   • Regions of maximum influence on inequality: the Batken Region, the Jalal-Abad Region, and the Osh Region (2016); the Batken Region and the Osh Region (2017–2018); the Batken Region, the Naryn Region, and the Osh Region (2019); the Batken Region, the Jalal-Abad Region, the Naryn Region, and the Osh Region (2020); the Batken Region and the Osh Region (2021);
   • Regions of minimal influence on inequality: the Talas Region and the Naryn Region (2016); the Jalal-Abad Region, the Naryn Region, and the Talas Region (2017–2018); the Chui Region, the Talas Region, and the Jalal-Abad Region (2019); the Talas Region and the Chui Region (2020); the Jalal-Abad Region and the Naryn Region (2021).

Thus, during this period, the Bishkek's role has been gradually increasing. The Issyk-Kul Region and the city of Osh are even considered regions with fairly high GRP per capita. However, these regions have an insufficient impact on nationwide inequality.

DISCUSSION

In the future, regional policy in the sustainable development context should be aimed at increasing GRP in the whole country, especially in the Chui, Jalal-Abad, Naryn, Batken, Osh, and Talas Regions, which will lead to an increase in employment and improve people's incomes. Despite the fact that the indicated problem is complex and multifaceted, reducing the level of interregional inequality requires certain measures. The government should create favorable conditions for business in the regions, including assistance in obtaining loans and developing technologies.

It is necessary to continue investing in infrastructure development and ensure equal access to it in all regions. The development and implementation of plans to improve transport, energy, and communication infrastructure in less developed regions can contribute to their economic development, expand accessibility, and reduce the gap between regions. Attracting investment from other regions and countries can contribute to the development of highly effective specific industrial clusters on a regional basis based on the geographical concentration of industries, considering innovative features. This will increase the inflow of foreign investment, especially if additional benefits are provided.

Small and medium-sized enterprises contribute to the reduction of interregional inequality. Therefore, the government should support their development in underdeveloped regions, simplify bureaucratic procedures, and reduce the tax burden. This will help create new jobs and increase the incomes of the population. Supporting entrepreneurship, creating specialized jobs, and expanding services in the regions can help increase employment and improve the economic situation.

Kyrgyzstan has a great tourism potential. It is necessary to invest in tourist infrastructure, promote tourist routes, and attract more tourists to the regions.

Agriculture is an important source of income for many residents of less developed regions. The government should invest in the development of agriculture in the regions and provide access to advanced technologies and financial and technical support to farmers and rural cooperatives to increase productivity and profitability.

The authorities should provide social support for the most vulnerable groups and reduce the level of poverty as the main cause of interregional inequalities. The government should also facilitate the migration of labor resources to various regions where there is a need for workers because migration can be an important source of income for many residents of the regions.

Elaboration of regional development strategies for each region can help identify priorities and ways of development based on the unique features and specifics of each region and the structural transformation that has taken place in it.

Thus, reducing regional inequality is a rather challenging task. The above recommendations can contribute to a more sustainable socioeconomic development in the Kyrgyz Republic.

CONCLUSION

Based on the results of the spatial and temporal analysis of interregional inequality in the Kyrgyz Republic, we can draw the following conclusions:

- In recent years, the level of interregional and intra-regional center-periphery inequality has remained high in the Kyrgyz Republic. Particularly, there is an interregional differentiation between Bishkek and the rest of the Kyrgyz Republic, which is the cause of the decline in the population's living standards in the regions.
- To achieve interregional inequality, the government pursued a policy of redistributing budgetary resources with equalization grants, which often led to dependency effects and slowed economic development.
- Based on the above, the authors note that the dynamics of the correlation coefficient and the Tail's and Atkinson's indices are similar. Divergence processes prevailed in the Kyrgyz Republic from 2016 to 2019; convergence processes prevailed in the subsequent period until 2021.
- It is necessary to implement a balanced regional policy aimed at stimulating the competitive advantages of the regions.

REFERENCES

Abdyrov, T. Sh. (2017). Formation of innovative clusters – As an effective tool for the development of the regional economy. *Science, New Technologies and Innovations in Kyrgyzstan, 3*, 88–94.

Abdyrov, T. Sh., & Toktogulov, A. K. (2017). Cluster as a major factor in the development of the regional economy. *Engineering and Construction Bulletin of the Caspian Region, 2*(20), 54–58.

Alymkulova, A. S. (2012). Economic alignment of regions as the basis for sustainable development of the Kyrgyz Republic. *Bulletin of Bishkek Humanitarian University, 2*(22), 164–166.

Alymkulova, A. S., & Kemeldinova, J. M. (2016). Development of conceptual foundations and directions of effective reforms of regional economic management. *Bulletin of KEU named after M. Ryskulbekov, 1*(35), 198–202.

Atkinson, A. B. (1970). On the measurement of inequality. *Journal of Economic Theory, 2*(3), 244–263.

Boyne, G., & Powell, M. (1991). Territorial justice. A review of theory and evidence. *Political Geography Quarterly, 10*(3), 263–281. https://doi.org/10.1016/0260-9827(91)90038-V

Cabinet of Ministers of the Kyrgyz Republic. (2022, April 28). Presentation of the main goals and objectives of the draft Regional Policy Concept for 2023–2027. https://www.gov.kg/ky/post/s/21234-2023-2027-zhyldarga-regionaldyk-sayasat-kontseptsiyasynyn-dolboorunun-negizgi-maksattarynyn-zhana-mildetterinin-betach-ary-boldu. Accessed on April 15, 2023.

Kolodina, E. A. (2019). The research of regional leveling policies effectiveness in the Russian Federation. *Regional Economics and Management: Electronic Scientific Journal, 4*(60), 6007. https://eee-region.ru/article/6007. Accessed on April 14, 2023.

Kovarda, V. V. (2018). Improvements to the system of the balanced social and economic development of a region by regional financial fund. *Society: Politics, Economics, Law, 7*(60), 37–40.

Kydykbaeva, A. K. (2019). Investment climate and its impact on attracting foreign capital to the Kyrgyz Republic. *Bulletin of the Kyrgyz State University named after I. Arabaev, Anniversary issue,* 65–71.

Maslikhina, V. Yu. (2013). Quantitative evaluation of economic and social spatial inequality in the Volga Federal District. *Online Journal "Scientific Studies", 4.* https://naukovedenie.ru/PDF/22evn413.pdf. Accessed on April 12, 2023.

Menshikova, V. I. (2010). Regional socio-economic policy in Russia: New imperative possible implications. *Bulletin of the Tambov University. Series; Humanities, 11*(91), 181–192.

Moroshkina, M. V. (2018). Spatial development of Russia: Regional disproportions. *Russian Journal of Regional Studies, 26*(4), 638–657. https://doi.org/10.15507/2413-1407.105.026.201804.638-657

National Statistical Committee of the Kyrgyz Republic. (n.d.). Official website. http://www.stat.kg/ru. Accessed on April 14, 2023.

Novkovska, B. (2017). Regional development disparities and their connection with hidden economy. *UTMS Journal of Economics, 8*(2), 151–158.

Poluyanova, N. V. (2020). Regional socio-economic policy implementation issues aimed at recipient regions development. *Herald of the Belgorod University of Cooperation, Economics and Law, 3*(82), 125–135. https://doi.org/10.21295/2223-5639-2020-3-125-135

President of the Kyrgyz Republic. (2022). Decree "On further measures to improve the administrative-territorial structure and development of the regions of the Kyrgyz Republic" (October 18, 2022 UP No. 350). *Bishkek, Kyrgyzstan.* https://cbd.minjust.gov.kg/434830/edition/1287220/ru. Accessed on April 15, 2023.

Sayakbaeva, A. A., Sherbekova, A. A., Murzataeva, A. D. J., & Sayakbaev, T. D. (2018). The role of investment in the improvement of the macroeconomic situation in regions of the Kyrgyz Republic. *Eurasian Scientific Association, 12–4*(46), 272–276.

Shedko, Y. N. (2014). Factors and conditions of sustainable region development: Synergetics of interaction. Bulletin of the Moscow State Regional University. *Series: Economics, 4,* 7–10.

Shevchenko, K. S., & Sergeicheva, I. A. (2020). Characteristics of donor and recipient regions and their role in Russia's development. *Bulletin of the Council of Young Scientists and Specialists of the Chelyabinsk Region, 4*(31), 61–65.

Theil, H. (1967). *Economics and information theory.* North-Holland Pub. Co.

Zubarevich, N. V. (2020). Pandemic and regions: Results of January-August 2020. *Economic Development of Russia, 11,* 91–95.

REGIONAL ECONOMIC SYSTEMS: ENSURING ADAPTABILITY IN CONDITIONS OF UNCERTAINTY

Ekaterina A. Isaeva[a], Alexey V. Shleenko[b], Alexandra A. Chudaeva[c], Irina N. Shvetsova[d] and Ilya E. Pokamestov[a]

[a]*Financial University under the Government of the Russian Federation, Russia*
[b]*Southwest State University, Russia*
[c]*Samara State University of Economics, Russia*
[d]*Pitirim Sorokin Syktyvkar State University, Russia*

ABSTRACT

The planning of the strategic regions' development is hampered by numerous uncertainty factors, which creates problems for public administration bodies. This research aims to develop a method for assessing the abilities of the region's economic system to adapt to uncertain conditions as a methodological basis for implementing public administration measures. The authors conducted a study of the dynamics of the development of the federal districts of Russia in 2019–2021. The conducted study revealed the heterogeneity of the reaction of regional economic systems to the impact of uncertainty factors, although the overall dynamics of the country's development were positive. The research methodology includes the determination of relative changes in the main indicators of socioeconomic development of regions and their contribution to the country-wide dynamics from the beginning of the occurrence of uncertainty factors to the recovery stage; their adjustment, considering the rigidity indicators; ranking of regions by the level of adaptability of the economic system; development of a differentiated set of measures to improve the adaptability of each type of economic systems. The authors determined that a high level of rigidity causes a low adaptability of the economic system to changes. The authors tested the methodology for assessing the adaptability of the economic system on the example of the federal districts of Russia. The authors distinguish three types of regional economic systems, depending on their

Development of International Entrepreneurship Based on Corporate Accounting and Reporting According to IFRS
Advanced Series in Management, Volume 33B, 181–189
ISSN: 1877-6361/doi:10.1108/S1877-63612024000033B023

adaptability, and apply a differentiated approach to substantiating regional policy measures.

Keywords: Region; economic system; adaptability; rigidity; uncertainty; instability; regional policy; pandemic

JEL Codes: R11; R58

The life of today's society is conditioned by increasing uncertainty factors. Spontaneous events and unpredictable and random phenomena arise in the world, undermining the normal course of organized processes and taking subjects beyond their comfort limits (Anosov, 2022; Gukasyan et al., 2022; Karpunina et al., 2022b). The very fact of their occurrence creates conditions of limited visibility when it comes to planning economic activities. In such conditions, forecasting is difficult, and the dynamics of the development of the system remain unclear. Accordingly, it is difficult to determine the sequence of actions to achieve the region's effectiveness (Fraymovich et al., 2022; Usanov et al., 2023). Special attention is required to maintain the economic system's stability, ensured through developing its adaptive abilities (Nazarova et al., 2022). Adaptability is associated with the economic system's ability to self-preservation, structural adjustment, transformation, and confrontation in conditions of instability (Yachmeneva, 2008). To determine the adapt-ability of an economic system, a unified methodology for assessing its socioeconomic stability is required. Various approaches are used in practice for this purpose. However, they do not set the task of assessing a large number of adaptation effects, rather focusing their attention only on some of them (e.g., on economic or social effects for the region).

METHODOLOGY

Akoff (1972) connects the adaptability of the economic system with the selection of incentives for the consistency of the goals of all subjects of the economic system. Gukasyan et al. (2022) note that adaptation is achieved through purposeful managerial influence on the economic system. In conditions of uncertainty, an economic entity can implement one of three strategies:

(1) a reduction strategy;
(2) an investment strategy; and
(3) an ambivalent adaptation and development strategy (Karpunina et al., 2022a).

Orlova et al. (2016) believe that the adaptability of the region's economic system in conditions of uncertainty can be assessed using indicators of economic security. The authors propose an appropriate system of indicators for evaluation. An original approach is proposed by Maksimovich (2004) to assess the adaptability of the industrial structure of the region. Its matrix includes an assessment of the level of diversification of the economy's structure, the effect of agglomeration, the conjuncture of the leading sectors, and the population's income. Romanova and Huat Thi Phuong Zung (2015) highlight the insta-bility of the market capacity, the structure of activities, the change in the solvency of consumers, the isolation of competing entities, and the ambiguity of the choice of suppliers. Thus, adaptive behavior consists of regulating the economic system for changes through internal transformation in accordance with strategic goals.

The research hypothesis consists in the assumption that in conditions of uncertainty of environmental factors, when decision-making on the further development of the region is difficult, the implementation of measures aimed at reducing its rigidity to achieve a long-term effect of adaptation of the regional economy becomes a strategically important task of regional government bodies. The research aims to develop a method for assessing the abilities of the region's economic system to adapt to the conditions of uncertainty as a methodological basis for implementing public administration measures.

The research objectives are as follows:

- To study the ability of the region's economic system to adapt in conditions of uncertainty.
- To justify the choice of indicators for assessing the region's adaptability and develop a methodology.
- To assess the adaptability of the federal districts of Russia in conditions of uncertainty based on the proposed methodology and draw conclusions about the further vector of regional management.

The research methods are analysis, synthesis, economic and statistical analysis, graphical method, systematization, and systemic approach.

RESULTS

Factors of uncertainty appear due to (1) the existence of a considerable number of heterogeneous elements or (2) frequent and unpredictable changes in heterogeneous elements (Galieva et al., 2023). The existence of these factors leads the economic system to a state where it is impossible to foresee, control, and consider changes when making decisions regarding its future development.

The region's adaptability in conditions of uncertainty is the ability of its economic system to change parameters under a controlling influence in a certain period and return to a state of balanced development in the absence of clear guidelines for its further movement. The proposed approach is based on the following:

- Adaptive reactions to changing external factors manifest themselves in changing the region's behavior, reflected in the restructuring of its internal structure (resources, activities, methods of organization, etc.) through the implementation of management mechanisms (Khashir et al., 2023; Kuzmenko et al., 2022).
- It is necessary to consider the time factor: the speed of the economic system's response to changing conditions is important, which manifests itself by adjusting the parameters, structure of systems, or control actions to achieve optimal management quality with initial instability.
- The low adaptive capacity of the economic system is due to its high rigidity. The economic system's rigidity is its ability to remain within the previously formed determinants that determine the nature of functioning and management methods. If the economic system cannot change the tools used and adjust the behavior of participants to changing conditions, then it is rigid, and its level of adaptability will be minimal.

• The adaptation of the economic system presupposes the achievement of consistency of operational decisions and strategic actions in the process of its management. The methodology proposed by the authors uses weighted indicators of regional development, which makes it possible to identify "stress zones" and imbalances in the territorial development of the state despite the relatively prosperous dynamics of the development of individual regions (Babina, 2018).

The analysis is carried out in the period 2019–2021, that is, starting from the pre-pandemic period and ending with the stage of post-pandemic economic recovery. To calculate changes in social and economic indicators for the study period, the authors determined the share of each indicator in the all-Russian indicator at the beginning and end of the study period. Next, the authors calculated the ratio of the obtained share of the indicator at the end of the study period (recovery from the crisis) to the share of the indicator at the beginning of the study period (precrisis level). The cumulative change in economic and social indicators for the period is defined as the arithmetic mean of the changes received by groups of economic and social indicators. The authors introduced two indicators to assess rigidity (according to Raygorodsky (2001)): (1) the average recovery time of the system and (2) the probability of restoring the system by a given time as a result of the control action. Three types of economic systems will be distinguished: (1) mobile (scores from one and above), (2) rigid (below 0), and (3) transitional (simultaneously showing features of mobility and rigidity – such economic systems receive ratings in the range from 0 to 1) (Raygorodsky, 2001) (Table 1 and Table 2).

The dynamics of the gross regional product indicator in 2019–2021 remain heterogeneous in the context of federal districts. In five regions, there was an increase in the indicator. In three regions (the Volga, Ural, and Siberian Federal Districts), there was a decrease in this indicator in the pandemic 2020. Due to this the all-Russian gross regional product (GRP), decreased by 1.32% in 2020. By 2021, there was an increase in the indicator in Russia. However, its regional structure has changed. The volume of manufacturing production during the period of uncertainty caused by the COVID-19 pandemic also showed a multidirectional dynamic. In general, in 2020, the indicator value in Russia increased by 5.4%. However, in three regions (the Southern, Volga, and Ural Federal Districts), there was a decrease in the indicator. The share of regions in the aggregate indicator also changed. The COVID-19 pandemic has also affected retail trade. In general, in Russia in 2019–2021, there was a systemic increase in retail trade turnover by 17.4%. However, this growth was provided only by four regions of the country; the other four regions (the North Caucasus, Volga, Ural, and Siberian Federal Districts) reacted to the COVID-19 restrictions of 2020 by reducing the indicator. The volume of paid services to the population in 2020 in Russia decreased by 11.8%. All regions reacted to the situation by reducing the indicator. In 2020, investments in fixed assets increased by 5%. The all-Russian dynamics again did not turn out to be homogeneous. In the Far Eastern Federal District, it was possible to observe a decrease in the indicator (−0.5% relative to 2019). There were shifts in the share of regions in the all-Russian indicator. The most tangible consequence of the uncertainty caused by the COVID-19 pandemic was the disruption of international trade relations, which manifested itself in a reduction in the balance of import–export operations. Particularly, the indicator "exports with non-CIS countries" decreased in all regions and, in general, decreased by 22.1% compared to 2019.

The uncertainty has also affected the dynamics of social indicators in Russian regions. During the COVID-19 pandemic, the labor market was unbalanced; there was a jump in

Table 1. Indicators for Calculating the Adaptability of the Federal Districts of Russia, 2019–2021

Indicator/Federal District	Year	Central	North-Western	Southern	North Caucasus	Volga	Ural	Siberian	Far Eastern	Russia
Economic indicators										
Gross regional product (GRP), billion rubles	2019	33,139.8	10,577.6	6,611.7	2,294.8	14,103.7	13,272.0	9,090.3	5,970.6	95,060.7
	2020	33,637.0	10,644.0	6,710.0	2,404.0	13,669.0	11,675.0	9,027.0	6,044.0	93,810.0
	2021	41,685.3	16,611.9	7,952.0	2,695.6	16,878.4	16,699.0	11,287.2	7,373.6	121,183.0
Manufacturing industries, billion rubles	2019	16,610.4	6,267.1	2,989.3	434.8	9,585.1	5,384.6	4,904.1	1,260.6	47,436.0
	2020	18,323.6	6,994.5	2,951.4	482.0	9,395.9	5,318.7	5,165.4	1,386.5	50,017.9
	2021	22,740.1	9,778.5	3,343.2	592.8	11,703.0	7,332.3	5,860.0	1,628.1	62,978.1
Retail trade turnover, billion rubles	2019	11,678.6	3,302.0	3,504.3	1,626.0	5,839.7	2,849.2	2,946.0	1878.5	33,624.3
	2020	11,849.6	3,418.7	3,534.1	1,605.5	5,786.1	2,828.4	2,944.6	1906.7	33,873.7
	2021	13,874.4	4,071.9	4,336.5	1868.5	6,596.5	3,159.0	3,419.9	2,145.0	39,471.7
The volume of paid services to the population, billion rubles	2019	3,691.6	1,080.7	1,188.1	446.2	1,664.6	907.3	889.5	667.8	10,535.6
	2020	3,124.8	946.8	1,112.0	414.0	1,506.6	788.8	826.6	574.6	9,294.2
	2021	3,971.5	1,173.6	1,377.5	464.7	1728.9	965.0	962.9	677.1	11,321.2
Investments in fixed assets, billion rubles	2019	6,093.4	2083.0	1,378.1	629.7	2,718.6	2,967.3	1798.3	1,660.7	19,329.0
	2020	6,581.1	2,156.6	1,433.4	705.6	2,800.5	3,071.7	1902.7	1,652.4	20,302.9
	2021	7,871.1	2,297.8	1,501.0	723.9	3,075.4	3,190.7	2,241.2	1940.9	22,945.5
Exports with non-CIS countries, million US dollars	2019	184,920.1	45,223.4	14,896.2	873.4	30,872.2	33,067.6	32,458.7	28,200.7	370,512.2
	2020	140,140.6	37,354.9	13,651.6	797.9	22,868.8	23,593.0	26,834.6	23,271.4	288,512.9
	2021	218,934.8	54,781.5	19,450.9	1,194.3	34,397.9	36,525.6	35,041.9	27,835.2	428,162.1
Social indicators										
Average annual number of employees, thousands of people	2019	21,171.2	7,065.3	7,417.3	3,904.1	13,434.6	6,322.1	7,795.2	3,954.7	71,064.5
	2020	20,765.6	6,954.2	7,328.9	3,739.1	13,114.1	6,177.7	7,572.0	3,898.6	69,550.3
	2021	20,906.2	7,047.9	7,563.7	3,842.0	13,436.9	6,310.9	7,764.8	3,945.5	70,817.9
Total area of residential premises, millions of square meters	2019	1,086	393	418	217	800	321	429	194	3,857
	2020	1,104	404	429	222	814	326	436	196	3,931
	2021	1,157	413	437	229	832	334	443	199	4,044
The number of students enrolled in higher education programs, thousands of people	2019	1,268.5	418.9	404.6	208.6	807.9	299.2	475.9	184.8	4,068.3
	2020	1,284.4	424.2	395.8	206.1	798.2	290.9	471.6	178.0	4,049.3
	2021	1,312.5	428.2	386.0	203.1	790.8	282.7	468.6	172.4	4,044.2
Internal research and development costs from all sources, billion rubles	2019	576.6	165.2	29.2	5.3	186.3	68.6	85.9	17.8	1,134.8
	2020	621.9	155.8	29.8	5.8	180.9	74.5	86.5	19.4	1,174.5
	2021	672.0	171.9	33.9	6.5	215.2	85.4	95.3	21.3	1,301.5

Source: Compiled by the authors based on Rosstat (2022).

Table 2. Determination of the Adaptability of Economic Systems of the Federal Districts of Russia, 2019–2021

Indicator Change/Federal District	Central	North-Western	Southern	North Caucasus	Volga	Ural	Siberian	Far Eastern
Economic indicators								
GRP, billion rubles	−1.32	+24.5	−5.72	−7.7	−6.15	−1.3	−6.82	−3.11
Manufacturing industries, billion rubles	+3.17	+17.63	−15.74	+2.31	−8.01	+2.56	−10.06	−2.81
Retail trade turnover, billion rubles	+1.21	+5.05	+5.44	−2.19	−3.79	−5.51	−1.09	−2.79
The volume of paid services to the population, billion rubles	+0.11	+1.04	+7.87	−3.3	−3.35	−1.0	+0.77	−5.67
Investments in fixed assets, billion rubles	+8.83	−7.10	−8.25	−3.23	−4.67	−9.41	+5.03	−1.53
Exports with non-CIS countries, million US dollars	+2.45	+4.87	+13.01	+16.22	−3.56	−4.36	−2.62	−14.69
Total change in economic indicators	0.93	7.67	−0.57	0.35	−4.92	−3.17	−2.47	−5.10
Social indicators								
Average annual number of employees, thousands of people	−0.90	+0.12	+2.3	−1.18	+0.39	+0.13	−0.05	+0.20
Total area of residential premises, millions of square meters	+1.60	+0.22	−0.31	+0.58	−0.80	−0.73	−1.49	−1.97
The number of students enrolled in higher education programs, thousands of people	+1.04	+2.90	−4.08	−2.11	−1.54	−4.89	−0.88	−6.10
Internal research and development costs from all sources, billion rubles	+1.62	−9.29	+1.35	+6.26	+0.70	+8.46	−3.27	+4.24
Total change in social indicators	0.84	−1.51	−0.19	0.89	−0.31	0.74	−1.42	−0.91
Total change in economic and social indicators	0.89	3.08	−0.38	0.62	−2.62	−1.22	−1.95	−3.01
Rigidity indicators								
Average system recovery time	1	1	1	1	1	1	1	1
The probability of restoring the system by the specified time as a result of the control action (0, if Av≤0; 0.5, if 0≤Av≤1; 1, if 1≤Av)	0.5	1	0	0.5	0	0	0	0
The level of adaptability	0.45	3.08	0	0.31	0	0	0	0
Type of economic system	transitional	mobile	rigid	transitional	rigid	rigid	rigid	rigid

Source: Author's calculations.

the growth of unemployment. The average annual number of employed decreased in all regions, ensuring an overall reduction in the country by 2.1% during 2020. The negative dynamics of the number of students enrolled in higher education programs in 2019–2021 is evidence of consumer behavior in conditions of uncertainty. People are trying to save available resources, fearing adverse circumstances. Domestic expenditures on R&D in

Russia increased by 3.49% in 2020 compared to 2019. In the North-Western and Volga Federal Districts, the value of this indicator decreased.

DISCUSSION

Considering the contribution of each region to the recovery of the country's economy after the COVID-19 pandemic allows authors to distinguish the following three types of regional economic systems, depending on their adaptability:

(1) Mobile (indicator value 3.08): North-Western Federal District;
(2) Transitional (with signs of mobility and rigidity): Central (0.45) and North Caucasus (0.31) Federal Districts;
(3) Rigid: Southern, Volga, Ural, Siberian, and Far Eastern Federal Districts (0).

The North-Western Federal District adapts most quickly to the conditions of uncertainty, ensuring an increase in its contribution to the country-wide development. The implementation of public administration measures is required for each type of regional economic system.

For mobile regional economic systems, basic measures of public administration are as follows:

• Increasing the level of education of the population for the flexibility of the labor market (Okunkova et al., 2023).
• Digital infrastructure improvement for stimulating the activity of citizens in the global online markets (Karpunina et al., 2023; Plyasova et al., 2023a, 2023b; Plyusnina, 2023).
• Development of the sphere of R&D and innovation as a basis for increasing the investment potential (Kulikova et al., 2022).

The transitional regional economic systems are recommended to perform the following:

• To implement state programs to stimulate the capital expenditures of organizations on ICT (Alyokhina et al., 2022; Molchan et al., 2023).
• To implement financial and fiscal measures to increase the entrepreneurial activity of the population.
• To provide regional grants for the youth.

For rigid regional economic systems, the proposed measures should be strengthened by increasing the population's digital literacy and developing a retraining system.

CONCLUSION

The analysis of the regional dynamics of the Russian regions in 2019–2021 highlighted the heterogeneity of the response of their economic systems to uncertainty factors. The advantage of the proposed methodology is the ability to identify zones of tension and establish rigid regions that are least adaptive to uncertainty conditions to subsequently create incentives for their accelerated development. Russian regions are ranked according to their adaptability in conditions of uncertainty. The research proposes a differentiated approach to implementing public administration measures in relation to regions with different levels of adaptability.

REFERENCES

Akoff, R. (1972). *A concept of corporate planning* (G. B. Rubalsky Transl. from English; ed. by I. A. Ushakov). USSR: Publishing House Sovets Radio. (Original work published 1969).

Alyokhina, O. F., Ioda, Yu. V., Ponomarev, S. V., & Sharafutdinov, A. G. (2022). Digital transformation of regional economic systems: What has the pandemic changed. *Proceedings of the Southwest State University. Series: Economics. Sociology. Management, 12*(5), 132–143. https://doi.org/10.21869/2223-1552-2022-12-5-132-143

Anosov, B. A. (2022). Impact of the COVID-19 pandemic on the consumer market in Russia and China. *Economic and Social Changes: Facts, Trends, Forecast, 15*(6), 243–256. https://doi.org/10.15838/esc.2022.6.84.15

Babina, O. I. (2018). System of indicators of social and economic development of region. *The Newman in Foreign Policy, 44*(88), 31–33.

Fraymovich, D. Y., Konovalova, M. E., Roshchektaeva, U. Y., Karpunina, E. K., & Avagyan, G. L. (2022). Designing mechanisms for ensuring the economic security of regions: Countering the challenges of instability. In E. G. Popkova, A. A. Polukhin, & J. V. Ragulina (Eds.), *Towards an increased security: Green innovations, intellectual property protection and information security* (pp. 569–581). Springer. https://doi.org/10.1007/978-3-030-93155-1_63

Galieva, G. F., Sazanova, E. V., Dick, E. N., & Amineva, R. R. (2023). Study of current trends of participation of population of the BRICS and OECD countries in the global online labor market. *Proceedings of the Southwest State University. Series: Economics. Sociology. Management, 13*(3), 10–23. https://doi.org/10.21869/2223-1552-2023-13-3-10-23

Gukasyan, Z. O., Tavbulatova, Z. K., Aksenova, Z. A., Gasanova, N. M., & Karpunina, E. K. (2022). Strategies for adapting companies to the turbulence caused by the COVID-19 pandemic. In E. G. Popkova, (Ed.), *Business 4.0 as a subject of the digital economy* (pp. 639–645). Springer. https://doi.org/10.1007/978-3-030-90324-4_102

Karpunina, E. K., Moiseev, S. S., & Bakalova, T. V. (2022a). Tools for strengthening the economic security of the state in the period of socio-economic and geopolitical instability. *Drucker's Bulletin, 5*, 24–34. https://doi.org/10.17213/2312-6469-2022-5-24-34

Karpunina, E. K., Moskovtceva, L. V., Zabelina, O. V., Zubareva, N. N., & Tsykora, A. V. (2022b). Socio-economic impact of the COVID-19 pandemic on OECD countries. In E. G. Popkova, & I. V. Andronova (Ed.) *Current problems of the world economy and international trade* (pp. 103–114). Emerald Publishing Limited. https://doi.org/10.1108/S0190-128120220000042011

Karpunina, E. K., Okunkova, E. A., Molchan, A. S., Belova, E. O., & Kuznetsova, O. A. (2023). Management of personnel professional development as a condition of digital transformation of the organization. *International Journal of Learning and Change, 15*(4), 365–387. https://doi.org/10.1504/IJLC.2023.132135

Khashir, B. O., Shvetsova, I. N., Usanov, A. Yu., & Ponomarev, S. V. (2023). Specifics of digitalization in Russia and its regions under uncertainty. *Bulletin of Kemerovo State University. Series: Political, Sociological and Economic Sciences, 2*(28), 249–258. https://doi.org/10.21603/2500-3372-2023-8-2-249-258

Kulikova, M. A., Molchan, A. S., Polujanova, N. V., Balamirzoev, N. L., & Galieva, G. F. (2022). Smart social infrastructure as the basis for the long-term development of social entrepreneurship: Problems and prospects in Russia. In E. G. Popkova (Ed.), *Business 4.0 as a subject of the digital economy* (pp. 9–16). Springer. https://doi.org/10.1007/978-3-030-90324-4_2

Kuzmenko, N. I., Lapushinskaya, G. K., Lisova, E. V., Tleptserukov, M. A., & Karpunina, E. K. (2022). Russian regions: Assessment of factors of growth in the living standard and well-being of the population. In E. G. Popkova & B. S. Sergi (Eds.), *Geo-economy of the future* (pp. 619–639). Springer.

Maksimovich, A. P. (2004). *Adaptability of the economic structure of municipalities* (p. 106). Publishing house of the Ural State Economic University.

Molchan, A. S., Osadchuk, L. M., Anichkina, O. A., Ponomarev, S. V., & Kuzmenko, N. I. (2023). The 'Digitalisation trap' of Russian regions. *International Journal of Technology, Policy and Management, 23*(1), 20–41. https://doi.org/10.1504/IJTPM.2023.129468

Nazarova, I. G., Galieva, G. F., Sazanova, E. V., Chernenko, E. M., & Karpunina, E. K. (2022). Labor market and employment problems: Analysis of long-term dynamics and prospects of development in Russian regions. In E. G. Popkova (Ed.), *Imitation market modeling in digital economy: Game theoretic approaches* (pp. 711–722). Springer. https://doi.org/10.1007/978-3-030-93244-2_77

Okunkova, E. A., Kosorukova, I. V., Lazareva, T. G., Korolyuk, E. V., & Bogomolova, A. V. (2023). Global gig economy: Prospects and key growth threats for developing countries. *International Journal of Work Innovation, 3*(4), 403–417. https://doi.org/10.1504/IJWI.2023.128862

Orlova, A., Lyshchikova, J., Nikulina, Y., & Anokhin, Y. (2016). Assessment of the level of economic security in the conditions of uncertainty. *International Journal of Economics and Financial Issues, 6*(4), 1702–1706.

Plyasova, S. V., Bondareva, N. A., & Gridnev, Yu. V. (2023a). Assessment of the digital potential of the BRICKS countries in the formation of the new geopolitical order. *Journal of Volgograd State University. Economics, 25*(1), 128–142. https://doi.org/10.15688/ek.jvolsu.2023.1.11

Plyasova, S. V., Yazykova, S. V., Konishchev, E. V., & Araslanbayev, I. V. (2023b). Theoretical and methodical base for studying digital inclusion in Russia. *Surgut State University Journal, 11*(2), 46–60. https://doi.org/10.35266/2312-3419-2023-2-46-60

Plyusnina, O. V. (2023). Digital technology potential of economic recovery in post-COVID reality. *Bulletin of Tver State University. Series: Economics and Management, 1*(61), 15–25. https://doi.org/10.26456/2219-1453/2022.4.015-025

Raygorodsky, D. Ya. (2001). *Practical psychodiagnostics: Methods and tests.* Saratov, (Bakhrakh-M).

Romanova, A. T., & Huat Thi Phuong Zung (2015). Models and algorithms of the adaptive business increase – Subjects of the transport market to the external environment. *Transport Business of Russia, 1*(116), 3–6.

Rosstat. (2022). Regions of Russia. The main characteristics of the subjects of the Russian Federation: Statistical collection. https://rosstat.gov.ru/storage/mediabank/Region_Sub_2022.pdf. Accessed on August 13, 2023.

Usanov, A. Yu., Mazunina, M. V., Abalakin, A. A., & Grudneva, A. A. (2023). Study of the pandemic influencing economic systems through the prism of economic security. *Surgut State University Journal, 11*(1), 52–63. https://doi.org/10.35266/2312-3419-2023-1-52-63

Yachmeneva, V. M. (2008). Formation of a system of indicators for assessing the adaptability of the economic system. *Economics and Management, 1*, 60–67.

ANALYSIS OF PUBLIC DEBT POLICY AND ITS EFFECTIVENESS IN UZBEKISTAN

Bobir Tashbaev, Bunyod Usmonov and Sanjar Omanov

Tashkent State University of Economics, Uzbekistan

ABSTRACT

The authors study public debt policy based on the reports for 2011–2022 and examine the factors affecting the public internal and external debt growth rate using several methods. The research results demonstrate that internal and external debts have changed significantly under the influence of socioeconomic factors. The authors provide scientific recommendations and conclude that public debt is one of the vital instruments of the macroeconomic regulation system through the budget-tax policy. The main features of the debt financing system of the budget deficit are considered. It embodies the redistribution system of national income expressed through its activity as a "state debtor agent" to attract funds for financial support for the requirements of specific segments. Debt financing of the country's primary budget deficit affects the consumption, savings, and investment environment and usually depends on various aspects of the economy. During an economic downturn, the government revives aggregate demand by raising gathered funds (via the sale of securities) and funding governmental operations, which has a stimulative impact. To stabilize the national economy in terms of the country's foreign debts, global funds will have the opportunity to "infect" financial resources in exchange for funds. In a period of stable economic development, the activation of the state as a borrower in the financial market will have the character of crowding out private investments. This ultimately shows that public debt has the characteristic of limiting the scientific views of economists regarding state debts.

Development of International Entrepreneurship Based on Corporate Accounting and Reporting According to IFRS
Advanced Series in Management, Volume 33B, 191–195
ISSN: 1877-6361/doi:10.1108/S1877-63612024000033B024

Keywords: Debt policy; Uzbekistan; socioeconomic factors; stability of state finances; strategic investments; private investments

JEL Code: F34

As can be seen from the strategic goal (President of the Republic of Uzbekistan, 2022), state debts, ensuring their mutual harmony and defining their threshold criteria will appear as a guarantee of the stability of state finances in the future (Ministry of Preschool and School Education of the Republic of Uzbekistan, 2023).

The implementation of reforms in this direction requires attracting large and strategic investments in the country's economy. The further acceleration of the state debt policy should serve as a financial factor of future development due to the attraction of these debt funds for investment purposes.

LITERATURE REVIEW

One of the founders of the school of classical economists, Adam Smith, based his views on limiting the state's intervention in the economy. According to him, the internal debt has an equally negative impact on the economy. A. Smith commented on the debt policy of the countries of Europe in the 17th century. He opined that the economies were carrying the burden of heavy debts, which could ruin all great European countries in the future.

According to the author, the use of public debt to finance budget expenditures leads to a corresponding reduction in private capital. It is argued that if the funds spent on paying the public debt remain in the private sector, they can be used more efficiently (Golovachev, 1998; Smith, 2003).

Another economist, David Ricardo, agreed with Adam Smith's view of public debt as a purely negative phenomenon. David Ricardo evaluates public debt to finance the budget deficit in the economic crisis as an instrument for attracting internal and external financial resources without increasing additional budget revenues in exchange for increasing the tax burden. Looking at the view of economist B. Tashbaev, it is considered important to stimulate domestic consumption during economic crises or cyclical economic decline. It is recognized that increasing the tax burden to cover the budget deficit will negatively affect it (B-Study, 2023; Buchanan, 1976; Tashbaev, 2021).

Jean-Baptiste Say also supports the position of the classical economic school regarding public debt. According to his principles, the increase in public debt will ultimately not increase the amount of money in circulation. In our opinion, J-B. Say's opinion refers to the economic function of government debt instruments. Through this function, public debt instruments also serve as an important financial instrument for the regulation of the economy by the government. An increase in public debt does not mean an increase in national wealth.

Thomas Robert Malthus recognizes the debt financing of the budget deficit as a macroeconomic factor of increasing aggregate demand. John Stuart Mill admits that attracting "excess accumulated foreign investments" as public debt does not seriously affect macroeconomic stability when the public debt is efficiently utilized within the nation's economy (Blaug, 2008; Rohe, 1997).

Speaking about public debt policy, D. Hume (1875), along with those of other economists (Burkhanov & Mansur qizi, 2021; Burkhanov et al., 2022; Usmonov, 2023), recognizes that inefficient (wasteful) use of borrowed funds leads to the impoverishment of society. Through these thoughts, he clarified the criteria of the classics' negative view of public debt. According to the researcher, directing debt funds to cover government expenses related to effective investment has a prospective financial return for the economy, which leads to the creation of financial and economic opportunities to repay current debts in the future.

The description of the conceptual foundations and objectives of the contemporary theory of public debt is intricate. In this scenario, public debt encompasses not just economic concerns but also political and social interests in the scope of the international movement of capital.

RESEARCH METHODOLOGY

When preparing this research, the authors conducted a comparative analysis of data. By collecting national and global funds, projects that are implemented at the expense of public debt will ensure employment and increase the population's well-being by creating new jobs. We are equally interested in the collection of national and global funds.

The stabilization function of public debt is manifested in quantitative and qualitative impact on macroprudential indicators to ensure a balanced economic growth rate. It is noteworthy that this is not only stimulating but also regulatory tools. It has been theoretically and empirically substantiated that it is impossible to ensure sustainable economic growth in the conditions of high inflation. The achievement of financial stabilization and inflation equilibrium requires a tight limitation of monetary issue. One of the important ways to contain prices is the transformation of the economy from the monetary management system into the system of management of public debt policy by "transferring" (a) emissions and (b) operations in the open market. However, these methods for achieving macroeconomic stability also have a number of problems. State debt instruments are an important stabilization tool.

State debt also has a control function. This includes the country's credit rating, debt service, and debt efficiency monitoring system. Particularly, during the implementation of preliminary control measures by evaluating the credit rating of the borrower in the state debt policy, the current system for monitoring debt service and the economic efficiency of public debt is being implemented. Current financial control is organized through a constant monitoring system for duty. The increase in prices affects the economic balance by reducing the real value of financial assets and reducing total demand.

ANALYSIS AND RESULTS

Public expenditures, growing through debt financing of the state budget, create a crowding out effect with respect to private investment activity in the country. The public debt servicing system affects the balance of money supply and demand by influencing the market conditions of debt instruments.

The allocative function of public debt implies the ability to collect and concentrate the country's savings (savings in the hands of certain individuals) for investments related to the financing of large and strategic projects in various phases of the cyclical development of the economy. Also, the allocation function is an important financial instrument for collecting

Table 1. The Matrix Characteristics of the Allocation Function of Public Debt.

	Indirectly	Directly
Social	$S{\rightarrow}D_p{\rightarrow}I(r){\rightarrow}Un_e{\downarrow}$	$S{\rightarrow}D_p{\rightarrow}I(r){\rightarrow}P_g{\uparrow}$
Economical	$S{\rightarrow}D_p{\rightarrow}B_d{\rightarrow}W_g{\uparrow}{\rightarrow}D_c{\uparrow}(SRAS)$	$S{\rightarrow}D_p{\rightarrow}I(r){\rightarrow}G_{GDP}{\uparrow}(LRAS)$

Source: Created by authors.

internal and external global funds to finance projects and programs for specific purposes (Table 1).

By collecting national and global funds (S), the projects (I(r)) realized at the expense of state debt funds (Dp) will provide employment (Une) and increase the well-being of the population due to the creation of new jobs.

An increase in prices affects the economic balance by reducing the real value of financial assets and reducing aggregate demand.

In rapidly developing countries, the proportion of public debt in the gross domestic product (GDP) shows a consistent annual increase.

Based on these data, we can see the dynamic trends. There was a significant metric in the dynamic trend of the change in the share of public debt in relation to GDP in Uzbekistan in 2016–2020. The trend equation was equal to the following:

$$y = 0.6193\, x^2 - 2,493.4\, x + 3\text{E} + 06.$$

The coefficient of determination was equal to $R^2 = 0.9907$. This indicator is expected to increase in developed and developing countries by 2020.

Regarding the public debt strategy in Uzbekistan after 2010, foreign debts were given priority. As a result, the state debts formed in the last decade were mostly foreign debts.

DISCUSSION

In practice, short-term government bonds were used as domestic debt instruments. These debt instruments fulfilled the task of ensuring the current liquidity of the state budget in the literal sense by covering the temporary cash gap. The short-term nature of these obligations provided the possibility of their complete extinguishment during the current year.

The government shifted its attention first to the nation and subsequently to the execution of large-scale investment projects from the financial resources obtained at the expense of placing medium-term debt obligations.

Particularly, in 2018, 71.5 million treasury bonds with a nominal value of $147.37 million were issued in exchange for the issuance of state treasury bills in 2020. It is planned to issue bonds with a nominal value of 1.4 trillion sums. In this process, the central bank acts as a fiscal agent and confirms that the debt instrument has included funds in the state budget for the investor.

It can be seen that the national debt was $9.9 billion in 2018 and $30.1 billion in 2022. The total debt is mostly foreign debt. During the entire analyzed period, foreign debts were the main part of the gross public debt. Enhancing the external debt management system within the medium- and long-term framework is a matter of strategic significance in state debt management.

CONCLUSION

Public debt is one of the vital instruments of the macroeconomic regulation system through the budget-tax policy. It embodies the redistribution system of national income expressed through its activity as a "state debtor agent" to attract funds for financial support for the requirements of specific segments.

Debt financing of the country's primary budget deficit affects the consumption, savings, and investment environment. It usually depends on various aspects of the economy. During an economic downturn, the government revives aggregate demand by raising gathered funds (via the sale of securities) and funding governmental operations, which has a stimulative impact. To stabilize the national economy in terms of the country's foreign debts, global funds will have the opportunity to "infect" financial resources in exchange for funds. In a period of stable economic development, the activation of the state as a borrower in the financial market will have the character of crowding out private investments. This ultimately shows that public debt has the characteristic of limiting the scientific views of economists regarding state debts in the paradigm of historical development, which had a polysemantic description.

REFERENCES

B-Study. (2023). Development of financial science in the XVII–XVIII centuries. https://bstudy.net/729599/ekonomika/razvitie_finansovoy_nauki_xviixviii. Accessed on October 26, 2023.

Blaug, M. (2008). Mill, John Stuart, *Great Economists before Keynes: An introduction to the lives and works of one hundred great economists of the past* (pp. 214–217). Russia: Economics.

Buchanan, J. M. (1976). Barro on the Ricardian equivalence theorem. *Journal of Political Economy*, *84*(2), 337–342. https://www.journals.uchicago.edu/doi/10.1086/260436

Burkhanov, A. U., & Mansur qizi, M. E. (2021). The ways for improvement of investment strategy in the period of digital economy. In *Proceedings of the ICFNDS 2021: The 5th International Conference on Future Networks & Distributed Systems* (pp. 655–662). Association for Computing Machinery. https://doi.org/10.1145/3508072.3508202

Burkhanov, A. U., Tursunov, B., Uktamov, K., & Usmonov, B. (2022). Econometric analysis of factors affecting economic sustainability of chemical industry enterprises in digital era: In case of Uzbekistan. In *Proceedings of the ICFNDS '22: The 6th International Conference on Future Networks & Distributed Systems* (pp. 484–490). Association for Computing Machinery. https://doi.org/10.1145/3584202.3584274

Golovachev, D. L. (1998). *Public debt: Russian and global practice*. HSE University.

Hume, D. (1875). Vol. 3). *The Philosophical Works of David Hume: In four volumes*. Longman.Essays moral, political, and literary.

Ministry of Preschool and School Education of the Republic of Uzbekistan. (2023). Decree of the President of the Republic of Uzbekistan "On approval of the Concept for the development of the public education system of the Republic of Uzbekistan until 2030" dated April 29, 2019 No. UP-5712. https://www.uzedu.uz/ru/announces/94. Accessed on October 26, 2023.

President of the Republic of Uzbekistan. (2022). *Decree "On the development strategy of the new Uzbekistan for 2022–2026"* (dated January 28, 2022. No. PF-60). https://lex.uz/ru/docs/5841077. Accessed on October 26, 2023.

Rohe, J. F. (1997). *A Bicentennial Malthusian Essay: Conservation, population and the indifference to limits*. Rhodes & Easton.

Smith, A. (2003). *The wealth of nations*. Bantam Classic.

Tashbaev, B. (2021). Analysis of functional elements of public debt management. *Annals of the Romanian Society for Cell Biology*, *25*(2), 21–30. https://www.annalsofrscb.ro/index.php/journal/article/view/901. Accessed on October 26, 2023.

Usmonov, B. (2023). The impact of the financial ratios on the financial performance. A case of Chevron Corporation (CVX). In Y. Koucheryavy & A. Aziz (Eds.), *Internet of things, smart spaces, and next generation networks and systems* (pp. 333–344). Springer. https://link.springer.com/chapter/10.1007/978-3-031-30258-9_28

VECTOR OF DEVELOPMENT OF EQUAL COMPETITION IN THE UZBEKISTANI MARKET FOR AUDITING SERVICES

Minovar M. Tulakhodjaeva[a] and Mutabar Kh. Khodjayeva[b]

[a]Board of the National Association of Accountants and Auditors of Uzbekistan, Uzbekistan
[b]Tashkent State University of Economics, Uzbekistan

ABSTRACT

This chapter considers the stages of development of the audit services market in Uzbekistan and the process of improving the system of state regulation of audit activity, taking into account modern standards of international practice and ensuring information transparency of the audit services market, its stability, increasing the authority of the audit profession as a key factor of sustainable development of the audit services market and quality effect. It is crucial to remember that healthy competition promotes economic growth and increases the accountability of an audit company for the caliber of the provided audit services. New digital technologies are being developed and gradually implemented in accounting and auditing processes. Most businesses are working to maximize all contractual economic activities by automating accounting processes. Economic digitalization makes it possible to establish a national accounting system, wherein indicators will be collected to characterize the state of the firm's internal socioeconomic processes. This chapter investigates Uzbekistan's accounting and auditing regulations and how digitalization affects them. It emphasizes the necessity of digitalization and the benefits of using blockchain technology.

Keywords: Audit; audit services; audit activities; fair competition; quality control; digitalization; auditing profession; international auditing standards; auditing operations

JEL Code: M42

The transformation of Uzbekistan to market relations highlighted the necessity for new economic institutions that govern the interactions between different commercial

Development of International Entrepreneurship Based on Corporate Accounting and Reporting According to IFRS
Advanced Series in Management, Volume 33B, 197–204
Copyright © 2024 Minovar M. Tulakhodjaeva and Mutabar Kh. Khodjayeva
Published under exclusive licence by Emerald Publishing Limited
ISSN: 1877-6361/doi:10.1108/S1877-63612024000033B025

companies, among which the auditing institution holds a respectable position. Reliable information regarding an enterprise's operations is crucial in a market economy. The following is required:

- Government agencies to monitor compliance with tax laws.
- The owner of the enterprise to determine the development strategy and ways to improve the efficiency of its activities.
- Banks and insurance companies to assess the solvency of the enterprise and the likelihood of repayment of loans, determining the insurance risk.
- Suppliers, buyers, and other enterprises and organizations that have business relationships with a business entity, for confidence in payment for supplies, in receipt of goods, services, and works.
- Potential investors to assess income on deposits.

Audit is a component of market interactions. Like any other element of the market, it appears whenever any market participant makes a demand. Due to the growth and complexity of production and the expansion of the market, investors, creditors, and company owners (shareholders and founders) were previously unable to independently verify that all financial and economic transactions of the economic entity they were interested in complied with the legal prerequisites and were reliably reflected in the accounting records.

In this regard, on the one hand, it is necessary for stakeholders to have confidence in the integrity of the financial statements as they are used to make responsible decisions.

On the other hand, there are the following aspects:

- The cost of accessing organizational documentation.
- The possibility of biased information coming from the management and accounting departments of the company in conflict situations.
- The lack of free access to organizational documentation.
- The lack of specialized expertise and experience among interested users.

The institution of independent and highly qualified auditors was established in response to the vulnerability of financial declarations to distortions brought on by inevitable factors (subjectivity of the compilers, ambiguity in the explanation of regulations, etc.), which led to the establishment of independent, highly qualified auditors whose opinion on the reliability of the company's financial declarations could be relied upon by interested users (Khodjayeva & Maxmutjanovna, 2020).

The financial sector of the Uzbek economy is not complete without the audit system. The government is highly concerned with the growth and development of this region. As of now, a thorough regulatory framework for auditing operations has been established; the licensing process has been greatly streamlined and liberalized.

MATERIALS AND METHODS

The Law "On auditing activities" (February 25, 2021 No. O'RQ-677) (Republic of Uzbekistan, 2021) states the following:

(1) Only international standards for assurance assignments, reviews, quality control, auditing, and related services serve as a guide for auditing activities. The International Federation of Accountants of the International Auditing and Assurance Standards Board is in charge of distributing the standards. The Cabinet of Ministers determines the process for recognizing international auditing standards for use on Uzbekistani land.

(2) The requirement for obtaining a license to conduct auditing operations was removed. From the time that information regarding a particular audit company is entered into the Register of Audit Companies, this company is authorized to conduct audit activities. As before, it is permitted to establish it and carry out its operations in any organizational and legal structure permitted by law, except joint-stock companies (JSC). In this case, the following conditions must be met:

- There must be at least four full-time auditors whose audit company serves as their primary place of employment.
- The authorized capital of an audit company is comprised of property, including money spent especially for the audit company's operations.
- Unless an audit company is founded as a branch or subsidiary business company of a foreign audit company, the share of the authorized capital (authorized capital) owned by the auditors must be at least 51%.
- All files pertaining to the authorized capital (authorized capital) should be signed by the head of the audit company.
- Changes have been made to the list of companies subject to mandatory audits, as well as the rights, duties, and responsibilities of the audit company. Therefore, commercial companies that concurrently meet the following prerequisites at the end of the reporting year are now subject to mandatory assessment: over 100,000 basic calculated values (BCV) in book value of assets, over 200,000 BCV in revenue from sales of goods and services, and over 100,000 BCV in average annual employment.

A list of comparable services offered by auditing firms is also provided. It consists of the following:

- Establishing, repairing, and upholding accounting, creating financial declarations, and providing guidance on issues related to their preparation and upkeep.
- The auditor of an audit commission of a legal company serves as a trustee for investment assets.
- A tax consultant who works for the audit company or is hired by it may offer guidance on how to apply the law, compute, file tax and duty declarations, and perform other related tasks.
- The results of the audit will only be used to produce an audit report.
- The process for maintaining a registry of audit companies and auditors has been determined.

The research employed various methods, statistical tools, scientific observation, and logical and scientific reasoning to investigate the relevant statistics and hypotheses. The authors used the statistics from the State Committee on Statistics of the Republic of Uzbekistan for the analysis.

RESULTS

The process of growing the market for audit services demonstrates how the legislative framework for auditing is continually changing to consider the contemporary needs of the day and the business community.

The Law of the Republic of Uzbekistan "On auditing activities" stipulates that only auditing companies may perform auditing services, as well as the rights and obligations of the auditing company.

Let us look at the main phases of developing the regulatory framework governing auditing activities.

On December 9, 1992, the Republic of Uzbekistan passed a Law "On auditing activities" that established the initial legal framework for developing a market for audit services. There was a dearth of professionals and businesses capable of offering audit services (Khodjayeva & Muqumov, 2019); the next step was on May 26, 2000, when the Law of the Republic of Uzbekistan "On auditing activities" was amended. These amendments optimized the state regulation of auditing activities by introducing a straightforward and permanent system of licensing auditing activities.

Eight years of audit development have resulted in the establishment of more than 400 audit companies.

Next, starting on January 1, 2008, the government developed a system of difference for audit licenses for the following categories of audits to restrict the market access of dishonest companies:

- Proactive and necessary business entity audits, excluding those of banks, insurance companies, and JSC (auditing firms with a minimum of four full-time auditors, a minimum approved capital of three times the minimum salary, and a minimum of one auditor with a certificate in international accounting).
- Proactive audits (conducted by audit firms having a minimum of two full-time auditors and a minimum of 1,500 times the minimum salary in permitted capital).
- Audits of all businesses (auditing companies with at least five times the minimum wage and at least six full-time auditors).

The requirement for a minimum number of full-time auditors ensured that the minimum number of audit staff established was fully staffed with auditors whose primary place of employment is this audit company.

Most audit companies stopped operating as a result of changes made to the audit regulation framework and fierce competition.

Additionally, Uzbekistan's government has implemented several efficient economic incentives to encourage the active expansion of auditing operations. These incentives include the following:

- Auditing firms were excluded from paying income tax and the single tax payment until 2017.
- Decisions on the revocation of licenses for offenses are made only through the judicial procedure.
- The cost of the license fees paid by audit companies has been cut in half or more.
- Small business owners are no longer needed to have round seals. Audit companies are given the chance to correct any issues with licensing prerequisites and post-licensure terms within three months after acquiring their license.

ANALYSIS

There are still unexplored prospects in the domain of audit regulation, notwithstanding the actions done. Particularly, there was little active growth in auditing activities between 2009 and 2018. The auditing profession continues to participate in limited international activities. The measures' effectiveness was insufficient to guarantee the emergence of more competitive new audit companies (Table 1).

The analysis of the development of audits in Uzbekistan revealed several problems and deficiencies that hinder the growth of auditing operations, raise the importance of audit services for management decisions, and raise the bar for corporate governance, including the following:

- A low level of trust in audit companies and the perception of audit as an unnecessary procedure.
- Prohibition of tenders for the selection of audit companies that encourage unfair competition, particularly price competition that reduces the quality of audit services.
- The inability of audit companies to respond swiftly to information about the provision of mediocre audit services and dishonest activity on the part of auditors, etc., was caused by the lack of an effective external quality control mechanism for their work.

An important step toward improving the system of auditing activity regulation was the approval of the Resolution of the President of the Republic of Uzbekistan "On measures for the further development of auditing activities in the Republic of Uzbekistan" (September 19, 2018 No. PQ-3946), which eliminates the following prerequisites as of January 1, 2019 (President of the Republic of Uzbekistan, 2018):

- The minimum amount of authorized capital for audit companies, etc.
- The certification of heads of audit companies (before, heads of audit companies were certified every three years).

A new protocol has been implemented as of 2019 and is as follows:

- Previously, there were three different sorts of licenses based on the type of audit. Currently, anyone can obtain a license to conduct auditing activities.
- Four full-time auditors are now the bare minimum (before, depending on the type of license, two to six auditors were needed).
- An audit of the same business entity is carried out for no more than seven years in a row (previously – no more than three years), etc.

Table 1. Number of Auditing Firms (as Listed in the Registry).

Quantity	Years									
	2009	2010	2011	2012	2013	2014	2015	2016	2017	2018
Audit companies	*114*	*106*	*104*	*104*	*101*	*104*	*101*	*101*	*102*	*98*

Source: Compiled by the authors based on Tulakhodjaeva and Khodjaeva (2021)

According to paragraph 15 of the Decree of the President of the Republic of Uzbekistan "On additional measures to support the population, economic sectors and business entities during the coronavirus pandemic" (April 3, 2020 No. UP-5978), during the COVID-19 pandemic, the deadline for conducting an audit based on the results of 2019 of business entities subject to mandatory audit has been extended until October 1, 2020. Moreover, the requirement for a mandatory annual audit of limited and additional liability companies with a book value of assets of more than 100,000basic calculated values was introduced based on the results of 2020.

The Decree of the President of the Republic of Uzbekistan "On measures to radically improve licensing and permitting procedures" (August 24, 2020 No. PF-6044) removed licensing for audit activities as of January 1, 2021 (President of the Republic of Uzbekistan, 2020b). The Law of the Republic of Uzbekistan "On auditing activities" was amended on May 27, 2021.

As soon as an audit company's information is entered into the Register of Audit Companies, it can start doing audits. Audit services are provided in compliance with international auditing standards. Additionally, starting on August 15, 2021, republican public associations of auditors will have the power to hold qualification exams for them and issue, reissue, extend, and terminate the validity of auditor qualification certificates. Starting in 2021, the audit market is gradually coming to life (Table 2).

In accordance with Article 27 of the Law of the Republic of Uzbekistan "On auditing activities," an audit company may be established and carry out its operations in any organizational and legal form permitted by law, with the exception of a JSC, subject to the following requirements:

- Minimum number of auditors whose main place of work is the audit organization is four permanent auditors.
- An audit company's authorized capital is made up of assets, inclusive of money that is utilized by the company to carry out its operations.
- With the exception of situations when an audit company is created as a branch or subsidiary of a foreign audit company, the share of the authorized capital owned by the auditors (auditor) must be at least 51%.
- Only an auditor whose primary place of employment is this audit company should serve as its head.

Table 2. Details on the 2021–2022 Market for Audit Services.

	Years	
Number	2021	2022
Audit companies	96	126
Auditors	651	881

Source: Compiled by the authors based on National Association of Accountants and Auditors of Uzbekistan (n.d.).

DISCUSSION

The National Association of Accountants and Auditors of Uzbekistan and the Chamber of Auditors of Uzbekistan (nongovernmental and nonprofit companies founded based on voluntary membership) are the primary institutions of the auditing profession.

Being commercial entities, audit companies are accountable for the inappropriate or incomplete fulfillment of contractual commitments, as well as for adhering to laws governing auditing activities. Thus, the law sets a requirement for the supply of audit services in the presence of an audit company's liability insurance policy. Additionally, the auditing firm is required to do the following:

- Abide with the auditing standards and the Code of Ethics for Professional Accountants' requirements.
- Abide by the rules outlined in legislation aimed at preventing the use of earnings from crime to finance terrorism, as well as the financing of the spread of weapon of mass destruction (WMDs).
- Make sure auditors attend advanced training sessions once per year.
- Make sure audit services are provided independently.
- Give information on the prerequisites of international auditing standards for performing an audit, also the laws and regulations upon which the auditor's conclusions are based, upon request from an economic entity.
- Protect the privacy of data acquired while providing audit services.
- Assemble the audit findings in line with the prerequisites for auditing and keep copies of the audit reports in the audit company for at least five years.
- The company's management, persons responsible for corporate governance, and the audit commission should report in writing any violations of accounting legislation or facts clearly indicative of corruption offenses.
- Create and adhere to an internal quality control system for auditors' work.
- Refrain from interfering with the external quality control of the work of the audit company.
- Within five days after changing postal or email address, the audit company or the makeup of the auditors must notify the appropriate state body in writing or electronically.
- Maintain and keep the company's website current.
- Provide the designated state authority with paper or electronic information about audit activities annually before January 20.

CONCLUSION

The market for audit services is currently competitive, which helps strengthen the accountability of audit companies for the caliber of the delivered audit report based on the audit's findings.

Offering related audit services also provides competitive chances because of the sector's changing environment. Assistance with creating financial declarations that adhere to international standards and tax considerations is the most frequently requested service.

The audit company may also offer related consulting services for the application of tax legislation, such as developing computations, tax declarations, and fee declarations, if it employs a tax consultant or involves a tax consultant under a written contract.

As a unique area of entrepreneurship, auditing is effectively growing in Uzbekistan. As of January 1, 2023, there were more than 800 auditors working for 126 audit companies, with Tashkent housing the majority of these firms at roughly 65%.

The local subsidiaries of international auditing firms "Ernst & Young," "Pricewaterhouse Coopers," "Deloitte & Touche," and "KRMG" also run profitable operations in the country thanks to their superior reputations abroad and use of cutting-edge technologies and best practices.

It should be mentioned that 26 Uzbekistani audit groups belong to important networks and alliances on the worldwide level. Approximately 70% of auditing firms have been engaged in auditing work for 10 years or more.

It is logical to assume that the auditor's duty to society and the country should be as broad as possible, given the function of the audit in the interaction of management, owners of the firm, and the state, as well as its high authority in the current economic environment. In this context, it is objectively necessary to establish a mechanism for holding audit companies accountable for breaking the law regarding auditing activities. This mechanism must be effective and proportionate.

The market for audit services benefits from robust competition, which raises service quality, improves cost effectiveness, and promotes adherence to ethical norms for the profession.

REFERENCES

Khodjayeva, M. X., & Maxmutjanovna, K. D. (2020, April 30). Audit reporting: National standards of Uzbekistan and international practice. *Religación: Revista de Ciencias Sociales y Humanidades, 4*(14), 287–290. https://media.neliti.com/media/publications/331648-audit-reporting-national-standards-of-uz-854b9b27.pdf. Accessed on October 20, 2018.

Khodjayeva, M. X., & Muqumov, Z. A. (2019). Features of obtaining audit evidence in accordance with international audit standards. *Journal of Advanced Research in Dynamical and Control Systems, 11*(7), 978–981.

National Association of Accountants and Auditors of Uzbekistan. (n.d.). Official website). (https://naaa.uz/). Accessed on October 20, 2018.

President of the Republic of Uzbekistan. (2018). Resolution "On measures for the further development of auditing activities in the Republic of Uzbekistan" (September 19, 2018 No. PQ-3946). https://lex.uz/docs/3914504. Accessed on October 20, 2018.

President of the Republic of Uzbekistan. (2020a). Decree "On additional measures to support the population, economic sectors, and business entities during the coronavirus pandemic" (April 3, 2020 No. PF-5978). https://lex.uz/ru/docs/-4780475. Accessed on May 3, 2020.

President of the Republic of Uzbekistan. (2020b). Decree "On measures to radically improve licensing and permitting procedures" (August 24, 2020 No. PF-6044). https://lex.uz/ru/docs/4966394. Accessed on September 20, 2020.

Republic of Uzbekistan. (2021). *Law of the Republic of Uzbekistan "On auditing activities"* (February 25, 2021 O'RQ-677). Tashkent, Uzbekistan. https://lex.uz/docs/-5307886. Accessed on May 25, 2021.

Tulakhodjaeva, M., & Khodjaeva, M. (2021). Features of digitalization and ensuring transparency of accounting and audit in Uzbekistan. In *Proceedings of the ICFNDS 2021: The 5th International Conference on Future Networks & Distributed Systems* (pp. 651–654). Association for Computing Machinery. https://doi.org/10.1145/3508072.3508201

ASSESSMENT OF FINANCIAL SECURITY OF JOINT-STOCK COMPANIES: THE CASE OF UZBEKISTAN

Aktam U. Burkhanov, Bobir O. Tursunov, Bunyod Usmonov and Shokhina U. Mamayusupova

Tashkent State University of Economics, Uzbekistan

ABSTRACT

In this chapter, the authors evaluated the financial security of "Kvarts" Joint-Stock Company (JSC) and "Kattakurgan oil" JSC operating in Uzbekistan, considering external factors. The authors tested two main hypotheses. According to the first hypothesis, the statistical panel model, which considers fixed effects and random effects in the cross section, is estimated using the least squares method of the cumulative model. Regression analysis is used in the panel data model. It is desirable to perform the calculation using the method of least squares in this model as well. According to the alternative hypothesis, it is a dynamic panel model. This model studies the dependence of the independent variable in the previous period. If there is an autocorrelation of the residual between the predicted independent variable and the actual independent variable in the regression line of the statistical panel model, then the dynamic panel model is used by the lagged independent variable. Based on the official reports of "Kvarts" JSC and "Kattakurgon oil" JSC, the authors created panel regression model indicators based on financial security indicators using the Eviews-9.0 program. Moreover, the authors developed forecast indicators of their financial security status indicators until 2025.

Keywords: Stock market; COVID-19 pandemic; financial security; dependent variable; factorial variables; pooled model; fixed effects model; random effects model

JEL Codes: F65; G32

In the conditions of globalization, distribution and redistribution of financial flows in joint-stock companies (JSCs) are ensured as a result of the increase in the volume of investment through the capital market on a global scale. In this regard, it is an urgent task

Development of International Entrepreneurship Based on Corporate Accounting and Reporting According to IFRS
Advanced Series in Management, Volume 33B, 205–213
ISSN: 1877-6361/doi:10.1108/S1877-63612024000033B026

to develop a system of indicators related to the assessment of financial stability and the provision of financial support to JSCs. (Antsiborko, 2007; Hausman, 1978). Specifically, the approaches for evaluating the financial stability of JSCs involve several key financial metrics, including the liquidity ratio, current liquidity ratio, financial leverage ratio, equity ratio, return on equity (ROE), financial independence ratio, dividend yield ratio, dividend shows the need to use solvency ratio, price-to-earnings (P/E) ratio, and P/B (price-to-book) ratio. Considering the level of external risks, the primary focus of scientific research in this area is on internal risks associated with the financial condition when assessing the enterprise's financial security using these ratios.

In the author's view, the status of JSCs has not been fully defined. The world practice shows that one of the main mechanisms for solving the problems mentioned above is that JSCs still have a high share of the state.

LITERATURE REVIEW

Research in the field of financial security at the microlevel is conducted by the world's leading universities, research centers, and reputable international financial and credit organizations (Chen et al., 2020; Xu & Li, 2020; Yang, 2020; Yildirim et al., 2011; Zeng & Koutny, 2019).

Issues of financial security, threats to financial security and their prevention strategies were researched by S. Ahmed (Ahmad et al., 2014), A. Amicelle (2017), L. Amoore (2011), M. -P. Arrieta-Paredes, A. G. Hallsworth, and J. A. Coca-Stefaniak (2020), C. Callahan (Callahan & Soileau, 2017), Cao Yu (Cao & Chen, 2012), and others.

Economists-scientists of the Commonwealth of Independent States (CIS), namely L. I. Abalkin (1994), G. E. Krokhicheva (Krokhicheva et al., 2016), E. Kuznetsova (Kuznetsova & Laptev, 2011), M. Yu. Kussy (2013), I. Lebedev (2008), D. Soboleva (Soboleva & Kozlova, 2019), O. L. Stepicheva (Stepicheva & Mamontov, 2011), S. G. Spirina (2016), and others, contributed numerous studies on the evaluation and management of the economic and financial security of enterprises, particularly grounded in the concept of competitiveness.

Ensuring economic and financial security at macro- and microlevels, as well as their assessment and management, are studied in the scientific works of Uzbek scientists – H. P. Abulqosimov (2006), A. Burkhanov (Burkhanov & Mansur qizi, 2021; Burkhanov et al., 2023), A. Kadirov (2023), B. Usmonov (2023), and others. The research of the mentioned authors undoubtedly contributes a great deal to the conceptual framework for safeguarding the financial security of the business.

A group of Chinese researchers evaluated the influence of five main types of climate risk on the financial stability of Chinese mining companies (Sun et al., 2020). According to their results, there is a correlation between climate change and the financial performance of mining companies.

A group of Ukrainian authors (Delas et al., 2015) propose financial security assessment indicators based on the adaptation of Maslow's pyramid to the hierarchy of business needs. In this perspective, the need for security is paramount, occupying the third position after the concepts of financial security and the imperative of its actualization. The methodology for assessing the financial stability of an enterprise presented by these scholars includes the following:

- Identifying and evaluating the influence of external risks through strengths, weakness, opportunities, and threats (SWOT), shareholder net worth (SNW), political, economic, social, and technological (PEST), and Environmental threats and opportunities matrix (ETOM) analyses.
- Evaluating the internal elements of financial security, which include examining the financial and asset status, conducting operational and SVP analysis, scrutinizing enterprise cash flows, and assessing enterprise risks.

Considering the components of existing methodologies and their components in assessing the degree of financial security of enterprises, we can come to the following conclusions based on a comparative analysis of scientific literature. The group of scholars focused on assessing the risks that are an element of financial security through risk management tools (Ahmad et al., 2014).

In contrast to them, Y. Cao and X. Chen propose a methodology based on the modeling of enterprise development plans under the influence of threats to financial security (Cao & Chen, 2012).

W. Li and X. Wang mainly refer to creating tools for managing financial risks through engagement in stock trading (Li & &Wang, 2020). Their investigation relies on extensive practical digital data, primarily focusing on the financial market.

W. Zhang and H. Jiang studied a specific mathematical model of risk and threat assessment, which has strong theoretical validity and methodological tools that are considered accurate (Zhang & Jiang, 2019). Typically, these studies share a commonality in being conducted within a singular enterprise, with insufficient emphasis placed on evaluating the extent to which external factors influence business activities.

In 2022, M. Guven, B. Cetinguc, B. Guloglu, and F. Calisir studied the direct impact of the COVID-19 pandemic on stock markets. Additionally, the daily increase in deaths and cases negatively affected stock returns. The government's response policies also had an indirect positive effect on stock returns by mitigating the negative effect of the daily increase in confirmed cases and deaths of COVID-19 (Guven et al., 2022).

P. M. Schnell and M. Bose proposed linear mixed models with associated errors in various fields. According to this study, researchers determined that adding random effects to a linear model can lead to changes. Particularly, adding random effects leads to unexpectedly large changes in fixed effect estimates compared to the same model without random effects (Schnell & Bose, 2019).

Looking at the research carried out in recent years, it has become imperative to investigate the effects of the COVID-19 pandemic on the economy, including stock markets. In the study of financial security, scientists have proposed various methodologies: mathematical models (Zhang & Jiang, 2019), scenarios (Cao & Chen, 2012), and risk approach (Ahmad et al., 2014). Econometric methods serve as an advanced tool in studying external factors that affect financial security, including fixed models (Usmonov, 2023), fluctuation correlation analysis (Jin et al., 2022), mixed models (Schnell & Bose, 2019), etc. Due to the high frequency of stock market data (daily and, in some cases, hourly), the world community of scientists found it necessary to use the statistical panel model.

RESEARCH METHODOLOGY

In this chapter, the authors studied the effect of coefficients affecting the profit of "Kvarts" JSC and "Kattakurgan oil" JSC in Uzbekistan. On this basis, the authors consider it appropriate to analyze the coefficients that provide financial security and their correlation as influencing factors for the benefit of the "Kvarts" JSC and "Kattakurgan oil" JSC. The collected data, including a special indicator (i.e., panel data), were analyzed. Particularly, the data were reflected in the years 2015–2020 as units of this panel (Brunner et al., 2020; Mayadunne & Park, 2016; Schatz & Bashroush, 2019). Based on panel data, the authors performed regression and correlation analysis.

According to the models created based on panel data, the authors analyzed two different ways in world practice:

(1) H_0 is a statistical panel model estimated using the pooled model least squares method, considering fixed effects and random effects over time. Regression analysis is used in the panel data model. It is desirable to perform the calculation using the method of least squares in this model as well.

(2) H_1 is a dynamic panel model that examines the relationship of the independent variable in the previous period. If there is residual autocorrelation between the predicted independent variable and the actual independent variable in the regression line of the statistical panel model, a dynamic panel model is used by making the independent variable (i.e., lag [interval distance]).

For the first time in this research, the authors found it appropriate to implement the effect of factors using the least squares method of regression analysis using a statistical panel model. We can see the econometric view of the panel model in the following formula:

$$Y_{it} = \beta_0 + X^I\beta + \in_{it} \tag{1}$$

where:

i – chosen objects;
t – chosen years;
X^I – the K_{it} dimension of the vector of random variables;
β_0 – intercept, as a function of t and i;
β – a (K×1) vector angle (slope), as a function of t and i;
$\in_{it}$ – errors, different variations of t and i.

Using the least squares method of the above econometric panel model, the authors use hypotheses testing iid $\in$_it(0,σ_$\in$^2), that the errors are independent and identically distributed. Using this hypothesis, the authors will analyze the indicators of the statistical panel model. Additionally, z_i is added to this model, considering the special characteristics of the indicators of the statistical panel model. As a result, the model looks as follows:

$$Y_{it} = \beta_0 + X^I\beta_1 + z^I\beta_2 + \in_{it} \tag{2}$$

Usually, when the indicators of the studied subject are calculated in the statistical panel model within the framework of the research object, the analyses are mainly carried out using the following three models:

(1) Pooled model;
(2) Fixed effects model;
(3) From the random effects model.

We can see the appearance of the cumulative model in the econometric formula in formula (2). We can see the econometric formulation of the fixed effects model in the following formula:

$$Y_{it} = \alpha_i + X^I\beta + + u_{it} \tag{3}$$

In this formula, α_i is a separate constant that is constant to the selected object. In this model, all constants are usually not considered. The influence of one variable on the independent variable is analyzed. This analysis is carried out under the assumption of time constant. The hypothesis of this model is that it determines the normal distribution of errors and the independent effects of the variables. Additionally, this model performs maximum likelihood estimation using the least squares method (Delas et al., 2015; Der Derian, 1995; Kiss et al., 2019; Langley, 2013).

The econometric formulation of the random effects model is carried out in the following formula:

$$Y_{it} = \beta_0 + X^I\beta + \alpha_i + u_{it} \tag{4}$$

In this formula, α_i is the dispersion indicator. The analysis is performed considering that $\alpha_i \sim \sim iid(0,\sigma^2)$ $u_{it} \sim iid(0,\sigma^2)$ with uniformly distributed errors. A random effects model is also found using the least squares method, which finds out the state of the effect over different periods of constant and normal error distribution.

RESULTS AND DISCUSSION

Since this research aims to form a multifactor linear function based on panel data, the authors created the matrix of correlation variables. However, in the formation of a multifactorial function, there is a correlation between the independent variables, which creates the problem of multicollinearity.

On this basis, the variables with high coefficients reflected in the matrix were excluded from the multifactor regression model. As a result, three regression model indicators were calculated.

Table 1. Results of Panel Regression Model Indicators Based on Financial Security Indicators of Joint-Stock Companies (JSCs) ($Y\_it = \beta\_0 + X\_it^I\beta + \in\_it$) (Based on 2015–2020 Data).

Involuntary Variable (ln_income)	(1) Assembled Model	(2) Fixed Effect Model	(3) A Random Effect Model
P/E coefficient	0.100 ** (0.009)	0.063** (0.009)	0.5841*** (0.0000)
P/B coefficient	0.566** (0.007)	0.051** (0.005)	0.3637*** (0.0000)
ROE coefficient	0.315** (0.009)	0.123 ** (0.004)	0.6692*** (0.0000)
C (constant)	6.944 ** (0.000)	7.305** (0.000)	6.1570*** (0.0000)
The number of observations	10	10	10
R-square	0.8178	0.8648	0.8556
Number of JSCs	2	2	2

Source: Compiled by the authors.

Note: Values in the brackets are standard error of the *p*-value, ***$p < 0.01$, **$p < 0.05$, ***$p < 0.1$.

From the data in Table 1, we can see that the *p*-value of the selected independent variables in the three models is less than 0.05. This indicator means that the chosen variables, namely P/E, P/B, and ROE ratios, are voluntary variables. They have a direct effect on the involuntary variable ln_income.

The econometric view of the above three models can be observed in the following formula:

(1) Assembly model:

$$\text{ln\_income} = 6.944 + 0.100 \, *P/E + 0.566*P/B + 0.315 \, ROE + e \tag{5}$$

(2) Fixed effect model:

$$\text{ln\_income} = 7.305 + 0.063 \, *P/E + 0.051*P/B + 0.123 \, ROE + e \tag{6}$$

(3) A random effect model:

$$\text{ln\_income} = 6.157 + 0.584 \, *P/E + 0.363*P/B + 0.669 \, ROE + e \tag{7}$$

Examination of the metrics of the calculated models with cumulative, fixed, and random effects reveals relatively modest differences. To determine the superior model, the authors performed calculations using the J. Hausman test (Dai & Cooper, 2007). As per the Hausman test, in the absence of a correlation between the regressor (independent variable) and the effects, fixed and random effects are present. However, fixed effects are considered ineffective. If there is a correlation between the regressor and the effects, then fixed effects are considered to be present. However, a random effect can be presented because it does not exist. The null hypothesis is basically determined by the following econometric formula:

$$W = [\beta_{RE} - \beta_{FE}][V(\beta_{RE}) - V(\beta_{FE})]^{-1}[\beta_{RE} - \beta_{FE}], \sim 2k \tag{8}$$

If W is significant (i.e., the probability is less than 5%), the fixed effects model is the better model. If this probability indicator is greater than 5%, the random effects model is deemed superior according to the Hausman test.

The trends of P/E, P/B, and ROE ratios can be disclosed in favor of JSCs. The first one is that the protected earnings providing security for the JSC increase yearly. In our work, the method of economic value added (EVA) in the management of JSCs is to restore the system of evaluation of the state of protected status (Table 2).

Table 2. Economic Value Added (EVA) Analysis of "Kvarts" JSC.

Criterions	Years					
	2020	2021	2022	2023	2024	2025
Net operating profit after tax (NOPLAT), billion som	22.28	63.55	78.55	97.34	122.38	143.95
The invested capital, billion soms	220	349	347	336	314	249
weighted average cost of capital (WACC)	17%	17%	18%	18%	18%	
Economic added value (EVA), billion soms	−16.12	2,68	17.40	37.59	65.84	98.33

Source: Compiled by the authors.

Table 2 illustrates the enduring performance of JSCs using the economic added value (EVA) method. The examination of the analyzed JSC reveals that "Kvarts" JSC shows how much capital is being added to the invested capital. This indicator shows the company's ability to withstand external and internal risks to implement its strategy.

CONCLUSION

To secure the financial stability and smooth functioning of JSCs, it is advised to adopt the following measures for enhancing the company's financial security:

- To assess the financial security of JSCs and ensure it, it is necessary to develop a system of indicators representing financial security, considering indicators such as working capital, debt and private capital, liabilities, and assets, as well as to determine their normative levels.
- To ensure the security of the market value of the company's shares, it is necessary to increase the value of the equity. For this purpose, it is possible to increase the net profit as a result of increasing the volume of product production and minimizing expenses. This leads to an increase in the value of private capital and, as a result, serves to provide financial security related to the market value of the company's shares;
- Third, the amount of dividends paid by companies should be in a progressive form in relation to the net profit. In its turn, this leads to the achievement of the standard level of the P/E ratio and, as a result, provides an opportunity to avoid the risk associated with the market value of shares of "Kvarts" JSC. When panel data were analyzed through three models, the fixed effects model was considered the most appropriate.

REFERENCES

Abalkin, L. I. (1994). Economic security of Russia: Threats and their reflection. *Voprosy Ekonomiki [Questions of Economics]*, *12*, 4–16.

Abulqosimov, H. P. (2006). *Economic poverty*. Academy.

Ahmad, S., Ng, Ch., & McManusc, L. A. (2014). Enterprise risk management (ERM) implementation: Some empirical evidence from large Australian companies. *Procedia – Social and Behavioral Sciences*, *164*, 541–547. https://doi.org/10.1016/j.sbspro.2014.11.144

Amicelle, A. (2017). When finance met security: Back to the war on drugs and the problem of dirty money. *Finance and Society*, *3*(2), 106–123. https://doi.org/10.2218/finsoc.v3i2.2572

Amoore, L. (2011). Data derivatives: On the emergence of a security risk calculus for our times. *Theory, Culture & Society*, *28*(6), 24–43. https://doi.org/10.1177/0263276411417430

Antsiborko, K. V. (2007). *Mathematical models of management of industrial and financial security of an industrial enterprise (Dissertation of Candidate of Economic Sciences)*. Russian Economic Academy named after G.V. Plekhanov.

Arrieta-Paredes, M.-P., Hallsworth, A. G., & Coca-Stefaniak, J. A. (2020). Small shop survival – The financial response to a global financial crisis. *Journal of Retailing and Consumer Services*, *53*, 101984. https://doi.org/10.1016/j.jretconser.2019.101984

Brunner, M., Sauerwein, C., Felderer, M., & Breu, R. (2020). Risk management practices in information security: Exploring the status quo in the DACH region. *Computers & Security*, *92*, 101776. https://www.science-direct.com/science/article/abs/pii/S0167404820300614?via%3Dihub

Burkhanov, A. U., & Mansur qizi, M. E. (2021). The ways for improvement of investment strategy in the period of digital economy, Proceedings of the ICFNDS 2021: *The 5th International Conference on Future Networks & Distributed Systems* (pp. 655–662). Association for Computing Machinery. https://dl.acm.org/doi/10.1145/3508072.3508202

Burkhanov, A. U., Tursunov, B., Uktamov, Kh., & Usmonov, B. (2023). Econometric analysis of factors affecting economic stability of chemical industry enterprises in digital era: In case of Uzbekistan, *Proceedings of*

ICFNDS '22: The 6th International Conference on Future Networks & Distributed Systems (pp. 484–490). Association for Computing Machinery. https://doi.org/10.1145/3584202.3584274

Callahan, C., & Soileau, J. (2017). Does Enterprise risk management enhance operating performance?. *Advances in Accounting, 37*, 122–139. https://doi.org/10.1016/j.adiac.2017.01.001

Cao, Y., & Chen, X. (2012). An agent-based simulation model of enterprises financial distress for the enterprise of different life cycle stage. *Simulation Modelling Practice and Theory, 20*(1), 70–88. https://doi.org/10.1016/j.simpat.2011.08.008

Chen, Y.-L., Chuang, Y.-W., Huang, H.-G., & Shih, J.-Y. (2020). The value of implementing enterprise risk management: Evidence from Taiwan's financial industry. *The North American Journal of Economics and Finance, 54*, 100926. https://doi.org/10.1016/j.najef.2019.02.004

Dai, L., & Cooper, K. (2007). Using FDAF to bridge the gap between enterprise and software architectures for security. *Science of Computer Programming, 66*, 87–102. https://doi.org/10.1016/j.scico.2006.10.010

Delas, V., Nosova, E., & Yafinovych, O. (2015). Financial security of enterprises. *Procedia Economics and Finance, 27*, 248–266. https://doi.org/10.1016/S2212-5671(15)00998-3

Der Derian, J. (1995). The value of security: Hobbes, Marx, Nietzsche and Baudrillard. In R. Lipschutz (Ed.), *On security* (pp. 24–45). Columbia University Press.

Guven, M., Cetinguc, B., Guloglu, B., & Calisir, F. (2022). The effects of daily growth in COVID-19 deaths, cases, and governments' response policies on stock markets of emerging economies. *Research in International Business and Finance, 61*, 101659. https://doi.org/10.1016/j.ribaf.2022.101659

Hausman, J. A. (1978). Specification tests in econometrics. *Econometrica, 46*(6), 1251–1271.

Jin, L., Zheng, B., Ma, J., Zhang, J., Xiong, L., Jiang, X., & Li, J. (2022). Empirical study and model simulation of global stock market dynamics during COVID-19. *Chaos, Solitons & Fractals, 159*, 112138. https://doi.org/10.1016/j.chaos.2022.112138

Kadirov, A. (2023). Theoretical and methodological foundations of ensuring financial and economic stability of enterprises. *E3S Web of Conferences, 402*, 08005. https://www.e3s-conferences.org/articles/e3sconf/abs/2023/39/e3sconf_transsiberia2023_08005/e3sconf_transsiberia2023_08005.html

Kiss, M., Breda, G., & Muha, L. (2019). Information security aspects of Industry 4.0. *Procedia Manufactoring, 32*, 848–855. https://doi.org/10.1016/j.promfg.2019.02.293

Krokhicheva, G. E., Arkhipov, E. L., Tevosyan, S. A., & Kopteva, Yu. I. (2016). Capital safety in economic security. *Internet Journal "Naukovedenie," 8*(6). http://naukovedenie.ru/PDF/139EVN616.pdf (Accessed 26 October 2023)

Kussy, M. Yu. (2013). Financial risks and financial security of the enterprise. *Scientific Bulletin: Finance, Banking, Investment, 4*, 35–40.

Kuznetsova, E., & Laptev, D. (2011). Financial security of the enterprise as a subject of financial planning. *Bulletin of the Moscow University of the Ministry of Internal Affairs of Russia, 5*, 52–57.

Langley, P. (2013). Toxic assets, turbulence and biopolitical security: Governing the crisis of global financial circulation. *Security Dialogue, 44*(2), 111–126. https://doi.org/10.1177/0967010613479425

Lebedev, I. (2008). *Methods of minimizing financial risks while ensuring the economic security of metallurgy enterprises (Dissertation of Candidate of Economic Sciences)*. Financial Academy under the Government of the Russian Federation.

Li, W., & Wang, X. (2020). The role of Beijing's securities services in Beijing–Tianjin–Hebei financial integration: A financial geography perspective. *Cities, 100*, 102673. https://doi.org/10.1016/j.cities.2020.102673

Mayadunne, S., & Park, S. (2016). An economic model to evaluate information security investment of risk-taking small and medium enterprises. *International Journal of Production Economics, 182*, 519–530. https://doi.org/10.1016/j.ijpe.2016.09.018

Schatz, D., & Bashroush, R. (2019). Security predictions – A way to reduce uncertainty. *Journal of Information Security and Applications, 45*, 107–116. https://www.sciencedirect.com/science/article/abs/pii/S2214212618303387?via%3Dihub

Schnell, P. M., & Bose, M. (2019). Spectral parameterization for linear mixed models applied to confounding of fixed effects by random effects. *Journal of Statistical Planning and Inference, 200*, 47–62. https://doi.org/10.1016/j.jspi.2018.09.004

Soboleva, D., & Kozlova, E. I. (2019). Analyzing and managing financial sustainability of the company in turbulent environment. *Innovative Economy: Prospects for Development and Improvement, 2*(36), 405–414.

Spirina, S. G. (2016). Financial security of priority development economic systems. *National Interests: Priorities and Security, 12*(8), 55–68.

Stepicheva, O. L., & Mamontov, V. D. (2011). Formation of strategy of management of enterprise economic safety in context of Russia's accession to the World Trade Organization. *Tambov University Review. Series: Humanities, 12*(104), 415–449.

Sun, Y., Yang, Y., Huang, N., & Zou, X. (2020). The impacts of climate change risks on financial performance of mining industry: Evidence from listed companies in China. *Resources Policy*, *69*, 101828. https://doi.org/10.1016/j.resourpol.2020.101828

Usmonov, B. (2023). The impact of the financial ratios on the financial performance. A case of Chevron Corporation (CVX). In Y. Koucheryavy, & A. Aziz (Eds.), *Internet of Things, Smart Spaces, and Next Generation Networks and Systems* (pp. 333–344). Springer. https://link.springer.com/chapter/10.1007/978-3-031-30258-9_28

Xu, X., & Li, J. (2020). Asymmetric impacts of the policy and development of green credit on the debt financing cost and maturity of different types of enterprises in China. *Journal of Cleaner Production*, *264*, 121574. https://doi.org/10.1016/j.jclepro.2020.121574

Yang, B. (2020). Construction of logistics financial security risk ontology model based on risk association and machine learning. *Safety Science*, *123*, 104437. https://doi.org/10.1016/j.ssci.2019.08.005

Yildirim, E. Y., Akalp, G., Aytac, S., & Bayram, N. (2011). Factors influencing information security management in small- and medium-sized enterprises: A case study from Turkey. *International Journal of Information Management*, *31*(4), 360–365. https://doi.org/10.1016/j.ijinfomgt.2010.10.006

Zeng, W., & Koutny, M. (2019). Modelling and analysis of corporate efficiency and productivity loss associated with enterprise information security technologies. *Journal of Information Security and Applications*, *49*, 102385. https://doi.org/10.1016/j.jisa.2019.102385

Zhang, W., & Jiang, H. (2019). Application of Copula function in financial risk analysis. *Computers & Electrical Engineering*, *77*, 376–388. https://doi.org/10.1016/j.compeleceng.2019.06.011

ASSESSMENT OF THE FINANCIAL SUSTAINABILITY OF ENTERPRISES: THE CASE OF UZBEKISTAN

Aktam U. Burkhanov, Mohichekhra T. Kurbonbekova, Bunyod Usmonov and Jahonmirzo Z. Nizomiddinov

Tashkent State University of Economics, Uzbekistan

ABSTRACT

This chapter examines the theoretical aspects of the financial stability of enterprises with different forms of ownership. The authors' approach to the financial stability of industrial enterprises is developed. Depending on the size (large, medium, small) and specific characteristics within sectors and industries, various indicators can be employed to evaluate the degree of financial stability. According to the authors, considering the specifics of construction materials enterprises, formed by seasonality of demand, capital intensity, investment volume, transportation costs, technological processes, etc., the assessment of their financial stability is based on the definition of absolute financial stability, normative financial stability, and precrisis level of financial stability. Using this methodology, the authors analyzed the financial stability of firms operating in Uzbekistan's construction materials sector. The outcomes resulted in crafting scientific recommendations and practical guidance to improve the financial robustness of these businesses.

Keywords: Sustainability; financial sustainability; financial status; financial ratios; solvency; financial resource

JEL Code: O16

The financial prosperity of businesses largely depends on the type and amount of funds at the disposal of the business and how these funds are injected into its operations. The employed capital is categorized into equity and debt funds depending on the chosen course. The necessity of meeting self-financing requirements justifies the company's internal funds and serves as the cornerstone of the company's autonomy.

Development of International Entrepreneurship Based on Corporate Accounting and Reporting According to IFRS
Advanced Series in Management, Volume 33B, 215–223
Copyright © 2024 Aktam U. Burkhanov, Mohichekhra T. Kurbonbekova, Bunyod Usmonov and Jahonmirzo Z. Nizomiddinov
Published under exclusive licence by Emerald Publishing Limited
ISSN: 1877-6361/doi:10.1108/S1877-63612024000033B027

However, it is important to note that exclusively financing the company's activities through internal funds is not always advantageous, especially in seasonal production. There are situations where significant funds accrue in bank accounts, while conversely, funds may be scarce at other times.

As a result, the enterprise's financial health directly depends on attaining the ideal equilibrium between internal and borrowed funds. The precise development of the financial strategy plays a role in improving the effectiveness of enterprises. Therefore, financial sustainability is closely linked to the funding sources for the company's operations.

It becomes essential to examine the limits of approaches to assess financial sustainability in enterprise activities and optimize the entire system, encompassing the algorithm of indicators and their interpretation. This exploration should account for the nuances of ownership structures and network characteristics.

LITERATURE REVIEW

There are several approaches to the financial stability of enterprises in terms of existing views and indicators that describe it (Bunea et al., 2019).

L. Schwab, S. Gold, and G. Reiner created a simulation model of customer receivables and credit limits provided by financial partners as factors affecting the financial stability of small and medium businesses (Schwab et al., 2019). S. Cantele and A. Zardini examined the relationship between financial performance and sustainability practices in a firm's sustainable development (Cantele & Zardini, 2018).

T. Balezentis and L. Novickyte (2018) revealed the examination of profitability, regarded as a key factor in the financial sustainability of farms. Their study was conducted using the DuPont model, which takes into account the influence of profit margin (profitability), asset turnover, and capital multiplier (leverage) (Borodin et al., 2015; Burkhanov et al., 2022; Usmonov, 2023).

G. E. Pinches, K. A. Mingo, and J. K. Caruthers developed empirically based classifications of financial ratios for industrial enterprises and examined the long-term stability of these classifications (Pinches et al., 1973). Other researchers analyzed the financial sustainability of waste companies mainly through cost structure and cost efficiency (Burkhanov & Mansur qizi, 2021; Lohri et al., 2014).

M. Gombola and J. E. Ketz (1982) analyzed the sustainability of financial ratios for several industries based on factor analysis. N. R. Castro and J. P. Chousa (2006) proposed an integrated method for the financial analysis of sustainability-oriented value creation in companies. This method is based on three aspects: (1) accounting, (2) cash, and (3) market. The study concludes that ratio analysis and causal reasoning can be an alternative option for developing financial analysis of sustainability.

P. P. Drake and F. J. Fabozzi (2008) suggested the utilization of the following five financial ratios to assess the financial performance of companies: (1) return on investment, (2) liquidity, (3) profitability, (4) activity, and (5) financial leverage.

M. E. Öcal and others identified about 25 indicators that are important for construction companies despite the fact that there are more than 50 financial ratios for evaluating the financial condition of companies (Öcal et al., 2007).

V. Bobinaite (2015) focuses on the comparative evaluation of the financial robustness of wind energy firms. The health and viability of companies were determined using the Altman, Liss, and Tafler bankruptcy forecasting models using financial ratios.

S. McLeay and D. Trigueiros (2002) studied the theoretical foundations of financial ratios of enterprises. S. B. Stone and others (Stone et al., 2015) carried out a comparative analysis of financial ratios on the example of Detroit company.

According to T. A. Khudyakova and A. V. Shmidt (2019), the financial ratios of companies depend on the external environment. Moreover, the economic decline strongly depends on these relationships, while the decrease in the company's financial stability is reflected in its financial ratios.

W. Bowman (2011) analyzed the financial capabilities and sustainability of ordinary nonprofit enterprises, separated into long and short periods. R. N. Nyabwanga, P. Ojera, O. Simeyo, and N. F. Nyanyuki analyzed the financial position of small and medium enterprises (Nyabwanga et al., 2013).

V. I. Romanchin and I. V. Skoblyakova proposed indicators related to investment composition for evaluating financial stability. These indicators encompass turnover and fixed asset metrics, reflecting their perspective that it signifies the capacity to meet loan interest payments and the reserve of financial stability (Romanchin et al., 2002).

T. P. Carlin determined that the assessment of financial stability includes the study of changes in the composition of capital, methods of its distribution, and forms of its formation. Carlin also considered the effectiveness and intensity of capital utilization, alongside factors such as solvency and creditworthiness. The author employed a set of descriptive indicators to assess the reserve of financial stability (Carlin, 1997).

According to E. S. Stoyanova (2003), the key coefficients for financial sustainability encompass those derived from liquidity, active business, efficient resource utilization, capital structure, and operational analysis. L. V. Dontsova and N. A. Nikiforova (1998) advocate for a set of indicators with a point-based rating, offering a comprehensive evaluation of financial sustainability. It is crucial to justify indicators that depict the financial sustainability of enterprises scientifically, considering specific characteristics such as industry and specialization (Hedderwick, 1996).

In connection with the above-mentioned, the scientific substantiation of financial stability and classification of its indicators requires an approach that considers the peculiarities and specialization of the studied organization, including its industry affiliation.

METHODOLOGY

Based on the exploration of scientific literature, the authors aim to create a set of financial stability indicators using enterprises in the construction materials industry as a model. Given the unique characteristics of businesses in this sector, the authors propose categorizing financial stability, differentiating between absolute and relative indicators, specifically presented as financial ratios.

Absolute indicators of financial stability essentially represent the surplus or deficit of funding sources contributing to reserves and expenses. This is reflected in the contrast between the volumes of reserves and expenses, serving as an indication of the abundance or insufficiency of funds available for forming reserves and covering expenses.

The subsequent indicators are employed to elucidate the origins of reserves and expenses:

• Availability of working capital. This indicator is expressed by the following formula:

$$AWC = AWC - LTL - STL \tag{1}$$

where:
AWC – available working capital; LTL – long-term liabilities; STL – short-term liabilities.

• Availability of sources of own working capital and long-term liabilities. This indicator is expressed by the following formula:

$$WCLTL = AWC + LTL \tag{2}$$

where:
WCLTL – working capital and long-term liabilities; LTL – long-term liabilities.

• The general indicator can be expressed by the following formula:

$$GI = WCLTL + STL \tag{3}$$

where:
GI – general indicator of the main sources of formation of reserves and expenses; WCLTL – working capital and long-term liabilities; STL – short-term liabilities.

The metrics reflecting the accessibility of the mentioned sources for forming reserves can be articulated through three indicators representing the supply of the reserves they constitute. These are:

(1) Excess (+) or deficiency (−) of working capital (S_{AWC}):

$$S_{AWC} = AWC - Z \tag{4}$$

(2) Excess (+) or deficiency (−) of working capital and sources of long-term liabilities (S_{WCLTL}):

$$S_{WCLTL} = WCLTL - Z \tag{5}$$

(3) An indicator of the general surplus (+) or lack (−) of the main sources of reserve and expenditure formation (S_{GI}):

$$S_{GI} = GI - Z \tag{6}$$

The three-component form of the financial stability of the enterprise is determined using these indicators.

$$S1\,(S) = \begin{cases} 1, \text{if } S > 0 \\ 0, \text{if } S < 0 \end{cases} \tag{7}$$

The authors believe there are four categories of financial sustainability for assessing the financial state of enterprises, including absolute financial stability (S1 = {1,1,1}).

In this scenario, the enterprise relies entirely on its working capital to meet all reserves. As a result, the company is not reliant on external creditors because there are no grounds for payment challenges or violations of internal and external financial controls. Such situations are extremely uncommon. Furthermore, the enterprise's management might not be informed, motivated, or have the chance to use external funds for its primary activities.

RESULTS AND DISCUSSION

Assessing the financial sustainability of "Kvarts" JSC and "Bekabadcement" JSC involves examining absolute and relative indicators to determine the level of their financial stability, which are part of the building materials industry operating in Uzbekistan (Table 1).

In 2021, the own funds of "Bekabadcement" JSC increased by almost two times compared to 2014; debt funds increased by 13.7%. In 2014, the level of self-funding of the enterprise was 58.6. By 2021, this indicator was 71.0% (Bekabadcement, 2023).

During the analyzed period, the net assets of "Kvarts" JSC and "Bekabadcement" JSC were at a high level compared to the authorized capital. In 2021, the authorized capital of "Kvarts" JSC increased 120 times compared to 2014. The authorized capital of "Bekabadcement" JSC remained unchanged. The net assets of enterprises increased by 4.8 and 2 times, respectively.

This factor serves as a positive factor in securing the financial stability of network enterprises. That is, it fully meets the requirements of the standard value of enterprises' net assets.

Table 1. The Level of Equity and Debt Financing in "Kvarts" JSC and "Bekabodcement" JSC in %.

Years	Funding Sources	"Kvarts" JSC	"Bekabadcement" JSC
2014	Own funds	90.9	58.6
	Debt funds	9.1	41.4
2015	Own funds	92.8	4.0
	Debt funds	7.2	96.0
2016	Own funds	89.9	28.8
	Debt funds	10.1	71.2
2017	Own funds	91.4	52.4
	Debt funds	8.6	47.6
2018	Own funds	92.6	54.2
	Debt funds	7.4	45.8
2019	Own funds	90.0	58.1
	Debt funds	10.0	41.9
2020	Own funds	90.0	66.2
	Debt funds	10.0	33.8
2021	Own funds	86.0	71.0
	Debt funds	14.0	29.0

Source: Calculated by the authors based on the data of "Kvartz" JSC and "Bekabadcement" JSC.

Therefore, by examining the company's financial state, we assess its degree of financial stability.

The analysis indicates a positive growth trend in all absolute indicators of financial stability for both companies. However, "Bekabadcement" JSC faced a shortage of working capital until 2019.

Absolute liquidity ratio. During the analyzed years, this coefficient has steadily grown in "Kvarts" JSC. The analysis shows that this enterprise has a high possibility of timely and full repayment of short-term obligations (Table 2). However, this situation also indicates that excess funds are not used efficiently in enterprises.

"Bekabadcement" JSC exhibits a considerably lower absolute liquidity ratio than the standard benchmark. This suggests that the volume of short-term liabilities in the enterprise surpasses the available cash.

In 2015, only 0.15% of the enterprise's short-term liabilities can be settled in cash. Such a scenario indicates potential inefficiencies in financial management within the enterprise, which could lead to concerns and objections from suppliers of goods and services.

Current liquidity ratio. This coefficient is much higher than the standard value in "Kvarts" JSC. Although certain fluctuations were observed during the analyzed years, it has a stable growth trend (Table 2). The primary cause for the surge in liquidity can be attributed to the upswing in receivables at enterprises in recent years. Nevertheless, the substantial decline in 2016 and 2019 can be accounted for by the abrupt increase in the payables of these enterprises.

Table 2. Analysis of Financial Ratios of "Kvarts" JSC and "Bekabadcement" JSC.

Indicators	Company	Years							
		2014	2015	2016	2017	2018	2019	2020	2021
Absolute liquidity ratio	Kvarts	5.35	2.72	3.56	3.15	4.46	4.43	5.33	7.87
	Bekabadcement	0.12	0.11	0.004	0.19	0.06	0.07	0.17	0.06
Current liquidity ratio	Kvarts	8.83	9.42	7.53	8.92	10.40	8.40	9.16	11.79
	Bekabadcement	8.55	8.81	4.47	2.34	2.02	2.16	2.12	1.53
Financial independence coefficient	Kvarts	0.91	0.93	0.90	0.91	0.93	0.90	0.90	0.86
	Bekabadcement	0.59	0.04	0.29	0.52	0.52	0.58	0.66	0.71
Equity and debt ratio	Kvarts	10.03	12.90	8.94	10.64	12.45	9.36	9.74	13.09
	Bekabadcement	6.53	0.50	1.80	4.02	2.87	4.04	3.57	2.97
Equity ratio	Kvarts	0.88	0.73	0.84	0.85	0.84	0.90	0.94	0.90
	Bekabadcement	1.31	17.53	2.48	0.58	0.71	0.53	0.59	0.52
Turnover ratio of receivables	Kvarts	34.88	13.23	16.75	13.10	11.76	22.53	39.01	28.96
	Bekabadcement	7.11	16.84	24.66	11.50	18.61	22.58	17.98	23.12
Accounts payable turnover ratio	Kvarts	14.26	15.26	8.97	13.48	18.30	18.74	21.49	16.84
	Bekabadcement	6.88	10.45	7.41	9.43	7.39	9.58	9.93	9.63
Balance profit rate coefficient	Kvarts	0.38	0.38	0.39	0.40	0.41	0.38	0.41	0.53
	Bekabadcement	0.45	0.58	0.61	0.60	0.50	0.34	0.51	0.47
Net profit rate ratio	Kvarts	0.25	0.25	0.12	0.16	0.18	0.19	0.24	0.30
	Bekabadcement	0.17	−0.50	0.23	0.27	0.06	0.00	0.08	0.02

Source: Calculated based on the data of "Kvarts" JSC and "Bekabadcement" JSC.

Financial independence coefficient. During the analyzed years, this indicator was higher than 0.5 in "Kvarts" JSC (Table 2). In "Bekabadcement" JSC, this indicator is higher than the standard value except for 2015–2016. This indicator has had a steady growth trend in recent years.

Equity and debt ratio. The coefficient of equity and debt ratio of "Kvarts" JSC and "Bekabadcement" JSC was higher than the standard value during the analyzed period and had a significant fluctuation tendency. However, this indicator has steadily increased in the last three years in "Kvarts" JSC. In "Bekabadcement" JSC, it is decreasing (Table 2).

Equity ratio. In the analyzed years, this indicator was in the range of 0.84–0.94 in "Kvarts" JSC and 0.52–17.53 in "Bekabadcement" JSC. It was higher than the standard value (Table 2).

Turnover ratio of receivables. Calculations show that during the analyzed years, the turnover ratio of receivables was at different levels in "Kvarts" JSC and "Bekabadcement" JSC (Table 2).

The turnover ratio of accounts payable represents the speed of timely payments of debts by the enterprise. Calculations show that the turnover ratio of accounts payable in the analyzed enterprises increased in 2021 compared to 2014. Nevertheless, the fluctuation has an unstable trend (Table 2). This shows that enterprises are paying their creditors on time. However, this indicator is significantly lower in "Bekabadcement" JSC than in "Kvarts" JSC.

Balance profit rate coefficient. During the analyzed period, this coefficient had a steady growth trend for "Kvarts" JSC (Table 2). Therefore, the management of production costs is well established in this enterprise, which ultimately ensures the economic and financial stability of the enterprise.

The fact that this indicator was at the lowest level in 2019 at "Bekabadcement" JSC can be explained by a sharp decrease in the volume of product sales and problems in managing production costs at the enterprise.

Net profit rate ratio. This coefficient has been steadily growing since 2016 at "Kvarts" JSC. During the analyzed years, a negative trend is observed in "Bekabadcement" JSC; even in 2019, it was −0.50. Starting from 2021, it has a steady downward trend (Table 2).

CONCLUSION

Drawing from the analysis, it is fitting to enact the following measures to fortify the financial stability of enterprises:

- It is advisable for enterprises to devise a system for acquiring securities using a portion of their funds to boost the existing liquidity level. This facilitates the settlement of obligations in cash to other enterprises and economic entities through the rapid sale of securities and conversion into cash.
- The instability in the level of investments and their self-recovery indicates the need for refining the future investment policy of the enterprise to achieve greater stability.
- There is a need to enhance the prospect of financing extended reproduction in today's enterprises. This involves expanding production by utilizing acquired profits and undertaking the modernization and re-equipping of the enterprise.

- To address the capital requirements within enterprises, it is fitting for them to utilize appropriate internal and external sources, encompassing long-term and short-term funds. This necessitates the establishment of a mechanism for the prompt repayment of received loans.
- The turnover ratio of enterprise reserves is notably high in the examined enterprises, indicating effective asset management. However, the heightened risk of insufficient reserves is apparent. Consequently, it is advisable to integrate asset management in conjunction with reserve considerations.
- It is recommended for enterprises to establish a proficient system for transforming working capital into cash, enabling them to eliminate their liabilities. Additionally, it is preferable for enterprises to formulate and execute a mechanism for the early recovery of sales and receivables, converting reserves and costs into finished products.

The results of these activities will be as follows:

- The proportion of equity in the property's total value and the volume of sources of working capital will increase.
- The share of cash increases, the circulation of working capital accelerates, and the provision of working capital will increase.
- The amount of reserves and expenses will decrease.
- Sales profitability will increase.
- The amount of funds received from debtors will increase.
- The company's solvency level will improve.

REFERENCES

Balezentis, T., & Novickyte, L. (2018). Are Lithuanian family farms profitable and financially sustainable? Evidence using DuPont model, sustainable growth paradigm and index decomposition analysis. *Transformations in Business and Economics, 17*(1), 237–254. https://www.researchgate.net/publication/324171120_Are_Lithuanian_Family_Farms_Profitable_and_Financially_Sustainable_Evidence_Using_DuPont_Model_Sustainable_Growth_Paradigm_and_Index_Decomposition_Analysis. Accessed on October 26, 2023.

Bekabadcement. (2023). Annual report information of JSC "Kvarts" and "Bekabadcement" JSC. https://bekabadcement.uz/admin/adminfiles/sushfakt6.pdf. Accessed on November 12, 2023.

Bobinaite, V. (2015). Financial sustainability of wind electricity sectors in the Baltic States. *Renewable and Sustainable Energy Reviews, 47*, 794–815. https://doi.org/10.1016/j.rser.2015.03.088

Borodin, A. I., Shash, N. N., Tatuev, A. A., Galazova, S. S., & Rokotyanskaya, V. V. (2015). Model of control of financial results of the enterprise. *Mediterranean Journal of Social Sciences, 6*(4S2), 578–583. https://doi.org/10.5901/mjss.2015.v6n4s2p578

Bowman, W. (2011). Financial capacity and sustainability of ordinary nonprofits. *Nonprofit Management and Leadership, 22*(1), 37–51. https://doi.org/10.1002/nml.20039

Bunea, O.-I., Corbos, R.-A., & Popescu, R.-I. (2019). Influence of some financial indicators on return on equity ratio in the Romanian energy sector – A competitive approach using a DuPont-based analysis. *Energy, 189*, 116251. https://doi.org/10.1016/j.energy.2019.116251

Burkhanov, A. U., & Mansur qizi, M. E. (2021). The ways for improvement of investment strategy in the period of digital economy. In *Proceedings of the ICFNDS 2021: The 5th International Conference on Future Networks & Distributed Systems* (pp. 655–662). Association for Computing Machinery. https://doi.org/10.1145/3508072.3508202

Burkhanov, A. U., Tursunov, B., Uktamov, K., & Usmonov, B. (2022). Econometric analysis of factors affecting economic stability of chemical industry enterprises in digital era: In case of Uzbekistan. In *Proceedings of the ICFNDS '22: The 6th International Conference on Future Networks & Distributed Systems* (pp. 484–490). Association for Computing Machinery. https://doi.org/10.1145/3584202.3584274

Cantele, S., & Zardini, A. (2018). Is sustainability a competitive advantage for small businesses? An empirical analysis of possible mediators in the sustainability–financial performance relationship. *Journal of Cleaner Production*, *182*, 166–176. https://doi.org/10.1016/j.jclepro.2018.02.016

Carlin, T. P. (1997). Quality of life and competitiveness of Russian enterprises. In *Materials of the scientific-practical conference*. Orel State Technological University.

Castro, N. R., & Chousa, J. P. (2006). An integrated framework for the financial analysis of sustainability. *Business Strategy and the Environment*, *15*(5), 322–333. https://doi.org/10.1002/bse.539

Dontsova, L. V., & Nikiforova, N. A. (1998). *Annual and quarterly financial statements*. Delo I Servis.

Drake, P. P., & Fabozzi, F. J. (2008). Financial ratio analysis. In F. J. Fabozzi (Ed.), *Handbook of finance. Valuation, financial modeling, and quantitative tools* (Vol. 3, pp. 581–595). John Wiley& Sons. https://doi.org/10.1002/9780470404324.hof003054

Gombola, M., & Ketz, J. E. (1982). Cross sectional stability of financial ratio patterns in industrial organizations. *The Financial Review*, *17*(2), 24. https://doi.org/10.1111/j.1540-6288.1982.tb00053.x

Hedderwick, K. (1996). In D. P. Lukichev, A. O. Lukicheva, T. from English, & Yu. N. Voropaev (Eds.), *Financial and economic analysis of enterprises*. Finance and Statistics. (Original work published 1988).

Khudyakova, T. A., & Shmidt, A. V. (2019). Impact of the global recession on financial and economic sustainability of industrial companies. *European Research Studies Journal*, *XXII*(1), 143–157.

Lohri, C. R., Camenzind, E. J., & Zurbrugg, C. (2014). Financial sustainability in municipal solid waste management – Costs and revenues in Bahir Dar, Ethiopia. *Waste Management*, *34*(2), 542–552. https://doi.org/10.1016/j.wasman.2013.10.014

McLeay, S., & Trigueiros, D. (2002). Proportionate growth and the theoretical foundations of financial ratios. *ABACUS*, *38*(3), 297–316. https://doi.org/10.1111/1467-6281.00111

Nyabwanga, R. N., Ojera, P., Simeyo, O., & Nyanyuki, N. F. (2013). An empirical analysis of the liquidity, solvency and financial health of small and medium sized enterprises in Kisii municipality, Kenya. *European Journal of Business and Management*, *5*(8), 1–15. https://www.iiste.org/Journals/index.php/EJBM/article/view/5090. Accessed on October 26, 2023.

Öcal, M. E., Oral, E. L., Erdis, E., & Vural, G. (2007). Industry financial ratios – Application of factor analysis in Turkish construction industry. *Building and Environment*, *42*(1), 385–392. https://doi.org/10.1016/j.buildenv.2005.07.023

Pinches, G. E., Mingo, K. A., & Caruthers, J. K. (1973). The stability of financial patterns in industrial organizations. *The Journal of Finance*, *28*(2), 389–396. https://onlinelibrary.wiley.com/doi/10.1111/j.1540-6261.1973.tb01782.x

Romanchin, V. I., Skoblyakova, I. V., & Smirnov, V. T. (2002). *Venture capital in crisis management strategy*. Orel State Technological University.

Schwab, L., Gold, S., & Reiner, G. (2019). Exploring financial sustainability of SMEs during periods of production growth: A simulation study. *International Journal of Production Economics*, *212*, 8–18. https://doi.org/10.1016/j.ijpe.2018.12.023

Stone, S. B., Singla, A., Comeaux, J., & Kirschner, C. (2015). A comparison of financial indicators: The case of Detroit. *Public Budgeting & Finance*, *35*(4), 90–111. https://doi.org/10.1111/pbaf.12079

E. S., Stoyanova (Ed.) (2003). *Financial management: Theory and practice* (5th ed.). Perspective.

Usmonov, B. (2023). The impact of the financial ratios on the financial performance. A case of Chevron Corporation (CVX). In Y. Koucheryavy & A. Aziz (Eds.), *Internet of things, smart spaces, and next generation networks and systems* (pp. 333–344). Springer. https://doi.org/10.1007/978-3-031-30258-9_28

EFFICIENCY OF THE GREEN ECONOMY: MONITORING BASED ON INTERNATIONAL EXPERIENCE AND PROSPECTS FOR IMPROVEMENT IN UZBEKISTAN

Ismail U. Rakhimberdiev[a], Rustam F. Urakov[a], Raykhona A. Artikova[a], Nasiba N. Ismatullaeva[a] and Saltanat T. Seytbekova[b]

[a]Tashkent State Transport University, Uzbekistan
[b]Kazakh National Agrarian University "Higher School of Business and Law", Kazakhstan

ABSTRACT

Drawing on international experience, the research monitors the effectiveness of the green economy in Uzbekistan and determines the prospects for improving this efficiency in Uzbekistan. The theoretical significance of this research lies in developing a new methodological approach to assessing the green economy's development level. The novelty and uniqueness of the author's approach consist of the consideration of the development of the green economy from the perspective of efficiency, with a systemic consideration of costs and benefits. The successful testing of the author's approach in the case of Uzbekistan in 2023 confirmed its high quality and reliability. The main author's conclusion is that the efficiency of the green economy in Uzbekistan in 2023 is sufficiently high: ecological investments are profitable, which promotes the development of the green economy. To enhance the efficiency of the green economy in Uzbekistan, it is recommended to use a new methodological approach to monitor the green economy from the standpoint of its efficiency and integrate green economic indicators into corporate reporting using green International Financial Reporting Standards (IFRS). The practical significance of the results obtained is expressed in the fact that the results of the conducted monitoring of the efficiency of the green economy in Uzbekistan in

Development of International Entrepreneurship Based on Corporate Accounting and Reporting According to IFRS
Advanced Series in Management, Volume 33B, 225–233
ISSN: 1877-6361/doi:10.1108/S1877-63612024000033B028

2023, based on international experience, as well as the proposed recommendations for improving the management of the green economy, will help increase its efficiency in Uzbekistan by 2030.

Keywords: Efficiency; green economy; Uzbekistan; environmental investments; return on investment; performance management; green IFRS

JEL Codes: D61; D92; Q57

The green economy embodies concern for the environment and the fight against climate change. Its importance is difficult to overstate. Currently, countries worldwide have achieved significantly different results in developing the green economy. There are leaders with well-established green economies (e.g., EU countries), rapidly catching up, dynamically developing green economies (e.g., BRICS countries), and countries demonstrating restrained successes in developing the green economy (e.g., some African countries).

The problem lies in the fact that the existing methodological approach to monitoring the green economy considers its benefits and costs for development separately. For instance, the achievements of global leaders are evaluated in terms of the advantages they have gained (e.g., the reduction of carbon emissions into the atmosphere or the decrease in energy consumption in the economy). Similarly, countries worldwide are compared based on the volume of environmental investments. It is believed that the larger this volume, the more developed the green economy.

However, an in-depth analysis of the cause-and-effect relationships in the development of the green economy indicates that considering costs and benefits separately is incorrect. For example, reducing carbon emissions into the atmosphere may be achieved not through the growth of the environmental friendliness of production but through its closure (deindustrialization of the economy). Similarly, the reduction of energy consumption in the economy may be achieved not through increased energy efficiency but through strict energy savings at the expense of the population's quality of life.

Thus, given the limited capabilities of green innovations, economies that specialize in the extraction and export of natural resources and are characterized by extensive territorial expanses (abandoning automobile transport is challenging in large cities) cannot reduce carbon emissions at the same rate as economies specializing in the service sector, predominant in small cities where it is possible to move on foot or by bicycle.

Similarly, a large volume of environmental investments may be justified by a high return on these investments. In this case, environmental investments support the altruism of green investors and are also profitable, characterized by high profitability and low risk. In countries with emerging institutions of the green economy, the return on environmental investments may be significantly lower; the investment risk may be high, which will impede environmental investments.

Another problem is that public authorities are considered to be solely responsible for the development of the green economy because the state of the environment and climate are seen as a public good. This entails a significant and burdensome load on the state budget associated with financing projects for developing the green economy. The above determines the relevance of scientifically practical elaboration of the following issues:

• Improving the methodological approach to monitoring the green economy to increase the accuracy and objectivity of its assessment and international comparisons.

- More active involvement of the private sector in national initiatives to develop the green economy.

The novelty of this research lies in rethinking the development of the green economy from the standpoint of efficiency, making it possible to systemically consider costs and benefits and reliably interpret the level of the development of the green economy in each country, considering its specifics. The view on developing the green economy from an economic perspective is more comprehensive, enabling the inclusion of relevant indicators in corporate reporting. The research aims to monitor the efficiency of the green economy in Uzbekistan based on international experience and determine the prospects for increasing this efficiency in Uzbekistan.

LITERATURE REVIEW

The research is based on the fundamental provisions of the green economy concept (Inshakova & Solntsev, 2022; Muraveva et al., 2021; Popkova, 2022; Popkova & Sergi, 2023; Popkova & Shi, 2022; Zhak, 2021). In accordance with the established concept in the available publications, the development of the green economy is assessed using the following indicators, which are systematized and reinterpreted by the authors in this research. The following are the indicators of costs (C) for the development of the green economy:

- "Investment in water and sanitation with private participation (current US$)" (Tolmachev et al., 2023; World Bank, 2023e)*.
- "Investment in energy with private participation (current US$)" (Morozova et al., 2018; World Bank, 2023d)*.

The following are the outcome (B) indicators for the development of the green economy:

- "Energy use (kg of oil equivalent per capita)" (Andersen & Silvast, 2023; World Bank, 2023a)*.
- "GDP per unit of energy use (constant 2017 PPP $ per kg of oil equivalent)" (Mertzanis, 2023; World Bank, 2023c).
- "Total greenhouse gas emissions (kt of CO_2 equivalent)" (Ma et al., 2023; World Bank, 2023h)*.
- "Renewable energy consumption (% of total final energy consumption)" (Bogoviz et al., 2017; World Bank, 2023g).
- "Renewable electricity output (% of total electricity output)" (Bogoviz & Sergi, 2018; World Bank, 2023f).
- "Forest area (sq. km)" (Popkova et al., 2022; World Bank, 2023b).
- "CO_2 emissions (metric tons per capita)" (Li et al., 2023; World Bank, 2023i)*.

Nevertheless, from a scientific–methodological perspective, the issues of monitoring the effectiveness of the green economy are insufficiently developed. The existing literature and the reflected methodological approach fail to form a comprehensive understanding of the costs, benefits, and, more importantly, their relationship concerning the green economy.

This serves as a gap in the literature. The scientific foundation for studying economic efficiency is laid out in many works (Bogoviz & Mezhov, 2015; Khakimova & Kayumova, 2022; Litvinova et al., 2017; Turginbayeva et al., 2018). The experience of developing the green economy in Uzbekistan is also disclosed in publications (Abdurakhmanova et al., 2021; Ergasheva et al., 2021).

Building upon the mentioned publications, this research develops its own methodological approach, overcoming the noted shortcomings of the existing approach. This will fill the identified gap in the literature and enable precise and objective monitoring of the effectiveness of the green economy in Uzbekistan based on international experience.

MATERIALS AND METHODS

To achieve the goal set in this research, the authors developed a new methodological approach to monitoring the effectiveness of the green economy. The peculiarity of the new methodological approach is the systemic accounting of costs and benefits according to the following formula:

$$GE_{eff} = \frac{\left(\sum_{i=1}^{n} B\right) \Big/ n}{\left(\sum_{j=1}^{m} C\right) \Big/ m},$$ (1)

where:
GEeff – indicators marked with "*".
B – benefits (i.e., the results of the development of the green economy).
n – the number of outcome indicators (B) of the green economy development (in this methodological approach, $n = 7$).
C – the costs of developing a green economy.
m – the number of cost indicators (C) for developing the green economy (in this methodological approach, $m = 2$).

Formula (1) uses the given values of the above indicators (in percent). This is necessary for their unification (to ensure comparability of data on indicators having different measurement units). For the indicators not marked with "*," the present values are obtained by the following formula:

$$B = \frac{B_{country}}{B_{world}} * 100\%$$ (2)

where:
Bcountry – the value of the indicator in a given country (e.g., Uzbekistan).
Bworld – arithmetic mean of the indicator for the world.

For indicators marked with "*," the given values are obtained by the following formula:

$$B = \left(\frac{B_{world} - B_{country}}{B_{world}}\right) * 100\%$$ (3)

The interpretation of the GEeff indicator value is as follows:

- At GEeff<1, environmental investments in the economy do not pay off, which constrains the development of the green economy.
- At GEeff = 1, environmental investments in the economy have zero profitability, which does not make it possible to fully unlock the potential of the development of the green economy.
- At GEeff>1, environmental investments in the economy are profitable, which favors the development of the green economy.

To achieve this goal, this research monitors the effectiveness of the green economy in Uzbekistan with reference to the statistics of the World Bank in 2023 (based on the results of 2022). Qualitative interpretation of the assessment results, as well as the determination of the prospects for improving the efficiency of the green economy in Uzbekistan, is made using SWOT analysis, which also allows the authors to offer recommendations for improving this efficiency.

RESULTS

Based on the developed methodological approach, the authors monitored the effectiveness of the green economy in Uzbekistan in 2023. The results of the monitoring are presented in Fig. 1.

According to the monitoring results from Fig. 1, private investments in water supply and sanitation in Uzbekistan in support of the implementation of Sustainable Development Goal (SDG) 6 are at a high level – assessed at 10.41% in 2023 (the lower the value of this indicator, the better, according to the author's methodology for efficiency assessment).

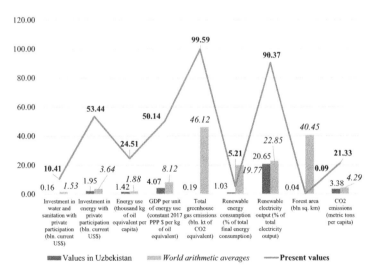

Fig. 1. Monitoring the Effectiveness of the Green Economy in Uzbekistan in 2023.
Source: Calculated and compiled by the authors based on World Bank (2023a, 2023b, 2023c, 2023d, 2023e, 2023f, 2023g, 2023h, 2023i).

Private investments in the energy sector in Uzbekistan in support of the implementation of SDG 7 are at a moderate level – assessed at 53.44% in 2023 (the lower the value of this indicator, the better, according to the author's methodology for efficiency assessment).

Energy consumption in Uzbekistan's economy in support of the implementation of SDG 7 is at a high level – assessed at 24.51% in 2023 (the lower the value of this indicator, the better, according to the author's methodology for efficiency assessment). The energy intensity of Uzbekistan's GDP in support of the implementation of SDG 7 is at a moderate level – assessed at 50.14% in 2023.

The consumption of renewable energy in Uzbekistan in support of the implementation of SDG 7 is at a very low level – assessed at 5.21% in 2023. The production of renewable electricity in Uzbekistan in support of the implementation of SDG 7 is at a very high level – assessed at 90.37% in 2023. The forest area in Uzbekistan in support of the implementation of SDG 15 is at a very low level – assessed at 0.09% in 2023.

Carbon emissions in Uzbekistan in support of the implementation of SDGs 11–13 are at a high level – assessed at 21.33% in 2023 (the lower the value of this indicator, the better, according to the author's methodology for efficiency assessment). Greenhouse gas emissions in Uzbekistan in support of the implementation of SDGs 11–13 are at a very low level – assessed at 99.59% in 2023 (the lower the value of this indicator, the better, according to the author's methodology for efficiency assessment).

Based on the values of these indicators from Fig. 1, the authors evaluated the efficiency of the green economy in Uzbekistan in 2023 using formula (1):

$$GE_{eff} = \frac{\frac{24.51 + 50.14 + 99.59 + 5.21 + 90.37 + 0.09 + 21.33}{7}}{\frac{10.41 + 53.44}{2}} =$$

$$= \frac{41.61}{31.93} = 1.30.$$

The obtained value of GEeff>1 (1.30 > 1). Consequently, environmental investments in the economy of Uzbekistan in 2023 are profitable, which favors the development of the green economy.

DISCUSSION

The research contributes to the literature by developing the concept of a green economy by proposing an improved methodological approach to its monitoring and management. SWOT analysis of Uzbekistan's green economy performance in 2023 is conducted in Table 1.

As shown in Table 1, the strengths (S) of Uzbekistan's green economy, contributing to its high efficiency in 2023, are as follows:

- A large volume of private investments in water supply and sanitation, actively supporting the implementation of SDG 6 (in support of Tolmachev et al. (2023)).
- A low level of energy consumption in the economy, actively supporting the implementation of SDG 7 (in support of Andersen and Silvast (2023)).
- A large volume of renewable electricity production, actively supporting the implementation of SDG 7 (in support of Bogoviz and Sergi (2018)).

Table 1. SWOT Analysis of Uzbekistan's Green Economy Performance in 2023.

Strengths (**S**):	Weaknesses (**W**):
• Large amount of private investment in water supply and sanitation. • Small amount of energy consumption in the economy. • Large amount of renewable electricity generation. • Low carbon emissions.	• Small amount of renewable energy consumption. • Small forest area. • Large amount of greenhouse gas emissions.
Opportunities (**O**):	Threats (**T**):
• Use of a new, author's methodological approach to monitoring the green economy from the perspective of its efficiency. • Integration of green economy indicators into corporate reporting using green International Financial Reporting Standards (IFRS).	• Preservation of current problems due to preservation of monitoring approach and lack of business involvement.

Source: Developed by the authors.

• A low level of carbon emissions, actively supporting the implementation of SDGs 11–13 (in support of Li et al. (2023)).

The weaknesses (W) of Uzbekistan's green economy, reducing its efficiency in 2023, are as follows:

• A low level of renewable energy consumption, indicating weak support for the implementation of SDG 7 (in contrast to Bogoviz et al. (2017)).
• A small forest area, indicating weak support for implementing SDG 15 (in contrast to Popkova et al. (2022)).
• A high volume of greenhouse gas emissions, indicating insufficient support for the implementation of SDGs 11–13 (in contrast to Ma et al. (2023)).

A threat (T) to the development of the green economy in Uzbekistan by 2030 is the conservation of current problems due to the preservation of the monitoring approach and the lack of involvement of businesses. Opportunities (O) are associated with the implementation of the following author's recommendations (to overcome weaknesses and strengthen strengths):

• Utilizing a new, authorial methodological approach to monitoring the green economy from the perspective of its efficiency.
• Integrating indicators of the green economy into corporate reporting using green International Financial Reporting Standards (IFRS).

CONCLUSION

The main conclusion of this study is that the efficiency of the green economy in Uzbekistan in 2023 is sufficiently high. Environmental investments are profitable, fostering the development of the green economy. The theoretical significance of this research lies in developing a new methodological approach to assessing the level of green economic development. The novelty and uniqueness of the author's approach lie in its first-time consideration of the development of the green economy from the perspective of efficiency, with a systemic consideration of costs and benefits. The successful application of the author's approach in the case of Uzbekistan in 2023 confirmed its high quality and reliability.

The practical significance of the results obtained in the research is expressed in the fact that the outcomes of the conducted monitoring of the efficiency of the green economy in Uzbekistan in 2023, based on international experience, along with the proposed recommendations for improving the management of the green economy, will help enhance its efficiency in Uzbekistan by 2030. The social significance of the author's scientific, methodological, and applied developments presented in the research lies in the perspective disclosed for improving the efficiency of the green economy in Uzbekistan, supporting the practical implementation of SDGs 6, 7, 12, 13, and 15.

REFERENCES

Abdurakhmanova, G. Q., Jeong, J. Y., Oqmullayev, R. R., & Karimov, M. U. (2021). The impact of tourism on employment and economic growth in Uzbekistan: An ARDL bounds testing approach. In *Proceedings of the ICFNDS 2021: The 5th International Conference on Future Networks & Distributed Systems* (pp. 431–439). Association for Computing Machinery. https://doi.org/10.1145/3508072.3508158

Andersen, P. D., & Silvast, A. (2023). Experts, stakeholders, technocracy, and technoeconomic input into energy scenarios. *Futures, 154*, 103271. https://doi.org/10.1016/j.futures.2023.103271

Bogoviz, A. V., Lobova, S. V., Ragulina, Y. V., & Alekseev, A. N. (2017). A comprehensive analysis of energy security in the member states of the Eurasian Economic Union, 2000–2014. *International Journal of Energy Economics and Policy, 7*(5), 93–101.

Bogoviz, A., & Mezhov, S. (2015). Models and tools for research of innovation processes. *Modern Applied Science, 9*(3), 159–172. https://doi.org/10.5539/mas.v9n3p159

Bogoviz, A. V., & Sergi, B. S. (2018). Will the circular economy be the future of Russia's growth model?. In B. S. Sergi (Ed.), *Exploring the future of Russia's economy and markets: Towards sustainable economic development* (pp. 125–141). Emerald Publishing Limited. https://doi.org/10.1108/978-1-78769-397-520181007

Ergasheva, S. T., Mannapova, R. A., & Yuldashev, E. I. (2021). Accounting – A system for managing economic information in agriculture. In E. Popkova & E. Zavyalova (Eds.), *New institutions for socio-economic development: The change of paradigm from rationality and stability to responsibility and dynamism* (pp. 173–181). De Gruyter. https://doi.org/10.1515/9783110699869-018

Inshakova, A. O., & Solntsev, A. M. (2022). Modification of international mechanisms for protecting human rights under conditions of anthropogenic environmental impact with the intensive development of technology of the sixth technological order. In A. O. Inshakova & E. E. Frolova (Eds.), *The Transformation of Social Relationships in Industry 4.0: Economic Security and Legal Prevention* (pp. 267–276). Information Age Publishing.

Khakimova, M. F., & Kayumova, M. S. (2022). Factors that increase the effectiveness of hybrid teaching in a digital educational environment. In *Proceedings of the ICFNDS '22: The 6th International Conference on Future Networks & Distributed Systems* (pp. 370–375). Association for Computing Machinery. https://doi.org/10.1145/3584202.3584255

Li, X., Zheng, Z., Shi, D., Han, X., & Zhao, M. (2023). New urbanization and carbon emissions intensity reduction: Mechanisms and spatial spillover effects. *Science of the Total Environment, 905*, 167172. https://doi.org/10.1016/j.scitotenv.2023.167172

Litvinova, T. N., Kulikova, E. S., Kuznetsov, V. P., & Taranov, P. M. (2017). Marketing as a determinant of the agricultural machinery market development. In E. Popkova (Ed.), *Overcoming uncertainty of institutional environment as a tool of global crisis management* (pp. 465–471). Springer. https://doi.org/10.1007/978-3-319-60696-5_59

Ma, R., Zhang, Z. J., & Lin, B. (2023). Evaluating the synergistic effect of digitalization and industrialization on total factor carbon emission performance. *Journal of Environmental Management, 348*, 119281. https://doi.org/10.1016/j.jenvman.2023.119281

Mertzanis, C. (2023). Energy policy diversity and green bond issuance around the world. *Energy Economics, 128,* 107116. https://doi.org/10.1016/j.eneco.2023.107116

Morozova, I. M., Litvinova, T. N., Przhedetskaya, N. V., & Sheveleva, V. V. (2018). The problems of financing of entrepreneurship infrastructure in developing countries and their solutions. In E. Popkova (Ed.), *The impact of information on modern humans* (pp. 277–283). Springer.

Muraveva, N. N., Belokon, L. V., Ignatova, M. A., Shuvaev, A. V., & Yakovenko, N. N. (2021). Making marketing decisions in an unstable economic environment. In E. G. Popkova, & V. N. Ostrovskaya (Eds.), *Meta-scientific study of artificial intelligence* (pp. 599–607). Information Age Publishing.

Popkova, E. G. (2022). Case study of smart innovation in agriculture on the example of a vertical farm. In E. G. Popkova & B. S. Sergi (Eds.), *Smart innovation in agriculture* (pp. 303–309). Springer. https://doi.org/10.1007/978-981-16-7633-8_34

Popkova, E. G., Litvinova, T. N., Karbekova, A. B., & Petrenko, Y. (2022). Ecological behavior in the AI economy and its impact on biodiversity: Lessons from the COVID-19 pandemic and a post-COVID perspective. *Frontiers in Environmental Science, 10,* 975861. https://doi.org/10.3389/fenvs.2022.975861

Popkova, E. G., & Sergi, B. S. (2023). Green supply chains. In B. M. Haddad & B. D. Solomon (Eds.), *Dictionary of ecological economics: Terms for the new millennium* (pp. 254–255). Edward Elgar Publishing. https://doi.org/10.4337/9781788974912.G.33

Popkova, E. G., & Shi, X. (2022). Economics of climate change: Global trends, country specifics and digital perspectives of climate action. *Frontiers in Environmental Economics, 1,* 935368. https://doi.org/10.3389/frevc.2022.935368

Tolmachev, A. V., Lifanov, P. A., Ketko, N. V., & Smetanina, A. I. (2023). The model of organisation of green entrepreneurship and the climate-responsible management of production factors in the digital economy markets. In E. G. Popkova (Ed.), *Smart green innovations in industry 4.0 for climate change risk management* (pp. 145–153). Springer. https://doi.org/10.1007/978-3-031-28457-1_15

Turginbayeva, A., Ustemorov, G., Akhmetova, G., Kose, Z., Imashev, A., & Gimranova, G. (2018). Financing aspects of an effective strategy for innovative enterprise development. *Journal of Advanced Research in Law and Economics, 9*(2), 714–720. https://doi.org/10.14505//jarle.v9%202(32).33

World Bank. (2023a). Energy use (kg of oil equivalent per capita)). (https://data.worldbank.org/indicator/EG.-USE.PCAP.KG.OE?view=chart). Accessed on November 3, 2023.

World Bank. (2023b). Forest area (sq. km)). (https://data.worldbank.org/indicator/AG.LND.FRST.K2?view='''chart). Accessed on November 3, 2023.

World Bank. (2023c). GDP per unit of energy use (constant 2017 PPP $ per kg of oil equivalent)). (https://data.worldbank.org/indicator/EG.GDP.PUSE.KO.PP.KD?view=chart). Accessed on November 3, 2023.

World Bank. (2023d). Investment in energy with private participation (current US$)). (https://data.worldbank.org/indicator/IE.PPI.ENGY.CD?view=chart). Accessed on November 3, 2023.

World Bank. (2023e). Investment in water and sanitation with private participation (current US$)). (https://data.worldbank.org/indicator/IE.PPI.WATR.CD?view=chart). Accessed on November 3, 2023.

World Bank. (2023f). Renewable electricity output (% of total electricity output)). (https://data.worldbank.org/indicator/EG.ELC.RNEW.ZS?view=chart). Accessed on November 3, 2023.

World Bank. (2023g). Renewable energy consumption (% of total final energy consumption)). (https://data.-worldbank.org/indicator/EG.FEC.RNEW.ZS?view=chart). Accessed on November 3, 2023.

World Bank. (2023h). Total greenhouse gas emissions (kt of CO_2 equivalent)). (https://data.worldbank.org/indicator/EN.ATM.GHGT.KT.CE?view=chart). Accessed on November 3, 2023.

World Bank. (2023i). CO_2 emissions (metric tons per capita)). (https://data.worldbank.org/indicator/EN.-ATM.CO2E.PC?view=chart). Accessed on November 3, 2023.

Zhak, L. (2021). Life is grey, but the tree of theory is evergreen. In E. G. Popkova & V. N. Ostrovskaya (Eds.), *Meta-scientific study of artificial intelligence* (pp. 69–73). Information Age Publishing.

PERSPECTIVE ON ADAPTING INTERNATIONAL FINANCIAL REPORTING STANDARDS (IFRS) TO THE LATEST TRENDS IN INTERNATIONAL BUSINESS DEVELOPMENT: CONCLUSION

Mansur P. Eshov, Gulnora K. Abdurakhmanova, Aktam U. Burkhanov, Nodira B. Abdusalomova and Shakhlo T. Ergasheva

Tashkent State University of Economics, Uzbekistan

International Financial Reporting Standards (IFRS) have strengthened their leading role in supporting the development of international entrepreneurship in the transition to a new era of globalization – the era of flexible international trade partnerships in the context of limited freedom in international trade. The main conclusion of this book is that IFRS should not solidify business traditions but break patterns, constantly adapt in harmony with changing cross-border trade needs, and organically integrate into evolving practices of corporate management, accounting, and reporting.

The theoretical value and practical utility of this book are expressed in its determination of the current needs of dynamically developing international trade partnerships, exemplified by the Eurasian Economic Union (EAEU) and the expanding Brazil, Russia, India, China, and South Africa (BRICS) bloc, in relation to IFRS. It also explains how to meet these needs most effectively. However, one should not stop at what has been achieved. Several other international trade partnerships, currently functioning or emerging in the contemporary global economic system, remain beyond the scope of the research conducted in this book. Their experiences should be studied in future scientific research.

Development of International Entrepreneurship Based on Corporate Accounting and Reporting According to IFRS
Advanced Series in Management, Volume 33B, 235–236
Copyright © 2024 Mansur P. Eshov, Gulnora K. Abdurakhmanova, Aktam U. Burkhanov, Nodira B. Abdusalomova and Shakhlo T. Ergasheva
Published under exclusive licence by Emerald Publishing Limited
ISSN: 1877-6361/doi:10.1108/S1877-63612024000033B029

In the future, new international trade partnerships will emerge, each with specific needs for IFRS. Therefore, it is necessary to continue a series of productive IFRS research and foster a fruitful academic discussion on IFRS development issues, as supported by this book. Subsequent research should identify emerging international trade partnerships, determine their IFRS needs, and provide scientific and practical recommendations for creating new IFRS and adapting existing ones to these growing needs.

Printed and bound by CPI Group (UK) Ltd, Croydon, CR0 4YY

17/07/2024

14529486-0001